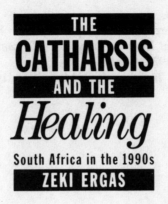

THE
CATHARSIS
AND THE
Healing
South Africa in the 1990s
ZEKI ERGAS

THE
CATHARSIS
AND THE
Healing
South Africa in the 1990s
ZEKI ERGAS

JANUS PUBLISHING COMPANY
London, England

First published in Great Britain 1994
by Janus Publishing Company
Duke House, 37 Duke Street
London W1M 5DF

British Library Cataloguing in Publication Data.
A catalogue record for this book is available from the British Library.

ISBN 1 85756 079 5

Printed and bound in England by
BPC Wheatons Ltd, Exeter

for 'Mone, Dave and 'J'

Contents

Part Two

A Supplement: a Brief Introduction to South African History
and Politics

Author's Note

This is a people-oriented book, which means that it owes a lot to a lot of people. As a matter of fact, it was not until I finished it that I realised how much. In other words, and simply put, this book would not be what it is – I hope good, or good enough, without false modesty – without their contributions. It is, therefore, appropriate that I should start by expressing my heartfelt gratitude to all those, more numerous than I first thought, who went beyond the call of duty and offered me friendship and hospitality because they trusted me and they liked what I was doing. They are: K Cremer; J S Mfabana; G Z Goniwe; R Barayi and G M Makaula (who passed away unfortunately); all community leaders from Cradock and its African 'location' Lingelihle; Jayne and Raoul Beaumont, farmers at Botriver who opened their house and their hearts; Friday France, from *Monitor* magazine, who did not mind spending a weekend showing me the reality of life in the townships and squatter camps of the Port Elizabeth/Uitenhage area; Robert Berold, the poet and idealist from Grahamstown; Sam Dube, who took time out of his business for the interview and to take me around in Khayelitsha; Ellison Kahn and his charming wife Adele, who were invariably friendly and supportive; Mosie Moolla, a member of the Transvaal Indian Congress, who I met at CODESA and with whom we discovered kindred souls; Stan Kahn, the genial former Funda Centre director, now an independent consultant; Tony Ngwenya and Vuyisile Mafalala, my friendly and competent Soweto guides; the inimitable Cecil Cook of the Transkei Appropriate Technology Unit (TATU), based in Umtata; Themba Passiwe, the owner of a small business consultancy firm in Guguletu, near Cape Town; Barend and Renée who work at the ANC's Western Cape Office and thanks to whom I could attend the Sharpeville rally in Khayelitsha; Piet Cillié ('the Professor') whose erudition and sense of humour made the Afrikaner history almost palatable; Evelyn Sagor, Adele's best friend, a charming lady, still seductive, whom I sometimes wished was twenty years younger; Thulani Manyoni, a sensitive soul from Sebokeng whom I met by chance in a CNA bookstore in Cape Town and who became my friend; Jan Rabie and Marjorie Wallace, delightfully entertaining; Jessica Landman, the social worker from Fort Beaufort with a great deal of goodwill; W A ('Bill') de Klerk, the philosopher and man of letters who at age 75 (he was born in

1917) retains a childlike enthusiasm; Ian Wyllie, the journalist, a shrewd observer of the South African political scene; and Ted and Shirley Tollman from Durban who were graciously helpful.

There were also those who agreed to be interviewed, who provided help and/or useful contacts and gave good advice. This is a fairly large group and, as I will inevitably miss some of them, I ask in advance for their indulgence.

The interviews with Rory Riordan, Es'Kia Mphahlele, F Van Zyl Slabbert and Pallo Jordan turned out to be substantive enough to form complete chapters. Those with Rachel Breytenbach, Bill Davies, Arnold Stofile, Peter Vale, Ms Nombeko Mlambo, Paulus Zulu, Dan Taylor and Jeremy Evans form significant parts of other chapters. There were other discussions, no less valuable, which, while not specifically mentioned in the book, enlightened me in a general sort of way and influenced my thinking and writing. These were with: Sheena Duncan (from Black Sash and the South African Council of Churches), H W (Harvey) van der Merwe, Tom Lodge, Neville Alexander, André du Toit, Moeletsi Mbeki, Simon Bekker, Gavin Maasdorp, Seymour Kapelowitz, Irene Menell, Z B du Toit (editor of the Conservative Party's mouthpiece, *Die Patriot*), Jan Marais (the owner of a consultancy firm in Cape Town), Eloff Theuns (consultant at CODESA), Francis Wilson, Arena Botha (from the South African Foundation) and Carl Nöffke.

I am thankful to Ina Perlman, the director of Operation Hunger, for having arranged a trip for me in the poor, drought-stricken area of Winterveld, north of Pretoria. Wolfgang Thomas, a director with the SBDC (Small Business Development Corporation), was very helpful in providing contacts; so were Casper Venter, the PR officer to President De Klerk and Roelf Meyer, the youthful and media-genic minister of Constitutional Development and the government's chief negotiator at the Multi-party Talks.

It is not perhaps too late to mention some of those – if not already mentioned above – who provided friendship and assistance in 1986. I can think of Joe Menell, Barry Streek, 'Laurie' Schlemmer, Beyers Naudé, Deon Geldenhuys, Chris Heymans and Mike Rantho, but there were several others.

I would like to thank the following:

University of California Press for permission to use material from *White Tribe of Africa: South Africa in Perspective* by David Harrison, published by University of California Press.

Weidenfeld and Nicolson for permission to quote from *The Boer War* by Thomas Pakenham, published by Weidenfeld and Nicolson.

Random House UK Limited for permission to use material from *My Traitor's Heart* by Rian Malan, published by The Bodley Head.

André Brink for permission to quote from *Looking on Darkness* by André Brink, published by W H Allen & Co.

The task that remains is a relief as well as a pleasure. It is to express my gratitude to my family for having put up, not only with my long absences in 1986 and in 1992, but also for my occasionally erratic temper in the long months that it took to write this book. Simone, my wife has an additional claim to my gratitude, having borne the larger part of the responsibility for providing for our needs in the last five years or so.

Z E, Geneva
June 1993

Introduction

I hesitated a long time before putting the word 'catharsis' in the title of this book. I thought it sounded presumptuous, even pedantic, besides being pessimistic and implying large-scale violence in the transitional period. Furthermore, it also seemed to me, in a superstitious and fatalistic sort of way, that I would, by using it, conjure up, precipitate even, the very violence that I wished could be avoided. Catharsis is a Greek word that Aristotle among others used in the sense of the cleansing or purification of the soul that the spectators of a Greek tragedy experienced during or immediately after the performance. In those days, the Greek tragedy was close in time and in spirit to the rituals and ceremonies which had to do with myth and religion, and the Greek spectator was not a mere onlooker but an active participant in what was going on. Freud, that great admirer of Greek antiquity, borrowed the term to describe his new psychoanalytical tool or technique (which indeed he called the 'Cathartic Method') the purpose of which was to help patients under hypnosis to remember and tell about their repressed experiences.

In retrospect, I realise that the idea of catharsis, if not the word itself, is present in practically all the seventeen chapters of the book. From the very first chapter – where Rory Riordan explains why De Klerk and the Nats cannot really afford to transfer power to the blacks without iron-clad guarantees as to the whites' future; which, of course, the black leaders cannot agree to because it would compromise their credibility; they can and will concede a power-sharing arrangement for a limited period of time (the so-called 'sunset clauses' in the future constitution), but that only postpones the inevitable outcome which, 'at the end of the day' (a favourite expression in South African English) is black power. To chapter seven where the vital question of violence is discussed at some length. To the very last one, where Pallo Jordan attributes the whites' refusal to recognise the 'essential humanity' of the blacks to a 'question of moral universe'; ie, they do not believe that white and blacks belong to the *same* moral universe.

As for the word 'healing' in the title, I wanted, at an earlier stage and in an outburst of innocence and optimism, to call the book simply *The Healing of South Africa*. But that would have been unwarranted and naive optimism, given the constant and growing violence that now involves the whites too and the enormous magnitude of the problems that lie ahead. However, in the course of the writing of the book I slowly came to realise that while *The Healing of South Africa* would not do by itself as a title, the concept was quite appropriate *after* the introduction of the word 'catharsis' into it. Not only for reasons of balance and symmetry, but also as a message of hope which is justified if certain conditions are fulfilled. Sticklers for semantic precision will object that the word 'catharsis' already incorporates that of 'healing' and, therefore, that the latter is redundant. Well, that is true to some extent. In psychoanalysis the concept of catharsis does imply that the patient will heal. But not necessarily, and he or she may relapse into the psychosis. It is thus, preferable, I believe, to mention the two words in tandem together. Besides, the word 'healing' has a magical quality for me.

During my travels in South Africa I did encounter a great deal of goodwill on the part of blacks and whites alike. But a peaceful resolution of the conflict will depend essentially on the sacrifices that the whites are willing to make to compensate for the injustices of the past. Both the catharsis – a devastating civil war at worst, serious but controllable disturbances at best – and the healing – the achievement of a viable society in which the various communities tolerate one another – will be the function of that will to sacrifice. The more they are prepared to sacrifice, the shorter and milder the catharsis, and the more complete and definitive the healing, and vice versa.

The structure and contents of this book reflect my belief that to understand the South African reality an eclectic and comprehensive approach is necessary. I thus looked into as many aspects of that reality as I could. I also hope that somehow the whole (the book) is more than the sum of its parts (the twenty-one chapters). The political, economic and social realities are disseminated in all of them. However, the first three chapters: 'U-Turn on 2 February 1990', 'CODESA' and '*Quo Vadis* Van Zyl?' as well as a section of Chapter 15, 'Travel Notes Two', deal exclusively with political questions. 'U-Turn' is an introduction to the new politics of South Africa. Why did F W de Klerk and the Afrikaner power elite change their minds? What do they hope to achieve? How has the ANC adapted to the new situation? What is the likely outcome of the confrontation/accommodation between the two? These are some of the crucial questions that this chapter attempts to provide answers

to. 'CODESA' is an analytical and descriptive summary of the negotiations between the minority government, the ANC and several
other participants to the Convention for a Democratic South Africa
(CODESA) between December 1991 and May 1992. *'Quo Vadis'* is a
candid and in-depth discussion of the nuts and bolts of South
African politics with F Van Zyl Slabbert, who is a progressive and
charismatic intellectual and politician.

Chapters 9 on 'The Burning Issue of the Land', 13 on 'Being
Super Rich in South Africa' and 17, 'Wrapping It Up With Pallo'
focus on economics. Chapter 9 poses the thorny question of the
land, then presents the tentative portraits of two white landowning
farming families in Western Cape as case studies. The Menells are
one of the two families that control Anglovaal, one of the seven
'Majors' (biggest conglomerates) in South Africa. Through them the
role and position of big business in South Africa are examined.
Pallo Jordan is one of the five or six top ANC leaders. This concluding chapter is based on a lengthy conversation with him which
itself is based on SAIRR's *Race Relations Survey 1991–2*, considered
generally to be the best and most reliable source of information and
statistics on South Africa.

The social problems, principally the appalling conditions under
which the large majority of Africans live in the townships, the
squatter camps and the rural areas, are examined in chapter 10 'The
Story of Crossroads/Khayelitsha', 11 'Notes on Soweto', 12 'Back
in Cradock Six Years Later' and parts of three 'Travel Notes' chapters 14, 15 and 16. The destruction of Crossroads, a shanty town
area near Cape Town in the 1970s and the creation of Khayelitsha,
both in the 1980s, are closely related. Perhaps 80 per cent of Khayelitsha's million or so residents live in shacks. This chapter includes
an interview with Sam Dube, a businessman from Khayelitsha, who
is a remarkable example of African entrepreneurial ability in the
face of overwhelming odds. Soweto, with its 3 million plus inhabitants, in one sense is the biggest slum in the world but in another
sense it could be a nascent African megalopolis. 'Back in Cradock
Six Years Later' is the story of my friendship with four African and
one white community leaders in that inland town of the Eastern
Cape. One of them is the uncle of Matthiew Goniwe, the young
black activist leader who was assassinated by the security services
in 1986; another, the brother of E Barayi, the former president of
COSATU (the Congress of South African Trade Unions, the biggest

labour confederation in the country). The pre-eminent leadership factor is analysed in chapters 6, 'The *Dopper* vs the Magnanimous Man', 7, 'The Buthelezi Conundrum', and 8, '*Nkosi Sikelel' iAfrika*'. The *Doppers* are members of a small and very conservative Calvinist church. De Klerk is a *Dopper*. Mandela is seen as Aristotle's Magnanimous Man. The chapter probes into the lives, personal histories and character of the two men. Buthelezi is the big enigma of South African politics. What does he really want? The subject is tackled dialectically: thesis (arguments of those who support him), antithesis (arguments of those who are against him) and synthesis (a balanced, objective view). Chapter 8 revolves around the author's three hectic days in the Cape during which the March 1992 referendum of the whites and the Sharpeville Rally in Khayelitsha took place in which Mandela participated; it also contains the brief profiles of some of the main leaders of the ANC-COSATU-SACP alliance.

There are two full chapters – 4, 'Being a Black Writer in a Racist Society' and 5, 'Afrikaner Literati on Language and Politics' devoted to culture and literature. In the former, Es'Kia Mphahlele, a grand old man of black South African letters, extemporates on the relationship between literature and politics in the situation of apartheid. The latter is a round-table discussion with Jan Rabie, a well-known Afrikaner writer, Marjorie Wallace, his wife and Hermien Dommisse, an actress, on literature and politics and the central role that the so-called Coloured people have played in the development of the Afrikaans language.

The three 'Travel Notes' chapters are perforce very eclectic and cover a number of different subjects including: the life of Robert Sobukwe, the PAC (Pan-Africanist Congress) leader; some original research on District Six, the Coloured district of Cape Town which was destroyed under the Group Areas Act; a visit to the politically radical, largely Coloured, University of Western Cape (UWC); a summary of my two days in Port Elizabeth's and Uitenhage's black townships, which are among the worst in South Africa; the reminiscences of Rachel Breytenbach about her brother Breyten, the great Afrikaans poet; a description of grass-roots development efforts – in Grahamstown, Robert Berold's Power Station Co-operative and, in Umtata, the work of Cecil Cook's TATU; a summary of my brief incursions into the Zululand and the 'Berg' (Drakensberg mountain resorts for the well-to-do).

Finally, there is the Supplement at the end of the book, made up of four chapters on the South African political history, which is intended mainly for readers who consider themselves unfamiliar with that subject. It should be read before the main text as an introduction to it. But, for those who *are* familiar with South Africa, reading it after the text might provide a pleasant, revelatory effect that is characteristic of rediscovering something that we knew once but which has receded to the back of our minds. Chapter 18, 'Early Days', is about the first inhabitants of the Cape Peninsula – the Strandlopers, the Hottentots and the Bushmen – and the arrival of the Dutch East India Company (DEIC) in 1652. Chapter 19, 'The Imperial Century', has sub-sections on Old and New Imperialism, both in the UK and in South Africa. The cultural imperialism of the British and the history-changing consequences of the discoveries of diamonds and gold in close succession at the end of the nineteenth century, which eventually led to the bloody Anglo-Boer War, are all examined therein. The era of the Generals (Botha, Smuts and Hertzog), Malan's watershed victory in 1948, the fascinating story of the *Broederbond*, apartheid's golden era up to Verwoerd's assassination in September 1966, Vorster and the beginning of the reform movement in the mid–1970s, are all in the Chapter 20, 'The Afrikaner Era'. The last chapter, 'The Liberation Struggle', starts with the naïve and innocent years at the beginning of the twentieth century, and then continues with the coming of age of the ANC in the 1940s and 1950s, the creation of *Umkhonto we Sizwe* (the military wing of the ANC) and the armed struggle, the split of the PAC and the Sharpeville Massacre in 1960. Then come the rise of the Black Consciousness (BC) movement in the late 1960s and early 1970s, the Soweto explosion of 1976 and its bloody aftermath. The chapter ends with a thorough look at black labour: its incredible growth in fifteen years or so, from the Durban strikes of the early 1970s, to the formation of the mammoth COSATU in the late 1980s.

This book is based essentially on my research trip that took place in the first half of 1992. Its true genesis, however, goes back to the autumn of 1985, when I was a visiting research professor with the African Studies Programme of Georgetown University in Washington, DC. It is then that I started writing the four chapters that form the Supplement in this book. In March 1986, I left for South Africa for a research trip that lasted a little over three months. It was an academically oriented trip, unlike that of 1992 which can, I believe, be called – as a South African journalist friend put it judiciously – 'deep journalism'.

I have decided to put the Notes singly at the end of each individual chapter, and not together at the end of the book. The main reason for this is that, in the main text, each chapter is a self-contained and independent subject – even though part of a larger whole. A related reason is that I have used the Notes sections to update and upgrade the chapters, roughly six to nine months after I finished writing the book. So it makes sense to read them right after the chapters and not to wait until one has read the whole book. Besides, I know from experience that searching for notes at the end of he book can be an unwieldy and frustrating activity.

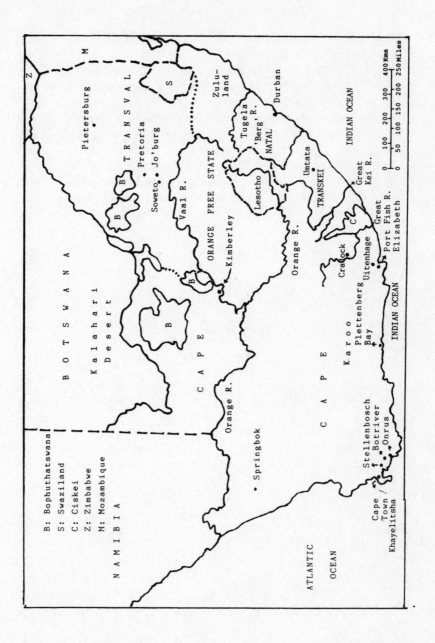

Part One

The Catharsis and the Healing

1

U-Turn on 2 February 1990: A *Cognoscente* Explains

'The referendum was a big gamble. I thought he was mad.'
Rory Riordan

Rory Riordan is the director of the Human Rights Fund in Port Elizabeth and the editor of the *Monitor*, a quarterly publication which provides in-depth coverage of the South African political scene by means of well illustrated interviews and well researched investigative articles. The Fund was started in the mid-1980s by Andrew Savage, a wealthy liberal businessman-cum-politician, who died in July 1990. Riordan is a neat-looking fellow of about forty. Tall, blond, clean-shaven (he used to sport a beard in the more revolutionary climate of the late eighties), extremely articulate, quick-witted, he is an excellent journalist of a liberal persuasion.

The following conversation took place in April 1992 in his office on the second floor of a modest two-storey building which houses the Fund's total staff of five or six. It is essentially an *ex-post-facto* commentary on the radical transformation of the South African political scene in the aftermath of De Klerk's famous speech in February 1990, in which he announced the unbanning of the ANC, PAC and SACP, and the liberation of Nelson Mandela. It is also a hard-headed, feet-on-the-ground assessment based on balance of power realities, unencumbered by any ethical or moral considerations; the 'what is' reigns supreme, uncluttered by the 'what should be'. In retrospect, the overwhelming impression that I derived from the conversation is that the best way to describe what is going on in South Africa today is that it is a power struggle, and that the Afrikaner power elite would like to hold on to real power until they become convinced that they have minimised the risk of retribution. They are also likely to procrastinate because they think that the passage of time acts in their favour: they would like to organise a non-racial coalition of conservative/liberal forces (a combination possible in the South African context) that could challenge the ANC at the polls.

I met Riordan at about five o'clock in the afternoon, after having spent the day visiting the infamous black townships of Port Elizabeth which are among the worst in South Africa.

'I found the townships very quiet and peaceful,' I said. 'A pleasant surprise after the Western Cape. . . .'

'The primary reason of the quiet and peace here in the Eastern Cape,' he answered, 'is that there is no Inkatha here, this an ANC stronghold. Secondly, the great revolt against the state is over, because it has been won. So, the ANC is into politics now.'

I asked him to summarise the politics of the transition: first, from De Klerk's and the National Party's perspective, and then from the ANC's perspective.

'All right,' he said, 'the new era began on 2 February 1990. Before that we had ten, twelve years of autocratic, militaristic rule by a government headed by P W Botha who was a man whose political tradition was the military. He was the man who built the South African military machine. He came into the presidency from being minister of Defence and was president for ten years through the Soweto riots when the military option was the big thing. He was the man who presided over: the 'total onslaught, total response' strategy; the growth of the South African arms industry; and the destabilisation campaigns in Southern Africa, especially in Mozambique and the war in Angola. All that was Botha's response to a political dynamic. That was the way he saw the world. But, as is inevitable with military/autocratic regimes, the government's behaviour became such that it made it difficult for its traditional allies to continue supporting it. And so it was that, after the institution of the tricameral system and the United Democratic Front (UDF)-organised resistance to it in the mid 80s, a whole range of pressures began building up round the South African government. Pressures for change which range from the obvious ones, like those induced by changing demographics – in 1948, for example, when the Nats came to power, the single biggest of group of people in Port Elizabeth were the whites who formed 40 per cent of the total;

now they are 20 per cent, and there are three times as many Africans – to less obvious ones like international sanctions, of which some worked, some didn't. Among those which did, the financial embargo by the international banks was perhaps the most effective. The UN-imposed military embargo caused an unbelievably large amount of the South African GDP to be diverted to an arms industry that the country could ill afford. Then came the Soviet/American accord on Angola which meant that, willy-nilly, South Africa had to get out of Angola. There were other things that were pretty effective too, such as: the sports boycott, cricket, rugby and the Olympic Games particularly; and the spectacle of South African ambassadors and foreign dignitaries being vilified all around the world – in Sydney, Australia, there were crowds of people spitting at the staff of the South African Embassy when they came to work and there were constant vigils in front of the embassy in Washington that lasted for months. On top of all that was the deterioration of the terms of trade of our base minerals and gold industry, as well as of our manufactured and agricultural products. We could continue to export but it cost much more. . . . On the home front, the endless and ongoing township revolt. They couldn't stop it no matter what they did and how much they tried. In Port Elizabeth, for example, one out of every hundred Africans was in gaol at some point after the national State of Emergency of June 1986. They beat them, they tortured them, they murdered the leaders in the middle of the night, others went into exile, but the revolt continued rolling.

'So, these were, in a nutshell, the pressures building up on the National Party, and the response of Botha was to dig a deeper trench and to buy a bigger gun. Then he had a stroke and was forced to resign, and De Klerk took over. He is a very good Afrikaner civil politician – not a military man at all – a lawyer by training, a conservative but also pragmatic man. De Klerk got into that big office and looked around, and I am sure he had never been told before what the pressures were. Botha was like Ian Smith, the stuff got stuck on his desk: it never got out, not even to his cabinet. There were things like the Department of Foreign Affairs seriously considering building a harbour on the Turkish coast at a cost of $450 million that De Klerk had probably never heard about [to get iron and other minerals into the European Community]. The resources of the country were being wasted to keep a system going that couldn't be kept going anyway. In real terms the GDP had been shrinking for about ten years.

'I am convinced that De Klerk looked at all this and his eyes were opened, he had never seen it before, and he said: "My God, there must be a solution to all this!" He is a civil politician, so he looked for a civilian solution. Being an intelligent man, he said right from the beginning that you can't negotiate only with black leaders that you like and disregard the others; you have to negotiate with those leaders that can deliver those constituencies that are giving you trouble. It was the ANC that was delivering the revolt in South Africa, that was delivering the international sanctions, so he knew that he had to negotiate with them. Hence the speech of February of 1990. He threw the thing open then, but he didn't throw it open blindly or stupidly. He threw it open with a whole range of strategies which were going to allow him to control the process. No politician ever surrenders control easily, as you well know. You must also remember that the whites in South Africa have had control of the territory in which they lived for almost 350 years. They've had exclusive control and they've manipulated the resources of that territory exclusively for their own benefit. They've behaved like farmers on a farm: it is their property, they own it, they can do with it what they like; they can move the cattle to this pen when they want, and to that pen when it suits them; that's the way they've always behaved. So, there is an enormous amount of tension involved in this process.'

'What you are saying is that they will try to hold on to power. How are they going to go about it? What is the strategy?' I asked.

'As I see it,' he responded, 'this is the way De Klerk looks at it: whether or not the ANC can deliver the vote, and I shall do my best that it doesn't, I must control the process and end up with a situation that I can live with. What is that situation? It is one in which real power remains in white hands in the predictable future. How do you do that? You do it through the continued control of the civil service, the security establishment, the parastatals (state-controlled enterprises), the media, and so on. The oldest political trick in history is to reward your followers with governmental jobs and the Nats have done that: in more than forty years in power they've crammed those institutions with their own people. I am not sure of the figures, but something like 1,200 top civil servants out of 1,350 are white Afrikaans-speaking males. It is the same thing with the security establishment. In South Africa about a third of the GDP is spent through the public sector, and that is effective control no matter who is in government. A parallel strategy is that which sometimes is called the DTA Option (after the Democratic Turnhalle Alliance in Namibia). It consists of getting together the second largest political coalition in the country after the ANC: the business community and the Democratic Party will be part of it; as well as Inkatha and the other conservative homeland governments; and possibly between half and two-thirds of the Coloured and Indian voters. So, even if the ANC wins a majority at the polls, they will turn around and say: "We can't govern this bloody place by ourselves! We haven't got the skills, and the connections, the means. So we have got to do it with somebody else." And who do they do it with? With De Klerk obviously. At the end of the day, if one party controls the votes, and another party practically everything else, that other party governs. You see, from the very beginning De Klerk's strategy has been predicated around maintaining real power, but through a system that would be acceptable to the international community.'

'Right. Let's now look at things from the ANC's point of view. Surely, they must have a counter-strategy, or something?' I asked.

'February 1990 was a big shock for the ANC,' he said. '1990 was a year of enormous tensions and pressures. They were an exiled organisation who saw themselves as waging an armed struggle and suddenly the rules of the game were changed. What were they going to do? Bring the head office to Jo'burg? They didn't trust De Klerk and his gang, not for an inch; who knows what could happen if they closed down in Lusaka and came here. Leadership? It was scattered all over the place: Lusaka, Robben Island, UDF, SACP, COSATU, underground, in the townships; how were they going to bring all these people together? Meanwhile, Oliver Tambo was struck down with a stroke and he was out of the picture. Opening a new office in Jo'burg, raising money, handling the guys coming out of gaol, dealing with the exiles coming back home. There was the violence in Natal they had to contend with, the strikes in East London and the riots in Port Elizabeth. They were under great pressure throughout 1990.

'There was a hell of a lot of self-inflicted injury as well: Mandela should've arranged to meet with Buthelezi and sort things out with him, but he didn't; they insisted on nationalisation and alienated the business community; they did not try to win the hearts and minds of the whites. They made countless mistakes, shot themselves in the foot regularly, there can be no doubt about it. So, in the end of 1990, the ANC looked weak and De Klerk strong.

'But in 1991, the winds started blowing in the other direction, the ANC began picking up momentum. In April, Mandela stopped co-operating with the government, accusing it of helping Inkatha in its violent campaign against the ANC. Gangs of hostel-dwelling Zulus were sweeping through the ANC communities in the townships, murdering, burning and maiming indiscriminately, and the police would always be somewhere else. The ANC could not mobilise under those circumstances, they couldn't get their organisation up and running. The ball was now in De Klerk's court. A big plus was when the ANC acquired the Shell building in downtown Jo'burg and installed its national headquarters there. Then, in July they had their first national congress in Durban where they brought 2,200 delegates together. I was there, it was a bloody good conference. For the first time ever, people from Lusaka, Dar es Salaam, London, Washington, Robben Island, the townships were united. You could sense the organisation coming together. The ANC left Durban with a fully elected, properly mandated national executive, including Mandela, who was elected president and who was clearly in charge.

'As fate would have it, this is when the Inkatha funding scandal broke out. Incontrovertible evidence surfaced that the government had been financing the IFP (Inkatha Freedom Party) illegally to the tune of many millions of rands for years. De Klerk's position was weakened significantly. So when the ANC sat down with the Nationalists for the National Peace Commission's first meeting in Pretoria, it had achieved full parity with them. The Inkatha funding scandal also hit Buthelezi where he was most vulnerable: his international reputation. It did not hurt his support base at home because that was made up primarily of a number of tribal arrangements, but his international reputation, which is so important to him, suffered. On 5 and 6 November came the VAT strike during which the ANC was able to almost paralyse the country for two days. De Klerk was again weakened, because plainly the old National Party style of politics, which was telling the country what was going to happen in advance, was not working any more. One more event that strengthened the ANC was that they were responsible for ending the sports boycott: the All Blacks (the famous New Zealand rugby team) came to South Africa, the national cricket team went on an international tour, the Springbok (here rugby but all national sports teams are called that) travelled to Europe and the international Olympic committee decided that South Africa could participate in the next Olympic Games. Meanwhile De Klerk was being savaged by the white right inside and outside parliament: they said, correctly, that he didn't have a mandate from the white electorate to do what he was doing; and they defeated him badly in all the by-elections that took place between February 1990 and December 1991. In conclusion, at the end of 1991, the ANC was much stronger than at the beginning of it, and it was the opposite for De Klerk who was clearly in trouble, and then he pulled the big one on us. . . .

'The referendum [whether or not to negotiate with the ANC] was a big gamble. I thought he was mad. I couldn't believe that he was doing it! I thought that three outcomes were possible: one, the least likely one, he would win a big majority and that would be a personal triumph; two, he would win by a small majority which would not solve the problem at all; three, he would lose, which would be a total disaster for him and the rest of us. Personally, I favoured the second possibility. To grasp the importance of the referendum, you must realise that De Klerk was facing at the time a full-scale revolt from within his own National Party caucus and from within the security forces. So he had to pull a big one, and he did. The Sunday night before the referendum (17 March 1992), I saw him on television in *Agenda*. God, did he look worried. As a rule, he looks very much in control of himself. But the news was bad: as late as Friday, there had been reports that the 'Nos' were gaining in the Transvaal and the Free State and that it was dangerously close in the two provinces. The National Party machine was in tatters. But, in the end he saw it through and won very big: almost 70 per cent of 'Yes' vote. It was better than what they were hoping in the wildest of their dreams. Now, what follows from this? I believe that De Klerk has achieved two major results with his victory in the referendum: one, he clobbered the white right wing; he has left the Conservative Party absolutely shredded, I don't think they will ever recover from it; two, he has made himself a much stronger bargaining opponent for the ANC; he can now claim a mandate from the white electorate for a range of policies which nobody knows much about. There will be also a certain euphoria and arrogance that will last a couple of months probably and then it will be back to serious business.'[1]

'What about the future? How do you see it?' I asked.

'First of all you've got to realise that we are in Africa, not in Scandinavia or Switzerland,' he said. 'I've been to Norway twice lately. They have a five million population who all look alike, all speak the same language, 90 per cent of them go to the same church and all adore the same king. It's a club. Here in South Africa, we've got nine languages, each of which is the home language for more than three per cent of the population. The cultural gulfs, whether we want to admit them or not, are stunning. This is really a very diverse country and to build a nation out of this mix is a considerable task which will require a lot of time and effort. Politically, the daunting challenge is to have a government that can effectively govern while at the same time not being destroyed by the opposition. Let's assume that we have a purely ANC government. If the Nationalists, the Conservatives, the business community and Inkatha wanted to destabilise it, they probably could. In other words, a purely ANC government would leave too many elites unsatisfied. Now, let's assume that we have an ANC/NP national unity government. That would leave Inkatha and a lot of activists in the townships unsatisfied. We must somehow structure a government that gives satisfaction to all the forces and factions that could otherwise destabilise it. It is going to be an unbelievably complex and complicated task. Something similar is true for the economy: we must somehow work out a system which is fiscally responsible, while at the same time responding to the urgent needs of the African community. It's a huge task which will require enormous amounts of brains and political courage and compromise.'

'I have this fear,' I said, 'that South Africa may come to resemble Brazil before the democratisation of the 1980s: a system of government that Latin-American scholars conceptualised as "bureaucratic authoritarianism", which is essentially either a military government with civilian support, or the reverse: a civilian government with military support. An unfortunate characteristic of such a system is that it results in the exclusion of a large minority of people – something like 30 to 40 per cent of the population – from the mainstream economy. These people are the left-out, the marginalised, Fanon's "Wretched of the Earth", who live in the vast northeast region, as well as in the slums around the big cities. They are the victims sacrificed on the altar of modernisation. There are, for all intents and purposes, two separate countries within the same Brazil: one is industrialised and belongs to the First World, while the other is a backward, poor Third World country. The two co-exist without really coming together. To a significant extent, the same situation exists in South Africa too: the white cities and sub-urbs could be in America somewhere, while the black townships, the squatter camps and rural areas could be in Nigeria or even Zaire. South Africa does not appear to have the means to fundamen-tally alter the situation, so a bureaucratic-authoritarian system would be the logical outcome. If that assessment is correct, what will power-sharing come to mean? Co-opting some African elites into the leadership structures? The creation of a new black middle class? Both?'[2]

'The business of transferring [real] power to the ANC has never been on their agenda,' he said emphatically. 'That does not mean, however, that things will come out in the end the way they want them to come out. They might've created a dynamic that they will not be able to control in the end. The Nats think, whether they are right or wrong, that the initial elections in South Africa will turn on Third World symbolism: personalities, flags, national anthems, and so on; and not on the issues.'

'Yes, but,' I asked, 'what happens later when the expectations and aspirations of the people are not met?'

'Well, that's the question that we shall have to face eventually, isn't it? You've probably heard that story about that woman in Khayelitsha who said: "Well, it's been more than two weeks that Mandela has been out of prison, *where* is my house?" Even if it is apocryphal, the story does tell you something about the situation: what are those people going to do when they find out that there won't be any houses for most of them? It's going to be tough. Particularly if the ANC leadership is seen driving the big cars, living in the big houses, sending their kids to the exclusive schools, and so on. That's what the 'Pan-Africanist Congress (PAC) – ANC's political nemesis – and the Azanian People's Organisation (AZAPO) – a radical, BC-oriented group popular among intellectuals – people are waiting for. They know they are not going to win many votes in the first elections, they are banking on the discontent, the disil-lusion that will follow them. It might happen, but, on the other hand, the ANC constituency has remained very loyal and solid through the most incredible attacks, and massacres, and infiltrations, and exile, and homelands being set up, so it might last a bit longer yet. I wouldn't sell them short at this point.'

It was getting late and Rory Riordan rose, signifying the end of the interview. We went down the stairs and out onto the street. I left him after thanking him once more. As I was driving back to the Humewood hotel on the Summerstrand, I thought that I was impressed by his wit, intelligence, articulateness and analytical ability. It was an excellent performance honed by repetition like that of a good actor in a good play. One thing obscurely bothered me, however. What was the connection between that performance and the dismal reality that I had seen in the townships and squatter camps of the Port Elizabeth/Uitenhage area?[3] I suspected him, unfairly probably, of playing a role, doing a job, in other words of having lost the true commitment, the passion, that he had earlier in the mid and late 1980s. But, on the other hand, that was life: to survive one has to adapt to changing circumstances.

Notes

1 In retrospect, Riordan turned out to be wrong in his prognostication that the right wing was 'clobbered' and the CP 'shredded'. Not only have they recovered from the shattering defeat of the referendum, but they have gained much ground. The latest polls (June 1993) suggest that as many as two-thirds of the whites support the right wing despite the election of the hard-liner Ferdie Hartzenberg to the presidency of the CP in replacement of Andries Treurnicht, who died at age 72 after a heart by-pass operation.

Two right-wing organisations came into being in April 1993 that are natural allies: the Afrikaner Popular Front (*Volksfront*), which unites virtually all the white right-wing political organisations (including labour unions) in the country; and the Concerned South Africans Group (COSAG) made up of the CP, Inkatha, Mangope's Bophuthatswana and Gqozo's Ciskei. The *Volksfront* wants a separate state for the Afrikaner nation; COSAG, a very loose, decentralised political system which suits their sectarian interests. What gives the *Volksfront* more credibility this time is that it is headed by General C Viljoen, the swashbuckling and beloved former commander of the SADF in Angola in the 1980s.

2 In his preface to *Reform and Revolution: South Africa in the 1990s*, published by Skotaville, 1991, Johannesburg, Gordon Naidoo, the editor, writes that there is a danger 'that the more things change the more they will remain

the same for the majority of the black population'. He also asks the question of whether what will emerge is 'a deracialised but unchanged economic system'. A theme that is common to all the contributors of the book is the fear that many leaders in the national liberation movement (read ANC) may be co-opted into the dominant and privileged class.

3 See Chapter 15 for an account of the dismal reality of the townships and squatter camps of the Port Elizabeth/Uitenhage area.

2

CODESA: Round One Was a Tie

There was a fairy-tale quality in this improbable gathering of erstwhile implacable enemies now socialising together . . .

On 21 December 1991, nineteen delegations of twelve persons each, plus a number of experts and journalists, met at the World Trade Centre in Kempton Park, a commercial and industrial area near Jo'burg's Jan Smuts Airport. Officially they all had equal status and represented the various political constituencies in the country. Ostensibly, the equality of status derived from two main reasons: one, it was desirable, at least at the beginning, for the negotiations – for a new, non-racial and democratic South Africa – to be as broadly based as possible; this was, after all, a country for so long torn apart by racism, discrimination, factionalism, mistrust, hostility and so on. Secondly, since a nation-wide, non-racial election was never held before, there was no way of knowing the real force of the parties in presence. In reality, of course, everyone knew that South Africa's future would primarily be determined by the two leading protagonists, the ANC and De Klerk's Nationalists, with Buthelezi's Inkatha playing a spoiler's role. Besides these three major forces, the participants to the conference included: the Democratic Party of the white House of Assembly, the National People's Party (NPP) and Solidarity of the Indian House of Delegates, the Labour Party of the Coloured House of Representatives (the three Houses of the moribund Tricameral Parliament); the extra-parliamentary Indian and Coloured opposition movements: the joint delegation for the Natal and Transvaal Indian Congresses (NIC and TIC); the South African Communist Party (SACP); and the governments of the four TBVC states 'Transkei, Bophuthatswana, Venda and Ciskei,' and the six homelands (Lebowa, KwaNdebele, KaNg-wane, Gazankulu and Qwa Qwa). Among the no-shows in Kempton Park were the 'respectable' right-wing Conservative Party (official opposition in the white House of Assembly since 1987 and a formidable rival of the ruling National Party), the PAC, AZAPO and the neo-Nazi or fascist AWB (the Afrikaner Resistance Movement in Afrikaans).

During the two days that the plenary sessions lasted, the two-hundred-plus delegates mingled in the cavernous halls of the World Trade Centre, trading jokes (gallows humour?), backslapping one another (at least metaphorically) and pinching themselves (literally) to make sure that all this was really happening. For there was a fairy-tale quality in this improbable gathering of erstwhile implacable enemies now socialising together as if they were bosom friends who had lost track of one another for a very long time. The over-zealous practitioners of apartheid of not so long ago, the gaolers and the torturers; the leaders of the liberation struggle, the freedom fighters, the militants, the activists, those on the receiving end of the big stick, those who had spent big chunks of their lives on Robben Island, Pollsmoor, Pretoria Central, or the other maximum-security prisons across the land; those who had betrayed the cause, the collaborators; those who had benefited handsomely from apartheid while they were paying lip service to human rights; they were all there like in a class reunion, thirty, forty years after graduation. It was almost absurd, like a surrealistic painting, to see Joe Slovo (for decades Public Enemy Number One of the government; a man whose wife, Ruth First, was killed by the Security Services; a man whose very name is anathema to Big Business) chatting amicably with Kobie Coetzee, the justice minister, and Zach de Beer, the leader of the Democratic Party and, for a long time, a protégé of Harry Oppenheimer, the Anglo-American's former chairman and the richest man in South Africa. And Chris Hani,[1] for many years the chief-of-staff of *Umkhonto we Sizwe*, rubbing elbows with Adriaan Vlok, minister of Law and Order in the mid to late 1980s – during the national State of Emergency – and the man responsible for the detention of an estimated 30,000 political activists.

CODESA did not happen one day out of the blue.[2] It came about more or less as the logical conclusion of a number of breakthroughs between the ANC and the government, the first of which was, according to H W van der Merwe, director of the Cape-Town-based Centre for Intergroup Studies, the direct talks that he was able to arrange, in 1984, between 'Piet' Muller, the assistant editor of the *Beeld*, who travelled to Lusaka to meet the ANC's national leadership. After his return, Muller published a series of articles which were favourable to the idea of negotiations.

Then came, between 1986 and 1989, the direct meetings between Nelson Mandela (who had been moved from Robben Island first to Pollsmoor prison and then to a warden's house in Victor Verster prison) and National Party bigwigs; beginning with Justice Minister Coetzee, followed by the minister of Constitutional Development, Gerrit Viljoen and, finally P W Botha himself. One of the first things that F W de Klerk did after replacing the 'Old Crocodile' was to meet the leader of the ANC. Meanwhile, things were also happening outside the official circles: it was in 1987 that Van Zyl Slabbert's Institute for a Democratic Alternative for South Africa (IDASA) organised its famous Dakar expedition to which some seventy prominent *verligte* (enlightened) Afrikaners (as well as some Anglos), academics, journalists, churchmen and businessmen participated. The ANC delegation was led by Thabo Mbeki and included first-drawer intellectuals such as Pallo Jordan and Mac Maharaj. The Dakar meeting was a turning point, leading to a change of heart and of perception on the part of the white public opinion concerning the ANC; the latter was now seen – to borrow Lady Thatcher's famous expression about Gorbachev – as an organisation one 'could do business with'. IDASA continued with its facilitating, mediating role and several meetings were organised between UDF, on the one hand, and the business community and liberal politicians on the other. Later Big Business was instrumental in the creation of the Consultative Business Movement (CBM), which was to play a key management role within CODESA.

After his liberation in February 1990, Mandela went to Lusaka and was named deputy president of the ANC. For all intents and purposes he was the new leader, because of Oliver Tambo's incapacitation. As winter approached in the southern hemisphere (in May), Mandela and F W were face to face again in Groote Schuur, the state president's official residence in Cape Town. The two leaders acknowledged once more that they needed each other and signalled their readiness to make compromises so that an agreement could be reached. There were other meetings that reinforced this commitment and the so-called 'pillars of apartheid' – the Land Acts of 1913 and 1936, the Group Areas Act of 1956, and the Population Registration Act of 1950 – were abolished. The stage was now set for the negotiations that would determine the future of South Africa to begin. They were at first called All Party Congress, then a Multi-party Conference and, finally, Convention for a Democratic South Africa, whose acronym CODESA quickly became a household word across the country and even overseas.

January and February 1992 were clearly a honeymoon period. The magic began to wear off in more or less direct proportion to the tackling of substantive issues. The single most important achievement of CODESA One (in anticipation of CODESA Two, the Plenary Session of which was scheduled to be held on 15 and 16 May, but which never was) came in March: all the participants, with the exception of KwaZulu and Bophuthatswana (Buthelezi and Mangope were rattled because their proposal to include the principle of federalism was not accepted), signed a Declaration of Intent. According to this, the new South African constitution would protect civil rights and personal freedoms; would be non-racial and non-sexist; there would be appropriate checks and balances as well as a separation of powers between the legislative, executive and judiciary branches of government; and the judiciary itself would be totally independent. The Declaration was hailed as a great achieve-ment because, it was said, all these principles might be as common-place as 'motherhood and apple pie' in America, but this was South Africa, a country that had never experienced democracy before, and so on. So, self-congratulation was the order of the day until the shoals of incompatibility were hit after 17 March. (This was the date of the whites-only referendum on whether or not the govern-ment should negotiate with the black opposition to bring about a new, power-sharing constitution (it was won by a landslide by De Klerk, see Chapter 1). The government, emboldened by its unex-pectedly big victory, made a series of tough demands (which amounted to a white minority veto) that were unacceptable to the ANC, and there was a deadlock, which was solidified by the Boipatong and Ciskei massacres of June and September 1992.

How did CODESA work? How was, in other words, the argu-ment carried forward? Its mechanics – secretariat, management and administrative services – are similar to those in all large conferences. More substantively, five working groups were established to deal

with the main issues of transition to democracy which were perceived to be: one, the creation of a climate conducive to free, unhin-
dered political activity; two, the definition and shaping of new,
democratic constitutional principles; three, transitional arrangements, ie, the accord for an interim government which would over-
see the period leading up to and including the drawing up of the
new constitution; four, the reincorporation of the four TBVC states
and six homelands back into South Africa; and five, time frames and
stages of implementation. Predictably enough, these five working
groups hatched a large number of offsprings (twenty-four in the
latest count) to look into the snags, the details and so on.

Were there any specific results? Well, Group One came to the
conclusion that as long as political violence continued, the whole
process of transition to democracy was endangered – a pretty logical
conclusion that was confirmed by the Boipatong, Ciskei and several
other massacres that came later; there was a lot of talk about a third
force manipulating and fomenting the violence to make it look as
if it was a black-on-black violence; the ANC and its allies believed
that the problem could not be solved without a radical restructuring
of the security forces which had to include, at some point, the
merging of *Umkhonto* and SADF at all levels. Other contentious
issues were: the release of the remaining political prisoners (some
of whom had blood on their hands); the return of the political exiles
and their families, which was hindered by an absence of funds (the
UNHCR was running out of funds, the government was slow in
releasing money); and the control of the South African Broadcasting
Corporation (the government has the prerogative of naming the
SABC's board of directors).

Group Two made no less than a hundred or so different proposals
as to the nature of the new political system that the new South
Africa should adopt, covering the whole gamut from an extremely
decentralised confederal/consociational system to a fairly central-
ised and unitary one. The government was in favour of a nominated
and broadly based group of experts drafting much of the constitution *before* the election of a constituent assembly (they were
against an elected body to begin with but they later relented); the
ANC, protesting that that would reduce the assembly to a rubber-
stamping parliament, was adamantly against it.

In Group Three, the Nationalists insisted that the present government should remain in power during the interim period which

they envisaged as a very long one (ten years). For the ANC both requirements were absolute non-starters: power had to be shared in an interim government of short duration (three or four years at the most). There were interesting developments in Group Four: the ANC and its allies wanted the reincorporation of the TBVC states and the homelands by a stroke of the pen, because they were artificial, illegal structures recognised by nobody outside the apartheid government that created them. The government, using the argument of constitutionality, dragged its feet. It also demanded that the populations concerned be consulted (by way of referenda) on whether or not they wanted to rejoin South Africa. The ten governments concerned were split right down the middle: five – KwaZulu, Ciskei, Bophuthatswana, Gazankulu and Qwa Qwa – supported Pretoria; the remaining five – Transkei, Venda, KaNgwane, KwaNdebele and Lebowa – the ANC. After the bloodbath of Ciskei the stage seemed to be set for more confrontation, not compromise.

In Group Five, the battle lines were drawn between the government, who wanted a long transitional period, and the ANC, who wanted a short one.

What happened after CODESA was stalemated? Even before Boipatong, the hardliners within the tripartite alliance ANC/ COSATU/SACP were calling for a more confrontational approach to be adopted because there was a growing gap between the angry mood of the people and the conciliatory attitude of the ANC leadership: 'We are losing touch with the grass roots. We are being seen as too soft. We are running the risk of our disappointed supporters moving to the left, ie the PAC and AZAPO.' Boipatong was the last straw and the alliance launched a mass-action campaign which would culminate in a two-day general strike at the beginning of August. The campaign and the strike were successful and just when the conditions seemed to be ripe for the negotiations to resume, the Ciskei massacre happened. De Klerk was forced into making major concessions: the release of the political prisoners, the constitution drawn by a democratically elected constituent assembly, a power-sharing interim government, and so on. But, as a quid pro quo, he pushed for a general amnesty for all political crimes committed during the apartheid era. Such a blanket amnesty would absolve the security services, the police and the politicians who were behind them, from the thousands of crimes that they committed in the

defence of white supremacy. Whether it is feasible politically for
the ANC to accept that those guilty of the torture and death of
Steve Biko and the assassination of Matthew Goniwe and many
others will never be prosecuted remains to be seen.

In conclusion, it is clear that the ANC will return to the negotiating table in a stronger position. This is mainly so because the
government's Achilles' heel – vulnerability to mass action – was
revealed during the period while the stalemate lasted, even if it is
true that the basic constant of the transitional equation remains
valid in the medium to long term (five to ten years): neither side
is strong enough to impose its will on the other. But it now appears
that the government needs the negotiations more than the ANC
does, because it is in a stronger position negotiating than not negotiating. This is mainly so because it is the very essence of negotiating
that the parties involved in it must make compromises. The ANC
has at its disposal a dual-mode strategy: it can alternate between
negotiating and applying pressure through mass action. The equivalent is not true for the government; it cannot alternate between
repression and accommodation: repression as a strategic tool is out.
In the absence of negotiations, the economy will continue to weaken
and the morale of the whites will deteriorate – ergo, the looming
spectre of mass emigration. While it is true that the blacks do not
benefit from a weakening economy, it is hard to see that their living
conditions can get much worse than they are already. ANC's main
vulnerability as a negotiating partner is that it has conceded power-
sharing as an over-arching principle. That means that the whites
will have the power of saying no to policies that they see as inimical
to their interests, because otherwise the negotiations would be about
transferring power, not sharing power. As long as power-sharing
remains a theoretical concept, it is not a serious obstacle to progress.
But when the time comes to translate it into practical realities, it
might prove a very tough nut to crack, perhaps even a Gordian
knot.

So what does the future hold? The negotiations, called simply
Multi-party Talks this time, were resumed in April 1993 after a
hiatus which lasted ten months. Twenty-six delegations, seven more
than CODESA in December 1991, representing virtually the whole
political spectrum (including the CP, the PAC and the AWB) were
present. The following items are on the agenda: One, the setting of
a date for the first non-racial general elections in the history of the

country – probably April or May 1994. This will be for the election of a constituent assembly that will be responsible for the writing of the constitution. An important provision here is that a 66 per cent (two-thirds) majority will be needed to do it (for a long time the Nats insisted on 75 per cent but gave up in the end), so that the ANC will not be able to dictate things. Two, the determination of the new regions of the country. It looks like there will be ten in the end. Three, the formation of a Transitional Executive Council (TEC) that will prepare for the election. The government and the ANC will be the main participants in it, possibly with representatives from the DP and some independent personalities, but not Buthelezi's Inkatha which will insist the principle of federalism be agreed upon before and the Afrikaner *Volksfront* which wants a separate state.[3]

After the constituent assembly election will begin a five-year transitional period between 1994 and 1999 during which the new constitution will be written (1994–6), regional elections will be held (1996) and the 1999 national elections will be prepared. That five-year period will probably be characterised by a power-sharing situation between the whites (the NP unless it is trounced by the CP in the constituent assembly election) and the blacks, almost certainly the ANC. It has been agreed that all parties polling a minimum of 5 per cent of the vote will participate in a national-unity government (they will receive ministerial portfolios; Inkatha will certainly make it and possibly the CP and PAC, but not the DP).

The coalition government that will be born from the 1994 election will be faced by the daunting task of meeting the aspirations and high expectations of the people. My guess is that those aspirations and expectations cannot be met to a significant extent in the next five years, it will take much longer than that. What then? It appears to be logical that a fairly authoritarian government will be needed in this period.[4]

Notes

1 Chris Hani was assassinated in April 1993. For the details see Note 3 at the end of Chapter 8.

2 For a comprehensive summary of the discussions and debates of CODESA, see: M Motlhabi, *Toward a New South Africa: Issues and Objects*

in the ANC/Government Negotiation for a Non-Racial Democratic Society,
Skotaville, 1992, Johannesburg. Motlhabi is also the author of *The Theory
and Practice of Black Resistance to Apartheid*, which has good chapters on
the PAC and the Black Consciousness movement and was published in
1984 by Skotaville which is a black-owned publishing house.

3 There is a substantial note on the *Volksfront* at the end of Chapter 1.

4 See my comments on bureaucratic authoritarianism towards the end of
Chapter 1.

3

Quo Vadis Van Zyl? Mr Mediator at a Crossroads

*'The ANC is not [a] party ... that knows who its constituency is ...
For the time being the ANC is still a [liberation] movement.'*
F Van Zyl Slabbert

Frederik Van Zyl Slabbert, born in 1940: former leader of the Progressive Federal Party (PFP, since defunct and replaced by the Democratic Party) and of the parliamentary opposition in the white House of Assembly. Presently a professor at Witwatersrand University's (Wits) Business School. An intellectual with the common touch. An excellent speaker. A handsome, witty and charming man. Charismatic. Has preserved his credibility with the blacks at the cost of alienating academic and political colleagues and friends in the PFP. In the last two years (1991–3), has played an important mediating role as chairman of the Witwatersrand Metropolitan Council (Metro for short) between the Johannesburg City Council, the Transvaal Provincial Authority and the civic organisations of the Witwatersrand area which includes Soweto.[1] He is also the founder of IDASA and the initiator of the famous meeting in Dakar in 1987.

It occurred to me, while I was in South Africa in 1992, that it would be a good thing if Van Zyl joined the ANC. This idea was based on the belief that De Klerk and the Nats needed to be persuaded that the whites' best bet was to accept the full consequences of majority rule and not to try to emasculate the latter by all sorts of gimmicks, like minority vetoes and excessive regionalism aimed at diluting the legitimate powers of the winner and that, if powerful and credible white political personalities like Van Zyl joined the ANC, that could prove helpful.

Only days before my scheduled departure from South Africa (3 May 1992), I managed to secure an interview with Van Zyl at the Braamfontein Hotel, across the street from the massive Johannesburg City Hall, where we had breakfast together. I found him noticeably greyer and thicker than six years earlier when I had met him at his house in Rondebosch, Cape Town. I started in an oblique way telling him that I had been at the CODESA talks the day before, where I had met Michael Sachs (both of whose parents are heroes of the liberation struggle: his mother was one of the principal defendants of a famous terrorist trial; his father, Albie, was blown up in Maputo by BOSS (Bureau of Security Services) and lost an arm; he is presently an ANC negotiator at CODESA in the group that deals with constitutional matters). Michael Sachs is an interesting and knowledgeable young man who worked as minutes-taker there, with whom I had talked, among other things, about the question of leadership. First, about the ANC's, COSATU's and the SACP's – about people like Joe Slovo, Thabo Mbeki, Jay Naidoo, Chris Hani – and then Slabbert's name had come up and Michael had said: 'He fascinates me. He is someone I would like to see involved with the ANC.' 'Involved with the ANC?' repeated Van Zyl as if to make sure that he had heard correctly. 'Yes,' I said and told him how, in the course of my investigations, I had raised the question of his playing a national role in politics with leading academics, politicians, businessmen and so on, most of whom had expressed regret that he had marginalised himself after his resignation from the PFP. 'Now it's time,' I told him with conviction, 'to re-enter the national political scene with a bold action: joining the ANC will send an unequivocal message to the liberals sitting on the fence that that's the way to go.'

Van Zyl launched into a long explanation of his position that made me realise that this was not the first time that he had been confronted with the idea of joining the ANC. 'The first point that I'd like to make,' he began, 'is that when I left parliament it was not just a matter of personal pique. To be sure, there was a degree of frustration, but that has to be expected in party politics. It had also nothing to do with my not having the stamina, the staying power, even if twelve-and-a-half years in any kind of job is a long time. For me it was a political decision, an intensely political decision, born of my analysis of the political situation. I felt that we had reached a stalemate in the political dialogue of this country and that we were polarising at enormous rate. People were trapped in political positions which were fixed and dogmatic and I couldn't get out of it. So, by resigning, I wanted obviously to make a statement. I wanted to say that this parliament is not going to do the job, that we would have to find a new way to get the dialogue going. And it was with that in mind that I saw myself more and more in a mediating, facilitating role. That's what IDASA was practically all about. I understood from the outset that two major forces were pitted against each other in this country: the National Party, which had been the carrier of Afrikaner nationalism for a long time but which would have to change, to fundamentally re-shape itself – but it couldn't do it alone; and the ANC, which was a liberation movement with a mix of Socialist/Marxist and strong African/nationalist elements in it. If you read *Comrades Against Apartheid* by Ellis and Sechaba you get some idea of what I am talking about.[2] You must understand that I have no fundamental prejudice against Marxism, I am simply saying that that was the political tradition in which the ANC evolved. In other words, the ANC was a liberation movement committed to a revolutionary paradigm because it was confronted by a nationalist movement in power using repression. It was a classical situation. Now when the government started relaxing the situation, the real question was how these two major political forces were going to change vis-à-vis one another; more prosaically, how they were going to tackle the process of negotiation; but, even more importantly, how the debate could now be deepened to address the fundamental questions of the transition which were not only constitutional, but also ones of development, of stability, of viability, and so on. So, to cut a long story short, both the government and the ANC are involved in a process of fundamental realignment: the NP has moved some way from being an exclusive white party to an inclusive non-racial party, but it still sits with a lot of its old elements in it; the ANC is experiencing the pressures of having to become a constituency organisation, in other words, a political party.

'I've always said that if I should one day return to active politics, I would do so to a party that knows who its constituency are, that knows what it is saying to that constituency in rather unambiguous terms. For the time being the ANC is not that party. The ANC is still a movement. It is still allied with the SACP – I don't for a moment deny the SACP the right to operate freely as a party and to seek its membership, I just happen to fundamentally disagree with its basic premises. So, as long as the SACP plays a significant role defining the policy positions of the ANC; or, at a minimum, as long as the ANC has not sufficiently clarified where it stands ideologically with respect of economic and financial policies, and political structures, I cannot join it. But if and when it does, and I happen to agree with them, then I will be happy to engage, to become part of it. So, it's not being precious, or anything like that. It's a question of time ultimately and there is little that I can do to accelerate it. But it will come. I am sure that it will sooner or later. Meanwhile, there is plenty that I can do which I find worthwhile doing, like my work at the Metropolitan Chamber, for example.

'One more point that I want to stress, which I know from experience, is that once you become a member of a political party, an enormous amount of your time and energy is consumed by the organisation and ritual of that party: you have to raise funds, you have to visit constituencies, you have to go to party meetings. I am quite willing to do that, to accept that kind of discipline, if I think that joining a party is the most important thing to do. At the moment, I don't think so. I think that there are other things that I am doing that, while not being as dramatic and sensational as CODESA, can be just as important. This battle that is going on at the Metropolitan Chamber (the merging of white and black municipalities), if we can pull that one off, if we can stabilise part of the country which is responsible for 70 per cent of its GDP, that would be a great achievement.'

He had made his opening statement. It was a good one, a convincing one, and I had no reason to doubt his sincerity. Still, I wanted to get to the bottom of his mind, so I kept hammering at it. 'I don't know if I agree with you fully,' I said. 'My intuition tells me that now is the time for you to join the ANC. Now is the time to take the plunge.'

'It's getting there, it's getting closer,' he said politely, he didn't seem annoyed.

'Don't you agree that the future of the country is with the ANC?' I insisted.

'I agree,' he said directly, candidly.

'And that the future of the country is at stake *now*? And that people like you can make a big difference by showing the way. The value of the example. There are a lot of confused, hesitating people

out there and this could be the signal that it is all right to join, that
the time is ripe to do it. I think you're carrying a great responsibility
on your shoulders.'

He took seriously what I was saying. 'Yes, you might be right,'
he said. 'But the question is: what am I joining in?'

'I think it's a mistake to look at the ANC as a Communist-
dominated organisation,' I countered. 'Besides, the Communists
themselves are not the rigid, Stalinist doctrinaires that they used to
be. The world is changing and the Communists are changing with
it. If you say that Socialist ideology is a big influence with the ANC,
yes, but it is a pragmatic, flexible sort of Socialism. It would be
strange, indeed abnormal, if they were not Socialists, given the
situation that prevails in South Africa, don't you agree?'

'Yes. And I said to Valli Moosa [one of the brilliant young leaders
of the ANC; born in 1957 and a graduate of physics and maths
from the University of Durban-Westville in Natal; of Indian origin],
to Cyril Ramaphosa [secretary-general of the ANC; born in 1952], to
Jacob Zuma [deputy secretary-general; born in 1942], to Thabo
Mbeki [now national chairman of the ANC, replacing Oliver Tambo;
heir apparent to Nelson Mandela; born in 1942]: "I am available 24
hours a day to help in whatever capacity that I can, to do the things
that need to be done," and I still mean that. But they feel you have
to become part of the movement before they actually rely on you to
give any assistance.' He suddenly blurted out, saying what was
really in his mind: 'Don't underestimate the need to have the
National Party as part of the solution. Don't make that mistake.
Because you sit with this enormous dilemma of having to find
some sort of working coalition.'

'You know as well as I do that the problem with the Nats is that
they are not really prepared to give up real power. Sharing power
is a vague, nebulous concept and they are using it to the hilt to
hold on to power and to preserve white privilege.'[3]

'That's not going to help. You see, there is a funny kind of
political mating dance going on: the Nats want to give the ANC
the responsibility, but not the power; the ANC want the power, but
they are not all that keen to take up the responsibility because of
the legacy of the past; so they are playing games with one another.
Taxpayers are paying millions for that cosy club called CODESA to
negotiate the real issues, but they are not doing it.'

'The Nats are playing for time,' I said. 'They are using the negotiations as a means to gain time. They reckon they need time to organise black political support: the Coloured community, the conservative Africans that follow the Zion Christian Church, some of those who live in the homelands. They appear to be banking on the idea that they might even be able to deny the ANC an outright victory at the polls. That would allow them to retain significant power.'

'I think it's inevitable that they both treat each other as negotiating partners as well as political competitors,' Van Zyl observed. 'But they are playing games with each other and it is my view that it is not going to work.'

'Can it be any other way? After all the Nats have not been really defeated in a war or in a revolution. The ANC doesn't have the power to throw them out of government.'

'It is essentially the same for the Nats, they cannot suppress the ANC. They are both strong enough to deny one another the fruits of the victory, but not to impose their will on the other side. That's why they have to find a deal that will take us through the next four or five years. Nobody is going to win it over the next four or five years. If we can find a deal to manage the transition for the next four or five years, then maybe we stand a chance.'

I told Van Zyl that Piet Cillié (the former editor of *Die Burger*, the influential Afrikaans-language Cape Town daily newspaper and, until 1992, chairman of the *Nasionale Pers*, the Afrikaans media conglomerate) and W A (Bill) de Klerk (a philosopher, playwright and novelist) had both told me that what was needed was a change in the mental attitude of the Afrikaners.[4] They had to realise that, in the long run, their salvation in South Africa was predicated on their ability to transform themselves from a ruling, governing minority into one that is indispensable for the development and welfare of the country. In the long term, political power cannot be withheld from the black majority.

'Yes, that's absolutely true,' Van Zyl agreed emphatically.

'But they are still resisting the idea,' I said. 'They are still thinking in terms of control and, therefore, their mental attitude is wrong. And that's why they need to be pressured, even perhaps be forced into that frame of mind.'

He grinned. He saw of course what I was driving at. He answered me with a charming metaphor: 'The worst thing that you can do is to try to jump on a merry-go-round before it has stopped. Because you might not get on the right horse if you do that. And I am not saying this because I have any delusions of grandeur, because I see myself as a great saviour, or anything. It's simply that an enormous energy has been released because of the transition and it is very important that one doesn't dissipate that energy, that one doesn't waste one's time. You want to stay focused. And it doesn't have to be forever. If we can get through the current crisis on the Metro [-politan Chamber], if we can get this thing up and running, then we will be building a framework that is usable at the national level. If we can get the Jo'burg City Council to take responsibility for Soweto, then for the first time changing the quality of life in Soweto will become a reality. Also, there is one thing that we've discovered on the Metro that they are bound to discover at CODESA one of these days: it's fine to negotiate and reach agreements, but it is the next step that is more difficult: administration. The moment CODESA moves into admin with an interim government, they will run into exactly the same problems that we have been running into: how do you deliver the goods to your constituency? Who do you transfer power to? Who is prepared to accept the other person's bona fide? and so on. All that stuff is still to come.'

'Yes. But are the civics interested in admin? I think they are rather playing the power game,' I retorted.

'True enough. But reality is catching up with them. They've discovered that it is much easier to mobilise people not to pay than it is to mobilise them to pay (for rent, water, etc). They've discovered that if they overplay their hand they run the risk of losing their constituencies. You know, it's nice to talk about dignity and justice up there when it doesn't mean anything. When you measure your dignity against the possibility of being kicked out of your house, it's a different story altogether. Suddenly the people are saying to the civics: "Hey, what are you going to deliver for us? What is it?" Now, that in itself is a very important moment in politics. Because, eighteen months ago, the civics were sort of toyi-toyi-ing through the transition: "Ra-ra-ra, let's give them hell! Let's show these guys! It doesn't matter if we promise the sky because nobody is going to ask us to deliver anything." And suddenly the thing is becoming very real for them. I think we are in a far more serious bargaining phase now than we've been for a very long time. I know Moses [Mayekiso, the newly elected president of SANCO] is saying: "Let's work this thing out at the national level." So now we have a national

working group on local government. What are they going to do?
They are going to sit for three months. They are going to throw up
terms of reference, they're going to chat, they're going to have
lunches and cocktail parties, they are going to start eyeballing one
another; and then, finally, they are going to say: "Maybe it's not
such a bad idea to go out there and ask the people: what's going
on here?" And who are they going to run into? Us. And we are
going to say: "Well, this is what we've done." "Oh," they will say,
"that's very nice," and they will take our work, and go up there
and formulate a framework, and they will come back to us with it.
Because, let's be realistic, what magic have they got at the national
level that can solve the problems at local level? You've got to work
out solutions at local level, there is no other way to do it. And the
local level, it's water, it's electricity, it's sewerage, it's refuse
removal, it's roads, it's houses, it's schools. And these are very
concrete things.'

'OK. I want to be honest with you,' I said. 'What I think is: given
all the backlogs that have been accumulated over the decades in
education, housing, health, welfare, etc and the unbelievably high
unemployment rate, is the South African problem soluble really?'

Slabbert grew animated. 'You are now touching on what I regard
as the gut issue of the politics of transition,' he said. 'As long as
you have one side making demands that the other side cannot meet
because it is sitting on a supply-side crisis, the problem *is* insoluble,
even if a populist government comes to power. There are ample
examples all over the world – in Latin America, Africa. What does
a populist government do after it comes to power? It raises wages
across the board, shifts expenditures to the poor – subsidises food,
rents, energy, it controls other prices. As a result, the deficits soar,
capital flees the country, the exchange rate of the currency falls
dramatically, there is no new investment, inflation rages out of
control, production levels fall off, the GDP shrinks, and the poor
are worse off than they were to begin with. What does the government do? It clamps down, it suspends all the democratic advances
that they have achieved, and it goes to the IMF to ask them what
kind of structural adjustment programme they must impose on
their people to qualify for the loans that will allow survival.

'It's a sad story', he continued. 'How to avoid the same predicament from occurring in South Africa? By having an understanding,
a contract among the major parties prioritising the alleviation of

abject poverty: you've got to identify and target the groups which are the most deprived. And let me tell you something, they are not the organised workers in the mines and factories. These are privileged groups. The rural poor, the squatter communities, these are deprived groups in this country. When I listen to Jay [Naidoo, the secretary-general of COSATU] and all these people, I don't hear much about these groups. They talk about workers who are already part of a labour aristocracy. To help those Fanon called the 'Wretched of the Earth' you can have the Ina Perlmans [executive director of Operation Hunger] and others to bring food, blankets, clothing to them to solve the immediate problem. In the long run, you have to invest in human capital. We shall have to overhaul the educational system of this country on a massive scale: six years of basic primary education focusing on maths, the sciences, and then you can go into building skills. It will take ten, twenty years, and then we shall be getting somewhere. But, meanwhile, you've got to accept that there is going to be massive unemployment. There are many, many people who will never be able to have a job and you have to plan housing for them, and that's cheap, basic sort of housing. You have to identify the land, you have to provide elementary services, and hope that some kind of informal economy will develop that will carry them along. This is the kind of political contract that would work if the major political actors agreed to suspend these issues from the political debate. But instead of doing that they are playing funny buggers with one another. Barend [Du Plessis, the Finance minister, later replaced by Derek Keys, a liberal] unilaterally imposes VAT, without explaining it to the other side which goes against it. VAT is not a bad system because it is the only way to broaden the tax base. If Jay Naidoo was president tomorrow, he would have to invent VAT to cope with the kinds of problems that we've been talking about. But the way he introduced it, Barend effectively killed it. So, there are no short-term painless solutions, no long-term magical solutions, but there are short- and long-term painful and difficult solutions, but the political will to adopt them must exist.'

It was a good analysis of the situation which made sense. Perhaps that was part of the problem: it made too much sense. Also, I was left with the uncomfortable impression that the whites were let off the hook too easily. So I said: 'It seems that the government, Big Business and the whites in general are banking on a relatively painless redistribution through growth. The opposite approach: growth through redistribution is anathema to them. I agree that it has to be both, but the problem is that the whites are not prepared to make the kind of sacrifices that are necessary to make this thing work.'

'You're right. Sure, I agree with you,' he said. 'Look, there is a very good book edited by Mall, Natrass and Leroux called *Redistribution*, there are some excellent articles in it. The essential point they are making is this: what can you really redistribute in this country without cutting the very branch that you're sitting on, ie, the economy? You can redistribute land, of course. But if you're going to redistribute agricultural land, you better find the people with the expertise to farm it. Because if I give you a piece of land and you don't know how to farm it, what's the whole bloody point about it? So you've got to look at land redistribution in the framework of agricultural reform which is creating the skills of using the land effectively. But there you come up against white resistance. The white landowners have been a landed aristocracy in this country. Just like in feudal times, lording it over the black farm workers as if they were serfs. That's got to change, but it must be carefully negotiated. I don't think there is much joy in non-land redistribution. The whole nationalisation debate, that's dead. It's nonsense. Then you look at the revenue side: taxation. We are already very heavily taxed, so there is very limited scope for new taxes, except for the Value Added Tax. In the expenditure side, you can re-allocate resources to agricultural reform, housing, skills, and so on, and that's about it.'

I was astonished that he had failed to mention redistribution of wealth. After all, a couple of thousand of large investors owned perhaps as much as 98 per cent of all stocks listed on the Johannesburg Stock Exchange (JSE) worth hundreds of billions of rands. I had read recently in the *Race Relations Survey* 1991–2 (a very dependable annual publication by the respected South African Institute of Race Relations, SAIRR) that the twenty richest South African families had assets listed on the JSE worth R11 billion and that did not include all their holdings overseas. I told Van Zyl all that, adding, 'They made much of that wealth under apartheid, they have benefited from it,' and that they should perhaps give some of it back.

He smiled thinly, shook his head, and said, 'The rich are untouchable, my friend.' He explained that it was counter-productive to expropriate them – 'a remedy worse than the malady' – because their liquid moveable assets were in safe havens outside the country anyway and that if things got too tough for them they always had the option of leaving the country and taking all their know-how, contacts, the loyalty of their employees, and so on with them. So it was best to work with them through persuasion – besides they were contributing quite a bit on their own. He was right of course. I remembered I had read not long before the interview that De Beers had announced that it was transferring its foreign assets into the De Beers Centenary AG, a new Swiss-based company. Centenary and De Beers would be 'stapled' together, the financial analyst who was the author of the article had written. Should the need arise – the threat of nationalisation, for example – it would be very easy to unstaple the two companies. Some four-fifths of De Beers' earnings derived from outside South Africa. The move provided an almost watertight protection.[5]

'The people must be told the truth,' Van Zyl went on 'and both sides will have to do it. You can't have Nelson saying one thing and Chris Hani saying the opposite. You can't have De Klerk going around the country telling the whites that it is going to be painless. It's crazy. Whites must be told: "You are going to suffer." But I agree with you the toughest thing in politics is to sell sacrifice.'

I expressed doubts that the whole truth could be told to the black masses. 'We are not dealing here with a society that is politically mature and also they've suffered so much,' I said.

'Sure,' he responded, 'but do you compound their suffering by maintaining them in ignorance? By keeping them as political infants? Or do you help them to become politically mature? Because, you know, if they don't become politically mature, Nelson wouldn't last six months as president!'

'To be honest with you,' I said, 'I wonder if things have not gone too far in this country for things to work out without some form of catharsis that would cleanse all that fear, hatred, anger and resentment.'

'Revolution, you mean,' he said and went on, 'it would be horrendous. We must do all we can to avoid it. Our only chance is for De Klerk and Mandela to agree on and sell that programme of suffering and reconstruction to the people. If they can't, then it's too bad because we are going to inherit the whirlwind in this country. Yes,

I can promise you that: we are going to inherit the bloody whirl-wind in this country.'

We both fell silent. It seemed an appropriate end to our dis-cussion. Then Van Zyl said: 'Listen, by the way, there is a book launch tomorrow evening at the Wits [Witwatersrand University] Club. A book of mine is coming out, it's called *The Quest for Democracy*, about the dynamics of the transition, do come if you are interested . . .'[6]

It was quite crowded at the Wits Club when I arrived the next evening at about 7.30 pm. It is a big room in an old, squat building. The sort of architecture and decor that one often sees in the univer-sities and government buildings of the former British colonies in Africa. Red, or rather ochre-coloured, floors, wood panelling, a zinc bar. A table was set with canapés, petits-fours, soft drinks, wine. Beer was available at the bar. In clusters of two, three or more, about fifty people milled about. The kind of people one would expect to meet in a gathering such as this: fairly affluent-looking, intellectually sophisticated, presumably liberal. One thing that struck me immediately was that there were few blacks, not more than four or five in all. Could it be, I wondered, that they were tired of happenings like this one? Tired of being with earnestly liberal people self-congratulating for having the right attitudes, for being concerned, for caring; with people who would go back, after the launch was over, to their comfortable houses in the comfortable suburbs, while the business of eking out a miserable existence in the townships, the squatter camps and rural areas would continue . . .

After a while, people sat on rows of chairs and the three authors and the editor of the series took their places behind a long table before them. Three books were being launched that evening: one was Slabbert's, another was on AIDS and a third on the economics of the transition. They were slim volumes designed for a broad, non-specialist audience. The editor spoke first, followed by the three authors. It was all reasonable, rational and predictable. God, I thought, there are so many reasonable, rational and predictable people in South Africa!

I went up to Van Zyl with a copy of the book that I had just purchased to congratulate him. He wrote on it 'Zeki, Thank you for a stimulating talk' and signed it. I told him that I had seen Pallo (Jordan, the director of ANC's Department of Information and Publicity and one of the leading intellectuals of the movement; see

Chapter 17) who had said: 'Tell him, if I were in his shoes I would do it . . . [and] I will sign his membership card personally if he joins' (I had asked Slabbert's permission to mention our conversation to Pallo). He burst into a loud guffaw and then said laughingly, 'Is that what he said? . . . I will think about it. If I do it you will hear about it.'

What I didn't tell him was the rest of Pallo's comments. 'He won't do it,' he had said, 'because he sees himself as a mediator, as the man in the middle.' As I left Van Zyl, I wondered if and when he would make up his mind. Not too late, I hoped.

Notes

1 The civic organisations moved into the vacuum created by the loss of credibility of the Black Local Authorities (BLA) which had compromised themselves by dealing with the government after the establishment of the tricameral constitution in 1983. At the beginning they circumscribed their activities in the economic sphere – boycotts against the payment of rents and other municipal services, etc. But, increasingly, they came to play a political role, wanting to transform the society from bottom (grass roots) up. The South African National Civics Organisation (SANCO) was formed in April 1992 and Moses Mayekiso, a fairly radical labour union leader and prominent Communist, was elected president. More on the civics in Chapter 15, and my discussion with Bill Davies at the beginning of Chapter 16.

2 S Ellis and T Sechaba, *Comrades Against Apartheid: the ANC and the South African Communist Party in Exile*, 1992, London. It is about how the SACP took over the leadership of the ANC between 1960 and 1990.

3 That is not true any more. As I write these words in September 1993, it is clear that the Nats are prepared to give up real power. They are still hoping to preserve white privilege to a substantial extent, but that is only human.

4 More on Cillié and Bill de Klerk in Chapters 5 and 6. W A de Klerk is best known overseas for his book *The Puritans in Africa* (Rex Collings, 1975, London), which is a historical study of Afrikanerdom as seen by an enlightened Afrikaner thinker. He also wrote *The Thirstland* (Rex Collings, 1977), an epic, historical novel about an Afrikaner trek from the Transvaal to the dry lands of the southern Angola and northern Namibia.

5 In fact three large conglomerates/holding companies are controlled by the Oppenheimer family: the Anglo American, the De Beers and Minorco based in Luxembourg. In an article, 'Oppenheimers Shifting Assets from

South Africa,' *International Herald Tribune*, 29 September 1993, it appears
that all assets outside South Africa owned by Anglo and De Beers are
being transferred to Minorco. On whether or not this is to avoid possible
future nationalisation, the opinion of experts is divided. On this and
related subjects, see also the conclusions to Chapters 13 and 17.

6 F Van Zyl Slabbert, *The Quest for Democracy: South Africa in Transition*,
Penguin, 1992. Another book by him which I like is, *The Last White
Parliament*, H Strydom, 1985, Johannesburg, published in England by
Sidgwick and Jackson, 1986. It is a sincere, autobiographical account of
his life up to 1984. His childhood and adolescence were far from being
easy: his parents divorced when he was very young and both he and
his twin sister had to be taken away from their mother when they were
only seven years old – she died of alcoholism in 1974.

4

Being a Black Writer in a Racist Society: Es'Kia Mphahlele Speaks Out

'The economic and political empowerment of the black people, that's the real agenda now.'

Es'Kia Mphahlele

Es'Kia ('Zeke') Mphahlele's house was in Northcliff, an outlying middle-class suburb in the south-eastern part of Johannesburg. In that small, rented cottage, the grand old man of black South African letters was putting the finishing touches to his latest book in the company of Kefilwe, his only daughter – he has four sons, but all of them live in the US. Rebecca, his beloved wife of almost fifty years was already in the northern Transvaal (near Pietersburg) preparing their move there after Mphahlele's acceptance of a professorship at the University of the North at Turfloop.

Born in Marabastad, an African township near Pretoria that doesn't exist any more (it was a 'black spot' which had to be removed), the author of the classic autobiography, *Down Second Avenue*, spent much of his childhood in Maupaneng, a village seventy-five miles from Pietersburg, where he was raised by his maternal grandmother.[1] He became a teacher as well as a poet, a short-story writer and a playwright, but took the momentous decision to leave the country in 1957, at age 36, finding it impossible to continue after the Bantu Education Act was introduced in 1953 by Verwoerd, who was minister of Bantu Affairs. I had tried to see him in 1986, the first time I was in South Africa, but it had not worked out. This time, at the end of April 1992 after two or three telephone calls he agreed to see me. I wanted him to tell me, among other things, what it meant to be a black writer in a racist society.

In preparation for our meeting I had read the two volumes of his autobiography: *Down Second Avenue* about his childhood and young adulthood years, and *Afrika My Music* about the following 26 years (1957–83). The first twenty of these were spent in exile: in Lagos, where he was a teacher; in Paris and Nairobi, where he worked for Unesco (supporting the arts and culture in black Africa); and in the United States, where he was an academic, primarily at the University of Colorado at Denver.[2] I had also read some stories, the first volume of which was published in 1947 under the title of *Man Must Live*. Other significant works include: *The African Image, In Corner B and Other Stories* and *The Wanderers*, which were banned in South Africa for a long time. We spent two hours together in the early afternoon in his modest living room. This is the gist of what he told me:

'Literature is a reflection of the society in which it develops. To the extent that the writer is part of that society and writes of his or her experiences (which derive from membership of that society) his or her writings must be, of necessity, a reflection of it. However, to the extent that literature is a product of the imagination the writer must also *re*create that reality, which is a social reality. The relationship between society and literature does not have to be a dogmatic one: things must be allowed to take their natural course. The black writer is surrounded by an immediate reality which, in the South African case, is a white-dominated society. But he or she must go beyond it, he or she must have a vision of what a just and democratic society should be. That means that you have to develop a sense of Africanness which is negated by white society. In other words, to be an African in a white-dominated society means that you have always to assert that Africanness which involves the awareness that one is part of Africa, not just of South Africa. It is, therefore, very important that one should know about the rest of Africa: its geography, its politics, economics, sociology, and so on. Also, the black writer has a special responsibility to tell his people about the history of colonialism and domination in Africa. If he or she avoids that responsibility, deliberately or willingly, then there is, of course, something deficient in him as a writer. Because, he is made up by that history, he is part of it, and the present-day history is very much a reflection of the colonial history. The white man's position in South Africa is a colonial one in many respects, no matter how long he has been here. His mentality is still very much a colonial mentality. A black writer will recognise that, but also move beyond it. The greatness of a writer is in the moving beyond. That's where the vision thing comes in . . .

'One works against a very Eurocentric stream in this country. All the major universities are Eurocentric. The big influence in those universities is the textbooks which with few exceptions were written in Europe or America. That's the case not only in the biological and physical sciences, but also in the social sciences. Until very recently, the ultimate rationale for that situation was that this is a white man's country and, therefore, it is normal that the ideas should derive from a European centre, rather than an African centre. The universities thought of themselves as institutions that must be acceptable to their European counterparts, they never thought of themselves as African. And that is still true today, even if not acknowledged so openly any more. They still talk about South Africa becoming the leader of Africa, but not about it being part of Africa. That's the mentality. That's also why the black writer must be a teacher in this particular phase of our history; these two functions are linked, intertwined. As for myself, what I teach is often what I write, and what I write is often what I teach. I see the black writer as having a dual role in society: one is that he is a human being among human beings, a man or woman among other men and women who are entitled to make demands on him. Which means that he or she must be concerned with human progress, concerned with poverty and injustice, concerned with a number of things, issues, that the society is concerned with. As a human being and a political animal, he should be part of the liberation and emancipation processes.

'The writer's second role is that, as a writer he should draw into himself to internalise and recreate the social reality using his imagination. This is where the writer differs from the social reformer, from the revolutionary. Because then he is developing a craft, or exercising his craft as a writer. Even as a creative writer, however, he or she will remain a teacher, because he must try to broaden the minds of his readers, to show the way, tell them which way the society is going, and what kind of future is possible. A writer is not a social reformer, because he is dealing with the feelings, the heart and the soul; not only with reason, the mind and ideas . . .

'When I came back to South Africa after twenty years of exile, I found out that things had become much worse in the meantime. The repressive laws had been expanded, the institutional violence had increased – the detentions, the arrests in the middle of the night, the torture in the prisons had all been there before, of course, but now they were considerably magnified. When in 1990 De Klerk began abolishing a number repressive laws, that sort of eased the atmosphere, but that didn't empower the black majority. We still don't have the political power, the economic power. The economic and political empowerment of the black people, that's the real agenda now. And the white man is still hesitant to go into that agenda full steam, because he is still a slave of his own past, he is still haunted by the ghost of that past, he is still a prisoner of that past, which is white domination . . . They've got too much to lose and they cannot afford that, you see. Taking from other people, enriching themselves in all manner of ways. They've got themselves into the position that they've got to protect what they possess. Our reading of the situation is that they don't want to let go, and that they think the transition must not involve a painful sacrifice. They want to make sure of that. When I look at Terre Blanche's AWB (the neo-Nazi Afrikaner Resistance Movement), I think they express the deep sentiments of a large majority of the white people who don't want to dramatise those sentiments as they do, who don't want to act through them, at least for the time being. The white man in South Africa is confronted with a dilemma, an inner conflict, between his desire for peace and his fear of having to lose too much. Inevitably, the transition is going to be a stormy one; it will be an uphill struggle with its ups and downs. Like Sisyphus, we will almost reach the top of the mountain, only to find ourselves at the bottom again. The way I see it, the black people must be first empowered by the law – the law is important because it stipulates what can be done, and what cannot be done. It will fix new pegs in the social landscape. It will not be possible any more to discriminate against, molest or harass anyone on account of his race, of the colour of his skin. The attitudes will have to change too, but that's the long haul. It will take a very long time: a couple of generations at least, thirty, forty years. As new generations are born and raised, the injustices and inequities of the past will be more and more behind us. Look at America, we are probably in an equivalent stage as they were in the 1950s. Three, four decades later a lot of progress has been made, but much still remains to be done. Partly, this is so because African-Americans are claiming more, demanding more, it's in the nature of things: the country has grown more affluent, so the claims are bigger . . .

'Yes, the "lost generation" is a huge problem.[3] They are the angry young men of the townships who were, in the 1970s and 1980s, the youths who rejected Bantu education, who put liberation before schooling and who, as a result, are unemployed and unemployable. Those young men grew up in violence and now live by the law of the gun, they've got nothing to lose. It's a gigantic problem which we must confront and deal with as best we can. I am, myself, involved in a community development programme in Soweto which I started in 1980. We've tried to provide a learning environment for them where they could begin to realise their potential, to want to get back into the formal system. But, unfortunately, there are very few programmes like that, we are just a drop in the ocean. A lot more resources will have to be poured into projects of this kind – and other kinds – to develop skills: technical, communication, thinking skills, and so on. The toughest part is that the very people who need an education are the ones who don't want it. So, we must dig in, provide incentives. It's going to be a very long process. Meanwhile, this is going to be a violent country, a country with a very high crime rate. I don't see a full-scale revolution. Yet. It might come, but later. The violence will continue under a new government. Just think of the backlog that a new government will have to deal with in just all the social services that you can think of: health, welfare, education, housing, water, electrification, rural development. I mean, the rural people are the forgotten people. By far the largest proportion of the rural people are abjectly poor. They don't even have the will of getting out of the mud yet. In this country, the focus has always been on the modern sector, the industrial and urban areas. Except for the white farms, the rural areas didn't count really. The domestic workers too were terribly exploited. My mother, for example, was still in her twenties when she started working as a domestic worker, she worked until she was forty-five years old and then she died. She made very little money.

'One should not be misled by what is going on at CODESA. They still don't look at the average black as a fellow human being with the same thoughts, needs and aspirations as themselves. The attitude change that you see is at the leadership level, and even there it is minimal when you come to think of it. You see, at that level they are confronted with articulate individuals who are capable of making demands on them based on a valid rationale. The black man is challenging you and so you've got to sit down and listen to him, to see if you can work out something together. But you still don't have to admit him into your club. It's still a very superficial response to the black man's demands. You deal with him the same way you have to deal with a disease, a boil on your nose. They still look at us like a problem to be solved, not as a fellow human being with equal rights. All that talk about democracy, liberalism, human rights, it's just that, talk, high-falutin talk. It has nothing to do with what they are actually thinking and feeling. That's why I believe that they – the white power structure – have a double agenda, a secret agenda. We don't know what it is exactly, but they are working at it all the time. And this is what often pains me: we are not dealing with people who are telling us the truth. No, there is no basic trust between us, we are all engaged in double-talk and double-think. The double-talk from our side comes from the pretence that we take them seriously, that we believe them when they say "this is what we want".

'I can't even begin to speculate what the final outcome will be. But history will reveal the truth one day. True enough: there is a difference between the conservatives and the pragmatists, but it is one of degree, not one of substance. The pragmatist tells himself: I've been forced into this disagreeable situation, I must deal with it, it makes sense for me to do that. It's practical politics. The pragmatist's honesty is that of expediency, rather than one based on persuasion or belief. It is not a deep-seated honesty. In fact, one cannot expect deep-seated honesty from them, for the simple reason that they were born into their own system. They are the prisoners of their own past. They are not going suddenly to be emancipated. The blacks have the power of making life pretty miserable for them and they are dealing with the situation. But their strategy is one of containment, not one intent on revolutionising, overhauling the whole system. The old equilibrium has been shattered and must be replaced by a new one. But the search for a new equilibrium is going on at the leadership level. What about the masses? That's the problem, you see. CODESA is not reaching the people down there. It's a kind of game played by the leaders. Many people see the black delegates of CODESA as dancing to the tune of the white man. Like marionettes and the white man is pulling the strings.'

This is when the conversation shifted back to literature. We spoke about the African Writers Association (AWA) to which he belonged, about the ANC's COSAW (Congress of South African Writers), about white South African writers, about the black writers of the fifties (Mphahlele's generation), of the sixties and seventies (writers influenced by the Black Consciousness movement) and so on.

'The AWA was founded in 1978 after Biko's death,' Mphahlele said. 'COSAW came later. I didn't see the point of leaving the AWA and joining COSAW, but I do address their meetings when they ask me to. The AWA is not part of the BC movement institutionally, but we share their philosophy of black pride and self-reliance. In that sense, we are a child of the BC era. This is how the AWA came about: PEN International had two chapters in South Africa, one in Cape Town and one in Johannesburg. They were both segregationist and PEN insisted that they couldn't continue as PEN affiliates if they didn't admit blacks. The Cape Town chapter died of a natural death. The Jo'burg chapter tried to do that. There were two meetings where we came together, the whites and the blacks, and then the whites dropped out. The reason was that the white writers wanted only the published writers to be part of the new chapter, while we wanted to include the aspirant writers who had never been published before. They became impatient with this and the thing fell through, and we founded the AWA.

'You could probably say that white South African writers – people like Gordimer, Brink, Coetzee – would not have been accepted in the West the way they were, were it not for their stand against apartheid. Honestly, I can't see Gordimer winning the Nobel if apartheid never existed. But that's neither here nor there. She is a good writer and was involved in the struggle against apartheid and all its injustices. No, I don't see her as a Marxist. She is a fiercely independent writer who refuses to be bullied by an ideology, who wants to be the social conscience of her country. She is an active member of COSAW and has done a lot for it. My problem with her is that she is an elitist writer: she writes for the literary person, for the intellectual. Her books are not accessible to the general reader. I also find her fiction very cold. It lacks passion. Not necessarily emotional passion, but spiritual passion. She has come out publicly that she is an atheist. I am not a Christian myself, but I am a spiritual person. I have a spiritual life. If she had that kind of spiritual life and impulse, I think her fiction would be different. She is a stylist, her work is very cerebral . . . Alan Paton, yes, he did have a spiritual life. *Cry, the Beloved Country* is a very passionate work, in that sense. J M Coetzee solved the paradox of being a white writer writing about a black country by being intensely allegorical. Athol Fugard, by working with black theatre people, that's why there is a symbolism in his plays that works . . .

'People like Maishe Maponya, Matsemela Manaka, Zakes Mda are serious playwrights who have written good plays. But they seem to have come to the end of their creative periods. They've exhausted their subjects which had to do with apartheid: repression, torture, massacres, that kind of thing, and I don't think they have much else to say. Writers tend to get trapped inside a groove. I think it's Breytenbach who said that with apartheid dead many writers are going to run out of material. That's true. The black writers of the fifties and sixties never fell into that trap. Alex la Guma, Richard Rive [pronounced Reeve, it's a Cape-Malagasy name],[4] both so-called Coloured; Can Themba[5] and Bloke Modisane – they are both dead now; Arthur Maimane and Lewis Nkosi, who lives in America, and myself, we portrayed human life as human life. Oppression or no oppression, that human life had its own drama, its own distinctive drama, even though the general environment was that of apartheid. Also when we say that apartheid is dead, we should qualify that. Legal apartheid is on the way out, but not mental apartheid. But that is [a subject] more difficult to handle than "Casspirs [riot-control vehicles used by the security services] rumbling around in the townships", shooting, tear-gassing, sjambokking [a *sjambok* is a long whiplike baton], and so on.

'Njabulo Ndebele? He is a good short story writer and a very bright man, but he hasn't published much lately in the way of fiction. My own experience is that when you take on administrative duties, your writing goes out of the window.' He chuckled. Ndebele was the president of COSAW.[6] 'Then you have the BC-oriented writers and poets,' he went on, 'Sipho Msepamla and Mafika Gwala, among the older ones; Don Mattera, Mothobi Mutloatse – who directs the Skotaville publishing house now – and Miriam Tlali [pronounced Tladi] among the younger ones.[7] If you pick up a copy of the *Staffrider* [a quarterly magazine of the arts and culture published by COSAW], you will see that verse is stronger than prose. The reason for this apparent paradox is that you need a good mastery of the English grammar and syntax to write good prose, and Bantu education has destroyed that; in poetry you work in images mainly, grammar and syntax are not so relevant.'

After that Mphahlele rose to go to the bathroom. I noticed that he is a small man, slightly stooped, not overweight; he has a full head of white hair. His eyes are the most striking feature of his face, I thought: big, almond-shaped, brown under white bushy brows; but also soft, gentle, but penetrating, knowing and shrewd.

Kefilwe, Mphahlele's daughter, was in the living room making pastiche jewellery using some natural materials like dried petals, leaves and wood. We chatted a little waiting for her father to come back. It turned out that she was unhappy in South Africa, that she felt like living in a ghetto. She said that she wanted to go back to the States where she had lived most of her life. Life was too tense in South Africa and she was having a hard time in adjusting. Also, if I remember correctly, there was a sentimental problem, a man that she had left behind . . . It was quite a paradox, I thought, just when her father had, at long last, reached the apex of recognition and prestige in his own country, she was feeling like an outsider, forlorn and nostalgic of life in a foreign country.

Mphahlele gave me a lift to Auckland Park, closer to central Johannesburg than to Northcliff. I had to see Carl Nöffke, an old acquaintance of mine and the director of the American Studies Institute at the Rand Afrikaans University (RAU). There was also Deon Geldenhuys there, a young and brilliant political science professor who I might be able to catch.

We talked some more in the car. Here was a man in the twilight of his life, going back to the land of his origins, where he grew up as a child. He had had a long and productive life and everything had come together nicely in the end. He would conclude his life surrounded by the respect of his peers, the admiration of his students and the affection and love of his family and beloved wife Rebecca. It was a fate to be envied.

Notes

1 Es'Kia Mphahlele, *Down Second Avenue*, Faber & Faber, 1959.

2 Es'Kia Mphahlele, *Afrika My Music*, Ravan, 1984, Johannesburg.

3 Several agencies, such as the Get Ahead Foundation, are involved in trying to help the 'lost generation'. The Community Agency for Social Enquiry (CASE) has done some significant research on it and came up with a report in May 1993 which quantifies and categorises young people into those who are 'lost', 'marginalised' and 'at risk'. Meanwhile, the push for the introduction of a national development service, which would harness the energy of young people, while providing them with training and employment opportunities, is gaining momentum.

4 Richard Rive, who was born the same year as Lewis Nkosi in 1935, was deeply moved by the tragedy of his people removed forcibly from District Six by the racist Group Areas Act and about which he wrote, *Buckingham Palace, District Six*. There is a whole section on District Six in Chapter 14.

5 Can Themba committed a passive sort of suicide: he drank himself to death in Swaziland in 1969 at age 45. *The Will to Die* was posthumously published in London in 1972.

6 Njabulo Ndebele, who holds an MA from Cambridge and a PhD from Denver University, published a well-known collection of short stories, *Fools and Other Stories*, Ravan, 1983, Johannesburg. The book went through several editions (three in 1990). While head of COSAW, Ndebele published a remarkable collection of essays, *Rediscovery of the Ordinary: Essays on South African Literature and Culture*, in 1991. He was then appointed vice-chancellor of the University of the North at Turfloop whose chancellor is Mandela himself. In May 1993, he was chosen by an independent committee to be the chairman of the new South African Broadcasting Corporation (SABC) board to ensure neutrality in the coverage of the forthcoming national elections. His selection, which was vetoed by De Klerk on the grounds of his ANC connections, created a major political crisis.

7 A poet of significance not mentioned by Mphahlele is Wally Serote who replaced Barbara Masekela as head of the ANC's culture desk.

5

Afrikaner Literati on Language and Politics

*'I tried to be a ... protagonist, a conscience, for the Coloured people ...
there are three million of them and they are the real inheritors.'*
Jan Rabie

Onrus (*onrust*, in Afrikaans, ironically enough means 'unrest') is a
charming little village on the Atlantic Ocean favoured by Afrikaner
artists – writers, painters, weavers, pottery-makers – and yuppie
professionals. It is not far from Cape Town – about one-and-a-half
hours' drive at a leisurely pace.

We are in the garden of Jan Rabie's and Marjorie Wallace's house.
Four of us are sitting around a white iron garden table on which
stands a bottle of white wine. Jan, who was born in 1921, is an
important figure of Afrikaans letters. He is, I am told, still convalesc-
ing from tick-bite fever (which can be life-threatening) and feels
weak, is not his usual buoyant self. Marjorie, his wife, of Scottish
origin, is a well-known painter. She suffers from a hip ailment
which makes walking difficult, but that does not keep her from
being full of pep and her limpid blue eyes twinkle with childlike
malice. Jan and Marjorie live in close communion with nature. They
sleep outdoors on the verandah throughout the year, even in July
and August, the coldest months of the year when the temperature
can go down to almost zero degree centigrade during the night.
The second guest around the table, other than myself, is Hermien
Dommisse, introduced by Jan as 'a theatrical personality from
Johannesburg'. She is a thin, fragile-looking woman (like old
porcelain), in her sixties probably, with a wan expression on her
face. She speaks in an elegant, albeit slightly pedantic, English –
her diction is, of course, excellent.

'Jan, can we talk about the *Sestiger* movement?' I began.

He corrected me immediately and facetiously. 'It is pronounced *Sesticher* . . .'

'It's the French names that people are most troubled with,' interjected Marjorie, 'names like du Toit, which becomes du Toy; Labuchagne becomes Labusquachney,' she laughed. 'Leroux *reste le même* also Malan.'

'*Sestigers* means "the writers of the sixties", it was a real breakthrough,' Jan explained.

'He [Jan] is one of the two founders – with Bartho Smith of the Transvaal,' Marjorie said with some pride.

'Was Bill [W A de Klerk] part of it?' I asked.

'No, no,' Jan exclaimed. 'Bill stayed with the older generation. He never moved in with the *Sestigers*. Generations do not like each other and don't really meet, you know. The *Sestiger* movement was a reaction against the establishment. I've never met van Wyk Louw, for instance.[1] They were old fashioned, classical. We went to France . . .'

'And Jan came back with this book, *Een-en-twintig* (*Twenty-One Short Pieces*).' Marjorie intervened again. 'He was influenced by Henri Michaud and people like that. Before, all Afrikaans writing was the farmhouse novel, the kind of *platteland roman*, the sort of thing where they struggle to make a living on poor soil, and so on.[2] Jan's book was a sort of sensation to a lot of younger writers. So most people say that the *Sestiger* movement was started by Jan Rabie and the *Twenty-One Short Pieces*. And then Bartho came back. Later, André Brink and Chris Barnard, they all went to Paris. It was a new influence. It was not at all this old Dutch thing. They all started writing in a different way. They were all disenchanted with the old Afrikaans literature. The *Sestigers* was a movement of opposition; of young writers, poets who disliked apartheid. And Bartho started a little magazine which he called *Sestiger*, and he gave the movement the name of *Sestiger*; and it was Steven Leroux, André Brink, Jan, Chris Barnard, later Elsa Joubert, but never Bill, he was before.'

'In a sense we started the *Sestiger* movement at Ingrid Jonker's grave,' Jan said. 'Special Branch stood on one side and we stood on the other side. We buried her twice, a second time without the Special Branch. Ingrid Jonker is a very interesting and deeply felt example of this fighting the father figure who represents tradition and authority . . .'[3] He suddenly pointed at some trees in the back of the garden. 'You see olive tree there? Picking my first olives. 'That's our first crop. I have seven of them . . . Anyway I have something special to say about my work. It all boils down to a simple thing, that I tried to be a . . . protagonist, a conscience, for the Coloured people. To me the Afrikaans language, which is spoken by the Coloured people to a large extent, is the greatest inter-racial achievement that we've had in this country so far. It was done by the Malays, and Blacks, and Hollanders, and Huguenots. It was a real hodge-podge – the Hottentots largely disappeared into this mass – and the result was that they, the Coloured people, are the real inheritors.

'They are kind of left out today, they are not standing up for themselves – nobody likes to be called Coloured. So my books originate from as much as I could fish from the archives on how the Hottentots and the Hollanders became mixed, on how the Afrikaans language and the whole set-up more or less derived from that, and stayed Capey-Coloured to some extent. The light-skinned whites moved inland, they were then nomadic ones, you know, the ox wagon, the freedom, and so on. Anyway, the best of my work was writing about these people that were our first real South Africans, with a new language that they forged together with the whites. And they don't count today, because you don't say brown, you only say white and black. I feel the brown is the most important element and I tried to show it in my work. I wrote a series of five novels called *Bolandia* – *Bolandia One, Two, Three, Four*, and *Five*. It's still neglected, the role of the brown person, and it is not fair, there are three million of them and they are the real inheritors. In America the real inheritors are more or less extinguished, the Indians do not count. But the Coloured people do count, at any rate they should count. This is what I am trying to say: that they should count much more, and in writing too.'

After centuries of oppression the Coloured community of the Cape is now wooed actively by the Nationalists who hope that they will vote for them in the forthcoming non-racial national elections, scheduled for 27 April 1994. De Klerk visited Mitchell's Plain, a large Coloured township on the Cape Flats, and attracted big crowds.

'The Coloured people are scared at the moment,' Marjorie observed.

'They are very scared,' Jan confirmed.

'I don't mean the intellectuals, but the ordinary working class people,' Marjorie went on. 'They don't know if they are going to be better off under the ANC than under the Nats. They just see it as another alien thing that is going to be pushed up on top of them. It's different for the intellectuals, they reach out to the ANC, the BC movement, and so on.'

'You know, the black man always walked tall and the poor Coloured man always with his shoulders bent. That shouldn't be,' Jan said.

'The present generation of Coloured intellectuals walk tall enough,' Marjorie disagreed. 'People like Jake [Gerwel, rector of the University of Western Cape], Tony Links.[4] But they didn't used to ... The ANC has been very disappointed that they have such a low membership of Coloured people in the Cape. And some people say it's because they address all their meetings in English and not in Afrikaans, which is the home language of the large majority of the Coloured people. Now they have Boesak as chairman for the Western Cape, but even he speaks in English in public rallies. Something to do with Afrikaans being the language of the oppressor perhaps.'

'That's true for the Africans, who have always rejected Afrikaans, but not for the Coloureds,' Jan said. 'You see, Afrikaans to me is doubly important. It is my best weapon against apartheid. Instead of talking about the colour of the skin I talk about the language. It brings many more people together. I believe I must be very Afrikaans to fight apartheid. Most people don't see it that way, but it is true for me.'

'Breyten [Breytenbach] says that most whites in the Western Cape are in reality browns anyway because they have African blood in their veins,' I said.[5]

'Yes, some Coloureds are lighter-skinned than some whites,' Jan agreed.' Adam Small [a well-known Coloured poet] is very light-skinned, and he calls himself black. I said to him, "Adam, you can't be black, you are whiter than I am." "Yes. I am not black-black," he replied, "I am just black" '.

We all laughed. I asked Jan to tell me about his ancestry.

'I am a Capey from the West,' he said. 'French Huguenot. Some Hottentot blood – I hope so anyway. My mother was a Leroux. Rabie, that's a Czech or German name, I think, long ago. I feel ashamed, talking so much about Europe. Living in Greece in Crete for three and a half years, in Paris for seven. But Mother Africa hasn't given me much yet! You know, I can't avoid Europe. Europe to me is terribly important. As a matter of fact, when I was growing up in the Western Cape, I never saw a black [African] person. To us *they* are the immigrants. Fifty years ago there were no blacks in the Western Cape at all. The black man doesn't like to hear that, but he is an immigrant, not me. The settler is him!' He chuckled and continued: 'I was the first to write about apartheid. In *We, the False God*, in 1958. That's quite a while ago. Way before the whole hullabaloo of the last twenty years or so.' He fell silent for a moment and then said again: 'Language is for me the most important thing, not the skin colour.'

We spoke about Breytenbach. How 'terribly depressed' he was the last time he came to Onrus in December 1991. 'He just saw *Rooi Gewaar* ['Red Peril' in Afrikaans] everywhere,' said Marjorie. 'I think he felt that his role was not being appreciated. He was resentful of that.' The reference was to the seven years that he had spent in gaol trying to help the ANC and to all that he had done overseas while living in Paris. After the ANC was unbanned and the exiles came back home, Breytenbach didn't. Albie Sachs and Jeremy Cronin emerged as the 'great white heroes'. Breytenbach was left out in the cold. 'His period of usefulness is over,' Marjorie concluded.

'Can I interrupt and say that I think it is quite typical. De Klerk will also be dropped . . .' That was the first time that Hermien Dommisse was speaking.

'And Mandela will be dropped!' Marjorie said, as if overbidding in an auction.

'The Gorbachev syndrome?' I asked rhetorically.

'The people who initiate things get pushed to the sidelines,' commented Hermien sombrely. We fell silent for a while as if paralysed by the thought of what could happen to South Africa if De Klerk and Mandela passed from the scene.

'What do you think of André Brink's latest book, *An Act of Terror*?' I asked to break the silence.[6]

'It is good,' Marjorie said.

'He is no longer an Afrikaans writer,' Jan lamented. 'That means that he's disappeared from my orbit . . .'

'André writes in English for instant international recognition,'

Marjorie explained. 'He works very hard at his overseas image, but at the centre he is a very sincere guy I think, and *An Act of Terror* is good.'

'It would be a better book if it had 350 pages instead of 625 [I had just finished reading the book, so such details were still fresh in my memory]; but I must admit the Landman family chronicle [another 200 pages at the end of the book] is an ingenious way to introduce the Western reader to the Afrikaner history,' I said.

'It's the first time that André writes such a long book,' Marjorie remarked. 'It's true that he has become a bit verbose lately. When there is a Guild meeting, he will go on and on, he just can't stop!'

'Coetzee is not verbose. Precision, concision, great imagination, the three hallmarks of a great writer, don't you agree?' I said a trifle pompously, giving away my preference.

'Coetzee is a better writer artistically. He has a chance of winning the Nobel Prize, André has not. Though he would love one dearly,' Marjorie said maliciously.

'Your comments on Gordimer's Nobel?' I asked in a light tone.

'Nadine is a good writer,' she said. 'She is a sort of beady-eyed observer who then sits doing it like a fine tapestry on a frame like a fine needlework. I was very glad she got it. We all wrote a letter and said: "We are enchanted for literature, for South Africa and for women!" Because it was the first time that a woman got it for ages . . . She's had two or three books that are good. *Burger's Daughter* is good, *The Conversationalist* is quite good. But she's had some very bad ones too. *July's People*, for example is all wrong. It's such a wrong image altogether. I found it terrible.'

'Jan, there is something that has always puzzled me: how do you get to write really good literature when you are emotionally and politically so tied up?' asked Hermien. 'Of course, all writing, all art, must be passionate,' she went on. 'I deeply believe in that – that you cannot be really creative without having a passion for what you are doing, but emotional and political bias, isn't that a limitation?'

'I think the danger is that you fall into pamphleteering, like Jan did in *We, the False God*, which was bad because it was a pamphlet,' Marjorie said.

'My worst work is always political,' Jan agreed. 'But, a writer should be able to tackle any kind subject and do it well.'

'I guess the question is: how can a writer transcend his political

involvement to write literature that is of a more permanent nature?'
Hermien said.

'Yes, I know,' Jan acknowledged. 'I struggled with that thing
terribly sometimes. I rewrote a book four, five times, because of
that.'

'I think you must put a distance between yourself and your
subject,' Marjorie observed. 'You must find a symbol for it, a metaphor. A direct, realistic hammering, that's not literature. It's the
same thing for painting.' She looked at her husband. 'That story of
yours, Jan, what was it? The one where the house is suddenly
sinking into the earth which has become black and rotten. The earth
is pouring into the house through the windows, just like a boat
taking water in the middle of the sea. It's a much more powerful
image of apartheid that the Casspirs rumbling around in the townships and the soldiers shooting people. That's stuff for journalists,
not writers.'

'But there is quite a bit of that in André Brink, but never in
Coetzee. Perhaps that's one of the reasons he is a better writer,' I
said. 'He *is* a much better writer, you just don't mention them in
the same breath,' Marjorie admitted and then said: 'Do you know
about Elsa Joubert? Have you read *Poppie Nongena?*'[7]

I said that I was not familiar with the book.

'You should absolutely read it,' she said, 'it's a very important
book. It's about her own maid, about her struggles against apartheid: the pass laws, the oppression, the poverty; the day-to-day
reality of apartheid; it's a long chronicle of her life. She tape-
recorded everything she said. It was a tremendous breakthrough
because people who read it were unaware of what the black people
were thinking and feeling . . . This was suddenly a sincere book by
a woman about another woman.'

'And they shared the profits,' Jan said grinning.

'My feeling is that we are going through a tremendously important cultural change,' Hermien said. 'Maybe change is not a very
good word to describe it, maybe revolution is a better word, because
there is a development in which a new culture is being born. It is
neither English, nor Afrikaans, nor black. It seems to be coming
together and you can see it in some painting and in some sculpture
and in literature. But it is still very difficult to do it because everything is in a state of flux. My own feeling is that we are on the
verge of creating a totally new civilisation (if I can use a big word

like that) which will be the fusion of the European and the African heritage. The question is: what is African heritage? Not long ago I had a long conversation with Barbara Masekela [the head of the ANC's culture desk until she was replaced by Wally Serote, the poet], and she spoke to me about the necessity of the African culture becoming predominant in South Africa. She defined it as the African music, African sculpture, African folklore, and so on. "But", I told her, "your average African doesn't know anything about it, he has become urbanised, he has become Americanised." '

What about the supernatural dimension? I asked myself. What about the dimension that has to do with *muti*, or magic, that is the domain of the *inyangas* and *sangomas*? It is a dimension that plays a significant role in African life. How and where did that fit in a Western, American way of life. These thoughts crossed my mind but I didn't say anything.[8]

'There will be several different cultures but one dominant culture,' Marjorie said as if answering my unuttered question.

'It's like one lingua franca and several vernaculars,' Jan said returning to his beloved linguistic dimension. 'The lingua franca aims at generalisation and smoothing; making it easier, simpler, to communicate; whereas the vernacular aims at specialisation; it is more emotional, more particular. I think this is where Afrikaans will be heading in the future.'

'But,' Hermien said, 'Afrikaans is a truly indigenous language because it grew out of the earth, out of the people, of the country. English is an imposed language.'

'African English is often shallow,' Marjorie remarked. 'The African language traditionally was an oral language, and not a written language, and that's a problem with what is being written now in English by Africans. The best that has come has come from your Coloured poets, Adam Small and . . .'

Jan disagreed: 'Now, wait a minute. Wally and four or five other guys write good poetry in English too.'

'That's indigenous too,' Hermien conceded. 'Still, what will happen if English becomes the dominant language and Afrikaans is sidelined? That to me would be a desperate loss.'

'A great impoverishment surely,' Jan said gloomily.

I remembered my conversation with Mphahlele. 'There is a quite long tradition in South Africa,' I said, 'of black writers writing in English. I mentioned my talk with Neville Alexander [a Coloured extreme left-wing politician and intellectual, who is also a distinguished linguist] who was involved in a major study at UCT which apparently came to the conclusion that while English will become the dominant language of South Africa in the future, Afrikaans will survive as an important vernacular.'

Jan did not have the opportunity to comment on what I had just said for this was when Jayne Beaumont, a friend with whose family I was staying in Onrus, came and the conversation ended. But it was not the last time that I saw Jan and Marjorie. About six weeks later, when I came back to the Cape to stay for three days with the Beaumonts at their farm in Botriver, they took me one night to have dinner with some friends – two female artists, a potter and a weaver I believe – and there they were. It was a very pleasant evening.[9]

Notes

1 In fact it appears that N P van Wyk Louw – as well as Uys Kriege, Elisabeth Eybers and a few others – was himself one of the originators of a movement of renewal in Afrikaans poetry known as the *Dertigers* (the Writers of the Thirties). It is strange how the innovators of one era become the conservatives of the next. A fate unavoidable for most creators probably.

2 The classical example of the *platteland roman* is Olive Schreiner's *The Story of an African Farm*, 1883.

3 Ingrid Jonker died in 1965 at age 31. Her father, Abraham Jonker, who was also a well-known writer, belonged to the old school.

4 More on UWC at the end of Chapter 14 in my conversation with Peter Vale.

5 Breyten Breytenbach is widely considered as the most important Afrikaans poet since van Wyk Louw and D J Opperman. There is a whole section on him in Chapter 15 which is a conversation with his younger sister, Rachel.

6 He has published two more books: *First Life of Adamastor* and *On the Contrary* in 1993. He is a prolific writer.

7 *Poppie* was first published in Afrikaans in 1978. Jonathan Ball published it in English in 1980 under the title of *The Long Journey of Poppie Nongena*.

8 The subject of *muti* is a very complex one. See Chapter 16 for some of its most frightening and macabre ramifications.

9 For the story of my stay with the Beaumonts, see Chapter 9.

6

The *Dopper vs* the Magnanimous Man: Can the Two Win Together?

'You are my son – you are going to be president one day.'

Jan de Klerk

'Nelson is a good man. He can walk with kings and he can walk with beggars.'

Eddie Daniels

I met Frederik Willem de Klerk only once. It was in May 1986 when he was clearly one of the two or three strongest men in the regime, which meant that he was one of the two or three probable successors to the ageing President P W Botha.

De Klerk had accumulated a number of important positions: minister of National Education, leader of the National Party for the Transvaal Province, minister of the Budget, and chairman of the Ministers' Council at the House of Assembly, the white parliament. He had been a member of Parliament for Vereeniging in the Vaal Triangle south of Johannesburg for close on fourteen years. He had already practised law for eleven years in Vereeniging before deciding to take the plunge. Coincidence, some would say providence, played a determinant role in that choice. For he had just been appointed to a professorship at Potchefstroom University when the Nationalist MP for Vereeniging, a certain Blaar Coetzee, was appointed ambassador to Rome and his seat became vacant. F W was the perfect choice to replace him. After some soul searching he made up his mind and he was elected easily to the House of Assembly in November 1972.[1]

His office was on the eighteenth floor of the H F Verwoerd

Building on Parliament Street. Our appointment was at 9.30 in the morning and I had been forewarned that our meeting would have to be a very short one because he had to chair a meeting of the Ministers' Council at 10. It was a large, functional office which reminded me of a similar office that I had been in only weeks earlier, that of Professor J P de Lange, the rector of the Rand Afrikaans University and a former chairman of the *Broederbond*, a man who had President's, P W Botha's, ear. The first thing that struck me when he came in was his extraordinary baldness: he had but a narrow band of grey hair around the temples and the back of his head. He looked much older than his fifty years. He was also shorter than I expected. It didn't occur to me at the time but, in retrospect, I realise that his extraordinary baldness was a great asset to him during the referendum campaign. Let me explain: in the age of electronics and American-style politics, appearance counts for very much, at least as much as substance I would say, and De Klerk's baldness combined with the roundness of his face and the chubbiness of his cheeks and the particular quality of his smile gave him the look, in television and photographic close-ups, of a big, overgrown baby. Saatchi and Saatchi, the famous experts in publicity and public relations, have not failed to exploit that to the hilt in the March 92 referendum campaign.

We spoke at length about the issue of the succession to the ageing P W which was a hot topic at the time. The prevailing conventional wisdom was that F W, as the leading candidate of the hardline faction, had a better chance of success than Pik Botha, the perennial Foreign Affairs minister, who led the liberal faction. Other dark-horse candidates included Chris Heunis, the minister for Constitutional Development and Gerrit Viljoen, the minister of Education and Development Aid. Predictably enough, F W maintained that there were no factions within the government, which was united in its efforts to bring about reform. He also warned me not to expect too much too soon, as reform was difficult and bound to take a very long time. Less than three years later, in February 1989, after President Botha suffered a stroke and resigned as leader of National Party, F W was elected to that position, beating Barend du Plessis, seen generally as the *verligte* candidate, by just nine votes. He didn't smile much during our meeting, clearly wanting to convey the image of somebody very much in control, confident in his power and in his destiny. All in all, I came away from that meeting feeling that this was a hard man, a man who had it in himself to be ruthless if and when the circumstances demanded it.

Six years later, in March 1992, long after F W became president in August 1989, I went to see Piet Cillié (see Chapter 3). He is a charming, erudite, articulate and witty man whose conversation is peppered with quotations from the Bible, Shakespeare and various philosophers – one such quotation that I can remember now is from Whitehead: 'Great advances in civilisation all but wreck the societies in which they occur.' Whitehead, he explained, was thinking of the French Revolution, and the Russian Revolution, which was considered as a 'great advance' until the horrors of Stalinism became common knowledge in the 1950s and 1960s. Piet Cillié told me a revealing, if anecdotal story about F W which I summarise below:

'It was right after F W's historic speech in parliament. Three American journalists came to see me; one was from the *New York Times*, one from the *Washington Post*, and a third one from *Time* magazine I believe. They asked me what I thought of F W. Well, I told them about the De Klerk family history, I told them that it is a true political dynasty which began with F W's great-grandfather who was a senator in the Cape Colony and which continued with his grandfather who ran for parliament twice, but unsuccessfully. More recently, his aunt Susanna was married to Prime Minister J G Strijdom who succeeded D F Malan in 1954. His father was an important National Party politician, his career perhaps partly facilitated by the fact that he was the prime minister's brother-in-law. He held several ministerial portfolios and was president of the Senate between 1968 and 1976, which is the year of his retirement. He died three years later at the De Klerk family farm at Krugersdorp. It seems that when F W was only four years old, his father told him: "You are my son – you are going to be president one day." F W was clearly his father's favourite, while his brother W J ("Wimpie", eight years older than F W) was his mother's favourite. W J was always more liberal in his politics than his younger brother. He was for a long time the editor of *Rapport*, the largest-circulation Afrikaans Sunday newspaper in the country before he became, recently, a professor of journalism at the Rand Afrikaans University (RAU) in Johannesburg.

'W J de Klerk is credited with coining the terms *verkrampte* and *verligte* to describe the split, in the 1970s, of the Afrikaner establishment into two rival camps. The point of all this is that I told my American journalist friends that while I didn't have any doubts that De Klerk had the political skills and the leadership qualities to navigate the ship of state through the stormy seas of the transition, I was unsure whether or not he had enough steel in his teeth to withhold the pressure. The conversation was supposed to be not on the record, so you can imagine my surprise when I saw a few days later in the English-speaking press: "Piet Cillié, an old friend of P W" – another inaccuracy, because I never was a personal friend of P W Botha, only a political friend. You know, as the editor of a major paper you can ill afford to be personal friends with politicians; they will use you, manipulate you – so, "Piet Cillié, says that 'De Klerk doesn't have steel in his teeth'." That was of course, to say the least, a misrepresentation of what I had said. Anyway I wrote a little poem and sent it to F W. It goes like this:

> With steel in his backbone and teeth,
> and gold in his eyes and on his tongue,
> he crossed the Rubicon in one mighty jump.

He sent me back a note, thanking me for it. So that's my little story.'
    'Steel in his backbone and teeth and gold in his eyes and on his tongue . . .' I liked that. It was a good metaphor, the first part of which dealt with character, substance, and the second with appearance, the 'look'. Ultimately, of course, it is the former that counts. So the question is: who is De Klerk, what kind of man is he?
    A third De Klerk – W A de Klerk, writer – is a personal friend with whom I had long conversations in 1986 and 1992 in Paarl (in the Boland, not far from Stellenbosch), the first time at his famous farm 'Saffier' (which he later sold) and then at his house. I was particularly impressed by the central chapter of his book, *The Puritans in Africa*, 'The Promethean Afrikaner' on Dr H F Verwoerd, the high priest of grand apartheid, whom he described as a man with 'a flawed vision . . . a fanatic who sincerely and passionately believed that he had the Saviour's Gift, not only for his own people, but for everyone.' I remember well, he told me in the course of our 1992 conversation: 'The last person on earth that will sell out to the ANC in any way is De Klerk.' (see Note 4, Chapter 3 and Notes 10–11, Chapter 20.)

Ian Wyllie, the retired editor of Durban's *Sunday Tribune*, whom I visited at his home in Kloof in April 1992 to pick his brains on Buthelezi and things in general, told me the following about De Klerk:

'F W is going to try to hold on to power. There's no question in my mind that he is not going to sell his people down the drain. You must understand it, he comes from a very conservative Afrikaner background himself. I mean his whole life was built on the idea that the Afrikaner had to find his way to power, and then hold it. His father was a very conservative man. He was the minister of Interior under Strydom, and that was before there was a Ministry of Sports, so he was responsible for deciding issues like whether a black boxer could come into this country, and he would not give a black American boxer a visa, and his explanation was a simple one. He went public and said, I think in parliament: "Can you imagine what would happen in this country if a black boxer knocks down a white one?" This was De Klerk's father who was always adamantly against multiracial sports. I am just telling you that F W grew up in a climate which was very determined to keep the white man boss. He may've surrendered a great deal of this, but it may also be that some of it is still in him.'

While Ian Wyllie chuckled softly, I remembered having watched on South African television what De Klerk's father dreaded most: the destruction of a famous Afrikaner boxer in the ring by a black opponent. The Afrikaner boxer was Gerrie Coetzee, his black opponent, Frank Bruno, the British heavyweight of West Indian origin. It was April 1986 and the fight was held in the Wembley arena in London and transmitted live on South African television. There was great anticipation that Coetzee was going to teach Bruno a lesson, he was truly the 'great Afrikaner hope'. In fact, he was bigger than his opponent, but that didn't help him any; it was all over in less than two minutes in the first round with Coetzee knocked out and on the canvas. The following morning, Coetzee's lightning defeat was front-page news in all the South African newspapers. The sensationalist tabloids had devoted the whole of their front pages to it with colour photographs of the unfortunate loser who looked bad with a bruised and swollen face. He announced that he was retiring from boxing. It was inevitable that parallels would be drawn between what had happened to Coetzee and what might happen to the Afrikaner nation in the future. The trauma that De Klerk's father wanted to spare his people from had come to pass a quarter-century later.

Wyllie thought that 'Wimpie' de Klerk, F W's older brother, had played a significant role in his brother's conversion. 'I'm sure that he did, yes,' he said. 'I knew Wimpie well, we were both members of the same editors' conference, that of Sunday newspapers' editors. I believe he was quite sincere in his more liberal approach. But, again, I am not too sure that he would like to see the Afrikaner weakened to the extent that he lost his position of influence in the country. I think they are all working towards preserving an Afrikaner identity, it is a very strong thing in them.'

I think that religion has to be of paramount importance in De Klerk's deep-down personality and character. An assessment of that element requires that we go back a century and a half to the time when F W's great-great-grandfather Barend Jacobus was still alive. That was the time of the Great Trek (1836–8), but B J did not take part in it. Instead, he chose to do battle against what he saw as corrupting decadent tendencies in the Calvinist Dutch Reform Church (DRC). He and a few like-minded colleagues were instrumental in the founding of a traditionalist, conservative new church, which came to be known as the *'Dopper* Church' (*dopper* in Afrikaans means a little metal cap used to extinguish the flame of a candle or oil lamp). More formally and officially, the church is called the *Gereformeerde Kerk* (GK) which, with the *Hervormde Kerk* (HK), are the two much smaller churches of the DRC. By far the biggest arm of the DRC is the *Nederduitse Gereformeerde Kerk* (NGK), to which the majority of the Afrikaner political establishment belongs – to such an extent, in fact, that the NGK was dubbed by an irreverent press as 'the South African government in prayer'. It was in 1869 that the first *Dopper* theological school was established in Burgersdorp. It was moved to Potchefstroom in 1905 and it became the core of the Potchefstroom University (for Christian Education) in 1919. F W, who was born in 1936, graduated from Potchefstroom University cum laude in 1956 with a BA LLB. He met his wife-to-be, Marike Willemse, while they were both students at the university. She is the daughter of the late Professor W A Willemse, a pillar of respectability. After his marriage to Marike and his election to parliament in 1972, F W's political career quickly blossomed: he was re-elected unopposed in 1974, and in 1978 he began his education for a possible premiership. He occupied several ministerial posts: Social Welfare and Pensions, Home Affairs and National Education in 1984. Meanwhile, he was in 1982 elected leader of the National Party for the Transvaal Province to replace Dr Andries Treurnicht, who had resigned to protest against the new tricameral parliament and who later founded the Conservative Party. As late as 1988, De Klerk, as the minister of National Education, had tried to subdue the liberal English-speaking universities – Wits and UCT mainly – by threatening to cut their subsidies unless they proved capable of maintaining law and order on their campuses. De Klerk eventually lost that battle when the courts ruled in favour of the universities.[1]

So, there is precious little in the family history, life and professional career of De Klerk to suggest that he has in his inner being the ingredients that would make his 'crossing of the Rubicon in one mighty jump', as put so elegantly by Piet Cillié, logical or understandable. The question is, therefore, what happened to make this man act so out of character, throw caution to the wind, and take what is perceived to be enormous risks? Unless, of course, he didn't act out of character, he didn't throw caution to the wind and he didn't take enormous risks. Certainly, there were objective conditions that facilitated the move: the collapse of Communism in the Soviet Union and Eastern Europe was one; the severe deterioration of the economy due to financial and trade sanctions was another; the international isolation and the sports boycott were two more; and there were others. These were indeed some of the objective conditions that made a radical change of course necessary. But there is another reason, to which I have alluded at the start of this chapter and which has to do with the change of strategy in conflict resolution (throughout the world, in fact). It is now time to expand a little on this.

Stripped to its bare-knuckle essentials, that change of strategy involves a rejection of confrontation as a means of achieving a goal and the embrace of negotiation instead. Negotiation represents the modernisation of conflict management. The so-called civilised world has adopted it partly because it is a winning strategy: it plays well on television, the dominant medium of modern communications. One can hardly have politicians smiling and discussing credibly and reasonably about peace, while in the news programmes the police are shown busily tear-gassing people, cracking their skulls open or letting police dogs loose on defenceless

civilians. But, and that is an important 'but', an apparent willingness
to negotiate does not *necessarily* mean that one is prepared to make
major compromises or concessions on substance; certain things can
be declared non-negotiable, one can have a secret double agenda.
Furthermore, even if one causes the breakdown of negotiations
through intransigence, it is important to continue to insist that one
is ready to discuss, to negotiate. Then the ball is in the other side's
court. You wait and see what they are capable to come up with. In
South Africa they may resort to mass action 'because that is the
only language that the government understands', as Jay Naidoo,
the general secretary of COSATU, put it. But that is a dangerous
strategy, because it is confrontational, and therefore ugly and self-
defeating, particularly if it doesn't succeed. So, by carefully dosing
negotiation with intransigence, you will be able to weaken your
opponent, wear him down. Especially so, if you possess many
important trump cards: the army and the police, Big Business, the
civil service, the public sector, and so on. So time is on your side
and you can concentrate on building a coalition of forces: the whites,
the majority of the Coloured and Indian communities, the conservative blacks in the homelands and elsewhere, Inkatha, and so on;
that could be, in a free election, if not the outright winner, then at
least a very strong second that would be impossible to ignore. That
is the strategy. Will it work? The initative now seems to be with
the ANC. To summarise the following African maxim that I owe
to De Klerk, the writer: 'Tell me where you come from, tell me
where you are heading for but, please, don't waste you breath
telling me what will happen along the way.' F W knows where he
is coming from, he also knows where he would like to go, but will
he be able to get there? It seems increasingly unlikely.

In conclusion, it is well to bear in mind that it is a very intricate
game that is being played here, a game in which there is far more
than meets the eye, a game of hidden agendas, in which the mastery
of the art of negotiation as politics is at least as important as the
justice of one's cause, a game in which mistakes can be deadly. On
both parts . . .

I don't know Nelson Mandela. I've never spoken to him personally.
The closest contact I've had with him was in Khayelitsha, the
sprawling black township near Cape Town, on 21 March 1992,
the 32nd anniversary of the Sharpeville massacre. It was there, in

a soccer field, on a hot and sunny afternoon, with about 35,000 other people, that I witnessed a remarkable phenomenon, a magic moment: the communion of a great leader with his people. When he finally arrived, an hour late, at three o'clock in the afternoon – there had been rumours that he was not feeling well and might not come at all – it was as if a tremendous amount of energy was released. A massive din rose from the stadium like a hundred lions roaring together and the crowd surged forward to make a more intense physical contact with their hero. He flashed his trademark toothy smile and did not seem afraid that he might get crushed by the rowdy multitudes. (See Chapter 8.) He was charismatic in the true Weberian sense of the word, I thought, in the sense of a mystical and mysterious quality of the leader that makes the crowd to follow him. When he finally spoke it was a moderate, responsible speech – but he is also capable, when the circumstances demand it, of making fiery, even inflammatory, ones. Who is this man? Is he capable of leading South Africa to a new, democratic future?

Perhaps a few biographical details are in order to begin with.[2] Nelson Mandela was born in 1918 at Qunu, near Umtata, in the Transkei. His father was chief councillor to the paramount chief of the Thembu, the single largest tribe in the Xhosa nation. He was only twelve when his father died and he came under the guardianship of his cousin David Dalindyebo, the acting paramount chief. After graduating from a Methodist boarding missionary high school, he enrolled in the old Fort Hare University College at Alice, in the Ciskei. Fort Hare in the late thirties and early forties was still a prestigious college – it had not yet been hijacked by the Nationalist government and turned into a 'bush college' – which attracted, not only the black South African elite – Sobukwe, Buthelezi, Tambo, as well as Mandela, to name but a few – but future leaders from all over the African continent, such as Mugabe of Zimbabwe, Lule of Uganda, Njonjo of Kenya, and so on. In the third year of their studies, Mandela and Tambo were expelled from the college for having participated in a student strike. On his return to his ancestral home, Mandela found out that a tribal marriage was being arranged for him, that the bride had been chosen, the *lobola* (dowry) paid, and even the details of the ceremony worked out. Unable to deal with the situation, he fled to Johannesburg where he completed his legal studies and articled (training period) to the Jo'burg firm of attorneys – Witkin, Sidelsky and Eidelman in 1942. In 1952, Mandela and Tambo opened the first black legal practice in the country.

Meanwhile, Mandela had been politically active: with Tambo and Sisulu he was among the founding members of the ANC's Youth League in 1944. In fact, the driving force of the League in those early days was a certain Anton Lembede, a young Zulu teacher and intellectual who died of a mysterious illness in 1947.[3] In 1949, Mandela was elected to the ANC's national executive and a year later he became president of the ANC-YL. He played a prominent role in the Defiance Campaign of 1952, having been appointed volunteer-in-chief, and travelled widely around the country. That same year he was elected president of the Transvaal branch. Between 1953 and 1962, he was continuously banned, which meant that he couldn't attend large political gatherings; so he had to resign from the ANC officially and exercise his leadership secretly. This was a critical period that included the Congress of the People campaign, which culminated in the adoption of the Freedom Charter in 1955–6, and the four-and-a-half-year-long Treason Trial that followed it and ended with the acquittal of all the 156 accused in 1961.

A few months before this, however, one of the most traumatic events of the black liberation struggle occurred: the Sharpeville massacre – triggered by the PAC's anti-pass protests. In the national emergency that ensued, both the ANC and PAC were banned and there followed probably the most difficult decade and a half in the history of the struggle.

It was in 1957, during the Treason Trial that the 39-year-old Mandela met the 23-year-old Winnie Madikizela who was quite famous for her beauty, as well as for being the first African female medical social worker at Baragwanath Hospital in Soweto. Mandela had already been married once to Evelyn Ntoko, a nurse, who had given him three children, only two of whom survived. Winnie is the daughter of Colombus Madikizela, who was a teacher and later minister of Agriculture and Forestry in the Transkeian government. They were married in 1958 and two daughters, Zenani and Zindziva, were born in quick succession.

Mandela's family life was fated to be of very short duration, however: he was arrested during the National Emergency of 1961 and, after his release, he went underground to organise the campaign against the proclamation of the Republic, which severed all the ties with the British Commonwealth. After that, events accelerated: the three-day strike against the proclamation of the Republic failed and *Umkhonto we Sizwe* (MK for short), was founded, with Mandela named as its leader. A campaign of sabotage against civilian targets was launched just before Christmas 1961. Mandela left the country clandestinely and underwent guerrilla training in Algeria. He returned in the middle of 1962 but was arrested, tried and sentenced to five years' imprisonment. It was in 1963 that the single biggest blow came to the ANC as an organisation: its entire top leadership – Walter Sisulu, Govan Mbeki, Ahmed Kathrada, Raymond Mhlaba, Elias Matsoaledi, Andrew Mlangu, as well as Dennis Goldberg and Lionel Bernstein (Oliver Tambo was already outside the country) – was captured in a raid on Liliesleaf Farm, its underground headquarters in Rivonia, a Jo'burg suburb.[4] In a stroke of bad luck, the government discovered documents on the farm that incriminated Mandela and proved that he was the chief of MK: the diary of his tour in Africa and handwritten notes on Operation *Mayibuye* ('Come back' in Xhosa) and a plan for a possible guerrilla campaign. In the Rivonia Trial, which opened in October 1963, Mandela was given the honour of being named defendant number one. In April of the next year, at the close of the trial, he made his famous speech that ends thus: 'I have cherished the ideal of a democratic and free society in which all persons live together in harmony and with equal opportunities. It is an ideal for which I hope to live for and achieve. But if needs be, it is an ideal for which I am prepared to die.'

The trial was given worldwide publicity. Mandela became famous all over the world. The sentence that fell in June was life imprisonment for all the defendants (except for Bernstein who got 20 years). It was a relief, because it was feared that the Verwoerd government, which was at the height of its powers then, might, in a self-destructive disregard for the world public opinion, send the nine men to the gallows. But it didn't. The Afrikaner leaders have shown time and again, even in their wildest and maddest moments, that they are not prepared to commit suicide. Mandela spent the next eighteen years on the infamous Robben Island (known as *esiqithini*, 'at the island'). By all accounts, the first ten years were very hard: working in the limestone quarry day in day out; making do with one blanket in the summer and two in the winter; no underwear, no long trousers and no socks, even in the thick of the winter; no radio, no newspapers and no permission to study; visits by direct family only twice a year. His reputation as a magnanimous man grew on the island. This is what Eddie Daniels, a white man and a fellow inmate for fifteen years, wrote in an article published in the Communist journal *New Age* after his release:

> Nelson is a good man. He can walk with kings and he can walk with beggars. In prison Nelson carried himself impressively. Even the way he walked. He taught me how to survive. When I was ill, he could have asked anybody else to come and see me. He came personally. He even cleaned my toilet. He is a man of great integrity.

In April 1982, Mandela, Sisulu, Mbeki and others were transferred to Pollsmoor Prison, near Cape Town. That same year a massive Release Mandela Campaign was launched that lasted many years and culminated in 1988 at the famous twelve-hour concert in Wembley and elsewhere to celebrate Mandela's seventieth birthday; the concert, in which many world-class entertainers participated, was broadcast in fifty countries. The international pressure for his release was becoming unbearable. In August, there were stories in the papers that Mandela was being treated for tuberculosis in a Cape Town clinic. In December he was moved to a warder's house in the Victor Verster Prison near Paarl. The government was concerned – scared is perhaps a better word – that he might die in prison, and that all hell might then break loose. His health was monitored by a battery of doctors. Mandela's contacts with government representatives began as early as July 1986 when he first met Kobie Coetzee, the minister of Justice. That meeting was followed by one with Gerrit Viljoen, the minister for Constitutional Development. In July 1989, Mandela met P W Botha, the state president and, in December, his successor, F W de Klerk. He was released on 11 February 1990, which was a Sunday, and immediately addressed a mass rally in the centre of Cape Town.

Three and a half years have gone by since Mandela was released. It is time for an assessment. Not a final assessment, of course, that can come only after the current transition which will last until the year 2000. A preliminary assessment is all that is possible at this time, one that concerns his transformation from the state of a symbol: 'A living icon in the liberation culture of the whole continent ... the most uncompromising symbol of resistance and struggle against racial domination in the twentieth century',[5] to that of a mortal, fallible, 'human, all too human' politician who can, at best, if he is lucky and things don't fall apart, aspire to become one of the world-class statesmen of the last decade of the century.

H W (Harvey) van der Merwe wrote this in an article that was published in *Rapport* the very same day that Mandela was released from prison:

> When I visited Mandela in 1984, I summarised my impressions of him in three characteristics: warmth and goodwill, as expressed in the manner in which he inquired as to the condition of my sick wife; a strong and forceful personality, and the authority with which he spoke about politics; and dignity – although he was imprisoned behind a thick glass partition, I never for a moment felt that *he* was behind bars and that I was free. He transcended his detention.
>
> These impressions were reinforced when my wife and I enjoyed a meal with him in the Victor Verster prison in December 1989. Here I got to know the statesman who had emerged as a facilitator between divergent political groups in South Africa ...
>
> I can think of no other leader of the same stature who can achieve more to establish a government of national unity in South Africa.[6]

In June 1991, Arthur Miller, the famous American playwright, came all the way from New York to interview Nelson Mandela in his Soweto home. Miller wrote about 'his rather majestic poise, unmarred by rancor ... [of] his charm and civility, even if he was the man who set up the ANC's guerrilla force, the *Umkhonto we Sizwe.*' He noted that 'toward the end of his imprisonment he ran "Mandela University" on Robben Island, and white warders were among his pupils.' What struck Miller most was 'the absence in him of any sign of bitterness after 27 years in prison ... How does one manage to emerge from nearly three decades in prison with such hopefulness, such inner calm?' He asked and provided his own answer: 'Mandela, to put it simply, is a chief'.[7]

In other words, a man with aristocratic qualities, or a 'magnanimous man', to use Aristotle's famous categorisation of character. A magnanimous man 'will never do things that are hateful and mean',

Aristotle wrote in the *Ethics*, 'he will bear all his fortunes with dignity, take the most honourable course that circumstances permit. The tasks that he undertakes are few, but grand and celebrated . . . He is bound to be open in his likes and dislikes . . . He does not nurse resentment . . . The accepted view of the magnanimous man is that his gait is measured, his voice deep, and his speech unhurried . . . he is not highly strung . . .'

To conclude: Antony Lewis in an article in the *New York Times* saw in De Klerk what he called the 'Gorbachev flaw'.[8] Because, he wrote, 'he is aware that a repressive system no longer works but in the end [he is] unwilling to abandon it.' There are still remnants of truth in that statement even if the two situations, that of the former Soviet Union and that of the present-day South Africa, are fundamentally different. De Klerk and the Afrikaner Nationalists who support him have come a long way even if they are still incapable of fully accepting a simple truth: the whites must transfer power to the black majority some time around the end of the century and there are no guarantees. As Breyten Breytenbach wrote some time ago: 'We must give ourselves into the arms of the Great African Mother and trust she will not drop us'.[9] Lewis, in that same article, wrote that Nelson Mandela President would be 'the best guarantor of a stable and prosperous South Africa'. The problem for De Klerk and most whites is that Mandela is 75 years old in 1993 and, with the possible exception of Thabo Mbeki, they don't really trust anyone among his possible successors.[10] So it looks like negotiation and confrontation will follow one another in a not-so-merry-go-round until such time that the majority of the whites become convinced that their best bet is indeed to 'give themselves into the arms of the Great African Mother'. A complicating factor is the white right wing which will probably not give up without a fight.[11] However, in the end, whether alive and as president, or dead and from his grave, the Magnanimous Man will win. One wishes that that does not have to mean that the Dopper – who is fast becoming the Pragmatic Man – must lose. One wishes that the conditions were ripe for the two to win together and that the Dopper could welcome the Magnanimous Man to the Tuynhuis as . . . his successor.

Notes

1 Two books on F W are: *F W de Klerk: Man of the Moment*, by A Kamsteeg and E Dijk, Vlaeberg, 1990, Johannesburg, and *F W de Klerk: the Man in his Time*, by W J (Wimpie) de Klerk, Jonathan Ball, 1991, Johannesburg. The former is more objective and less hagiographic in its treatment.

2 There are several biographies on Nelson Mandela. I will mention two: *Nelson Mandela: the Struggle Is My Life*, International Defence and Aid Fund (IDAF), 1986, London, which is a compendium of 'Speeches, Writings and Documents', 'Memoirs on Robben Island' by Mac Maharaj and M Dingake, as well as a short but interesting autobiographical note by Mandela himself; and Fatima Meer's – she is a well-known sociology professor at the University of Natal in Durban and a political activist – *Higher than Hope*, 1989.

3 Lembede, who wrote an MA thesis on *The Conception of God in the Writings of Philosophers from Descartes to the Present Day*, was a brilliant thinker. He was one of the originators of the Black Consciousness (BC) philosophy in South Africa. He often spoke or wrote about the pathological state of mind – the loss of self-confidence, inferiority complex, frustration and the idolisation of the whites – that was brought about among blacks by racism. See: *No 46 – Steve Biko*, Hilda Bernstein, International Defence and Aid Fund (IDAF), 1978, London, page 12.

4 The Liliesleaf Farm was rented by a certain Arthur Goldreich, a colourful character who had fought in the Israeli War of Independence in 1948. He was a member of the Palmach in Israel, an elite fighting unit within the Haganah, the main military force. He was later arrested but managed to escape from prison.

5 F Van Zyl Slabbert, *The Quest for Democracy*, page v.

6 I had a long chat with Harvey on Mandela. I went to see him at his centre in April 1992. Among other publications of his centre, he gave me a photocopy of the English version of his article, 'Mandela After His Release'.

7 Arthur Miller's interview was published in the *Weekly Mail*, 5 July 1991, Johannesburg, under the title 'The Playwright and the Politician'.

8 4–5 July 1992.

9 Rian Malan, *My Traitor's Heart*, Vintage, 1991, London, page 410. First published in 1990, this excellent book was praised in *The Times Literary Supplement* as a 'magnificent book, an explosion of truth telling'.

10 Now that Chris Hani is dead and Thabo Mbeki is national chairman of the ANC, the whites ought to be reassured.

11 Alarmingly, the polls in June 1993 show that large numbers of whites – perhaps as many as two-thirds – are abandoning De Klerk's National

Party to flock to the right wing Conservative Party. There have been ominous developments lately such as the election of the hard-liner Dr Ferdie Hartzenberg as leader of the CP and the formation of the Afrikaner *Volksfront* under the leadership of General C Viljoen, a hero of the Angolan war (see also Note 1 at the end of Chapter 1). If that flight to the right proves to be a permanent one, a non-negligible possibility, then De Klerk may well woo the Coloured community turning the NP into a truly multi-racial party, possibly in the long run, one dominated by Coloured politicians.

7

The Buthelezi Conundrum: A Dialectical Approach

'I think that he acknowledges Mandela's primacy and would be content with second spot but I don't think the other leaders of the ANC would grant him that.'

Ian Wyllie

Durban, which handles more than half of South Africa's exports and imports, is by far the country's largest port. This tropical city on the Indian Ocean is sometimes described as the largest Indian city outside India: indeed, more than half of its million plus population is of Indian origin. The majority of the Indians were brought to Natal in the late nineteenth and early twentieth centuries as indentured labourers to work in the sugar-cane fields for a number of years and then go back to India. Most preferred (or were allowed) to stay at the expiration of their contracts. Others came on their own as 'passenger' Indians, became shopkeepers and traders and are the originators of Durban's prosperous Indian business community today. The 400,000 or so whites who live in Durban are largely the descendants of the early British settlers. Broadly speaking, they form the industrial and professional elites of the Natal Province.

In Natal proper, the Africans, the large majority of whom belong to the 'Zulu nation', live in the townships such as Umlazi (the biggest in Natal with a population estimated close to one million) and KwaMashu. Zulus are by far the dominant political and demographic element in Natal's power equation.

Natal's future is seen as being inextricably linked to that of the Zulus who, with a total population of more than seven million, are the largest black ethnic group in South Africa; they are followed by the Xhosas, with about five million; the Northern Sotho, 3.5 million; the Southern Sotho, 2.5 million; the Tswana, 2 million; and so on. Perhaps five million Zulus live within the borders of Natal; the rest are scattered in the hostels of the black townships and the mine compounds of the Transvaal and the Orange Free State (OFS). Natal is the smallest and, after the OFS, the least populated of South Africa's four provinces, but some crucial historical events took place there. In 1838, on the banks of the small Nkome River (which was rebaptised 'Blood River' after the battle), the Voortrekkers (those Boers that chose to leave Cape Colony) inflicted a heavy defeat on King Dingaan's army. In 1879, a regiment of Lord Chelmsford's army was ambushed by the Zulus at Isandhlwana and wiped out, close to 900 Redcoats were killed. After that the British crushed King Cethswayo's armies at Rorke's Drift and Ulundi, and Ulundi the Zulu capital was burned to the ground. Traditionally, Zululand begins north of the mighty Tugela River, that was the part that was unified by the great King Shaka, but today the KwaZulu homeland is made up of Zululand plus a number of enclaves that are scattered all over Natal.

It was not my first visit to Durban. I had come exactly six years ago, in April 1986, to be present at the launching of the KwaZulu/Natal *Indaba* (conference), whose purpose was to explore the possibility of a joint government. The idea had ripened slowly. The central government was at first against it, but later, when it became clear after 1984 that the new tricameral constitution was not going anywhere – it was in fact the beginning of the chronic wave of violence which still continues today – P W Botha had relented and a lot of whites began looking at the *Indaba* as a useful sounding board of a future federal solution for the whole country. After a long preparatory phase, forty-one regional and national organisations representing political, labour and business interests had agreed to participate.

The Achilles' heel of the *Indaba* was that it was categorically rejected by the UDF (the ANC was still banned of course) and COSATU on the black side, and by the Conservative Party and the other right-wingers on the white side. The two months or so preceding the inauguration were marked by several violent incidents: the delegates of the UDF-affiliated National Education Crisis Committee (NECC), who came to Durban for the annual conference, were attacked by Inkatha vigilantes and one delegate was killed and several others injured; two weeks later the theatre where *Asinamali* (We Have No Money), a play by Mbogeni Ngema, was being shown was attacked and the producer of the play killed. Eye-witnesses said that the *Impis* (Zulu warriors) were looking for Ngema but, luckily for him, he was not present that night. At about the same time, the offices of Professor Lawrence ('Laurie') Schlemmer, a close adviser of Buthelezi, were fire-bombed both at the university and his home.

At the inauguration, which took place at the historic Durban City Hall, Buthelezi himself led the KwaZulu delegation, while that of the Natal government was led by Frank Martin, senior MEC (Member of the provincial Executive Committee). Radclyffe Cadman, the Pretoria-appointed administrator of Natal, was also present, but only as an observer. Buthelezi had made a defiant speech explaining that he had changed his mind about not leading the KwaZulu delegation personally only at the last moment, because he wanted to show his enemies that he was not a man easily intimidated by threats (there had been rumours of a possible attempt on his life).

After the official ceremony, the delegates and some selected guests and journalists were invited to a cocktail party in an adjoining room; I managed to get in thanks to Schlemmer. I recognised some of the faces in the crowded room: Amichand Rajbansi, the leader of the Indian House of Delegates in the tricameral parliament; Reverend Joe Hendrickse, his counterpart at the Coloured House of Representatives; Harry Schwarz, an MP from the Progressive Federal Party at the white House of Assembly (later ambassador to the United States).

Buthelezi was naturally the centre of attention and I was impressed by the way he worked the crowd like a seasoned politician. With a fixed, slightly condescending smirk on his face he shook hands with people who assumed deferential poses, chatted briefly with them, and then moved on; the amount of time he spent with each person seemed directly proportional to his or her position on the global political scale. I was with Dr Oscar Dhlomo, his second-in-command (secretary-general of Inkatha and minister of Education in the KwaZulu government; in 1991 he resigned both his posts and set up the Institute for Multi-party Democracy, positioning himself as a mediator, a facilitator), who after a few unsuccessful attempts managed to introduce me to his boss. I mumbled a few words of congratulations, which he acknowledged silently while simultaneously offering me his hand distractedly. I clasped his hand energetically, but he didn't clasp it back; it was a soft and well groomed hand. He looked younger than his 57 years: his bearded face was devoid of wrinkles and I didn't notice any white hairs; but he was slightly plump, looking like a man who lacks exercise. His demeanour was clearly aristocratic. Mangosuthu Gatsha Buthelezi is the chief of the large Buthelezi tribe and has close family ties with the royal family; his mother is a princess and a daughter of King Dinizulu. He is known to be a proud and vain man, very ambitious politically, with a temper, capable of flying into a rage if challenged or crossed in any way. There is a story, possibly apocryphal, according to which a white journalist, who had dared to compare him to Bishop Muzorewa, was beaten up by his bodyguards in his capital Ulundi. In the first elections in Rhodesia/Zimbabwe after the civil war and independence in 1980, conventional wisdom among the whites – the British, the South Africans and the settlers themselves – was that the moderate bishop would emerge as a winner, and that is why he was financed heavily by the South African government. In the event, Muzorewa won only three out of the one hundred seats contested! Mugabe won an absolute majority with 57 mandates.

My main reason for coming to Natal in April 1992 was to try to learn more about the bloody, ruthless rivalry between the ANC and Inkatha, which is often portrayed as black-on-black violence. I had gone earlier to see Musa Myeni, the International Relations director of the Inkatha Freedom Party (IFP) in Johannesburg. Here, in Durban, I planned to see Paulus Zulu, a pro-ANC specialist of Zulu politics at the University of Natal and Ian Wyllie, a former editor of the Durban *Sunday Tribune*. I will, begin with Myeni, and then follow up with Zulu and Wyllie.

Musa Myeni is a man who speaks his mind forcefully, and, occasionally, even brutally. His self-confidence is sometimes pushed to the limit of arrogance. He is knowledgeable and articulate but also bent on hyperbole, because he is too concerned with scoring propaganda points. For instance, throughout our conversation he constantly referred to the ANC-SACP alliance, 'forgetting' the third member of that alliance, COSATU. I asked him what the IFP stood for, what were the main points of divergence with the ANC. What the IFP wants is to avoid at all costs a unitary state that is likely to be dominated by the ANC in the long run. Everything else derives from this central fact. For instance, it insists that the Multi-party Talks (once CODESA) should agree on federalism as the most suitable system for South Africa *before* a constituent assembly is elected because such an assembly would be dominated by the ANC and its allies, the SACP and COSATU. If that happened, Buthelezi could be reduced to the state of a regional player and that, of course, is anathema to a man with an ego as big as Buthelezi's. So he is using 'Zulu nationalism' as his principal weapon, because African nationalism is ANC's preserve. The IFP is against an elected constituent assembly writing the constitution, Myeni explained, because that would exclude from the process many parties, and that, given South Africa's history of factionalism and hostility, would be very dangerous. The IFP wanted an all-inclusive group, in which all the parties, big and small, were represented, to draw up the new constitution.

'You understand,' he said, 'at this point CODESA is not at all representative, because the Conservative Party, PAC, AZAPO and the traditional leaders are not part of it. So we propose that CODESA pause for a time to take stock [that was about two months before the breakdown of the negotiations in June 1992] and come up with new ideas to attract the recalcitrants. We must make sure that we don't rush the end-product,' he concluded, 'because the most important thing is for the end-product to be right.'

I asked Myeni if it was true that the ANC was making serious inroads into the traditionally Inkatha strongholds, such as the townships around Natal, and that Inkatha's presence at the University of Zululand was very small. He challenged me angrily: 'What is your research? What are you basing your statements on?'

'Polls, surveys, impressionistic evidence . . .'

'Polls! Surveys! What do they mean in the current climate of violence and intimidation? So I say there is only one way to test our strength, as opposed to ANC's strength, and that's through elections; but you can't have free and fair elections if the violence and the intimidation don't stop. The ANC is attacking our people. Look here,' he said, pointing at a newspaper on the desk, 'these are pictures of ANC people arrested yesterday in Sebokeng wearing police uniforms. In Empageni they caught the local ANC officials with A–47s and hundreds of rounds of ammunition. Have you heard about the speeches that Winnie Mandela and Harry Gwala [ANC leader of central Natal, also a self-avowed Stalinist] are making about liberating Ciskei and Transkei, using force if necessary. So, you will understand that we've told our people to be careful, not to admit openly that they are IFP members, because they can get killed if they do so.'

After that Myeni had launched on another pet subject: the strong bias against the IFP and in favour of the ANC in the print media. 'Did you know about the rule of adding a zero when counting the people who attend the ANC rallies and taking away a zero when estimating the crowds of the IFP rallies?' he asked rhetorically. 'Early last year,' he continued, 'I attended a media conference at Vista University [a new university for blacks with several campuses around the country] and the editor of the *Sowetan* who was there told me that his own journalists had complained to him that they were instructed by the ANC to do just that. Let me give you a typical example: in Port Elizabeth, where Mandela went after he was released from prison in February 1990, most papers said that there were half-a-million people to welcome him, when in fact there were only 50,000 people.' Major papers in the country estimated the crowds at between 300,000 and 400,000 people; anyway, Eastern Cape is ANC 'territory' and the example was badly chosen.

Perhaps sensing my reservations, Myeni changed course once more. 'Did you know that the ANC was started by Zulus?' he said vehemently. John Dube, its first president, was a Zulu. P I Seme, its third president, was also a Zulu, he was an uncle of Chief Buthelezi as a matter of fact!

I remembered having read that P I Seme had replaced the more left wing radical J Gumede in 1930. His leadership had proved to be quite catastrophic – the ANC had moved to the right and become irrelevant; its membership, just like that of the Industrial and Commercial Workers Union (ICU), had dwindled; the 1930s was possibly the worst decade in the history of the ANC.[1]

'Come to think of it,' Myeni went on, 'all the ANC presidents, except for two, were Zulu. The ANC is a product of the Zulu nation!' he almost shouted.

So that was perhaps the main reason of the no-holds-barred nature of the ANC/Inkatha rivalry, I thought: the belief by Buthelezi that the ANC had been hijacked by Xhosa leaders such as Mandela, Tambo and Sisulu. One shouldn't forget that Buthelezi himself was a prominent Youth Leaguer in the 1940s and that in those days the driving force of the ANC-YL was the Zulu teacher and intellectual by the name of Anton Lembede.

'There is a conspiracy against the Zulu nation and we know it,' Myeni continued, 'but we have many non-Zulu supporters. Of our total membership of 2.2 million, 43 per cent are non-Zulu. We have more than 100,000 white members; we have branches in Sandton, Randburg, Benoni. Our youth movement has almost one million members. [Some time later I was to learn that all the school children in KwaZulu were automatically members and that their member-ship fees were included in the school fees].[2] 'We have 600,000 card-carrying members on the Rand alone.' He paused. 'All this is reality,' he concluded. Why do people deny reality? Why are so many people trying to prove that Inkatha is nothing? It is psycho-logical warfare, a conspiracy against the Zulu nation.'

Somebody came into the room to tell Myeni that the journalist from the Associated Press had arrived. It was time to go. As I took my leave from him I felt distinctly that he didn't like me. Well, too bad, as the French say, *Nous n'irons pas passer nos vacances ensemble* ('We will not spend our summer holidays together').

Paulus Zulu is a professor at the Centre for Social and Development Studies of the University of Natal. Even though a strong ANC supporter, he is considered an expert of Zulu politics and it is for that reason that I went to see him in his office at the university. He is a slightly built, soft-spoken man, but the mildness of his speech and manner stand somewhat in contrast to the firmness of his views. Paulus conceptualises the violence in Natal – which has cost their lives to more than 5,000 people in the last eight years or so – as nothing less than a civil war between apartheid-created struc-tures on the one hand, and those that resist apartheid on the other.

'It is not a black-on-black violence,' he insisted, 'the forces involved in the conflict are black as well as white on both sides.' He explained that the struggle against apartheid had taken many forms: consumer boycotts; active opposition against Pretoria's policy of incorporation of the townships (like Umlazi, KwaMashu), which were part of Natal, into KwaZulu; and fighting the corrup-tion and the inefficiency of the Black Local Authorities and the educational system. The main participants in the struggle were the youth organisations, the trade unions and the civics. It was during that struggle that Inkatha had shown its true colours, which were those of an ally of the South African state.

'We must not forget,' Paulus said, 'that the KwaZulu government is an apartheid-created structure and that the KwaZulu government and Inkatha are one and the same thing. Suffice it to say that Chief Minister Buthelezi is also president of Inkatha. You must also understand why the perpetuation of violence is necessary from their point of view. Without violence the political players would jockey for position on the basis of policies and platforms which the electorate would be free to choose from. But that is exactly what is not possible in a climate of endemic violence and intimidation. The government has the means to stop the violence if they really wanted it. But they don't, because it is not in their interest to do so. They have this option of disrupting and disorganising the black opposition and they are exercising it. The Natal violence was exported to the Transvaal and the Free State through the apartheid-created migrant labour system. Huge numbers of lonely men living degrading existences in dehumanising single-sex hostels and mine compounds segregated along ethnic lines were the perfect instrument for the perpetuation of violence. Today the violence has become a monster which is feeding on itself, it generates its own momentum, the criminal element has moved into the law-and-order vacuum, but I still think that these aspects of the violence are not the essential ones and that it could be stopped if the government became convinced that it is in its interest to do so.'

I asked Paulus what the conditions were for a peaceful resolution of the conflict. 'Both parties must recognise that they need each other, that they must co-operate if chaos and even a civil war is to be avoided. The government needs the ANC for legitimacy, and the ANC needs the government for effectiveness; neither one of them will be able to dominate the other in the next five or ten years. So it is in their interest to form an interim government of coalitional balance which could deal effectively with the violence. The security forces must be brought under joint control, *Umkhonto we Sizwe* must be merged with SADF.'

'What about Buthelezi and Inkatha in all this,' I wanted to know. 'Can you really leave them out of a deal at the national level?'

'First of all, Buthelezi is Inkatha and Inkatha is Buthelezi,' said Paulus emphatically. 'Inkatha could not survive as a major political force without Buthelezi, and Buthelezi like everyone else has a limited lifespan, he is 64 years old.'

I was not convinced. 'Yes, but,' I retorted, 'that's still nine years younger than Mandela, and besides Buthelezi's mother is still alive I believe, and Banda [the dictator of Malawi] is still in power at 95 . . .'

'The critical factor is that the KwaZulu government is in large part financed by Pretoria. Take the money away and Buthelezi's clout disappears. Besides, what kind of political future can you expect if your support comes mainly from the old and the un-educated? He might also over-reach himself with his manipulation of Zulu nationalism, which might come to be equated with Inkatha and that's a no go for the young and the educated. The king is increasingly perceived as a pawn in the hands of Buthelezi whose government controls his salary. Buthelezi is a man in a hurry. One of the problems with him is that he is a very difficult person. If you read his speeches, it's always I did this, I did that, I will do this, I will do that. His politics is a one-man show; he is the Kwa-Zulu chief minister, minister of Finance, minister of Police, chief of the Buthelezi tribe in Mahlabatini, prime minister to the king and IFP president. It's always the same people in the Inkatha political rallies, they are simply bussed around from place A, to place B, place C, and so on, and they get support from the South African government. Even the UWUSA [the Inkatha-affiliated labour union] launching rally in a Durban soccer stadium (about 70,000 people were there) was organised with the help of the South African police, it came out in the recent revelations.'

'There has been talk about a new centrist party led by De Klerk, a coalition of whites, Coloureds and even conservative blacks which might constitute a credible political force. It is often said that many of the six million or so members of the Zion Christian Church (an African church led by Bishop Lekhanya) could vote for such a party.'

'I disagree with that,' Paulus said. 'My own research shows that there is no difference between the Zionists and the non-Zionists when it comes to ANC support. People are quite capable of differen-tiating between the religious and the political spheres. If you go to an ANC- or a COSATU-organised rally you will find the Zionists are not under-represented.'

We ended our conversation with some general remarks about

the future of South Africa. Surprisingly enough, Paulus Zulu is optimistic. He talked about the 'politics of sanity' according to which an uneasy but functioning relationship would prevail between the ANC and the government. 'The ANC must gain the acceptance of the business sector,' he said, 'that's why they've watered down their demand for nationalisation and replaced it with an American-style anti-trust legislation. They've made some foolish statements in the past. The large majority of Africans are not socialists at all. What we need is a mixed economy. In other words, a free market system in which the state has a responsibility to help the poor. . . .'

It is in Kloof (which means a ravine in Afrikaans) a quiet, leafy residential suburb between Durban and Pietermaritzburg, that Ian Wyllie has lived since he retired from the editorship of the *Sunday Tribune* in August 1989. These days he keeps busy helping edit *Reality*, a bi-monthly journal of political opinion of small circulation. He is a shrewd man, with a good instinct, or feeling, about the way the political wind is blowing in South Africa. We first talked about the *Indaba* and why it had failed, and then moved to more global issues: the violence, Inkatha, Buthelezi, and so on. He put the responsibility for the failure of the *Indaba* squarely on P W Botha's back:

'He wouldn't have anything to do with it. He was an obstinate man, he wasn't listening sufficiently. The *Indaba* had support from unexpected quarters, the *Broederbond* and the Afrikaner big business. There was a strong undercurrent of feeling that something had to be done, there was a huge rethink that was going on among the Afrikaner ruling class and intelligentsia. They realised that they had reached a deadlock, a logjam that needed to be broken. This is when the De Lange report on education came out, proposing for the first time, the gradual integration of the racially segregated schools. The pass laws were on the way out and the new constitutional dispensation, the tricameral constitution had been a disaster, I always thought that it was flawed from the start, a very stupid thing to do, if anything it entrenched apartheid instead of moving away from it.

'So, suddenly Buthelezi found himself in the middle of a vast movement searching for a solution. He was not coming from nowhere of course, he had been using the government for his own purposes for a long time. In the year or so after the *Indaba* was launched Buthelezi rode a true political high. I am sure he would've been elected easily to the presidency of Natal in a general election. He had an amazing amount of support among the whites. His political fortunes began to wane when it became clear that the *Indaba* was not going anywhere. His time has passed. The *coup de grâce* was the unbanning of the ANC and the release of Mandela. He must've felt as if his whole political rug was being pulled from under his feet. But the *Indaba* is far from having been a useless exercise. Many lessons were learned from it. CODESA really is nothing but another *Indaba* at a higher level. Of course, in comparison with it the *Indaba* was much simpler because it was dominated by Buthelezi.

'The problem with CODESA is the opposite: there are just too many second-rate, even third-rate, participants in it. But it is going to shake down, level down [the "levelling of the political field" is a favourite expression among the political *cognoscenti*]. I must say that I am very hopeful, more optimistic than I've ever been in my whole lifetime; but we have a very long way to go on this.'

I asked Wyllie to give me his assessment of the current violence, of Buthelezi's personality, of Inkatha's future.

'Inkatha, as you know, started as a Zulu cultural movement,' he began. 'Buthelezi moved it to the realm of party politics and supposedly he broadened it, but of course it remains a Zulu movement essentially, and I think that Buthelezi likes to keep it so. That way he is the undisputed leader. King (Goodwill) Zwelithini is intellectually nowhere near Buthelezi who really twists him around his little finger all the time. He is manipulating the king to infuse his movement with a solid nationalistic base, he has of course the largest ethnic community in South Africa to work with. Buthelezi has always played an interesting game. I think he had always had a great admiration for Afrikaner nationalism, because it has worked well for the Afrikaners, and he doesn't see any reason why it shouldn't work for the Zulu nation too. Buthelezi is no political philanthropist, of course. Whatever he has done in politics, he has done as a result of his political ambition. We have to accept the premise that he is in politics for himself, but he is not in this respect any different from many ambitious politicians. He has got to use something to serve his political ambition, and he has decided to use Zulu nationalism. The fact of the matter is that the Zulu nation cannot be ignored in this country. It is both their strength and their weakness that they are so strong regionally. Paradoxically, this is one the primary reasons why they express themselves at the national level much more vigorously than any other ethnic group in the country. Even the Xhosa are more divided – the Transkei, the Ciskei, the Border region, Eastern Cape. The Zulu unity is beginning to disintegrate, the ANC is making strong inroads in the Natal townships and among the youth. Buthelezi knows that he is losing ground, and that's why he is resorting to this use of the king. But he runs the risk of overdoing it. If he discredits the king by manipulating him too much, he can find himself with a much weaker base in the end.

'Nationalism can be a double-edged sword. Afrikaners used it successfully for a long time to grab economic and political power, but they went too far. The same thing could happen to Buthelezi. You've got to have a sense of timing in politics. Buthelezi knows that he must make a deal with Mandela, but he cannot bring himself to do it. The success of Mandela as a politician, as a statesman has been fatal to Buthelezi, who has a personality problem that complicates things for him enormously, he believes that he is entitled to a special reverence which stems from his claim to royal links; he thinks he should be treated like a prince; he expects people to accord him a dignity that goes beyond his ability as a man to win status. When Mandela came out of prison – and Buthelezi had actively campaigned for his release like many of us – he said: "We must get together." Buthelezi answered: "Yes, come to Ulundi." He wanted Mandela to go to his capital. He could've easily met Mandela in Durban, or even in Pietermaritzburg, but he wouldn't do it. Mandela was told by his advisers: "Don't do that, it's a ploy; you'll be seen by the Zulu people as Buthelezi's equal." '

'Do you really believe that Buthelezi sees himself as Mandela's equal?' I asked Wyllie.

'No, I think that he acknowledges Mandela's primacy and would be content with the second spot, but I don't think the other leaders of the ANC would grant him that. Another problem with Buthelezi is that he could've stopped the violence right at the beginning, kill it in the bud, so to speak, but he didn't do it. There was a deafening silence on the part of Buthelezi when the violence started in 1984–5. When the NECC people were attacked in Durban, Inkatha leaders said that it was a provocation for them to hold their meeting in

Durban. Now, who the hell do they think they are to determine that kind of a territorial prerogative? Ever since 1985, the violence has been incredibly destructive and perpetual. At least 5,000 people have died – that we know of; the real figure could be much higher because they've been manipulating information all the time. The police will tell you, for instance, that ten people were killed in Soweto, or in Alexandra, or in the Vaal Triangle, or on the Rand over the weekend; but they won't tell you how many people were killed in Umlazi, in Khayelitsha, or in Natal as a whole, during the same weekend. They will wait for three weeks and then give you a figure for Umlazi, and so on, for that particular weekend; but they won't mention Soweto, and so on, this time. I do believe that the government could stop the violence if they really wanted it, but they don't see it as being in their interest. They stand, in my view, to win quite a bit of support as a result of this violence, because they represent the only stabilising factor now, many black people are sick and tired of all that violence . . . '[3]

'Not if they, the Nats themselves are seen as partly to blame for the violence,' I felt obliged to interject.

'Yes, that's true,' Wyllie agreed. 'Furthermore,' he went on, 'one should not underestimate the Zionist factor, there are six million of them, you know. Suppose Bishop Lekhanya, their leader, tells his flock: better stick with the devil we know, than taking chances with the devil we don't know. He was always respectful of the white authorities, very supportive of P W Botha, in the past. F W and his all allies could, in a general election, end up with enough support to keep their nose just ahead, or at least as a formidable second. The ANC is an untested quantity electorally. I've always assumed that the ANC was the dominant black political organisation in this country, and I still believe that this is so – the PAC, I don't think they come anywhere close, but they have influential constituencies: the universities, the intellectuals, the youth. F W very cleverly has tested his strength. He was being taunted by the right, he accepted their challenge and cut them down to size. Even I went out and voted for him. I never even dreamed that I was going to vote for a man with his political record, to give him credibility. What we are going to see is a very protracted period of tough bargaining. The parliament is going to lose its relevance. F W is going to operate increasingly as an executive president. The international community will be prepared to help him. But he must be able to keep the talks going. That's a big "but", because if for some reason the talks are broken off, then he will be in big trouble. As long as he manages to keep the talks going we will see a growing confusion, a growing disunity among the blacks. Mandela himself may not last. After Mandela what? The ANC must be seen as capable of delivering the goods to the people. That carrot must always look fresh. I don't know how long it will be before it begins to look withered and old. Don't expect any solutions to the South African problem, there aren't any. Improvement, yes; but solution, no.'

After Mandela, what? That question stuck in my mind long after I left Ian Wyllie, the shrewd commentator of the South African political scene. I realised that a lot hinged on Nelson Mandela being 'alive and well' in the next, say, ten years. He, far more than F W, is the guarantor of a relatively peaceful future in that beleaguered country. . . .

Notes

1 For more details see Chapter 21.

2 See my conversation with Dan Taylor towards the end of Chapter 16.

3 The violence issue may well turn out to be a make or break one in South Africa. *The Economist*, 5 June, 1993, page 44, reported that there were 20,135 murders in 1992, up from 14,700 in 1991. That is roughly the same number of murders as in the US, a country about six times more populated in which the murder rate is one of the highest in the world. At the other end of the scale we find countries like Japan and Switzerland where it is, relatively speaking, ten times smaller than in the US. Some knowledgeable observers believe that even that horrific number, 20,135, is significantly inferior to the real number. What is almost a truism is that political and criminal violence has become the single most important and intractable obstacle on the road to a stable and prosperous South Africa.

8

Nkosi Sikelel' iAfrika: Three Hectic Days in the Cape

'We demand jobs at a living wage, we demand food at prices we can afford, we demand pensions that will allow us to feed our children and clothe them. And if these demands are not met, we are prepared to take to the streets in our millions to remove this government from power once and for all.'

Jay Naidoo

Huge, screaming headlines proclaimed his referendum victory in the English press: 'It's Yes!', 'Landslide for the Yes Vote!', '69%', 'De Klerk Has His Mandate!'[1] The Afrikaans press was equally enthusiastic. It was as if a gigantic sigh of relief was heaved in the predominantly white areas of the land. In the black townships the reaction was more muted, but overwhelmingly positive too. All the pundits, journalistic heavyweights, academics, politicians and professional pollsters who had predicted, at best, a modest win of between 55 and 60 per cent were proven to be widely off the mark. The white right wing, 'Treurnicht and his gang', was dealt a devastating blow.[2] This was a good thing because had the 'no' vote won the consequences certainly would have been terrible: 'If the "no" vote wins South Africa is going to burn. The violence that we have now is going to look like kindergarten stuff,' had said Sam Dube, a businessman friend from Khayelitsha, a man of moderate views normally, just hours before the results became known.

I switched on the radio in the car and fell on the speech that De Klerk was making to celebrate the victory. I noted the Churchillian (even vaguely Lincolnian) overtones of the speech: '. . . It does not often happen that in one generation a nation gets the opportunity to rise above itself. The white electorate has risen above itself in this referendum. The white electorate has reached out through this landslide for the yes vote to all our compatriots, to all other South Africans. And the message of the referendum is, in a certain sense of the word: today is the real birthday of the real new South African nation.' Applause, cheers; De Klerk was on the steps of the white parliament. He then came close to apologising for apartheid without actually doing so (that was more than a year into the future, he did it openly in April 1993). He said that apartheid was the fruit of a flawed vision but that the intention had been good. 'Therefore,' he concluded, 'it had to be abandoned, to be replaced by the only viable policy that can work in this country, and that is: power-sharing and co-operation, the building of one nation in an undivided South Africa.'

It was a good, ego-massaging speech. It was good rhetoric and the occasion clearly called for it. I wondered who his speech-writer was. Any help from Saatchi and Saatchi, who had run the referendum campaign?

On the following day, 18 March 1992, ANC's 'People Budget' rally was held on the parade grounds in front of the City Hall which normally is a vast, open-air parking lot with, on the one side, rows of food stalls (some *Hallal* underlying the fact that a significant minority of Cape Town's Coloured population is Muslim) and flower vendors and, on the other, across the street, the Castle, the old pentagonal fortress of the 'Mother City'. The rally was scheduled to begin at one o'clock but at 12.30 the place was already half-full and people continued arriving by the bus- and train-loads. Those who came by train formed columns and then streamed towards the parade *toyi-toyi*-ing (running, singing, stamping the feet and pointing clenched fists up to the sky as if in a war dance.) A platform was built near the City Hall and there were the usual ANC/COSATU/SACP slogans and the bank of loudspeakers, which were being tested. It was occupied by local political, religious and trade-union leaders. Presently a matronly-looking woman climbed on to it, grabbed a microphone and began belting out songs which were picked by a group of veterans sitting, forty-fifty deep, on folding chairs in front of the platform. They were all very respectable-looking in their Sunday clothes: many of the men wore suits, ties and hats; the women were in white blouses and skirts, dresses, colourful scarves and berets. They sang, clapped hands, swayed rhythmically, whiling away the time, waiting for the arrival of the national leaders. I recognised three of the songs: *'Mandela Sereletsa Sechaba Sa Hesu'* ('Mandela Protect Our Nation'), *'Ityala Labo Linzima'* ('Their Crime Is Serious') and *'Senzeni na?'* ('What Have We Done?'). So they repeated many times *Mandela sereletsa, Mandela sereletsa, Mandela sereletsa, sereletsa sechaba sa hesu*, and then *Ityala labo, ityala labo linzima, ityala labo linzima; Senzeni na? Senzeni na? Senzeni na?* – the rest I couldn't understand.

It all looked good-natured and innocuous enough, but it wasn't. On the roof of a nearby building (an indoor car park – I had gone there in search of a good vantage point to take photographs), security police in mufti had taken position, watching the crowd on the parade with their binoculars and occasionally whispering in Afrikaans into their walkie-talkies. The parade itself was surrounded by Casspirs, manned by crack troops in camouflage fatigues. Security was tight. This might be an era of negotiation and not of confrontation but the government was taking no chances and, besides, old habits die hard.

The commotion behind the platform was an unmistakable sign that the leaders were finally arriving. It was close to two o'clock and here they were: Cyril Ramaphosa, the secretary-general of the ANC; Jay Naidoo, secretary-general of COSATU; Chris Hani, the secretary-general of the SACP and ANC leader; and Allan Boesak, ANC chairman for the Western Cape.[3] No Winnie Mandela in sight. The 'Mother of the Nation' (not for long any more, but we didn't know that yet) was supposed to attend the rally, but for some reason she was not there.

Amidst all the tugging, shoving and ululating, the four leaders climbed on the platform and shook hands with the local leaders. They were all still young: Hani at 50 was the oldest, followed by Boesak who was 47; Ramaphosa was just 40, and Naidoo, at 38, was the youngest. Ramaphosa, by dint of position the most powerful of the four, is a Dantonian figure: big, muscular, he was the fiery leader of the National Union of Mineworkers (NUM) before he was appointed two years ago to his present post; he appears to have grown, matured even mellowed in the last year or so, as befits the number three man in the ANC hierarchy (since his election in August 1993 to national chairman, Thabo Mbeki is clearly number two). There is something ascetic, even Jesuitic, about Naidoo, I thought. He is a Robespierre: tall, thin, intense, seemingly burning with an inner fire. Hani's appearance – thick-jowled, a little plump around the waist (he gave me the impression of a man who didn't exercise much) – was misleading. He had probably the largest following in the ANC after the Grand Old Man himself. In July 1991, in the last elections for the ANC's National Executive Committee, he obtained the largest number of votes, beating Thabo Mbeki at the post. The man was something of a mystery: considered as one of the top contenders for Mandela's job after he retires or passes away, he made a decision that has puzzled many: he chose to accept the position of secretary-general of the SACP that Joe Slovo and his colleagues offered him. The decision did not make sense and the likeliest explanation was that he wanted to keep himself in reserve, as the leader the people will turn to if the current leadership of the ANC compromised themselves by making too many concessions to the whites or, if they were, in the long run, unable to deliver the goods. I glanced at Boesak, the epicurean. He had been a national leader with prestige and stature once, but he lost it with his constant philandering. His divorce from the mother of his four children and his remarriage to a white Afrikaner television producer was the last straw and he was forced to resign the post of president of the World Alliance of Churches. He is now seen by some as a political opportunist, unlikely to regain a leading national role.

Ramaphosa was the first to speak. It was a bland, predictable speech which reflected faithfully the current positions of the ANC. He was careful not to attack De Klerk and his government frontally. There was an unspoken, tacit rule that the ANC and the government, as the two principal protagonists at CODESA, would treat each other with respect, like two heavyweight boxing champions of more or less equal strength slugging it out in the ring. So Ramaphosa spoke responsibly, reasonably, moderately – a speech in marked contrast to those he used to make when he was the secretary-general of NUM: the 'restless masses' must not be excited. So he chose to kick again the white right wing, which, since the referendum, was already floored:

'Comrades,' he said, 'let me begin by saying that the yes vote is about to win in a landslide. The message we derive from this is that the right-wing element is about to be liquidated completely [very optimistic there]. . . . The right wing has been propagating policies that could take our country back to the dark ages. We are not going to allow our country to be taken back to *Baaskap*, we are not prepared to say *Baas* [Boss] to anyone any more. Those days are over.'

Mild cheers. Ramaphosa went on: 'We will never allow another right-wing government to rule this country. The right-wing and their supporters have been willing and prepared to commit national suicide by going to some dry, arid corner of our country called Orania and establish some funny state there. In the interests of all the people of our country, both black and white, we are not going to allow them to commit national suicide. Because they are our countrymen [too], we invite them to join [us in] CODESA, because CODESA is the only forum that can deliver a non-racial South Africa . . . Comrades, viva ANC viva! *Amandla!* [Power]' There were responses of *Ngawethu* (to the people).

Next, Boesak introduced Naidoo who, as is customary with him, was far more bellicose and demagogic. He began by shouting at the top of his lungs '*Amaaandla!*' and something else that I didn't understand and then went on: 'Comrades, we will only allow one more vote in this country, and that is the vote that will transfer the power to the people of our country. There will be no more racist votes in our country, because we are determined to march to a non-racial democracy. We have a message for De Klerk, and those in power who support De Klerk: we don't want any more racist elections, we don't want any more racist budgets. We, the people, reject the racism of apartheid. We reject the starvation wages that we are being paid. We reject the high food prices that are demanded from our people. We reject the fact that we don't have equal pensions. We reject the fact that we have unequal education [the crowd began coming alive]. What we are saying to this government is . . . the wealth of our country belongs to all its people; it is the workers that produce the wealth of South Africa. We've had an apartheid government in power that has criminally abused the tax-payers' money. They've wasted our money in organisations like Inkatha. They've wasted our money in hiring death-squad killers. They've wasted our money in the tricameral constitution. They've wasted our money in corruption and maladministration. And what we are saying, us workers, is that the time for De Klerk to go is now. [Loud cheers.] That is the message that we are sending him from all over the country. If they don't hear this message clearly, [they should know that] the workers of this country are mobilising to take the action that will remove them from power. [Cheers.] We are saying [to them] that: we demand jobs at a living wage, we demand food at prices that we can afford, we demand pensions that will allow us to feed our children and clothe them. And if our demands are not met, we are prepared to take to the streets in our millions to remove this government from power once and for all! Away with apartheid, away! Down with the present government, down! And forward to the people's government of the future. *Amaaandla! Ngawethu!'* A chorus of whistles and cheers.

Then Boesak took over. It was significant that Hani, who represented the SACP, did not speak. He seemed to be saying: I am here, I am with you, but I must keep a low profile, you know why. Boesak announced Mandela's arrival 'tomorrow' for a three-day visit of the Western Cape during which 'he will attend rallies at Saldanha Bay, Paarl and Khayelitsha, as well as meeting in the Methodist Church at Green Market Square in Cape Town'. He asked for volunteers to run an election campaign (for the Constituent Assembly) 'because you can't win an election without volunteers'. He then concluded: 'Comrades, you've gone to parliament [the hated tricameral parliament which excludes Africans, perhaps 200 metres from the parade] to tell these people to go. You've heard Cyril Ramaphosa, you've heard Comrade Jay. We are now saying that the next step is elections before the end of the year. And that means that the white racist referendum is over, the real elections are coming! That the white people's veto over our future is over, the real elections are coming! Votes for the white parliament are over, the real elections are coming . . .! The real elections are coming! The real elections are coming! The real elections are coming! The real elections are coming! The real elections are coming!' Five times! The crowd responded by cheering wildly and whistling.

'Thank you, comrades,' Boesak said, 'let us now be ready. Let us stand all those of us that can stand. Let us remove our hats, those of us that have a hat on. Let us get our hearts, our minds and souls ready to sing the national anthem.' He made a sign to an elderly man in the audience who clambered up the platform, cleared his throat and led the crowd into *Nkosi Sikelel' iAfrika: Maluphakamis uphondo lwayo. Yiva imithandazo yethu. Nkosi sikekela. Thina lusapho lwayo* . . . 'Let its horn be raised. Listen also to our prayers. God bless. Holy spirit, bless our people.') It is true that it is a 'hauntingly beautiful' song as, I believe, Alan Paton put it once. So they sang. Their right clenched fists pressed to their hearts, they sang. The veterans in the front rows – these men and women who fought the unequal battles of the 1940s and 1950s – they sang the song that they've sung hundreds, perhaps thousands of times; they sang the song that symbolises their hopes of freedom and social justice, their hopes for a better future, if not for them, then for their children, and their grandchildren. So they sang . . .

That night I finished reading *The Age of Iron*, J M Coetzee's last novel. It's the story of an old woman dying of cancer. She is a white widow who lives alone in a small house in Cape Town. One day she discovers that a tramp and his dog have taken up residence in a cardboard box next to her garage. For some reason she feels attracted to that man and she wants to help him, but the fact is that she needs even more help than he does. In an awkward, groping and bumbling way they try to help each other and are successful to a certain extent, even though nothing really is resolved. But that is largely because nothing really can be in this world of ours whose essential law is deterioration and death. *The Age of Iron* is also a metaphor of sorts for South Africa. The author seems to be saying: don't expect too much; don't aim too high; all that can be achieved is a modus vivendi of sorts. Nothing, however, is simple and cut and dried in Coetzee's work.

I have also read *Life and Times of Michael K* and *Waiting for the Barbarians*, which are both allegories of what might happen if and when normality collapses. *Life and Times* is about survival when disaster hits the support systems of the so-called civilisation and they fall apart. Then, it is a paradox: the ostensibly weak become strong; the ostensibly strong become weak. This is so because, in the so-called civilised societies, we have gone very far from our roots in nature. Also, in industrialised countries, the group may be stronger, but the individual is weak because he often lacks an interior, spiritual life. In normal times, Michael K is a half-wit, an idiot almost, somebody who is despised by society. But in times of crisis (civil war), he reveals himself as a superior human being because he is close to the earth, to the spring of life. *Waiting for the Barbarians* can be seen as a masterly allegory about P W Botha's time when the country was run by the State Security Council (SSC, similar in substance to the Soviet Politburo), which relied on the National Security Management System (NSMS), whose octopus-like tentacles covered the whole country, to make decisions. The Bureau in the book is nothing else but the SSC, and the magistrate a provincial official who refuses to be part of the NSMS. There is more to the *Barbarians* than that, of course. It can also be seen, for example, as a paradox in the relationship between the oppressor and the oppressed: the latter appear to be on the losing side but they may end up as winners because the former may self-destruct spiritually. If the soul is destroyed, the destruction of the body cannot be very far off.

I had read not long ago an interview with Coetzee, published in the *International Herald Tribune*, November 1990. He was asked what he thought about Fukuyama's *End of History and the Last Man*, whose main thesis appears to be that the victory of capitalism-cum-liberalism is complete in the world, now that Marxism/Communism has been exposed as the biggest swindle of 'history'. He answered that the capitalist West had little to brag about, that it was 'rapidly moving to a plateau of inconsequentiality or irrelevance' and that it was 'actually in the third world where history, real history, is happening'. I agree with that and share his anguish about the terrible predicament that Africa, tropical Africa, finds itself in. The endless sinking into the abyss – the violence, the social upheaval, the corruption, the misery, the despair, the starvation and death – while the first world stands by, watching, indifferent, throwing a few crumbs now and then to ease its conscience . . .

On the following morning, I drove to Langa to meet Themba Passiwe (pronounced Passiweh) a friend who would take me to see Nombeko Mlambo, a PAC cadre. I wanted to hear viva voce what the PAC positions were, particularly vis-à-vis the ANC, its much bigger rival. I waited by the side of the road in front of the police station for Themba to arrive. He had told me to wait for him there and not to take any chances by going into Langa on my own. The police station was just at the entrance of the township after one got off from the N2 highway. Themba arrived five minutes later in an old, banged-up car, not the new Toyota Cressida that I had seen parked in front of his house at Rondebosch in an alley shaded by leafy trees. He said that it was preferable that I leave my car at the police station. We went inside and he spoke in Xhosa to the three or four police officers behind the desk, a woman among them, who readily agreed, so we parked the car in the yard and left in Themba's car. The window next to the passenger seat did not open and it was hot, so I sat in the back seat. When I asked Themba why he had not taken the Toyota, he chuckled and said jokingly, but also with some embarrassment, 'This is my township car. You know, people drive carelessly in the townships.'

Themba Passiwe is a shrewd, ambitious and intelligent man not yet forty years old who 'made it' in this white-dominated society, partly because he played the game by the rules, and partly (a larger part probably) through his own efforts and diligence. He holds a commercial degree from the University of South Africa (UNISA), a huge institution near Pretoria from which thousands of Africans have received degrees after correspondence courses. Passiwe himself earned his while working at the same time. In 1985 he set up a firm specialising in 'financial and management services' for small businesses in Guguletu which presently employed about a dozen people. He bought his spacious, comfortable house in Rondebosch two years ago. His wife is a social worker and they have two small children. Themba is a thoroughly urbanised and westernised African who is still studying at UCT, this time towards a masters degree in business administration. People like him will have great opportunities in the new South Africa, unless, of course, things went wrong. When I asked him if his friends and relatives had not resented it when he had moved out of Guguletu and to Rondebosch, he replied that there were no problems, that people understood. 'I've done it primarily for the sake of the children,' he said. 'Schools are not good in Guguletu. It's still Bantu education: mediocre teachers, overcrowded classes, and so on. It's going to be like that for a long time.'

Langa (which means 'sun' in Xhosa) is the first African township that was built on the Cape Peninsula. There was an unmistakably run-down look about it: dusty, abandoned carcasses of vehicles rotting in waste grounds, ubiquitous rubbish piles and plastic wrappers flying about. As we drove towards Ms Mlambo's sewing workshop, I saw old and fading graffiti on the walls: 'Viva the ANC! Viva Oliver Tambo! One Settler One – ' (the rest was effaced, whether deliberately or not I couldn't tell). We passed old, barrack-like structures which used to be male single-sex hostels, but in which whole families lived now. There were long laundry lines from wall to wall, seven to eight deep, and the laundry on them fluttered in the wind while drying under the sun. Kids played around with toy cars they made themselves with wood and wire. Idle youths stood by doing nothing; unemployment is a terrible scourge in this country. Themba stopped the car in front of a nondescript little house and we went inside. We found ourselves in a large room full of young women in their upper teens and lower twenties, who were all busy sewing, by hand or by machine, cutting and ironing. They smiled coyly as we came in. They were neat-looking, some wearing headscarves, others not. Ms Mlambo was behind a screen talking on the phone. She was one of those ageless African women with a smooth-skinned round face – which was beautiful – but she was very fat, with huge hips that, paradoxically enough, did not prevent her from moving about quickly. Themba introduced us and I told her what I was up to and she spoke about herself: the first stage of social etiquette in Africa: getting to know each other before moving on to the business in hand. It was soon clear to me that she was a highly intelligent woman, very articulate in English; she was also well travelled, she had been to the US, England and Zimbabwe. I must say I was not disappointed by what she told me. I was taken aback, almost shocked by the virulence of her condemnation of the ANC. For the first time, I realised fully the extent of the animosity between the ANC and the PAC.

'The ANC is not a democratic organisation,' she said. 'They don't really consult the people. They don't educate the people, they don't tell the people what the real situation is in this country. This whole CODESA thing is a trick. Nothing will really change for the large majority of the people. What CODESA will do is that the ANC fat cats will get even fatter. Yes, it's going to work for them. The rich countries needed an excuse to stop the sanctions and now they have it. Foreign investment will come and there will be plenty of opportunities for them to get rich, but things will stay pretty much the same for the poor people.'

'But why do the people support the ANC then?' I asked her.

'People follow them because they have the money, they rent the buses to bring them to the rallies. Also, there is intimidation, they force people to come. People who oppose them get killed in the townships.'

'But I thought that the "third force" [rogue elements in the South African security services] and Inkatha were responsible for much of the violence,' I said.

'No, that is not true,' she disagreed. 'There is a war going on because the ANC wants to become the dominant political organisation in this country.' Wants? I thought. There is little doubt that the ANC *is* the dominant political organisation in the country. But, not wishing to antagonise Ms Mlambo, I kept quiet.

We then spoke about PAC's grass-roots community development programme – 'the PAC is close to the people' – about the sewing project that she was the director of, and we took our leave from Ms Mlambo; it later occurred to me that the name of Azanian People's Liberation Army's (APLA, PAC's armed wing which has not given up armed struggle) commander is Johnson Mlambo. Are they blood relatives, I wondered.

Themba suggested that we go and talk to an old friend of his who owned a repair shop of household appliances not far away. The place was bulging with refrigerators, cooking stoves, radios, television sets some of which overflowed outside the shop. The man who was behind the counter was no longer young; his hair was white and he wore thick prescription glasses. He greeted Themba exuberantly. He knew about Ms Mlambo and disagreed with her completely. He was a staunch ANC supporter and an optimist:

'De Klerk is the right man for the job,' he said, 'and things are moving in the right direction. But Rome was not built in a day and people will have to learn to be patient. We need time to turn things around. There are so many things that need to be done.'

We went back to the police station. Themba had to get back to his office where he had a business appointment and I had to go to Cape Town, to the Methodist Church in Green Market Square, where Mandela was scheduled to speak at three o'clock. It was already past two-thirty, so I would be late.

When I arrived in the Methodist Church Mandela was already half-way through his speech. The place was packed with older, respectable-looking, church-going, black (mostly African) people. To the right of the altar where a lectern was placed sat the white officials of the church. I got in, threaded my way through a bunch of standing people, walked up the aisle to the foot of the altar without anyone stopping me. Owing to the camera around my neck, the small tape recorder in my hand, the security people must have taken me for a reporter (I was also white) but I still found the security incredibly – dangerously – lax. In fact, I had been struck by the same thing at the People's Budget rally the day before. Anyone could, at any time, kill a major political leader. I shuddered at the thought of what could happen if a white fanatic assassinated Mandela. De Klerk is much better protected, of course, even though what happened at Potchefstroom University only days before the referendum when a white right-winger threw a canister of tear gas in his direction, wounding slightly a cabinet minister, shows that even he is not entirely safe, despite the elaborate security apparatus that accompanies him wherever he goes.

The acoustics in the church were bad; it was hard to follow what Mandela was saying. He was talking about the VAT strike (4–5 November 1991) in which 'we brought out three million South Africans into the street for two days'. He attacked Barend du Plessis (the Finance minister, later replaced by Derek Keys, a better-liked liberal English-speaker) for his 'rich man's budget'. He then said something that the newspapers made much hay of the following day: 'We would like to warn South African leaders in the government that we are not going to allow a Du Plessis to be so insensitive as to increase the difficulties of our people. Those who are poor, those who are unemployed, it is our duty to protect them, even if it means destroying the economy.'

'Even if it means destroying the economy', that was the line that was picked up and widely quoted by the media. Many assumed an 'I told you' attitude and repeated the shopworn accusation that the ANC was a Communist organisation which would not hesitate to wreck the economy to achieve its socialist goals. After he finished his speech Mandela was immediately escorted to his car and his small motorcade of three or four vehicles left, accompanied by two motor-cycled policemen who opened the way in front.

For me it was time to go to Locarno House in Woodstock where ANC's regional offices are located in an attempt to see Rosie, the PR officer whose name was given to me by an Indian journalist. I wanted to attend the Sharpeville rally on the following day which promised to be a memorable event.

I found the Locarno House easily. It's a plain, whitewashed, three-storey building across the street from the Something Good Bakery, as the Indian journalist had explained. There were an empty hallway and a conference room on the ground floor and various offices – Women's League, Youth League, Public Relations and Information, and so on – on the other two floors. The atmosphere was distinctly informal and convivial. The PR and I office was busy and Rosie Campbell, a genial blonde with an endearing smile (an invaluable asset in her trade), who appeared to be in her late twenties, was animatedly talking on the phone. She told me that

'Barend' was co-ordinating the rally and directed me to another room at the end of the corridor. I found Barend, a friendly young Coloured guy, in front of his computer. I told him that I had a car and offered my services for the rally. He said that I could help to transport some soft drinks and other stuff and asked me to come at twelve the next day, the rally being scheduled to start at one.

That night, to celebrate what I considered to be a scoop, I decided to go to the Waterfront (which reminded me the Wharf in San Francisco) to reward myself with a nice supper. I went there with Evelyn Sagor, a good friend of the Kahns in whose little flat I was staying. Evelyn was vivacious and a good conversationalist and so it was a pleasant evening.

Not wanting to take any chances, I arrived at twelve sharp on the following day. Barend was in his office, in front of his beloved computer. We took the stuff from the hall and put it in the boot of the car with the help of Renée, a young Coloured girl who was a volunteer. It's about half an hour from Woodstock to Khayelitsha, much of it on the N2 highway. As we zoomed along on the highway – being a Saturday, there was little traffic – I decided to provoke Barend into a political argument by playing the role of a devil's advocate. I told him succinctly what Ms Mlambo had told me about the ANC – an elitist organisation, no consultation with the grass roots, a leadership that was mainly looking after its own interests, and so on.

Barend almost choked with indignation. 'It's not true, it's not true,' he kept saying, 'it's the PAC that has little popular following. They are envious of the ANC, you see. They take extremist positions just to differentiate themselves from the ANC, because otherwise there wouldn't be any reason for them to exist, they wouldn't have a distinct identity.'

'But I don't understand,' I retorted with a contrived naïveté. 'Surely ever since Sobukwe seceded from the ANC in 1959 they've had a distinct identity based on the necessity of having a black leadership and on the land question: that it should be returned to its rightful owners without compensation.'

'Except for the compensation part, these are the same as the ANC's positions. Do you see anyone among the top ANC leadership who is not black? On the land question, we are simply more responsible. The confiscation of the land without compensation would be an unmitigated disaster, it's just not possible.'

'What about Joe Slovo, Ronnie Kasrils, Jeremy Cronin, Raymond Suttner, Gill Marcus, Albie Sachs?'

'These are the six whites among the fifty elected National Executive Committee members. There are none among the thirty *ex officio* members and among the six top leaders [Mandela, Sisulu, Tambo, Ramaphosa, Jacob Zuma and Thomas Nkobi]. Except for Marcus and Sachs, they are SACP members too. Slovo, I will admit, is an exception. His opinion does carry weight. Sachs is a constitutional expert very much admired, but he doesn't have real political power.'

'Gill Marcus is Mandela's personal assistant. That's a lot of de facto power, don't you agree?'

Finally, Barend more or less conceded the point: 'The ANC is a non-racial organisation, the future of this country belongs to a non-racial democracy. "One Settler, One Bullet" is an irresponsible slogan, besides being impractical. All it does is provoke the answer "One Bomb, Many Kaffirs".'

'That's not fair,' I said, 'the PAC has given up that slogan.'

'Yes, but it is still what the PAC is identified with in the minds of the black radical youths in the townships. As for elitism, you will soon see what kind of mass following that the ANC has.'

Throughout the conversation Renée had kept silent. But from the way that she bent forward – she sat in the back of the car – it was clear that she had followed it with keen interest.

As we reached Khayelitsha, the long lines of miserable shacks alongside the highway came into view. They hugged the sandy dunes like a bunch of beggars in one of Brueghel's paintings, a very perturbing sight. We turned off the highway and found ourselves on a wide tarred road, a bewildering contrast with the surrounding desolation. Barend stopped to ask directions on how to get to the stadium where the rally was being held. We passed a cemetery at the gate of which a big wooden cross had collapsed and lay between two pillars. Further away, several rows of concrete latrines with nothing around them stood still like soldiers at attention before a drill sergeant. Then we were on the Zola Budd Drive, dubbed so by Khayelitsha's residents because one had to run fast on it if one didn't want to get killed by a stray bullet. There had been a lot of violence here recently and the dark marks on the asphalt were those left by a burning vehicle or a tyre which was set ablaze. Shacks, shacks, shacks. Seemingly endless rows of shacks. Then a cluster of matchbox houses, a petrol station, a *spaza* shop (a small shop run from a shack), a police station surrounded by barbed wire, the large, modern Community and Resource Centre.

As we got closer to the stadium, the crowds began to thicken and we were soon stopped by MK (*Umkhonto we Sizwe*) marshals in khaki uniform who were directing the traffic. We were waved on when Barend explained that we were part of the ANC delegation and that we needed to get inside the stadium. At the gate, the sea of humanity opened a passage to let us inside, making me think of the Red Sea which had parted to let the Hebrews pass. The 'stadium' was very basic, to say the least: a piece of flat land with patches of meagre grass here and there surrounded by four brick walls; there was nothing for people to sit on. The platform for the leaders had been set up near the eastern wall. The bank of loudspeakers seemed to be much bigger than at the parade. A much larger crowd was expected here, of course. After we parked the car in a corner, Barend took the streamers and the banners from the boot and disappeared. Renée stayed behind with me. She has the sweetness that is characteristic of Coloured people and a soft and singing voice. She is quite attractive too: almond-shaped brown eyes, shapely bosom, long lean legs. She wore a scanty T-shirt, blue jeans and sandals. She said that she was an ANC member but that she supported the SACP too, 'there is no real difference between the two'. I understood better the close, almost organic, relationship between the ANC and the SACP. The reality of the South African situation is that just when Communism is in global retreat all over the world (with the possible exception of China) the SACP is thriving: membership is growing so fast that the party is having a hard time keeping up with it (the SACP has a tradition of being an avant-gardist, and not a mass, party; it also prides itself on its superior organisation). Renée told me that she was a sales girl at Woolworth's and that she lived at Elsie's River where her family had been 'removed' from District Six some twenty years ago.

The people continued to stream into the stadium. It was like a river flowing into a lake. I estimated the crowd already in the stadium at about twenty thousand. A local leader spoke in Xhosa presumably to warm up the crowd before the arrival of Mandela which was now imminent: he was expected at two o'clock. But the crowd did not seem to pay much attention. I continued chatting with Renée who said suddenly: 'The PAC is very quiet these days. I wonder what they are up to. I think they are lying low, waiting for the ANC to make a mistake.' And then: 'You shouldn't have upset Barend like that, he is very committed to the ANC, you know.' I told her that I had done it on purpose to see what was in his mind. She shook her head in mock disapproval.

Meanwhile, the crowd had grown bigger: at least 30,000 people now and it was beginning to grow restless. It was a hot day, the sun was beating down on the stadium relentlessly and Mandela was late. Rumours started to circulate that he was not well and that he might not be able to come at all. There were counter-rumours that he was on his way. Then, after fifteen more minutes of uncertainty and confusion, he was suddenly there. He came in from a small side door normally used by the umpire, the officials and the players. He was accompanied by Allan Boesak, Trevor Manuel (head of the Economics section at the national headquarters and a chief negotiator at CODESA) and three of four burly body-guards.

A massive cheer rose from the stadium and the crowd surged forward and the human chain of marshals trying to hold it back broke. Mandela was soon surrounded by a sea of people trying to touch him. He did not appear to be worried and smiled benevol-ently. He was wearing a traditional collarless African shirt embroid-ered around the neck and at the sleeves, which were short. I found that he was far more impressive than when he wore a suit, a shirt and tie. His high cheekbones and his eyes, which turned into slits when he smiled, gave him an oriental look. He was very charis-matic. His bodyguards and the ANC marshals had a hard time containing the crowd and opening a path for him to advance towards the platform. There was something profound, mysterious, poignant in this encounter between the hero and his people – it was his first visit to Cape Town since his liberation. Mandela was eventually able to reach the platform and he climbed on to it. He shook hands with the local leaders and then turned to face the crowd and raised his clenched fist in salute. The crowd roared its approval again, and the human chain of marshals threatened to break again; some of the marshals were using their *sjamboks* quite liberally now. The soccer field was more than three-quarters full with people: a crowd of 35, perhaps 40,000 men and women.

Suddenly, Winnie Mandela materialised on the platform as if out of thin air. I had not seen her arrive. She got up and grabbed the microphone. '*Makabane, Makabane* [Comrades],' she said, 'I've come

here to apologise for not having attended the Budget Rally the day
before yesterday. At the last moment I was assigned to another
rally in the Vaal [where Sharpeville is], so I couldn't come and I
apologise for it.' She repeated the same message in Xhosa and then
concluded: '*Makabane*, I can't stay, I must leave now because I have
a plane to catch. *Amandla! Ngawethu!*' The crowd cheered her noisily,
she is clearly popular with the masses. She then kissed her husband
and left. Whether it was deliberate or not, the impression made
was that she was a political leader in her own right, that she might
even have a different political agenda to that of her husband. She
is said to have a constituency of her own in the angry young men
of the townships, those who had rejected education by putting
liberation first, those who are disillusioned because they are on the
wrong side of the political fence, those who have little to gain from
a peaceful solution. Despite her involvement in the murder of a
youngster by her 'football team' bodyguards and, to anticipate
a little, her separation from her husband, she remains a political
force to be reckoned with.[4]

Finally, Mandela rose to speak. He appeared to be in top form
and spoke without notes in three languages: in English, Xhosa and
Sesotho. The acoustics were good and every word that he uttered
was intelligible:

'We are here today to commemorate those heroes and heroines
who fell, who were shot down by the white regime, in Langa here
and in Sharpeville in the Transvaal. They shot innocent, defenceless
people who engaged in a non-violent, orderly and disciplined protest. Those who have brought about apartheid, the most brutal
system of racial oppression this country has ever seen, did not even
want the blacks to engage in a peaceful protest. They regarded
then, as they still regard today, any form of protest by blacks . . . as
a declaration of war against white supremacy. And for that reason
[alone] they shot in Sharpeville sixty-nine innocent people, shot
and killed them, and injured 400 people. In Langa here they killed
fewer than that. Nevertheless even to kill one individual is a criminal offence, even if it is done by those who are supposed to protect
the very people they kill. One of the reasons why we are having
this violence today is that the South African police and the South
African defence force are taught a demonstration against the regime
is a declaration of war against white supremacy. We know that in
spite of that, there are policemen, there are members of the defence

force, both white and black, who are very keen to keep the name of their forces clean. . . .'

This is when the tape ran out but no real harm was done because the rest of his speech was a repetition of what he had already said at the Methodist Church about the 'rich man's budget', the 12 per cent VAT and the man responsible for them, Barend du Plessis. But, the reaction of the crowd to one thing that he said struck me. He said, and I am paraphrasing: 'The whites have nothing to fear from us. We are not out to take their houses, their cars, their jobs, their businesses away. All we want is a non-racial democracy where social justice will prevail.' It seemed to me that the statement was greeted by cold, even stony, silence by the crowd. It occurred to me that this was not perhaps what the crowd wanted to hear. What they wanted to hear was that it was now their turn to have a taste of the good life that the whites took as their birthright for such a long time. In other words, I sensed that there was a large mass (an iceberg, perhaps, would be a good analogy because nine-tenths of it is hidden below the water) of anger, resentment and frustration 'out there' which would be difficult to contain. Maybe Mandela could do that, at least for some time, because he is Mandela, but probably not his heir apparent, Thabo Mbeki. 'Now it is our turn!' is an obsessive idea which could easily turn into a dangerous and unstoppable political slogan. That is why the real agenda could well be the containment of the poor and angry masses.[5] The Afrikaner power elite knows that transferring controlling power to the ANC would be a risky proposition unless that problem is settled. The ANC leaders know that their own and their movement's positions as the pre-eminent political force in the country could be jeopardised if they openly abandoned the fundamental principles of the Freedom Charter concerning the sharing of wealth and the restitution of the land to the people. A complicating factor in this equation is the real possibility that the Afrikaner right wing will probably fight if it does not get what it wants: a separate state. After all, they are used to playing the game rough. Africans are capable of forgiving (but probably not forgetting), but for that to happen the whites as a whole must be willing to make much bigger sacrifices than they appear at this time prepared to make.

After Mandela finished his speech, they all rose on the platform and sang *Nkosi Sikelel' iAfrika*, and the magic worked once more, a mystical emotion swept the field, and it was the end. Mandela was escorted to his car which, with two other cars, had been brought up near the platform, and he got into it, after flashing for one last time his big smile and waving to the crowd. As the small motorcade slowly crawled towards the exit it was mobbed by the delirious crowd, and it was stop and go for a while, and then the cars disappeared from my field of vision. The sea of black humanity slowly drifted towards the gate of the stadium.

As I stood there watching the crowd and daydreaming, Barend and Renée suddenly materialised at my side. His eyes glittering with irony, Barend said, 'Do you still believe that the ANC is an elitist organisation and that its leaders have no contact with the grass roots?' He looked as pleased as a child who has just been given a piece of his favourite candy.

I smiled and said, 'No, I don't believe so any more. It was quite an experience.' I put my arm around his shoulders and added, 'Thank you for bringing me here.' I felt fulfilled in a special sort of way: I had witnessed the communion of a true great leader with his people. True great leaders are an endangered species now. They had all but disappeared in the industrialised rich countries (it is arguable that De Gaulle was the last of the giants). They are all politicians now. Some better than others. Some, more honest – or rather less dishonest. Some, more competent. But politicians they all are, without real charisma or vision.

Notes

1 Certainly the 'historic' victory that the Springbok (a small antelope, one of the national symbols of South Africa; all national sports teams and sportsmen are called Springbok) cricket team won in Sydney against the Australians – one of the big boys of world cricket – after decades of sports isolation two days before the referendum, was a crucial factor in the landslide. The news of the victory in the World Cup competition triggered an unbelievable wave of enthusiasm among the white South Africans. Kepler Wessels, the team's captain, became an overnight national hero and his teammates were on their return home a week or so later, honoured with a ticker-tape parade on Market Street, one of the main thoroughfares of Johannesburg. The point that the victory and the resumption of international sports ties would have been impossible without the co-operation of the ANC was not lost on the whites.

Even more so than the United States, South Africa is a sports-mad country. For the whites the most popular sports are rugby and cricket and for the blacks, football (soccer) and rugby, in that order (it used to be, roughly until the 1970s, that rugby was number one even among blacks, but that changed probably because of racial segregation in rugby).

A man who in the last four or five years has played a key role in the racial integration of sports in South Africa is Steve Tshwete, the head of the ANC's sports section. He is a bespectacled man of about fifty, with a big, booming voice and of great negotiation skills. He was a very talented rugby player himself in his younger days, probably Springbok material, but he was denied the chance because of the colour of his skin. Tshwete, like many ANC leaders, is an 'Island graduate', having spent 15 years in Robben Island between 1963 and 1978. In the late eighties, he was political commissar of *Umkhonto* under Chris Hani who was the chief-of-staff. Many see him as the sports minister in the first non-racial government after the general elections of (probably) April 1994.

2 The 'devastating blow' proved to be one of short duration. The political fortunes of the right wing appear to be on the rise again, this time led by General Constand Viljoen of the Afrikaner *Volksfront* and Ferdie Hartzenberg, the newly elected president of the Conservative Party. At the end of June, 1993, the World Trade Centre building in Johannesburg, where the negotiating parties were discussing the *Volksfront*'s demand for a separate state for the Afrikaner nation, was attacked by heavily armed militants of the *Volksfront* – mostly members of the AWB, which is part of the Front. High-ranking political leaders such as Ramaphosa, Roelf Meyer, the Constitutional Development minister and the government's chief negotiator, and Joe Slovo, were deeply humiliated. For more on the right wing, see Note 1, Chapter 1.

3 Chris Hani was assassinated in April 1993 by a right-wing fanatic with ties with both the CP and the AWB. The reverberations of his violent death will be felt for a long time. His main constituency, the angry young men of the townships with little education and no prospects for gainful employment, will now turn to more radical populist leaders such as: Peter Mokaba, the youthful president (he is only 35) of the ANC's Youth League; Tokyo Sexwale, the ANC's Witwatersrand region leader; Sydney Mufamadi who, at barely 35, is a former labour leader and presently a member of both the ANC's and SACP's national executives; and Moses Mayekiso, the new president of SANCO, also a powerful, youngish (he is in his mid 40s) Communist and labour leader. Last but not least, there is Winnie Mandela (see the following note).

4 Winnie was forced to resign her leadership position with the ANC after she was implicated in the murder of the fourteen-year-old Stompie M Seipei by her bodyguards. She made a political comeback of sorts in June 1993 with her election to the Witwatersrand region chair of SANCO.

5 I developed that theme, bureaucratic authoritarianism, in the course of my discussion with Rory Riordan in Chapter 1.

9

The Burning Issue of the Land and a Tentative Portrait of Two White Landowning Farming Families

'You don't simply say I am sorry to a man you have robbed. You return
what you stole or your apology takes on a hollow ring.'
Ernest Campbell

The land question, even more so than that of the wealth, lies at the very heart of the black/white conflict in South Africa. Unless it can be resolved in a satisfactory manner, it is difficult to see how the country could have a peaceful and prosperous future.

The 1913 Natives Land Act was in its essence the first formally segregationist law of the new state created in 1910 by the Union Constitution. It set aside about 10 per cent of South Africa's total land mass (roughly ten million morgen or hectares) for the Africans that formed 70 per cent of the population. The Act further ordained that in those 'Scheduled Areas' no white person could acquire any land – conversely, no black person could own any land in the 90 per cent of the country that was reserved for the whites. Despite the obvious, glaring injustice and its utter inadequacy, nothing was done about the Act for more than twenty years. It was only in 1936 that the new Trust and Land Act released 7 more million morgen to be added to the original 10 million, increasing the total percentage reserved for Africans to about 13 per cent.

Ever since, all the successive South African governments have been involved in an absurdly schizophrenic activity: on the one hand, buying land from white farmers in an effort to fill that quota of 17 million morgen; while, on the other hand, they were busily removing the so-called 'black spots' from 'white' South Africa. The total number of Africans – often whole communities – removed from places they had been living in sometimes for generations and dumped on land within the Scheduled and Released Areas is about 3.2 million. This story (as well as those of the Coloured and Asian peoples) is well documented in a remarkable report by the Surplus People Project.[1]

In the late 1950s and early 1960s came the Verwoerdian policy known as grand apartheid or 'separate development', which eventually led to the creation, in the 13 per cent of the country reserved for Africans, of the four 'independent' TBVC states and the six 'self-governing' homelands, the most important of which by far is KwaZulu. Grand apartheid, because it was essentially racist and prevented the Africans from developing in society, was a dismal failure and did enormous harm.

It must be added at this juncture that the 1936 Act caused much suffering because it had some stringent provisions concerning the 'labour tenants' (in other words, sharecroppers) and the 'squatters', as a result of which many Africans lost the rights and privileges as workers that they had enjoyed in white-held farms from time immemorial and could thus be fired at will. And this is precisely what happened: with the advent of the mechanisation of agriculture many of these workers were indeed simply kicked out of the farms without any compensation whatsoever. Those who were kept on were treated like slaves or feudal serfs.

According to SAIRR's *Race Relations Survey 1991–2*, 65,972 white landowners control a total area of about 77 million hectares, of which 63 million they own and 14 million they lease. It should also be noted that the state has, over the years, provided considerable financial and technical assistance to the white farmers.

So, that is the situation, which is obviously grossly unfair and unacceptable. The question is what is being done and what can be done about it?

After the quantum leap of February 1990, De Klerk's government has repealed the acts of 1913 and 1936. It has also appointed an Advisory Commission on Land Allocation and published a White Paper on Land Reform. The commission will have to deal with the two related questions of restitution and compensation. For the land that is still owned by the state – the famous Scheduled and Released

Areas held by the Development Trust – there should not be any major problems. Everyone agrees that it should be returned to the communities from which it was forcibly taken away and that these communities should be provided with financial and technical assistance. For the land that was taken away and then sold to the whites the problem is far more complicated: on the one hand, it is clear that that land was sold to the whites under very advantageous conditions: very cheaply and with little down payment, and with a considerable support system that included massive subsidies and significant technical help. On the other hand, however, the white farmers have worked hard and invested to develop the land, so they have a legitimate claim on it; moreover, in most cases the land has changed hands several times. Finally, large tracts of land that are owned by corporations and absentee landowners are currently unutilised.

The ANC, for its part, has proposed the establishment of a Land Claims Court which would deal with the issues of restitution and compensation. But as Pallo Jordan put it during our conversation in April 1992 (see Chapter 17), there is a 'bloody-minded opposition' on the part of the white farmers to the idea of a Land Claims Court, there is even a rush presently to convert the land currently unutilised into 'game reserves' to forestall any future expropriation. Jordan thinks that the negative attitude of the white landowners was encouraged by the government's White Paper on Land Reform which rejects the idea of restoring the victims of the forced removals to their old farms.[2] Meanwhile, several dispossessed African rural communities have been taking the law into their hands and attempting to reoccupy the land they once owned. The National Land Committee (NLC, a facilitator body sympathetic to the African cause) is working with twenty or so communities which are part of the Return to Land Movement. The reoccupation by force, the NLC fears, could lead to violence between the occupiers, the white landowners and the government.

For many left-wing religious organisations – such as the SACC (the South African Council of Churches), the SACBC (the Southern African Catholic Bishops Conference), the Institute of Contextual Theology and the Kagiso Trust – land restitution is the condition sine qua non for the healing of the still yawning apartheid wound. As Ernest Campbell, a leading theologian, put it in the mid seventies, and I am paraphrasing: 'You don't simply say I am sorry to a man you have robbed. You return what you stole or your apology takes on a hollow ring.'[3] This is also largely the PAC position, which holds that the land should be returned to its 'rightful owners' without compensation.

So, these, briefly, are the issues. The remainder of this chapter concerns my tentative portrayal, warts and all, of two white land-owning farming families in the Western Cape: the Brownes of Stellenbosch and the Beaumonts of Botriver, who have common roots in the nearby Elgin. The two families, particularly the two men, are close friends. Having lived with them for four days on two different occasions, I feel I know the Beaumonts better, in fact I consider them my friends.

The Brownes own a beach house at Seaforth near Simonstown on False Bay where the South African Navy has a big base. Further up north is Muizenberg, where Cecil Rhodes used to own a modest beach house in which he died. The caretaker of that house, which was turned into a small museum, a retired English gentleman, told me that that summer, the summer of 1902, was so hot and stifling that they had to punch a big hole in the wall facing the sea, so that a draught of air was created enabling Rhodes to breathe. The Brownes' beach house is a lovely place: an old, spacious, stone structure with a blue corrugated-iron roof and a large verandah overlooking a beach and a lagoon strewn with spectacular boulders, seaweeds and other large aquatic plants floating on its surface.

When I arrived in the late afternoon the men – Simon Browne, Raoul Beaumont and his son Sebastian – had gone out to swim in the sea in a boat with a small outboard motor. On the beach in front of the house I found Isabelle Browne, Jayne Beaumont and her daughter Arianne, sixteen years old. Isabelle was breast-feeding her four-month-old baby girl, Miranda. Later we went for a walk on the beach with Jayne and Arianne. In a cove behind some boulders was a colony of seals. After we came back we found that the men had returned from the sea and were showering. It was soon sundowner-drinks time on the verandah. While sipping our drinks – beer, wine – we chatted amiably and watched the sun, a big orange disk, slowly sink into the ocean. It was almost unbearably beautiful. The atmosphere was informal. The mood relaxed. The unspoken message appeared to be: we may be rich, but we are uncomplicated people who enjoy the simple, natural pleasures of life. I thought there was something Irish about Raoul Beaumont. He reminded me of John Huston, the good-old-sinner type. He is tall, with a white beard, a wrinkled, weatherbeaten face and neck, and clear blue eyes under bushy brows. Simon Browne is a giant of a man: six foot four or five, broad shoulders, thick neck, long blond curly hair; the epitome of the rugby player which he was in his younger days. Two diplomats from the British Embassy joined us for dinner. The whites-only referendum (on whether or not to negotiate with the blacks) was only three days away (17 March 1992).

'F W is going to win but by a small margin,' said one of the diplomats, giving thus expression to what was conventional wisdom at the time.

'What do you think is going to happen next?' I asked him.

He was noncommittal: 'Your guess is as good as mine.' Diplomatic prudence?

After supper, which was indeed simple but good, I chatted with Sebastian who is eighteen and goes to a boarding school in Cape Town, a school very much in the British public school tradition: single sex, uniforms and big on sports. He told me that the school had opted for the 'C-model' lately which meant that the admissions policy was in the hands of the PTA and the school administration. Non-racial in theory, but in practice the number of blacks admitted can be controlled by a variety of means, the most potent of which is the fees that have gone up dramatically: from R600 a term to R1,300 a term (there are four terms), plus the hostel cost for boarding students that can almost double that amount to about R10,000 per year. Only a tiny minority of blacks can afford to pay those kinds of fees.

It was front-page news when Chris Hani, about one year before his brutal death, had enrolled his twelve-year-old daughter at an exclusive boarding school, which charged R10,440 a year. 'Because they teach Greek,' had explained Hani, who himself had studied Latin and English at Fort Hare. Sebastian told me that there were two Africans in his class one of whom travelled daily all the way from Guguletu. He had to get up at four to take the train and then the bus to be in time for school, which began at eight. To make things worse, the poor boy was harassed by a gang of township toughs who accused him of betrayal. So some pupils and teachers had launched a fund drive to raise the money that would enable him to stay at the school's hostel. . . . Time passed quickly and it was getting close to midnight when I took my leave, it was a 45-minutes drive back to Cape Town. I practically invited myself to my hosts' farm on the following Sunday.

It was about eleven in the morning when I arrived at the Brownes' farm in Stellenbosch. It was a hot and sunny day. As I went inside the gate and drove on the dirt road towards the farmhouse I noticed down the hill the whitewashed, tin-roofed, neat-looking houses of the farm workers. The farmhouse was old Cape Dutch (I reckoned) but recently restored and in perfect condition. Next to it stood a big shed with a tractor and a Land-Rover in it. Bougainvillea bushes and some big trees provided shade both to the house and the shed. It was cool inside. Ochre-coloured tiled floors and furniture matching the architecture of the house (as far as I could tell). A good hi-fi system diffused soft classical music. The verandah at the back overlooked a nice-sized wooded lawn. Isabelle was feeding her baby when I arrived and Simon was not around. 'He is suffering from indigestion, he ate too much seafood last night,' explained Isabelle. At almost 40, she is a year and a half older than Simon and not very happy living on the farm. She has lived in Paris for many years (she is fluent in French) and misses the cultural environment of the French capital. Simon and Isabelle have two children: a little boy, Samuel, who is four and a half and Miranda, the baby girl. Simon appeared some time later, looking somewhat haggard. Before lunch we talked on the verandah about the farm and the history of his family. I provide below a summary of that conversation.

'My grandfather started farming in Elgin in 1927. My mother who grew up on the farm eventually met and married an Englishman, a cavalry officer, who took her to England and that's how I was born in London. When I was eight years old, in 1962, we came back to South Africa and my father went to work for my grandfather. After my grandfather's death, my father took over the farm for a while. After that my father retired and we went back to England. That was in the early 1970s. For about twenty years now that farm has been run by a general manager. It's a 650-hectare farm of which 240 hectares are planted with apples, pears, nectarines, kiwi fruit. It's a big operation, we pack our own fruit. It's the family farm, but none of us live in it – the rest of the family is not interested in farming.

'After Isabelle and I got married in 1985 we decided to come back and go into farming. There were many farms on the market then – there were big riots in Cape Town and many people were trying to sell their farms. Interestingly enough, they were all English speakers, none of them were Afrikaners. Anyway, we bought this farm for less than R400,000 [less than £10,000]. It has 72 hectares of land, plus all the buildings. The farmhouse was in bad shape, so we had to fix it up; we built some new houses for the workers, planted some new trees, constructed two dams; one has a capacity of 30 million gallons, the other is smaller; and put in micro-irrigation using Israeli equipment – the pumps, the filters – only the pipes are South African; we are fertilising through the water, it has revolutionised fruit farming, you know. Production per hectare, that's the bottom line in fruit farming; but one has to be patient, because it takes time for the trees to mature. The thing is to buy the land cheaply, which we did, so that you can afford to invest in improvements. It's a very good area, very good soil; it's in Stellenbosch, close to Cape Town; so it has very good possibilities. We were fortunate that the apple prices were very good over the years and we were able to pay back our bond [loan from the bank]. Our rand is weak, you see, we are exporting against strong currencies, so we can get a lot of rand for our product, which is good for us. We pick the fruit and take it to the central packing co-operative which is owned by the producers – 1,400 producers are co-owners, and then there is a central marketing organisation that does all the selling overseas. Ever since the controlled-atmosphere storage, it is pretty much a year-round operation now. The workers' salary averages about R90 [£22] per week, plus free housing and schooling, and a four-week bonus at the end of the year. They also benefit from a pension scheme: 15 per cent of their wages, half of it paid by the employer. Twenty-five people work on the farm of whom 13 are men and 12 women. Productivity is not very high for a variety of reasons. History has not been kind to the farm worker in South Africa. They've been very badly exploited. There were all sorts of laws against them and they couldn't organise themselves in trade unions. The educational level is very low; none of the workers on the farm has finished high school. That's why I am so serious about pre-school education, to give them a better start in life, I consider that my responsibility'.

'So, you're a bit like a feudal lord,' I interjected.

'You can't get away from it. You absolutely can't. Whether you like it or not.' At this point we stopped for lunch and then continued.

'Your standards must be high, you see,' Simon went on, 'and everybody's standards are quite low, so you've to impose your own standards. At the end of the day high standards will always take first place. We try to grow here a crop for an export market of great sophistication in the first world. Our fruit is being sold in Geneva, in Paris, in Frankfurt; we can't afford to grow a lousy product. Our challenge is to grow a terrific product with a very uneducated people. It's a very difficult thing to do. It's much easier to grow maize; sheep, cattle, it doesn't matter. Store the damn thing, take it to the abattoir. Fruit is an extremely complex operation. One has to work through people. It's only through people that you can get things going. For instance, with our plums: we pick plums around Christmas and every year it is the same; two or three chaps we have to rely on in our picking team just don't pitch up for two or three days because they are drunk. Now, I've worked as a picker in Washington State in America, in a fruit farm up there, and we picked apples for 28 days straight. There was no question of weekends being off, or anything like that. Here is the fruit, here are the bins, and off you go until it's over. The work ethic is very high. Here, it's very low. I really would like to go and farm in Morocco, you know, because there you're dealing with Muslims who have this incredible background of structure and of non-drinking, and of . . . yeah, directness, if you like, because Allah is everything, and if I'm working with a bunch of Muslims, I can get past first base easily, I haven't got any problems. Everybody knows his place in society, it's been going for two thousand years, it's fine. Here you're dealing with people with no background at all. No history. Two-thirds of the people had no father figure in the family, the mother is everything, which leads to a very disjointed population. Weak people. Latently ineffectual. By and large, the women are much stronger than the men, that's how it is, you see. I really wouldn't want to find myself on a tall mountain in a blizzard with a bunch of these chaps. They will never get you out of there if you're stuck. They will run away. The extended family is a big problem in this country. Women have children simply because they feel they must test their fertility. Along comes a child and he or she is given to the grandmother immediately. It's going on today, right here, right now. It's hopeless. There can't be any real progress while this is going on, the men take no responsibility for it. So the social side of farming is infinitely more difficult than it should ever be. When I was working in Washington State, they couldn't care less about you. You came to work in the morning, you got paid your money, and that was that. Because you are an American. You are an individual. You've got a place in society. You've got education. You know how things work. It's not always easy there, mind you, a lot of people would come and work for two days, get the money and go.'

Here I cut in with a question on undocumented Mexican workers and the struggle against exploitation.

'Yes, yes, Chavez and the United Farm Workers Union; yes, certainly, but Mexicans are wonderful farm workers. With dignity these people worked. In the evening they would come home at five o'clock and make tortillas. Lots of dignity. They were professional farm workers, you see, and that's the difference. The South African workers have still a long way to go before they attain that degree of pride. I try to build that self confidence. It's an uphill battle sometimes. But it's coming, you know. People are making decisions that they wouldn't be making earlier. But it's a different sort of level that you have to get through. It's very hard. You can't talk about anything but direct comparisons. I can't talk about *La Terre* of [Emile] Zola. Which I would be able to talk about with the Mexican workers because they would understand what I am talking about. Anyway, you know, at the end of the day, it is a secure existence here. I try to impress on people how nice it is to live on the farm. They could be living in Elsie's River, in Khayelitsha. It's hell there. I try to keep standards high. Now we can't afford to hire anybody who is not going to do a good day's work, who is not going to improve his position on the farm. I can't afford to hire somebody who is a half-assed individual. A tractor costs R75,000, a spraying machine R40,000. You can't afford a person driving those machines who is very poor quality. I advertise for my workers now. If somebody leaves me I advertise.

'I try to keep the place clean, not to have papers lying around, and rubbish. You saw how dirty was Khayelitsha yesterday [I had told him earlier I attended the Sharpeville Day rally there]. It's unbelievable, isn't it? There is no idea, no idea at all . . . We went on Friday with my workers to have a farm picnic at the seaside at Monwabisi ("place of comfort" in Xhosa, a recreation area on the beach), which is near Khayelitsha. We went into a area which we had to pay to get into and I thought that would be nice, because it would be nice and clean. From far it looks clean, but when you get close there are cigarette butts everywhere you look. There is a team of 15 chaps hanging out there like laundry on a line, doing nothing, except for changing the place of the sprinklers. It's really pathetic.'

At that point, deciding to be provocative, I said, 'The PAC thinks that the only way to deal with the land issue is to expropriate the white farmers without compensation. The rationale behind it is that they've had it too good for too long.'

I could see that Simon Browne was angered by that observation. 'If they come one day and say: "We want your farm," I'll say: "That's fine, here are the keys." Two weeks later they'll beg me to take it back. There are 15 families making a living on this farm. You need experience to run a farm such as this one. Yes, experience is everything in this business.'

After that, whether because of that last remark I had made or not, Simon Browne was less than the gracious host. Pretending he was not feeling good he returned to his bedroom. Isabelle too disappeared to nurse her baby. I took a walk by myself followed by the two dogs. I saw the two dams, one noticeably bigger than the other, the orchards, the micro-irrigation system. As I was taking my leave from Isabelle in front of the house, Simon, bare-chested and in his shorts, reappeared to say goodbye. That was the last time I saw them.

Compagnes Drift is the name of the Beaumonts' farm in Botriver, about an hour's drive from Cape Town. When, a couple of weeks later I drove there, I missed the main entrance and took a dirt road further up which soon became impassable. A group of men and women were working on a field at some distance from the road clearing it from the old vines and preparing it for the planting of new ones or some other trees. I shouted at them about the *Baas*. Some of them pointed at a small dot like a beetle way up on the hill. I could make out that it was a jeep-type vehicle which was moving in our direction. It took a good five minutes to come down to where I was and Raoul Beaumont jumped out of it. He gave some instructions to his white foreman in Afrikaans and then we went to the farmhouse. We passed through some apple trees on a dirt road. I saw two cottages on the right-hand side which Jayne told me later they rented out to visitors from Cape Town who wanted to get away from it all. On the left-hand side there was a big building with a couple of trucks parked in front of it and further down a big old wine cellar which was unutilised. The farmhouse, also old, had a less finished look than that of the Brownes'. In the big living-cum-dining room was a stone fireplace. We sat down in the spacious kitchen and had a long chat:

'My father arrived from the West Indies during the war [Second World War]. He had no money at all. He bought a small farm at Elgin for which he had to borrow the money; then he sold that and bought another farm which he developed and then sold half of it and put the money into the other half; then he sold that too and bought the farm where my younger brother and my mother are living now. I worked for my father for four years between the ages of 18 and 22, and then went to Europe and Australia for eight years, the dolce vita and all that, which lasted far too long. I was in Australia when my father became ill and I came back. In the meantime my younger brother had been for a year in Holland in an agricultural school and he was working on the farm. It was very difficult to have the two sons working on the same farm – the age gap, and so on. So, as a company, we bought this farm in 1973 which was completely on its knees. It was also a question of not putting all your eggs in the same basket: we had only fruit at Elgin, so we decided to buy a wine farm and spread the risks around. We didn't have to go too far, Elgin is just fifteen minutes from Compagnes Drift. We could exchange labour and equipment while we were building it up, so it made sense as a business undertaking. The farm was 500 hectares and we bought it for R200,000 [at that time, roughly £100,000]. It's good land and it's got two rivers running through it. The water is essential, you can't farm without it.

'We split the properties at my father's death. My brother took the Elgin farm, I took Compagnes Drift. I replaced all the old vines with new ones, built two dams, put in new orchards. This is an old wine farm, which goes back to the 1700s, but there never seemed to be enough money to get the winery going. In retrospect, I think I've made a mistake, I should've had the winery going. The cellar is old fashioned now, it needs R200,000 [in 1992, less than £45,000] to be spent on it and it would be all right. We diversified into soft fruits: apricots, nectarines, peaches; we also have a bit of almonds and wine grapes, and this is where we are today. This way our cash flow is spread throughout the year. With the grapes, the Co-op will pay you only twice a year: once at harvest time, and once at Christmas time. We have about 70 hectares planted and the rest is bare land, mountainside. You could run goats in it, or sheep, but I've never done it. I like keeping the mountain as it is; it is not a very high rainfall here, so your natural food in the mountains is not very high. You don't get a very high yield of wild flowers or anything like that. As for the labour situation, I've used the same amount of labour from the time I bought the farm, between 1973 and now: eleven men and eleven women, the wives – they always have a couple of daughters staying with them. I use outside labour sometimes. In fact, the men are sufficient to run the farm; the women work at special times, at harvesting and for special projects. All the wives are working now through July, for example. They are doing two things: one group is working at the oldest vineyard, which I am taking out to put a pear orchard there; the other group is working on the waterway, clearing it from all debris, so that the water can run unobstructed.

'I inherited some old houses which I fixed up and I built others for the workers. The average weekly wage is R75/80 [about £20] for the men and R65 for the women. I pay half of working clothes: overalls, gum boots, and half doctor fees. There is no pension fund – I did have one in the past, but it somehow fell by the wayside; they weren't really interested in it, maybe I should've continued it, maybe I will. Anyway my average salary is not far from double of what they make around here. I hired two guys from the Karoo where there is a severe drought and they were making R120 a month. It's a five-day week. I used to have a soccer team, but they were having too many injuries, so I had to drop it. The farm is probably worth more than R2 million [about £450,000] – if you can find a buyer – and in a good year I will gross half a million. Of this, two-thirds will go on expenses – labour, raw materials, repairs, depreciation, insurance, electricity, diesel fuel, and so on, which will leave me about R150,000. Part of that money I will use to plant three hectares of fallow land, which will cost me about R90,000. Because, you see, I refuse to pay any taxes on the farm, so I reinvest all my profits, it's all perfectly legal. It's the only way to beat inflation in this country [running at 16/17 per cent a year but, by August 1993, below 10 per cent].'

I failed to see the connection between inflation and reinvesting the profits, which would normally increase the value of the farm. Moreover, the fact that there is no capital gains tax in South Africa makes this option even more attractive.

After this conversation, Raoul took me on a guided tour of his farm. We drove through narrow dirt lanes around the vineyards and the orchards ending up on a *koppie* (little hill with a flat top), which commanded an unobstructed panoramic view of the surroundings; in the middle of the *koppie* was the second dam (big water reservoir) of the farm. He showed me the boundaries of his property: the undulating river, the mountain in the back, the village with its Coloured section, the Escom (electricity corporation) enclave within the farm, the farming co-op, the old hotel and the Botriver train station.

Later, we drove down to Onrus, about 20 miles from Botriver; Hermanus, a bigger village, a sort of South African Palm Beach, is at about ten minutes by car. Jayne had rented an old house on the beach. We found her cooking in the kitchen. Besides the family and myself there were three more guests to dinner. All three were middle-aged women involved with the arts: two, who lived together, ran an art school in Onrus which they had founded, one is a weaver and the other a potter, I believe, and next to their house is a small Greek Chapel considered a little architectural gem; the third guest taught art history in a Cape Town college.

The house was very old but had a lot of charm. One big room served as a living room, dining room and kitchen combined. There were a number of bedrooms in the back. In front of the house, stone steps led directly to the beach. It was a pleasant evening. We had grilled yellow tail, a local fish, and a good Boland wine. We talked about South African politics, literature and philosophy. I mentioned Aristotle's three forms of friendship: based on interest, pleasure and goodness which is, of course, the highest form. I wanted, I guess, my nascent friendship with Jayne and Raoul to be based on goodness. I wondered if this was possible given the particular circumstances of our relationship. Next morning we went after breakfast barefooted to have a long walk on the beach. I admired the fine white sand, the boulders with patches of greenish/grey moss rounded by the sea, the breakers with their foaming crests constantly crashing on them and, on the surf, the seagulls squawking. It was after that walk that Raoul took me on the visit to Jan Rabie and Marjorie Wallace that forms the whole of Chapter 5.

I left reluctantly. But it was not the last time that I saw the Beaumonts. A month or so later, after I finished my work in Jo'burg, I returned to Botriver and spent my last three days in South Africa with them at the farm. It so happened that the first three days of May (which is November in the northern hemisphere) were cold. We made a fire the night of my arrival. It was their second fire of the year, the first one they had made four days earlier (since 1980 they mark on a stone the date of their first fire every year; this year was the second earliest).

That same afternoon, as we had tea and snacks outside on the wharf, a wooden platform by the dam in front of the house. Three ducks, two white and one black, glided away and vanished behind the scrubby bush. 'We had many more, at least a dozen,' said Jayne, 'but they got eaten by the otters.'

Later we had 'Dam with Doms' (brandy and water) with Raoul while Jayne made a lovely moussaka for dinner. After that we watched the fire and television. At about midnight, Raoul and the kids went to bed; Jayne and I had a long chat. Despite the apparent calm, harmony and peacefulness, it turned out that there is constant unexpressed anxiety and fear.

'In the mid-eighties when it got real bad we considered seriously sending the kids out of the country,' said Jayne. The violence, the possibility of things exploding is always in the back of their minds. 'There is no way we could live in the farm if a civil war broke out, I don't know where we would go.'

The following day, a Friday, was 1 May, Labour Day, a public holiday, and the schools, the government offices and most businesses were closed. But it was a working day on the farm and Raoul was off to work at eight in the morning. I went for a walk with their two ageing dogs, both of nondescript ancestry. In the afternoon I played chess with Sebastian. He is a clean-cut, nice kid, respectful of his parents and good at sports, but only an average student. He wants to become a marine biologist, but is afraid that his grades won't be good enough to allow him to do that. Arianne, almost seventeen, is reserved, introspective, with a mind of her own, perhaps over-protected in some way; she is interested in the theatre. Lucien, who is twelve, is the most outgoing of the three children.

Friday night we went to a fundraiser for the Coloured community of Botriver which was held in a big room next to the church. There were raffles, homemade food and games. Jayne made a big cake for the occasion and Lucien brought one of his games which was very popular: a number of small plastic crustaceans lay on an electrified bottom and the game consisted of trying to lift them off without touching the bottom with the help of a pair of tweezers; each time a player touched the bottom a black plastic spider leapt from the side, startling the player to the delight of the onlookers, who then broke into hilarious laughter. At one rand a go, many tried their hands at it. But it was hard to do and most of the players (alas, including me) failed miserably. Another game, in which the goal was to get a small hoop at the end of a line (like an angler) into the neck of a bottle placed on the floor, was more my cup of tea; I won the second time I played. I also bought a piece of cake from Jayne and watched the card and domino players, who made a loud noise banging their dominoes on the table. Most of the Coloured people present were poor and backward. Except for a young guy whom Raoul described as a smallholder having a hard time making ends meet and married to a Coloured woman, the Beaumonts and I were the only whites present. When I pointed that out to Raoul he said that it was 'a tragedy'. The Boer farmers of the area have a long way to go before they change their old reactionary and racist ways.

Saturday morning we all got up late and had a leisurely breakfast at about ten. It was a grey and rainy day, the sort of weather they call 'a monkey's wedding' around here. In the afternoon Jayne, Arianne and I went to the hot spring baths of Caledon which is a half-hour's drive from Botriver. Raoul, Sebastian and Lucien stayed behind to watch a rugby match on television. The Caledon Baths had an archaic, turn-of-the-century air to it: an old, rectangular pool surrounded by old wooden cabins. But it was steaming hot in the water and I could almost feel myself penetrated by the goodness of the minerals.

That night, Raoul, Jayne and I went to Onrus to have dinner with the two art teachers I had met about a month earlier. We took Jayne's Merc. It was raining heavily and quite cold; there was little traffic on the road. It was a pleasant surprise to see Jan Rabie and Marjorie Wallace again – he was wearing the same old sweater and corduroy trousers, she was in a woollen, hand-woven, exotic-looking smock and Afghan slipper–socks that came up to her knees. A third guest was a middle-aged, loquacious, overweight and successful architect from Cape Town who owned a house in Onrus and came as often as he could. I missed part of the conversation because they lapsed into Afrikaans now and then, but if the part in English was an indication it must have been witty and enjoyable, at any rate they laughed a lot. The food – two main dishes, one meat and one fish, with rice and salad – was excellent as was the wine. We spoke French with Marjorie; she is of Scottish origin, but speaks quite fluent French, having spent some seven years in Paris with Jan in the 1960s. As we all went out together at the end of the evening I was a little surprised to see that Jan drove a vintage Austin or Morris (a true museum piece), an early 1950s model probably. The 'monkey's wedding' (it was raining 'cats and dogs') continued while we drove back to Botriver. Sunday morning I got up early and took the dogs for a last walk. The sky was grey and overcast but it was not raining. I went to the *koppie* where the second reservoir was. As I stood there watching, a train that belonged to another time and age rumbled into the station, the locomotive belching white steam. It blew its whistle twice and two guinea fowls, as if frightened by it, suddenly rose from between two rows of grapevines and flew away.

Notes

1 It is largely the story of the wholesale uprooting of the African communities. The 450-page report, entitled *The Surplus People: Forced Removals in South Africa*, was put together for the Surplus People Project by Laurine Platzky and Cherryl Walker and published by the Ravan Press in 1985. The total number of black people removed is given as more than 3.5 million, of which 3.2 million were Africans, 300,000 Coloured people and about 100,000 Indians. The bulk of the removals took place between 1960 and 1983, even though some communities such as Sophiatown in Johannesburg were destroyed even earlier in the 1950s. A pioneering study of the removals that deserves to be mentioned here is *The Discarded People*, by D Cosmas, published by Penguin in 1970.

2 See Chapter 17.

3 I think, but I am not sure, that Ernest Campbell's remarks came up during a conversation that I had with Father Smangaliso P Mkhatshwa in April 1986 (he was the secretary-general of the SACBC then, in 1988, he became general secretary of the Institute of Contextual Theology, he is also a trustee of the Kagiso Trust). Father Mkhatshwa, who was several times incarcerated in the 1970s and 1980s, was awarded an honorary doctorate in 1989 by Georgetown University, an institution I was affiliated to as a scholar in the mid 1980s.

10

The Story of Crossroads/ Khayelitsha and of Sam Dube – the Self-Made Man from Khayelitsha

'The poorest of the poor were robbed yesterday when thieves broke into the storeroom of Mother Teresa's nuns in Khayelitsha.'

Cape Times

'We are going to see. We are going to give them a chance to talk to our leaders, and we will see.'

Sam Dube

With a population of about a million and still growing fast, Khayelitsha is by far the largest African township in the Western Cape. More people live in it now than in Langa, Nyanga and Guguletu (the three older and more established African townships on the peninsula) put together. More than two-thirds of Khayelitsha's inhabitants live in abominable shacks some of which can be seen, like boils on an arse, from the N2 highway that goes east in the direction of Mossel Bay, George and Port Elizabeth. Nobody really knows at what rate the population of Khayelitsha is growing. It could be anywhere between five to ten thousand people a month including the natural increase. My educated guess is that the two-million mark can be reached before the year 2000.[1]

It is hard to believe that Khayelitsha is so recent a creation that there was nothing there ten years ago (in 1983) but an uninterrupted expanse of sand dunes often beaten by a howling wind. Its growth, fast like a terminal cancer in its metastasising phase, has in it both Orwellian and Kafkaesque elements, symbolic of the cruelties and absurdities of the apartheid system. Khayelitsha's genesis is inextricably linked to Crossroads' destruction. So, for a good understanding of the former, some knowledge of what happened to the latter is indispensable. For both stories I have relied heavily on old clippings of the local press, for the most part the *Cape Times* and the *Cape Argus*. I feel the Crossroads/Khayelitsha story is well supplemented by the conversation I had with Sam Dube, the self-made man from Khayelitsha that follows it.

I met Barry Streak, a journalist who works for the *Cape Times*, in May 1986. I had gone to the paper's offices to talk to Anthony Heard (then the editor) about Crossroads, which was being destroyed by factional violence. I had arrived in Cape Town only a day before and had actually seen the smoke billowing up from the still smouldering shacks near by the DF Malan Airport. Tony had said, 'You should talk to Barry about this, since he is the one in charge of the story.' Barry was precisely on location, working on it; but he came to see me on the following day at the Helmsley where I was staying and we spent two hours talking about Crossroads.

It is a long and complicated story, whose beginning goes back to the early seventies and which is quite revealing of the apartheid state's modus operandi, not only inasmuch as the influx control and relocation policies are concerned, but also in general, in the ideological sense of the word. It is a modus operandi that involves a curious, paradoxical combination of singlemindedness, even stubbornness, with flexibility, and a willingness to change when the going gets too tough. In other words, repression, but also accommodation, with constant attempts at manipulation.

There was, in the early 1970s, to the east of Nyanga, on the Cape Flats, a sprawling squatter camp known as Old Crossroads. This was the direct outcome of a 1967 government decision to freeze the construction of new housing for Africans in the Cape Peninsula, which was proclaimed a 'Coloured Labour Preference Area'. The policy did not, could not possibly, work because Cape Town acted as a powerful magnet for those impoverished rural Africans who lived in Ciskei and Transkei. By the end of the seventies, with the influx of new immigrants from the Eastern Cape relentlessly continuing, a number of satellite camps, among which were KTC (what the three letters of the acronym stand for is not known, probably Cape Town and Camp) and Portland Cement Works, sprang up around Old Crossroads. To deal with the situation, the government first launched New Crossroads, a new African township aimed at housing all the squatters living in the camps. When that proved to be insufficient, an even bigger township, Khayelitsha, was launched in 1983.

Despite the terrible living conditions prevailing in it, or maybe because of them, Crossroads came to symbolise African resistance against the pass and influx control laws (abolished in 1986). The government reacted by resorting to a divide-and-rule policy. In February 1977, Marais Steyn, the minister of Community Development, declared that 'in no circumstances whatsoever will any shack be bulldozed'. When that pledge was not kept only months later, there were massive local and overseas protests which forced the government to back down. Dr Pieter Koornhof, who was appointed minister of the newly renamed department of Plural Relations and Development, promised that the forced removals from Crossroads would be stopped. That same Koornhof, however, suddenly announced in 1983 that Khayelitsha ('Our New Home' in Xhosa), a new and bigger African township, would be built near Mitchell's Plain, about seven miles to the east of Crossroads and about 22 miles from Cape Town, which was designed to meet 'the consolidated housing needs of all the legal residents of Crossroads – the illegals would have to go back to where they came from'. The absurdity and duplicity of that statement was clear for everyone to see: 'legal residents of Crossroads' was an oxymoron, a contradiction of terms; the authorities knew that the large majority of Crossroads' residents were illegals.

The same scenario of international outcry and demonstrations in Cape Town was repeated. The government again retreated: Koornhof was replaced by Gerrit Viljoen, and the name of the department was changed again – this time to Co-operation, Development and Education. Even by their own cruel standards, an astonishingly brutal move was made in February 1985: a Tswana police detachment (virtually all the squatters in Crossroads were Xhosa), which was brought down from the Transvaal, was sent into the camp with orders to remove all the illegals by force. In the ensuing violence, 18 were killed and more than 200 wounded.

Again, expressions of disgust and indignation in Europe and America, followed by soothing noises made by the government. It was the epitome of hypocrisy for, at the same time they were making those statements, the authorities had already embarked upon a clandestine operation that consisted of supporting actively a right-wing vigilante faction – they came to be known as the *Witdoeke* after the white bands that they wore around their heads and arms so that they recognised each other in battle – which was engaged in a power struggle with the left-wing, pro-UDF, 'Comrades'. The kingpin of the operation was a certain Johnson Ntxobongwana (Nobs for short), the leader of the *Witdoeke*, who many think was bought off by the South African security services. Nobs rose to prominence when he was elected chairman of the Executive Committee of Crossroads in July 1978. Until then there was no political activity in Crossroads to speak of, except for three women's groups which organised community development projects with the aim of making life easier for the squatters. During the next seven years or so Nobs appears to have been a bona-fide community leader; he was even arrested a few times and did time in gaol. It is generally believed that it was during his last period of incarceration that a deal was struck between him and the government, the gist of which was that, in exchange for his help in ridding Crossroads and KTC of the Comrades, he would be recognised as the undisputed leader of New Crossroads.

The hostilities broke out in March 1986: with the active support of the South African security forces, Nob's *Witdoeke* militia attacked the Comrades in Old Crossroads and KTC, and defeated them after three months of intermittent battles. There were severe casualties: more than 70 killed and 400–500 injured. In the process, much of Old Crossroads and KTC was destroyed: an estimated 7,000 shacks were burned to the ground, and more than 70,000 people were left shelterless in the beginning of the winter which can be cold and very rainy in the peninsula. The operation was a success; the government's divide-and-rule policy was triumphant. Eventually, many of the 70,000 victims of the violence saw the writing on the wall and resigned themselves to moving to Khayelitsha. What happened was that, in the beginning, the squatter refugees (some of whom had taken refuge in the churches and schools of the area) were for several months cared for by church and welfare organisations. But these were on a collision course with the government and soon ran out of funds. In September, the Red Cross Society, which had spent more than a million rands in one of the largest relief operations yet seen in South Africa, announced that it was throwing in the towel: they were stopping the supply of cut-price food to the smaller relief agencies assisting the refugees. It was the beginning of the end. Some refugees were determined to move back to their old sites in Old Crossroads and KTC, but they were physically prevented by the authorities from doing so. This is when the first groups of people, wearied by the struggle, decided to go to Khayelitsha, allured by the one million rands worth of 'tents, mealie meal, samp, sugar beans, sugar, powdered milk, soup powder, blankets, pots, salt, [and] plastic bags for food' provided by the government.

Meanwhile, it was time to reward Nobs for his collaboration. Early in 1987, the authorities decided to upgrade Old Crossroads which was proclaimed a town after 1,400 of the 5,000 projected serviced sites were completed in June of that year. Nobs was appointed mayor. This brought a strong reaction by squatter leaders who, with the help of UCT's Legal Centre, took court action against the appointment, which was found eventually to be illegal by the Supreme Court. But the government could not afford to give up. It was a question of credibility for them, supporters had to be seen as reaping important rewards. So, they reappointed Nobs head of New Crossroads' Executive Committee this time. Before the year was out, New Crossroads was welcomed by Urban Councils Association of South Africa (UCASA) as a member.

The year 1988 augured well for the authorities: 'The winds of change are beginning to be felt in Crossroads, home to about 90,000,' trumpeted the *Cape Times*, 'Schools, infrastructure, houses, are popping out from the ground at an increased pace.' It was premature rejoicing: by the middle of the year, violence, that old scourge of Crossroads, had raised its ugly head again. An independent monitoring agency reported that '400 people have received gunshot injuries' in Crossroads and the adjacent KTC between May and July. With the excuse that 'radical elements existed in the township,' the security forces moved in early in 1989 to 'establish order'. The *Cape Times* reported ominously that 'conflict in Old Crossroads has reached a crisis point and could erupt any day'. Violence became endemic, chronic, 'part of everyday life that the residents have to put up with'. A prominent black leader, Themba Nyati, Member of the Executive Council (MEC) for the Cape Province compared Crossroads to 'a giant and festering sore'. With the unbanning of the ANC and the PAC in February 1990, the nature of the conflict changed and the violence intensified, as shown by the following headlines and quotes in the *Cape Times* and the *Argus*:

> Four killed in fierce battles at Crossroads. 150 shacks are burning fiercely.
> Strife-torn Crossroads focus of peninsula violence. Army called into Crossroads.
> Crossroads looters go on rampage.
> Crossroads teachers caught in crossfire.
> Three shot dead in Crossroads housing battles.
> New Crossroads violence, two die. Police baton charge Crossroads crowd.
> Townships sealed off. Security forces last night threw a ring of steel around the crisis-ridden townships of Old Crossroads and Khayelitsha.
> Youths fanning township violence – clash between the PAC and the ANC in the Crossroads area?
> ANC and PAC pledge peace in Crossroads.
> Youths burn 40 shacks in fights at Crossroads.
> Top level ANC probe of Crossroads.
> Both sides say they are ANC in the Crossroads war.

Things began to deteriorate seriously for Nobs and his faction even before the arrival of the ANC on the scene: 'Charges of corruption and exploitation are made against Nobs.' 'Police probe Crossroads rent irregularities.' 'Homes of Nobs and a senior committee member came under a hail of gunfire.' Nobs, fortunately for him, was not home when the attack took place. He had already gone into hiding and was away from the township. By the end of 1990, it was quite clear that Nobs had lost the power struggle that opposed him to J Nongwe, the chairman of the local, 5,000 members-strong, ANC branch; the *coup de grâce* was his ouster from his position as mayor. A few months later, an attempt was made by his supporters to reinstate him, but it was all in vain. The dénouement came in January 1992 when Nobs's house was razed and he was forced to leave Crossroads. He chose to go to Driftsands, a squatter settlement near the Fauré turn-off on the N2 highway, near Khayelitsha. A thousand or so of his supporters went with him.

Nobs's political saga appears to have ended. In March 1992, the *Cape Times* reported: 'Shanty town upgrading begins. 600 families moved to temporary sites. . . . The removal of 8,000 families will continue daily.' The wheel of *mis*fortune continued to turn. . . .

As mentioned above, it was in 1983 that the government announced its intention to create a vast new township called Khayelitsha between Macassar and Mitchell's Plain on the Cape Flats. All at once there were negative reactions from many quarters: 'Khayelitsha, a remote, sterile desert town is taking shape on the False Bay coast. It is a state-planned home for 250,000 blacks . . . Heunis's (minister of Constitutional Development) "Promised Land" – or the "last grave" for thousands of Cape Town's blacks?' wrote commentators in the local press. Professor D Dewar of UCT's Urban Problems Research Unit denounced it as a 'recipe for disaster'. The MP for the Garden constituency in Cape Town declared that 'Khayelitsha resembles something in a science fiction film'; Black Sash expressed 'reservations'. The government was not deflected from its objective. The same horrible Orwellian and Kafkaesque scene was re-enacted: 'Khayelitsha is based on sound planning,' Heunis said, adding that there would be 'no compulsion to move to Khayelitsha.' Be that as it may, the first '115 zinc homes' appeared on the forlorn, sandy dunes before the end of 1983, presumably as a Christmas present.

The 'big break' for the government came in early 1985 when Mali Hoza, the leader of a 12,000-strong group of the Cathedral Squatters (so nicknamed apparently because some of them squatted in a big church) announced that they were 'tired of running and hiding', and that they had decided to accept the government's latest package and move to Khayelitsha. The new arrivals were housed in 'Green Point Sites, a row of green tents in a dustbowl which became a sea of mud in the rainy season'. To sweeten the bitter pill, the government declared that the new township was to get a 'R12 million beach complex called Monwabisi ('Place of Comfort' in Xhosa). At the end of 1986, Louis Nel, the deputy minister of Information, predicted confidently that in a few years' time, 350,000 blacks would be living in Khayelitsha which 'is already home to 126,000'.

The private sector development agencies got in on the act. W H Thomas, director of the Small Business Development Corporation (SBDC), wrote a report that said: 'During the following weeks the SBDC will try to bring together some of the parties of the development process, hoping thereby to trigger off a process of grass-roots consultation and co-operation. Some may regard such efforts as naïve, others dangerous or meddlesome – yet it may be worth trying.'

Life was tough for Khayelitsha's early residents: the women had to go shopping in Mitchell's Plain, almost six miles away on foot: 'For thousands, food is a hot, dusty trek away.' 'Postal deliveries are non-existent in Khayelitsha. Mail is piled up carelessly on counters and gets lost. . . . There are only two post offices for the whole township.' Living conditions continued to deteriorate in 1987. A nadir of sorts may have been reached in the middle of 1988 when Mother Teresa established a mission station in the township composed of four sisters and a mother superior. The following report also dates from the same period: 'Tuberculosis and other poverty-linked diseases run rampant. One every 124 people in Western Cape has TB, compared to one to every 10,000 in the US. In Site B, a squatter section housing about 120,000 people in makeshift shelters, unemployment is rated at 80 per cent; malnutrition, kwashiorkor and TB are rampant.' 'Emergency home for Khayelitsha children and abandoned babies is being planned by the Children Welfare Society.'

Khayelitsha began to be seen as a dumping ground for undesirable squatters in white urban areas. For example: 'The Kraaifontein municipality will begin evicting the Bloekombos squatters and moving them to Khayelitsha tomorrow – where they face increased hardship.' The big news broke at the end of 1987: 'Khayelitsha rail line due to open in four months' time. Many of the 200,000 people living in the sprawling township will have a new alarm clock now: the 3.23 am Cape Town bound train. Within a decade Khayelitsha could be the size of Soweto and the railway link will be further strained. The Khayelitsha railway is of course subsidised, the cost of it all is astronomical, and there is no end in sight.' And so forth.

As was the case with Crossroads, 1988 is the year violence got out of control. Again, I reproduce below some of the quotes that appeared in the local press between 1988 and 1992:

In Lusaka squatter camp, where the shacks are so close together that walking between them is difficult, violence is just part of daily life.
Three killed: no motive for the shootings.
Khayelitsha blaze kills five.

More than 18 shacks have been burnt to the ground in Khayelitsha as groups supporting the PAC and ANC clashed at the weekend.

The agony of Khayelitsha. Police open fire on Khayelitsha marchers.

Khayelitsha burning. No-go area as offices, houses, barricades blaze.

Seven killed, 80 hurt in Khayelitsha.

Five dead, scores hurt in running battles with the police.

Stoning, arson in Khayelitsha.

Troops move into township.

The poorest of the poor were robbed yesterday when thieves broke into the storeroom of Mother Teresa's nuns in Khayelitsha.

Grieving Mr Solomon Tshuku, Site C Branch Chairman of the ANC, stands in his gutted house where his wife and four children were shot dead in a dawn attack last week.

Two more violent deaths in strife-torn Khayelitsha have brought the toll there to 12 in the past two weeks.

Night attacks in recent weeks in Khayelitsha, Cape Town's largest township, have left about 15 people dead and at least 100 injured. About 250 shacks were razed leaving more than a thousand homeless.

Mr Million Goniwe, 46, Lingelethu West Town Councillor, was shot dead on November 3 [1991], in an attack in Q Block, Site 13, at 8.10 am.

In the last days of 1991, two men were shot dead, one was wounded. About seven men set fire to shacks in A Block, Site C, at about 2.25 am on Wednesday. One woman and two men were shot dead, and three people wounded. 14 shacks were destroyed.

In an amazingly parallel development, Khayelitsha's mayor, Mali Hoza, travelled the same road as Nobs in Crossroads. In 1988: 'he and his nineteen men have won a landslide victory in Khayelitsha, the only black area in Cape Town where an election was held. Mr Hoza polled the highest number of the votes, 16,739. The poll was 43.4 per cent of the 67,867 registered voters. The next highest number of votes went to Mr Fulani with 7,277 votes. Mr Hoza is a businessman who owns a fleet of taxis.' But, barely a year later, 'The mayor who swept the polls is accused of thuggery.' And Mr Ngoboka, one of Mr Hoza's councillors, is stabbed to death in 1990.

Nelson Mandela attacked the state for not having suspended the corrupt mayor and his councillors. Two weeks later, the Town Council's offices were set on fire soon after midnight on a Saturday night.

In conclusion, despite some glimerings of light – for example, in 1991 the Western Cape Regional Services Council donated R30 million for development; the Catholic Welfare Bureau sponsored a project to plant at least a million trees to transform the desert-like environment of the peninsula townships and Khayelitsha will be a big recipient of this project; Khayelitsha which has 26 primary and four secondary schools, received its first library in Site B and six more are in the planning stage – making life more bearable in Khayelitsha will be a daunting, gargantuan task. According to a research project carried out by UCT, just the completion of basic infrastructural services there would require 'a further R900 million', (more than £250 million) and that was in . . . 1988. At the end of 1991, the overall picture remained a very bleak one: 'The deluge of the past two days has turned Khayelitsha into a virtual swamp, flooding 500 shacks and marooning more than a thousand people.'; Father Schneider, a Swiss clergyman who lived more than 40 years in South Africa, visited Site B in Khayelitsha (where between 100,000 and 150,000 people live) and said: 'Practically every bit of space has been occupied by squatters and the place is hopelessly overcrowded. The sewerage system is in a constant state of collapse, garbage collection does not function properly, and the streets are in a shocking state.' The problem is 'shack-dwellers form the bulk of Khayelitsha's estimated half-million population. Khayelitsha is mostly a shanty town with only 5,000 conventional and core houses.'

The terrace of Hard Rock Café on the esplanade of Sea Point in Cape Town. An early afternoon of a sunny and breezy day in mid March 1992. The waves beating on the rocky and sandy shore, seagulls circling overhead and occasionally squawking. Sam Dube is a big man not yet 50 who was a well-known rugby player in his younger days. His ears are crushed like those of a wrestler. He owns two businesses in Khayelitsha: a petrol station and a food-catering business managed by his wife. The Dubes (pronounced Du-bays) live in Guguletu, one of the more established black townships on the Cape Peninsula, not far from Khayelitsha. But Sam is thinking of moving out, of buying a house in one of the formerly white suburbs. He is an intelligent, self-taught man who has never travelled outside South Africa. He took time off this afternoon to tell me about his life, his feelings, his hopes.

'. . . Initially the black community did not want to go to Khayelitsha,' he said matter of factly, 'because, you see, at that time, in 1983, the government policy to keep the Western Cape as a Coloured Preferential Area was very much in effect. We simply thought that it was just another way of putting us in a transit camp where they could, if they wanted to, at a later stage, round us up and post us back to the Transkei and the Ciskei. I remember that a statement was made in the early sixties in the White Parliament to the effect that in 50 years' time there would not be a single African living in Western Cape, except for those with a valid work permit, as migrant labourers. So, there was a strong resistance among the people against moving to Khayelitsha. Later they went only because they didn't have any alternative. Their shacks were destroyed by the right-wing *Witdoeke* vigilantes. . . . They wanted a roof over their heads, so they moved, but unwillingly, against their will. . . .

'I was born and bred here in Cape Town. Never lived outside the area for a significant amount of time. I was born in 1946. I am supposed to be a Zulu if you want to talk ethnicity. But ethnicity in urban areas doesn't count, I don't even know what my next-door neighbour is. My father comes from Zululand. In fact, he lived at a border region between Zululand and Swaziland. I was born in a place called Elsie's River, which is not far from DF Malan Airport. Elsie's River is of course a Coloured area now. After the Group Area Act of 1953 we had to leave and went to Nyanga East where I went to primary school. And from Nyanga we moved over to Guguletu, where I live now. That was in 1959. I attended the Langa High School which at that time was the only high school for Africans in Western Cape. At a very young age I became involved in rugby. Strangely enough, rugby at that time was the dominant sport in Western Cape (even for blacks). We were very proud of our tradition. But, unfortunately, it sort of died out – with the youngsters who don't want to have their ears squashed [chuckles] . . . It is mostly soccer now. So I played rugby for the local club, then I became a provincial player. But sports was very segregated in those days. Until the mid seventies when things began to change. I remember, in 1970 I think it was, the All Blacks came to South Africa and we went to watch them at Newlands [a big stadium in a Cape Town suburb]. I was still a member of Newlands then. We used to go and train in the stadium. But there came a time when I had to ask myself whether I was not supporting racial sport by going to Newlands where I was not even allowed to sit where I wanted, where I wasn't allowed to use all the facilities provided for everybody. So some of us decided to put pressure on them. We joined up with the so-called Coloured community and we formed one single body: SARU, the South African Rugby Union. After that we refused to go to Newlands. We wanted to do our part to let the world community, especially the world rugby fraternity, know that rugby in South Africa was not only played by whites as it was perceived to be, and we succeeded.

'After I took my Matric [high school diploma], I wanted to continue with my studies. But I could not, unfortunately. I would've loved, at that time, to become a lawyer. But I lost my mother at a very young age and I had two sisters to support. I had to assist my father who was a labourer. He worked at the military hospital; what he earned was not sufficient to support us. So I had to go to work. I still remember my very first job, I was a petrol attendant [chuckles]. Life is a cycle, you know, here I am now the owner of a petrol station. The main reason for my taking the job was that I wanted to obtain a driving licence, which was expensive. I thought that at the petrol station, which also had a garage, I could learn for nothing. And that's what happened, and when I went for my driving licence, the owner of the garage even lent me his car. We are good friends now. So that was my first job. After that I went to work for a man called Allan H who is one of my best friends now. Yeah, he was a white guy; his brother-in-law was Reverend Peter S. You must've heard about him, he is in Johannesburg now, a Methodist. He's done a book as well, to make noise about the government policies. So, I joined this man, Allan, and that was also the time we were sort of politicising, in the sense that the Black Consciousness movement was at its peak. . . . I must really praise and give credit to Allan who allowed me to express myself as a human being. He restored my dignity, my self-respect. He never talked to me as to an inferior, even though he was my boss, and he gave me the latitude of trying to exercise my potential, which was something that was not normal in South Africa in those days.

'So, through Allan and BC, I instilled in myself some confidence in my capacities. I told myself: "Look, I know that as a black person in South Africa you're affected by those adverse political conditions, but you must not hide behind them, you must not try to cover up your failures using them as excuses." This is when I started looking for independency, and the only way to be independent is to be self-employed, right. So, when Allan had to close down his business, I became a furniture salesman. That also transformed my attitude, I now was able to work among my own people, service my own people. When I thought that something was not right in what the company was doing, I told them. I worked for them for about ten years, it was a big company, we were about 45. But they went under too, and I was faced with a situation of having to decide of what am I going to do with my life. For a while I was confused, after that I decided to go and strike on my own in Khayelitsha. Fortunately the SBDC had just built a shopping complex, and they were renting out the premises. I applied for a shop, a food-retail business, a kind of cafeteria, but for take-aways only. That was in 1985. I am still involved in that business, my wife runs it.

'Then I developed further by acquiring the right of a garage jockey. You know, that's the right to open and operate a service station and a garage business. It's a type of licence, you come to an agreement with an oil company, it's like a franchise. I did that with Trek, which is a local company owned by Afrikaners. Several of my friends said, "Why Trek? It's a *boere* company," and so on. "Look," I told them, "in order to know them better, be part of them [chuckles]". I must say my business relationship with them over the years has been excellent. I never had any problems with them, although their seminars are conducted in Afrikaans, but that has to be expected, it's a local company, and Afrikaans is an official language. So, that's how I got involved in business. . . . There are twenty-one of us at the service station. Twenty people that I look after. At the cafeteria they are fifteen, mostly ladies, of course. They prepare what we call soul foods – food must be good, not only for the body, but for the soul as well, it must have *muti* [magic].

'Yes, it is true that I have come quite a long way from my modest origins as you put it and I am quite satisfied with myself. But I feel I could have achieved more. I feel that my own personal growth has been hampered by what happened to me in the past. Because we were so poor I couldn't continue my education. You know, in Western Cape Africans were not allowed to own land, property. So, one couldn't go to the bank to acquire finance, because they would ask for collateral, you see. But how can you provide collateral if you are not allowed to own land and property?

'So, we had to take care of ourselves and started the *stokvels*.[2] They are community funds, sort of revolving funds, that people contributed to and drawed upon in turn; you had to wait for your turn to come, and then you could use it: to open a business, to make improvements on your house, to buy a car. And let me tell you that we had a very small default rate, much smaller than that of the banks, because, you see, one would lose face in the community if one defaulted, he would be shamed, his family would be shamed. We didn't have a permanent staff, work was done on a voluntary basis. We came together in churches, schools, community halls. . . . Today the banks are more willing to make loans to Africans, but the townships are still considered high-risk areas. Whose fault is it? As I said earlier, before the Group Areas Act we used to live in Elsie's River. That was not a high-risk area. That's what I mean, there are the scars. . . .

'So, Zeki, the question about how do I see the future of South Africa? I don't think that there could be any South African who could give you a straight answer. Unfortunately we've had our casualties. So, whether or not De Klerk is sincere in wanting to move towards a solution, there are the scars, there will always be the scars. . . . You know, the question of inequality, of the disenfranchised people, can never really be addressed in South Africa. Because, we will never have a big enough slice of the economic pie on our side. Many people will tell you: we cannot continue living by what happened in the past. But, unfortunately, the past keeps coming up. To a certain extent, it will be also a part of the future. The townships, they will be with us for a long, long time to come. That's present reality. It will be also future reality.

'However, we also know that violence cannot win. It's naïve to think that one can negotiate under the barrel of a gun. You know, the whites in this government are very, very strong militarily, we can only bring them to their knees by international sanctions, sports isolation. The South African whites have that competitive spirit. They thrive on competition. If you deprive them of that, you've killed their spirit, their will to live, this is why so many of them emigrated. So with the sports boycott we succeeded to break their will. I will tell you something else: militarily this government can, if they wanted to, squash all the violence in this country. They have the means. The black townships are designed in such a way that you have one, two, at the most three, entries, and you put soldiers there – one cap, one cap, one cap – and everybody is inside, and nobody can move. They are not like Claremont, like Sandton, where each and every road is an entry and an exit. So, they move in, close down the townships and say: "The hell with you, we've had enough of that violence, and it's got to stop", and it would stop. But they can't do it now, because if they do it, they will be seen by the international community as going back to their old, repressive methods, so they cannot afford to do it now. And let me tell you something else. We African people are not violent by nature. No matter what the whites will tell you about Africans being violent because of tribalism, because they are still primitive – you know, Shaka, the bloodthirsty tyrant, and all that. . . . What happened was that we tried to defend what was ours, we were sovereign nations. If you come barging into my house, without knocking on the door, and you say: "This house is mine", I am going to fight, I don't care who you are, I am going to fight. And that's what happened, and that's what's happening now. You know, Malcolm X said: "We don't want to be violent to any person who is not violent with us."

'Many affluent blacks are fleeing the violence in the townships. They also want to give a good education to their children. Most of the teachers in the township schools are not up to standards. It will take time to undo the damage done by Bantu education. So I am considering it [getting out] too. Even looking around. I know it's unfair to those who don't have the option, those who have to stay behind. But we shall have to go through that stage. The townships will probably get worse, because even those areas where the affluent people lived will become slums too. This is what happened in Alexandra township in Johannesburg. A lot of the people who had improved their houses moved out. My father used to own a house in Alex, it was a much better place to live in in the 1950s. But now those who could afford to do so have left, they went to live in inner-city areas like Hillbrow. It's an extremely violent place now. The crime rate is just unbelievable. In the white business district on Alexandra's border, people are afraid to walk the streets. Many are leaving, the place is paralysed. The majority of the unemployed youths survive by stealing, robbing. . . .

'So, when I hear talk about "New South Africa", I ask myself:

What new South Africa? I don't see any new South Africa that will be in a significant way different than the old South Africa. Yes, the people will have the vote. But, there will be even more class distinctions. I know, many people will say, it's natural to have class distinctions. That's true. But in South Africa they are man-made, in the sense that the government is giving substantial subsidies to its employees – so that they can buy houses – and thus creating a new middle-class black community. Class distinction should come about naturally, without the interference of the government that has its own agenda, which is not having to deal with the millions who will remain impoverished, in the townships, in the rural areas. . . .

'Do you know what we believe in the townships? We believe that Mr De Klerk is only interested in talking to Mr Mandela. The whites want to retain their standard of living, they don't want to be affected by the violence and poverty. What Mr De Klerk is really saying to Mr Mandela is: "Look, come in with us in the parliament, in the government. But, we would like you to talk to your people, tell them that they must be obedient." You know, the kind of independence, the kind of liberation that we were looking for, we will never achieve. What Mr Mandela and the other leaders were arrested for is not what they are fighting for today. Totally not. Because what the regime has done is that they have successfully addressed, not the major, but the petty apartheid that was being practised. Like, for instance, we are sitting here, you, a white man, and I, a black man, conducting our business at an ocean-side café in a so-called white area. Twenty years ago, we wouldn't be able to do that. I would have to come to your apartment, if you were a white South African. If you were a visitor from overseas, we would have to meet in a public parking lot, conducting our affairs like animals in a cage, because blacks were not even allowed to go into the hotels in the white areas, and you would have to have a special permit to go into a black township. Now, that type of apartheid was very much in force when the Mandelas and the Sobukwes were arrested. It's no longer. That's not an issue any longer. So, when Mr Mandela speaks about the inequalities, the people are thinking, not of petty apartheid, but of economic apartheid, and they are asking him to "Address it, please!" But that's a different kettle of fish. . . . For a long time, the whites of South Africa will remain on top. I am telling you, they will never allow their standard of living to drop sharply. What they are trying to do is to lift the standard of living of some of us to their level, or to half their level, and then they will be able to say: "Look, there has been development." But, but for the large majority of the people nothing much will have changed.

'Whites are not prepared to make the sacrifices that are required. They like their luxury. They have made this commitment to reform and all doors have opened, and the world has accepted them. Cricket tours, Olympic Games, business, trade, you name it. And nothing substantial has happened yet. It's unreal! So, this is how I see it, in a nutshell: the expectations are high, time will tell, but unfortunately we cannot forget what has happened in the past. Any attempt by the white community to go back to the *laager* mentality [circling the wagons, a defensive position] is going to spell big, big problems in this country. If, for instance, God forbid, the outcome of this referendum is a "No", South Africa is going to burn. There is going to be so much violence that the present violence is going to look like kindergarden stuff. A big "Yes" vote will give us some hope. We are going to see. We are going to give them a chance to address the problems, to talk to our leaders, and we will see.'

I thanked Sam Dube and walked with him to his white Toyota van and, after a triple-grip Comrade handshake, he was off. A few days later he gave me a tour of Khayelitsha: some of my impressions are described in Chapter 8.

Notes

1 In April 1992, when I was there, half a million was the generally accepted estimate of Khayelitsha's population. Jean-Claude Péclet, the editor of the French-Swiss weekly *L'Hebdo*, who visited South Africa in June 1993, mentions a population of more than one million. He also wrote that whole bands of unemployed rural people were arriving daily from the Eastern Cape in search of a livelihood. So it seems that: firstly, half a million in 1992 was probably an under-estimate and, secondly, Khayelitsha's population is growing at a phenomenal rate. It is now to Cape Town what Soweto is to Johannesburg, except that living conditions in Soweto *as a whole* are much better than in Khayelitsha. See *Le Temps du Partage Est Arrivé*, Jean-Claude Péclet *L'Hebdo*, 17 June 1993, Geneva, pages 22–4.

2 For more, see 'Bar None' in *Leadership*, W Ebershon and C Ryan, December 1991–January 1992, Johannesburg, pages 36–40. The *stokvels* (the word is apparently a derivative of 'stock fair' which existed in the Eastern Cape in the nineteenth century; it also means a party, like cocktail party) are about to become big business. Andrew Lukhele, the chairman of the National *Stokvels* Association of South Africa (NASASA) is exploring the use of the *stokvels'* funds as collateral to generate bank loans for its members. It is estimated that throughout the country the *stokvels* generate more than R200 million (roughly £45 million) a month in savings. Recent surveys suggest that there are about 24,000 *stokvels* in urban areas and hundreds of thousands more in rural areas.

11

Notes on Soweto – the Hybrid Metropolis

'They found two bodies yesterday . . . they were dumped from the train.'
Tony Ngwenya

Towards the end of the first volume of his autobiography, *Down Second Avenue*, which covers the first thirty-six years of his life, Es'Kia Mphahlele relates how Soweto, with its infamous males-only hostels, began with the Orlando township. It 'has been spreading west and south since 1934 in three-bedroom units; not east because that's the direction in which Johannesburg lies, twelve miles away; not north because that's where the line of the gold mines is. . . . As Orlando spreads into Meadowlands, Mofolo, Dube, Jabavu, Moroka, Molapo, Moletsane, holding more than 200,000 souls together, it also develops ulcers in the form of shanty towns. . . . Faction fights must be a source of amusement to some white supreme chief of the Bantu who decided to force people into ethnic compartments and threw thousands of single men into huge dormitories in hostels with high fences around them.'[1]

In the second volume, *Afrika My Music*, Mphahlele was 62 when he visited Soweto again in 1983 to find that things had much deteriorated since the late forties when he lived there for a few years while he taught in a secondary school.

'Soweto,' he writes, 'huge and slummy. Pipes burst and water irrigates the streets for days. Few lavatories work. Water hisses, swooshes and hisses ceaselessly for six months . . . and the West Rand Administration Board couldn't care less. Service payments are hiked periodically: what services? Garbage dumps keep shooting up all over the township, where children and elderly women continue to forage for cast-offs that may come in handy. . . . They are installing electricity to "improve the quality of life", as the official jargon goes. Might as well electrify a sewerage bog.... Soweto, home of maggots and rats and cockroaches, what are They doing to us?"[2]

André Brink, in his novel *Looking on Darkness*, gives a vivid description of Soweto in the seventies:

> Soweto with its phalanxes of identical houses, row upon row like the crosses of Delville Wood, with bare patches of bleeding red earth in between, erosion ditches, water taps, the stench of bad sanitation ... groups of teenagers in smart clothes or in rags, yelling at the passing women, occasionally grabbing one; children playing noisily with stones and wheels and broken dolls, children fighting, children pissing in the street. Cars parked beside houses and tatty gardens: enormous black American monsters from ten years ago, old wrecks with wide open doors.... Streetlamps protected by wire-mesh; a white goat; women breast-feeding their babies in front of their houses; a child beaten barbarously with a leather thong; and far away, far but visible, a barbed wire fence to hedge it all in, to stop the march of those regiments of houses. The muddy mess of early morning, half past four, five o'clock, six, when people go to work in the rain: the sound of thousands of feet, the low hum of voices ... those train journeys at five in the morning, five-thirty in the afternoon! We swarmed down the station steps like cockroaches, tumbled into coaches in a stench of perspiration, tobacco and stale beer; then pull off with a jerk, accelerate, speed on insanely, swaying round the bends, in a whirlpool of infernal noise: the roar and rattling of the train, deafening conversations, bursts of singing; afternoon papers, tins of curdled milk, food parcels, briefcases, shopping bags, nagging children.[3]

One day in mid-March 1986, Mike Rantho, a tall heavy-set man in his 40s, suffering from gout in his right foot, picked me up at nine in the morning in front of the Rand Afrikaans University (RAU) in Oakland Park. Mike worked for the Urban Foundation (UF) which was established by big business as a response to the Soweto uprising of 1976. Its purpose is to promote stability by helping the emergence of an African middle class 'with something to lose'. It tried to do that by a variety of strategies which included the support

of small-scale businesses, financially and otherwise; offering professional training schemes, building housing which would appeal
to the fledgling African middle class. It was Mike's job to take
foreign visitors 'worth the trouble' on a day-long tour of Soweto to
show them UF's achievements. Mike is an outgoing, articulate
fellow, well-suited to his job. I had phoned the foundation a few
days earlier and in response to my enquiries they had sent me a
folder full of information about the UF and Soweto.

Not unpredictably, the UF's Board of Directors reads like the
Who's Who of South African big business, with Anglo's Harry
Oppenheimer and Rembrandt's Anton Rupert heading the list. I
was surprised to find out that its 'net current assets' were only R33
million (about £11 million), clearly small potatoes compared to the
size of its ambition. I was 'disappointed' to learn that Soweto,
made up of 32 separate townships, is an acronym for *South West
Townships*. I expected something more colourful, I guess, like the
name of an exotic flower in an African language. (This is precisely
what the social engineers of apartheid had done in the Cape Peninsula, for example: Khayelitsha, the biggest African township in the
Western Cape, means 'Our New Home' in Xhosa; Langa and
Nyanga, two of the older African townships, mean 'the sun' and 'the
moon' respectively; several of the Coloured townships in the Cape
Flats where the residents of District Six were 'removed' after the
latter was destroyed were given names like Lotus River, Grassy
Park, Panorama and Monte Vista). . . .

I went through some of Soweto's statistics. Its population is given
as between 1.5 and 2.5 million but nobody really knows. In mid-
1993, numbers as high as 3–5 million were being bandied about;
for each and every one resident living in a house or shack, another
one, or even two, live in makeshift structures in back yards. There
are about 125,000 matchboxes – small three- and four-room brick
houses which were built between the early 1930s and the mid 1960s.
After that, the government stopped building any new housing for
Africans because it wanted to 'encourage' them to go back to the
homelands 'where they belonged'. Apparently, about a third of
Soweto's inhabitants are Zulus, with roughly an equal number
of Xhosas; then come the Sothos, Tswanas, Swazis and the others.
Most of the Zulus live in the dreary males-only hostels. The relationship between the hostel-dwellers and the other residents of the
townships has never been easy: constant tension and friction at

the best of times, which from time to time flares up into open violence. Part of the reason is social: the hostel-dwellers live brutal, isolated lives far from their families. But, increasingly, politics is the predominant reason: many of the Zulu migrant workers are Inkatha supporters, while the majority of the others support the ANC. Soweto is not a 'normal' city in the accepted sense of the word. It is still essentially a bedroom community with little economic activity in it, even though that is rapidly changing. It does have a large Central Business District (CBD) and a few smaller ones; and hundreds, if not thousands, of *shebeens* (bars, liquor outlets) and *spaza* shops; but the large majority of those who hold a regular job leave in the early morning and come back in the evening. It was estimated in 1983 that more than 70 per cent of all the income earned by Soweto's residents was spent outside Soweto in the Greater Johannesburg area where close to 50 per cent of the total purchasing power is reckoned to be non-white; that, too, is rapidly changing – the proportion is significantly larger now. The health needs of Soweto are met primarily by the huge Baragwanath Hospital which, in 1983, had a total of 2,740 beds and served more than 120,000 in-patients and 700,000 out-patients. There were, in 1983, 320 primary and 61 secondary schools in Soweto.

Historically, Soweto's development paralleled that of the Witwat-erstrand, known as the Rand or the Reef and one of the richest gold-mining regions of the world. About 64 miles long and 23 miles wide, it includes both Johannesburg and several other cities – Benoni, Boksburg, Springs and Germiston. With the growth of mining and manufacturing (and the related services sector), black labour became increasingly indispensable and housing for it was provided in Soweto. Those who came looking for jobs and did not qualify for official housing started building shacks that grew in time into squatter camps. Also, in those days, a large number of Africans (as well as some Coloureds and Indians) lived in the inner city areas of Jo'burg such as Sophiatown, Martindale and Newclare, which were known as 'freehold suburbs'. These blacks had a right to be there because they had acquired their properties before the 1923 Urban Areas Act, which forbade non-whites to buy property in white South Africa. So, at the end of the Second World War, a mixed population of 50,000 Africans, 3,000 Coloureds and 1,500 Indians were still living in the freehold suburbs. To be sure, the whites living in the neighbouring areas complained about the 'slums' and agitated for their removal but no action was taken by the authorities. That policy of 'benign neglect' came to a brutal end, however, with the Nationalists' watershed victory in the general elections of 1948. A new hard-line policy whose two cornerstones were removal and relocation became the order of the day. Soweto was earmarked as the principal relocation area for the Africans expelled from Johannesburg's inner city. By 1960, Sophiatown, Martindale and Newclare no longer existed . . .

Mike and I took the N1 freeway south and at Potchefstroom Street we turned west to enter Soweto. It was as if from one moment to the next we had changed continents, moving from North America to tropical Africa; from Los Angeles or San Diego, for example, to Lagos or Kinshasa. Our first destination was Katlehong Industrial Park, which consisted of forty or so small-scale businesses that employed between one and five workers each in panel-beating, brick-, fence- and wreath-making (a flourishing business, given the funerals of the violence victims). The budding entrepreneurs that we spoke to appeared reasonably content and hopeful about the future. Mike said that several of the businesses had reached the viability stage, others still needed to be subsidised. It took between three and five years for a business to become viable, some never made the grade, of course. The UF provided the initial loan to launch the business and technical assistance for as long as necessary.

Our next stop was a middle-class housing project still under construction. The houses looked nice, built with quality materials, spacious, with well-appointed kitchens and bathrooms, and small lawns outside. I was to learn six years later that the UF had run into serious trouble with its housing schemes and that many people had lost their jobs as a result, including Mike. What happened was that they had over-extended themselves, creating thus a severe cash-flow problem: the houses were expensive and not many Africans could afford to buy them; some of those who did buy them could not keep up with the payments; and so on.

We went to Funda Centre in Orlando next, both to have lunch and to visit the place. It is a modern teacher-training and adult education facility whose director in 1986 was Stan Kahn, a former academic and a genial man. I noticed on the wall of his office a large framed photograph of Teddy Kennedy, who visited the Centre in 1984. Stan said that, while his older brother Bobby was given a hero's welcome in 1968 (the year he was assassinated), Teddy's reception had been cool, bordering on the hostile. The reason was that 1984 was the year the tricameral parliament was inaugurated and the American government's opposition to it was not seen as being vigorous enough.

Stan showed us around after lunch. The classrooms were bright, spacious and well equipped. There was a well stocked library with a large number of periodicals and magazines. The students and the trainees appeared to be keen, interested. Back in Stan's office, Mike told me that he would like to take me to 'Beverly Hills', a part of Orlando West where the wealthy Africans lived. 'Some of the houses are real mansions, you will see,' he said. As we prepared to leave, Stan came up with the news (he had just made a phone call) that it was not safe to go there right now, some rioting had broken out in Orlando West, the Comrades were on the rampage again. Mike said that, given the circumstances, it would be better to put an end to our visit of Soweto. Before he dropped me off at the guest house belonging to RAU where I was staying, Mike promised to arrange a meeting with Es'Kia Mphahlele, who was a good friend of his. My efforts, however, to reach Mphahlele were unfruitful. I had to wait six years before meeting the famous writer and educator.

Six years later. February 1992. The offices of the United States/South Africa Leadership Exchange Program (USSALEP) in Johannesburg. Stan, who left the Funda Centre in 1990 to become an independent consultant, is the manager of the Transition to Democracy project financed by the American government to the tune of $7.5 million. The two main recipients of the American largesse are the ANC and Inkatha, which means a delicate negotiating role, but Stan is well suited to it both by temperament and training. It is 8.30 in the morning (Stan is not in) and I am with Tony Ngwenya who used to work for the Urban Foundation (another victim of the disastrous housing schemes) and later the American embassy but is currently unemployed. Stan's secretary, who is a blood relation of Tony's, had arranged our meeting. Tony is the person I am going to Soweto with. According to Stan, he knows Soweto like his pocket and has many friends there. He borrowed a car from a friend, he said and, after agreeing for a payment for his services (R200 for the day, including the car), we hit the road. We took the Soweto Highway south and then the Klipsruit Valley Road which leads to Orlando West.

Tony insisted that I should see the Mandela 'mansion', which was worth the detour. All I could see were some ten-, twelve-foot high brick walls and in the back some more white walls, this time of the house itself. It seemed to me more like a fortress than a luxury mansion. I was to learn the reason for it only much later when I read Arthur Miller's article on his meeting with Mandela at the same house in July 1991. The house's 'large, chesty configuration,' he wrote, is due to security reasons, 'its vulnerable dining and living rooms with their glass doors are protected by a deep brick veranda.'

Tony said he would stop at the house of an old friend of his, the secretary of the local branch of the ANC, and ask him to join us. It would be safer that way. The traffic was fluid on the main arteries which were tarred, even if dusty, and covered with potholes. Much of it was made up by 'combis' (route taxis) full of passengers. Clusters of youths stood around in street corners, seemingly idle. The side roads were red earth and very bumpy. One can easily imagine them turning into muddy bogs in the rainy season. Rows of rundown houses surrounded by half-collapsed walls, broken fences, sagging twisted chicken or barbed wire. But, suddenly, without warning, as it were, one entered areas of decent-looking housing, with tidy little yards, some trees, flower beds.

Tony stopped the car in front of one of the nice-looking houses and went inside. After a while he re-emerged with a handsome young man whose European features and light complexion suggested that some white blood flowed in his veins. Racial purity is largely a myth. It is not only the Afrikaners that are a 'bastard race', as the poet Breytenbach put it, and the Coloureds of the Western Cape (see page 58 for the joke about the distinction between blacks, meaning the Afrikaners and the Coloureds, and the black-blacks, meaning the Africans), but also the Africans themselves, even if to a much lesser extent. Vuyisile Mafalala, Tony's friend, in his early 30s, is a law graduate who still has to do his articles in a legal firm, but he has so far been unable to find one that also offers a reasonable salary.

'This is the notorious Meadowlands Hostel,' Tony said pointing with his hand to three or four grey, sinister-looking, squat brick buildings at a distance. Between it and the houses of the township was a wasteland: no vegetation, just rubbish and the ubiquitous plastic wrappings fluttering around. The back of the hostel was also waste ground, open land which belonged to the gold mines and which separated Johannesburg from Soweto. There had been several petrol-bomb attacks lately carried out by the hostel dwellers on the houses near to the hostel. We got out of the car to have a look at one of the houses that had been completely destroyed a few days ago. The roof had collapsed and the charred remains of beams and tiles were scattered on the ground; from a gaping hole in one of the walls one could see the room inside, which was barren; the residents had fled taking with them whatever they could.

'Who are these people and what are they trying to achieve?' I asked even though I knew the answer in advance. Most credible sources agreed that it was Inkatha-related, Zulu vigilantes that were carrying out the attacks.

'Inkatha has taken over the hostels and is waging an all-out war against the ANC, and the government is not doing anything about it, because it suits its interests. It wants to give the impression that black-on-black violence can plunge the country into chaos and that only the government can prevent that,' Vuyisile said. In reality, it is all about power, of course. A bitter, no-holds-barred power struggle about who will get how much of it in the new South Africa. I saw three more hostels in the course of my visit to Soweto: Dube, Nancefield and Jabulani. They were less dreary-looking than Meadowlands, but still unfit for human habitation.

After the Meadowlands hostel, the Ipelegeng (Anglican) Centre in Jabavu was a welcome contrast providing visual and mental relief. A modern, elliptical church stood in front, a big cement courtyard in the back, surrounded by an L-shaped building with a large auditorium and smaller classrooms for community development activities and a US Information Service library which looked like an oasis of sorts. The usual combination of propaganda and service. On the shelves, the great American classics of the nineteenth – Thoreau, Walt Whitman, Herman Melville, Mark Twain – and the twentieth – Dos Passos, Faulkner, Hemingway, Tennessee Williams, James Baldwin – centuries. On the walls, large framed pictures of Martin Luther King and J F Kennedy, posters of African-American celebrities such as Diana Ross, Bill Cosby, Spike Lee and Oprah Winfrey exhorting black youth to 'Read'. News magazines, old copies of the *New York Times*, the *Washington Post*, the *Wall Street*

Journal. Not many people around though. The director, a clean-cut, soft-spoken black man with an easy smile, explained that many kids came at the end of the school day.

Regina Mundi, the biggest church of Soweto, is not far from the Ipelegeng Centre. During the unrest in the late seventies and eighties, many big funerals of the victims had started here with fiery speeches denouncing the repression and praising the struggle. A large painting of a black *Madonna and Child of Soweto* hangs above the altar. The child has his two hands raised: the right one makes a V sign, which represents the ultimate triumph of Good over Evil; the left one holds a small black cross. In the lower part of the painting, there is an abstract rendition of Soweto in the shape of a giant eye, the pupil of which is a barely visible white cross; the iris is held by two elongated, pincer-like black arms. On our way out, we stopped to say hello to a white priest who lives in a small flat in the back of the church. A grey-haired, clean-shaven, ageless man, he has lived in Soweto for more than thirty years. He said that he prayed for a future South Africa in which racial harmony would prevail. I thought of the paradox of the white missionary in Africa. With the soldier, administrator and trader, he was one of the four pillars on which the temple of colonialism was built. He had wanted to suppress the indigenous African culture, and yet so many Africans received an education in missionary schools, even if they paid a high psychological and spiritual price for it.

Perhaps quarter of a mile south of Regina Mundi is Kliptown, where the famous Congress of the People was held in 1955. It was one of the watersheds of the black liberation struggle. More than three thousand delegates from all over the country congregated here on an open field to discuss the Freedom Charter and adopt it in the end. It is a sad irony that Kliptown today is the location of one of the worst squatter camps in Soweto: hundreds, perhaps thousands, of shacks built with an incredible hodge-podge of materials including planks, cardboard, canvas, cement blocks, corrugated iron and black plastic sheets. Depressingly, the most colourful part of it was the blue plastic portable latrines which could be mistaken for telephone booths. Rubbish everywhere and ca .asses of cars, but also laundry on a line put out to dry. I suggested that we go to Funda Centre for lunch. I wanted to see it again. Tony said that it has an African director now. We went straight to the restaurant. Fish and chips, and a salad, and a coke, for about ten rands (just over £2). Tony and Vuyisile introduced me to two or three young men who were all ANC activists. Funda, like many of Soweto's civic and educational institutions, was an ANC stronghold now.

In the very heart of Soweto, between Jabulani and Jabavu, sprawls the Central Business District, known simply as the CBD, which covers a huge area. Many of the buildings were constructed in the last five or six years. Taken separately, the Telephone Exchange, the Fire Station, the Soweto Council Civic Centre, are perhaps nondescript and impersonal architecturally, but they are not ugly; however, collectively, the place doesn't have any aesthetic coherence. Clustered about the middle of the CBD are, among other buildings, the Soweto branch of Standard Bank, a Kentucky Fried Chicken outlet and a McDonald's. At some distance, I could see the stalls of a massive African market; next to it was the soccer stadium. In the opposite direction, at the edge of the CBD, the hulking Jabulani Hostel. And, in between all those buildings, large tracts of empty land full of people and vehicles going from one place to another.

What I had in mind when I asked Tony to take me to a *shebeen* was the kind of place Mphahlele described in *Down Second Avenue*: a smoke-filled back-room in a matchbox house or a shack where ten, fifteen men huddled together to drink home-brewed beer and perhaps smoke *dagga*. The place we went to was new, big and ostentatious. A well stocked bar surrounded by mirrors (there were mirrors everywhere), marble-topped tables, plastic-upholstered chairs, a big colour TV in a corner; the dominant colour was pink. Being still early in the afternoon, the place was almost empty, only two or three tables were occupied. The big fat man at one of them was the owner, Tony said and added: 'It starts to fill when people come back from work beginning at about five. At night, until one, two o'clock in the morning it is very crowded. On Friday and Saturday nights one can barely get in.' Parked outside, a big truck from the South African Breweries looked like a three-storey house made of beer bottles. Against the outside walls of the *shebeen* were propped the hundreds of crates full of empty bottles that would replace the full ones on the truck.

After a second round of beers it was time to go to the Nancefield railway station to witness the arrival of the first commuters back from work in Johannesburg. Every day for about two hours between five and seven in the afternoon, the railway stations of Soweto disgorge tens of thousands of workers returning to the townships. I had seen them, at the other end of their journey, pouring down Hoek Street in downtown Johannesburg, so compact a human stream that it almost looked like a flow of black lava, in the direction of the East side of the Central (Park) Station, to catch the trains that would take them not only to Soweto, but also to the townships of the Vaal Triangle much further south, Sebokeng, Sharpeville, Evaton. The loudspeakers blared constantly in English, but in an Afrikaans accent, the departure times of the trains every five or ten minutes. . . . Two railway lines enter Soweto from the northeast and continue to the south west. There are about fifteen stations in all, one station for every one or two miles, depending on the density of the population of the areas crossed by the lines. The northernmost line ends in Naledi after crossing Orlando, Dube, Mofolo, and so on; the southernmost one goes to Lenasia, the Indian township, after crossing Orlando East, Klipspruit, Eldorado Park.

At the Nancefield Station it was eerily quiet. The 'station' consisted of a small, rundown brick building surrounded by barbed wire, nothing else but waste ground around it. Tony pointed to a hole in the ground in front of it. The travellers would be emerging from it, the railway tracks being below the ground level. 'They found two bodies here yesterday,' he said suddenly. 'They were dumped from the train.' There were constant attacks on the trains by professional killers who were never caught. Death squads. The famous 'Third Force'.[4] Most blacks believe the police, the security forces are behind it. What is still unclear is how much the top leadership is involved in it. After ten minutes or so, the first train arrived making clanging, rattling noises; then the strident screeching made by iron wheels braking on iron tracks was heard. After a brief hiatus and they started coming out of the hole. Mostly men, wearing old, baggy, threadbare clothes, dusty and greasy hats, and old shoes worn out at the heels. The women were in old smocks and woollen jackets, big, colourful berets and headscarves. They carried bags, parcels of – I presumed – groceries. They looked grim, devoid of hope. We were the only car at the station but they didn't pay any attention, filing by on their way to the matchbox house, the shack, they lived in, one, two miles away, unless they stopped in a *shebeen* before getting there. . . . Soon they were gone and again the eerie silence, the emptiness. We waited for the next train to come. It seemed longer than the ten, fifteen minutes that we had to wait. Then again the clanging noises, the braking. Again, the interval and the people emerging from the tunnel. Two, three hundred of them, exactly like the first time. Again, they passed by, ignoring the car. It was as if the same crowd had returned to the station taking some mysterious, invisible road and was exiting again from the same hole. Indeed, the same scene would be repeated ten, fifteen times in the following two or three hours in the Nancefield Station alone. How many more times in the whole of Soweto and in the rest of South Africa in a single day? 500? 1,000? More? And that does not include the same numbers travelling in the opposite direction every morning. That was the reality of apartheid and whatever the outcome of the negotiations for a 'new' South Africa it would remain so for many more years to come.

Notes

1 Es'Kia Mphahlele, *Down Second Avenue*, Faber & Faber, 1959, page 203.

2 Es'Kia Mphahlele, *Afrika My Music*, Ravan, 1984, Johannesburg.

3 *Looking on Darkness* was first published in 1974 by W H Allen and Co. The quote is from the Flamingo edition published in 1984, pages 223–4. Brink is well known in the West. Born in 1935, he has published more than a dozen books in English and several in Afrikaans. *A Dry White Season* was made into a very successful film. Steve Biko's role was played by Denzel Washington. There is a wonderful cameo performance by Marlon Brando – immensely fat – in the role of a disgruntled but very human lawyer. More on Brink in Chapter 5.

4 The 'Third Force' exists, of course. It is probably largely made up by rogue elements in the security services, not a formally organised entity. Left-wing intellectuals believe that its purpose is to destabilise the country, to show that a democratic system, evidently dominated by blacks, is not workable in South Africa. The subject is dealt with seriously, albeit with an axe to grind, in: *The Heart of the Whore: Apartheid's Death Squads*, J Pauw, Southern Books, 1991, Johannesburg. It was reviewed in the ANC journal, *Mayibuye*, in February 1992.

12

Back in Cradock Six Years Later: They Were Right All Along, Of Course

'Yes, there is only one snake now, the cash. If you have it, you, can move to town.'

J S Mfabana

I didn't find Mfabana much changed. He was 68 six years ago, so he must be 74 now. His paunch is a little bigger now, but otherwise he is the same. Goniwe, who is perhaps five years younger than Mfabana, has aged more: his hair is grey on the temples and he is thinner, which makes him look older somehow. Makaula, who at about 50 was by far the youngest of three in 1986, is not present. 'He has unfortunately passed away,' Mfabana informed me even before I had the time to enquire about him. He was very thin and already seriously ill, he had TB I think, but I am not sure. Mfabana introduced me to a new man that they had brought along. His name is R Barayi, he looks to be in his sixties. He is the older brother of E Barayi who was, until about a year ago, the president of COSATU.

'He is our replacement of Makaula,' Mfabana said, grinning. Barayi, who is much shorter than the other two, is wearing a suit, but no tie; Mfabana and Goniwe are in sweaters, with open-collared shirts. The three men are community leaders from Lingelihle, the black location or township of Cradock, a white town of about 5,000 inhabitants in the Eastern Cape, about 130 miles from Port Elizabeth. Lingelihle has a population of about 20,000, while roughly 10,000 people live in the Coloured township of Michausdal.

I had arrived in Cradock in the late afternoon of the previous day and spent the night at the Victoria Hotel which, I had found, had in the meantime been renovated. It was a true museum piece in 1986, more than a century old. I recall, the room I had stayed in had a high ceiling and a tiled floor. The iron bed was old fashioned and its springs had kept squeaking throughout the night. There was a small washbasin in the room, but the bathroom was outside, at the end of a long corridor. The curtain on the only window was of light material and so couldn't keep the light out. I had thus awakened at dawn and watched the sun rise. It was a delightful experience: the air was cool and crisp, and then the sun had gone up in a symphony of golden-orange hues. Now, all the rooms had carpets on the floor, private bathrooms and heavy curtains hung on the windows. While in the lobby checking in, I had noticed with a tinge of sadness that the old Victorian dining room with the big crystal chandelier in which we had made history – minor history, but history just the same – my three African friends and myself, had been converted into a billiards room. The crystal chandelier was gone, ordinary plastic chairs lined the four walls.

'We hope to attract the young people,' said the new manager a bit anxiously. He was white like the previous one, but what I didn't know yet was that the Victoria Hotel, that epitome of British colonialism, where only six years ago they were still refusing to serve blacks, had been sold to . . . an African. But more about this later, first I want to tell briefly about the 'minor history' that I mentioned above.

It was on the second morning of my stay in Cradock that Mfabana, Goniwe and Makaula had picked me up in a white minibus, which belonged to Goniwe, to take me on a tour of Lingelihle. But first they had made a point of stopping at Michausdal, the Coloured township, so that I could see the difference between the two. Michausdal was very much like a blue-collar suburb in England: rows of little houses, colourfully painted, each with its shrubs and flowers and its small lawn in front. All the streets were tarred and all the houses had electricity and water, Mfabana had told me. I had seen mothers pushing their babies in prams, bicycles and bright plastic toys were in the alleys, a car or two parked by the pavements.

In Lingelihle, by contrast, even the main street was untarred, with yawning potholes, and the small matchbox houses had a run-down look: whatever paint there was, was fading, the plaster was coming unstuck on the walls, many windowpanes were broken and replaced by rags. Carcasses of abandoned cars, refrigerators and cooking stoves littered the landscape amidst overgrown weeds and scrawny trees. Dust was everywhere, rising with each passing vehicle, and then settling back where it was before. The dominant colour was grey. But, being a Saturday, the streets, were alive with groups of youngsters playing soccer and womenfolk attending to their usual housekeeping chores of cleaning, washing and cooking. We had then gone to the shopping centre: a long row of ramshackle shacks selling groceries and other basic goods. Piles of garbage were everywhere, with mangy dogs sniffing at promising pieces. Finally, we had seen the squatter camp area, so wretched as to make the township itself seem decent in comparison. It had been an edifying experience and so I had decided to invite Mfabana and Goniwe to have lunch with me at the Victoria.

'But we can't,' had exclaimed Mfabana. 'Africans are not allowed to eat at the Victoria.'

'But how come?' I had retorted, 'hotels, restaurants and movie theatres are desegregated everywhere.'

√ 'This is a small town, nothing has changed here so far; the Boers are still in control,' Mfabana had explained. But I had insisted, I did not want to lose face. So we had gone to the hotel, I feeling like Don Quixote about to charge one of the famous windmills. At the hotel, to cut a long story short, after a brief argument with assistant manager, and then with the manager himself, during which I had threatened to make trouble 'with my journalist friends', we were allowed to have lunch, not at the restaurant, but at the Victorian dining room which had been opened especially for us. I still remember how the significance of the event was not lost on Mfabana who had felt inspired enough to launch on an impromptu speech on the inevitable liberation of his people.

'I don't know if you read your Bible,' he had said, 'but I do. Look what happened to the Pharaoh's army chasing the Israelites, they all perished in the Red Sea. Might is not always right. The Boers may well have a powerful army, but when the time comes it will not be of much help. Moses was able to lead the Israelites out of bondage because God was with him. The time will also come for us and we will be free.'

I had thought free . . . free . . . and then it had come: 'Free at last! Free at last! I have a dream . . . Thank God Almighty, we are free at last.' I had asked myself if Nelson Mandela could one day become the Martin Luther King of South Africa? The rumour in those days was that his health was not very good.

Later in the evening, as I was leaving Cradock, I had asked my friends if they needed, wanted something from America. The other two had not said anything, but Mfabana, who had shaken my hand at length, had said: 'Yes I need something. A dictionary. Can you send me a dictionary?'

'But,' I had said, 'I'll buy one in Durban, or Jo'burg, and send it to you.'

'No, no,' he had said emphatically, 'I don't want a South African dictionary, not even one from England. I want one from America, from the land of free men.'

I had been in South Africa for about two months when I had first read stories in the papers about the consumer boycott in the Eastern Cape which was getting 'out of control', and about how, in Port Elizabeth alone, about fifty white businesses had had to close their doors. The whites were scrambling to deal with the situation by negotiating with the activists and putting pressure on the authorities to release some of the militants who had been arrested and kept in prison without having been charged. I had read that in Cradock the whites had formed an Employers Federation which had reached an agreement with the local black leaders, bringing the consumers' boycott to an end. In fact the situation had been very tense and volatile in the Eastern Cape ever since that fateful night (17–18 June 1985) when four young black activists had disappeared on their way back to Cradock from Port Elizabeth after having attended a political meeting there. Their badly burned bodies – presumably to make identification more difficult – had been found several days later. Three of the activists – Matthew Goniwe, Fort Galata and Samuel Mkonto – were from Cradock (the fourth one, S Mhlawuli, was from nearby Graff Reinet). The four victims were given a big funeral in the soccer field of Lingelihle, with many important black leaders travelling all the way from Johannesburg and Cape Town to honour 'the heroes who had fallen fighting the brutal apartheid regime'. The event had been covered extensively by the national media, electronic as well as print, which had made a big deal out of the fact that during the ceremonies the red banner of the Communist Party had been raised above the crowd. Later, those guilty of the 'outrage' had been arrested by the police and thrown into gaol.

At the time of my arrival in Cradock in April 1986, the murders were still unresolved. The police had claimed to have investigated the case but to have found no suspects. The judge in charge had rejected the demands for an independent enquiry, giving the impression of wanting to cover the whole thing up. As I was reading about it in the papers, it had occurred to me that the affair could provide me with a good case study of African resistance against state fascism. I was lucky enough to find a good contact in Cradock who had told me on the phone that he was prepared to help me with my investigations. He was Keith Cremer, an Englishman in his mid-sixties and a lawyer by profession. Upon my arrival in Cradock he had rapidly filled me in on the situation and suggested that I should have meetings with both the African community leaders and a white member of the Employers' Federation 'to have the two sides of the story'. And this is how I had first met Mfabana, Makaula and the older Goniwe, who was the uncle of Matthew Goniwe – who himself was the president of the Cradock Residents' Association (CRADORA) – killed eight months earlier with three other activists. Matthew Goniwe was a charismatic young man who seemed to be destined to a great future, some even seeing in him the makings of another Steve Biko. Cremer had phoned me at the hotel to tell me that he had arranged meetings for me with Faith Collett, a white farmer who was the secretary of the Federation, and the three community leaders from Lingelihle. We were to have dinner with Faith Collett that very same evening at the Victoria.

She was younger than I had expected. Either in her late thirties or early forties, it was difficult to tell, and still attractive. She had dressed up for the occasion, using make-up liberally but not excessively; she smelled of a good perfume. After we had ordered lamb chops and a bottle of Stellenbosch wine, I asked her to tell me about her family and the farm. I summarise below what she has told me.

'The Collets go back a long time in Cradock. I belong to the fourth generation. We own a 2,500-hectare farm. It may sound a lot, but this is semi-arid land and one needs a large area to raise livestock, sheep and goats mostly, and a few cattle. We also grow some lucerne, which you call alfalfa in the States, I believe. We have three African families living on the farm. They have their own separate quarters. The men look after the herds and the crops in the fields, the women work as maids and cooks in the house. Their money wage is small, but they also get a sheep or a goat per family every month, as well as a bag of flour – mealie meal – some sugar and cooking oil. They prefer it that way. If you gave them everything in money, they would spend it during the first two weeks of the month and have nothing to eat in the last two. We also give them some clothes. All in all, I should think that the average family income is about R200 [less than £50] a month, which is not too bad. I admit that my lifestyle is a privileged one and that the system is essentially a feudal one. We live in a very big house and I couldn't imagine life without the servants. My two children go to a boarding school in Grahamstown at a total cost of about R11,000 a year. These days I can't afford to go to the UK every year, only once every two or three years. I have enough to fall back on, even if "they" took the farm away.'

Faith Collett did not have any conscience problem because she believed she was a much better employer than her Boer neighbours. I had shuddered at the thought of how the Boers might be treating their own workers. . . .

On the following morning I had an appointment at 10 o'clock with the three African community leaders and I was beginning to get worried because they were more than a half an hour late, when a white minibus had pulled up in front of Cremer's house and three elderly-looking gentlemen had come out of it. They were Mfabana, Goniwe and Makaula. After the usual preliminaries we got down to business and I asked them about the murder of the four young activists. They were all certain that the security services were behind it.

'They wanted to get rid of them,' Mfabana had said, 'especially of Matthiew Goniwe who they thought was dangerous, from their point of view, like a bad apple contaminating the rest.'

'I saw my nephew's body,' Goniwe had added, 'right after they found them. He was all burned, but not his underclothes, which means that they were put on after he was killed and burned, probably to prevent identification. Also, after having attended an afternoon meeting at the UDF office in Port Elizabeth, they had left at 9.15 pm, saying that they were driving straight home and that they would not stop on the road, except for the police. There was some additional circumstantial evidence, like the posting of a new security chief in Cradock just before the killing, and so on. We then talked about the consumer boycott which had continued for about five months very effectively before it was called off just before the Christmas season. They had made four demands and threatened to resume the boycott if they were not met: higher wages for Africans; the end of the discrimination in favour of the Coloureds; a township improvement programme for Lingelihle; and the arrest and punishment of the murderers of the four activists. In the following four months or so there had been some progress insofar as the first three demands were concerned, but not the fourth. While the regional UDF leadership had been discussing whether to resume the boycott or not, they were overtaken by much larger events: the general State of Emergency which was proclaimed on 12 June 1986 and the thousands arrests of activists that had followed it.

All that had happened six years ago. Here we were again in April 1992, Mfabana, Goniwe and I, plus Barayi who had 'replaced' Makaula who had passed away, sitting around in the same room in Cremer's house. Cremer himself had looked in before going to the office to make sure that everything was all right and to inform us that 'you'll be served some tea in a while'. He was past seventy now but he had not changed much. 'Very busy,' he had told me when I had first seen him, 'what with all these changes, I have to work even during the weekends!'

I was pleased to see Mfabana and Goniwe again and they seemed to be pleased to see me. 'Six years can be both a long and a short time,' I said. 'There have been some very dramatic changes at the national level, to say the least, in the last two years or so. What about here in Cradock? Have your lives changed noticeably?'

'There have been some good and some bad things,' Mfabana said philosophically. 'They've tarred the main street in Lingelihle, that's a good thing. They have also built some houses with government subsidies. But we still have no electricity. You know the new policy is to bring Cradock and the two townships – Lingelihle and Michausdal – together in a single town council, but before that can happen we must elect our own representatives; we don't have any councillors since we rejected the Black Local Authorities that had been appointed by the government.'

'All that seems very promising indeed. What about the bad things that happened?' I asked.

'Well, there are no jobs. Unemployment is our biggest problem. Many people haven't got the money to pay their rents. Other people keep coming from the rural areas; they are losing their jobs because of the drought, and our squatter area is getting bigger and bigger.'

'Are there many Conservative Party supporters in Cradock?' I wanted to know.

'It is a Nationalist stronghold,' Barayi answered this time. 'About the new houses,' he added, 'only the government employees can afford them. Teachers, nurses, social workers. I myself live in a council house and we still have to use the bucket system, there is no underground sewerage.'

'What about the attitudes? Are the whites nicer, friendlier towards the blacks?'

'Some are moving with the tide, others are not,' Mfabana answered. 'It is human nature, some take longer. In America you have the Deep South, in South Africa we have the Deep North,' Mfabana chuckled. 'But blacks are moving into the white areas all the time. I know of four houses on Market Street alone that have been bought by blacks. So, you see,' he noted, rubbing his thumb and forefinger together, 'now the snake is one, it is the cash.' He chuckled again. 'Yes, there is only one snake now,' he repeated, 'the cash. If you have it you can move to town.' The other two nodded emphatically.

'But how are the white neighbours taking it?' I enquired.

'Some are taking it well, others not,' Goniwe answered this time. 'A few weeks ago a Coloured friend of mine bought a house over the hill in the upscale area. A few days later I was driving past and I saw a big van parked in front of the house next door. They were loading the furniture.'

'You see, they are going to do that for a long time, they are not going to accept you as a neighbour, but you cannot really blame them, that's the way they were educated in their schools for three hundred years. They were always told that the white man was the boss. They are going to have a hard time to change,' concluded Mfabana. 'By the way do you know that Mr Africa bought the Victoria Hotel?'

I was startled. 'They sold the Victoria Hotel to an African?'

'Yes, and not only that. Mr Africa also bought the Cradock Inn in Michausdal, the bakery near the charge office, the Savoy Inn downtown, and a big house on this very street, a little further up. So he is establishing a real presence over here in Cradock, you might say. In fact, I think that he is preparing to move back to

Cradock. He now lives in Port Elizabeth, but he is a Cradock-born fellow. As a matter of fact, we grew up together. We used to play football together, and all that jazz.'

I was nonplussed by all that I had heard. This was a quantum leap. Mfabana was right: there was only one 'snake' now, and that was money. 'Do you remember?' I asked, 'in 1986 you told me that the white businessmen were discriminating against Africans, hiring Coloureds whenever they could. How are things now in that respect?'

'Oh, they can't do that now,' said Mfabana, but he was interrupted by Barayi: 'We've got a supermarket here owned by Mr Tem. He is a Chinaman and a very progressive man and I don't have anything against him. But what surprises me is that although we supported him during the boycott, you don't see any of our people working in his store.'

'They are probably driving the lorries outside,' said Mfabana. 'Even so. I don't blame Mr Tem, the trouble lies with us, not with him. We have never approached him on this issue. We should go to see him and tell him, "Mr Tem, we've never boycotted your store during the troubled times. So why do you go only for the Coloureds? What about the blacks?" If you go to OK [Bazaar], you will find a lot of blacks inside.'

Cremer's maid, a black woman, brought tea and some cookies. The mood is very relaxed by now. 'Cradock must be a real ANC stronghold,' I said.

'There has never been any other [black] party branch here in Cradock for as long as I can remember,' Mfabana confirmed.

Playing the devil's advocate, I expressed some doubts as to the ANC's ability to deliver the goods once they came to power. Mfabana, misconstruing my meaning, said: 'Man, as far as I am concerned, and I am voicing only my own views now, if the ANC comes to power as the next South African government, I don't see any problems for the whites, or for the Coloureds, or for any other nation. But the whites will have to support the ANC, because no government can operate without money.'

'Yes, but what if they come to power and they look after their own interests only, and nothing much changes for the people,' I insisted.

'Honestly I can't see why the ANC would not fight for the people,' Mfabana said. 'But when I say people, I mean everyone.

As far as the ANC is concerned, the people is everyone, not only the blacks.'

'I've got one fear,' Goniwe said, 'and that is, when there is a black government, some of our people will want things without really working for them. We black people have sometimes a problem, and that is that we don't have enough respect for other black people. That, I am afraid can create problems for a black government.'

'What about the schools?' I asked, changing the subject. 'Did they open the white schools to the other races?'

'Yes, they did,' Mfabana replied. 'But how many blacks will be able to attend those schools? That's my problem. Because the school fees are too high now, and our people are poor. We have very few middle-class people. The whites don't want to share what they have. What is theirs is theirs. That's why Mugabe is going for the [white] farms now, because it is the only way. The ANC will have to do the same thing.'

Later they took me to Lingelihle so that I could see for myself all the changes that had taken place. It was 6 April a national holiday: the day Jan van Riebeek and his small band of colonists had first set foot on the Cape peninsula in 1652.

'You see,' Mfabana observed, 'all the holidays that we have are white holidays. All the public monuments that we have are white monuments. We blacks have nothing.'

I found the township much better than the impression of it that was stored in my memory. The main street was indeed tarred, the council houses somehow looked less run down; there were fewer rusting carcasses, fewer rubbish piles, fewer mangy dogs sniffing around; and everything was not covered by dust. The new housing development on the hill above the river bend was quite impressive: three-, even four-bedroomed houses, surrounded by lawns and flower beds that would not have looked out of place in a white middle-class suburb. As we walked by, Mfabana stopped to greet a woman who was watering her flowers. 'She is a social worker,' he told me later. 'That one over there is a teacher.' All the houses have septic tanks that need to be emptied once every two years or so. A few of the owners bought power generators for electricity. The houses are worth between R40,000 and R60,000 (approximately £10,000 – £15,000). Often the government pays 90 per cent of the bonds, or mortgages, the aim being to create a new black middle class, 'with something to lose'.

I wanted to see the Cradock Inn which was bought by Mr Africa, so we drove over to Michausdal. It is an ordinary motel type of establishment with fifteen rooms or so. But it was closed on account of the holiday. So we had some soft drinks in the only open place that we could find, a small 'supermarket' that sold practically everything that the residents of the township might need on a day-to-day basis. As I took leave from my three friends, dropping them off one after the other where they lived in Lingelihle, I wondered if I was ever going to see them again. I liked them. They were, I felt, fully human in a way that we Europeans sometimes are not. In our endless quest for more we have lost something which they haven't . . . yet.

Keith Cremer was reading Guy Butler's latest book when I arrived. Guy Butler is a local author who writes about local things, in Olive Schreiner's tradition. He used to teach at Rhodes, but he is now retired and lives in Grahamstown. I had been to visit Olive Schreiner's house in Cradock which has been turned into a small museum, but it was closed. It is an ordinary little house with a corrugated iron roof. Lunch with Cremer was pleasant: chicken, potatoes, vegetables and a fruit salad. We talked about politics, but also about personal matters. He told me that he had lost his sister lately; she had a cancer and it was difficult at the end. He is an old bachelor and has been living by himself for a long time now. A certain nostalgic feeling creeps over me when I meet people like him. They are the last of a breed, the last of an era. You know that when they are gone, they are not going to be replaced. He told me that in the heyday of grand apartheid, in Strijdom's days, they went to such grotesque extremes it was unbelievable. They wanted to move the entire African population back and forth between the white areas and the black bantustans at the end of every 'bloody week', so that the point that they were migrants, and not residents, was made plainly. 'It was no joke, you know,' he said, 'these guys were deadly serious. They were talking about hiring boats, trucks, and what have you. There were stories in the papers. Incredible absurdities of that sort.'

Later Cremer told me also about the day, not long ago, when his car was stoned at Lingelihle. 'I had finished my business there and was driving on the dirt road that leads from the edge of the township to the main road, when a stone hit the side window next to me. It was a big stone.' He cupped his hand to show the size of a tennis ball. 'And I can tell you I didn't stop to find out who it was, I just drove on. I was pretty shaken for a while.' Upon hearing about the incident the black leaders of Lingelihle had come to his office to apologise and that was that. 'You never know what is going to happen,' he said thoughtfully. 'We don't really know the blacks.' That is the same point that Rian Malan makes over and over again in his excellent book, *My Traitor's Heart*: blacks know the whites far better than whites know the blacks.[1] So what? So they can bide their time to settle some old accounts? Maybe. Anyway, it is not Keith Cremer's problem. The future doesn't belong to him.

The news broke long after I had left Cradock. *The New Nation*, a weekly journal whose editor is Zwelakhe Sisulu, son of Albertina and Walter, published a secret document that appeared to be authentic, dated 7 June 1985, authorising the 'permanent removal from society' of Matthew Goniwe and two of his fellow activists.[2] Three weeks later Goniwe and the three others were dead. Even more shockingly the document is signed by Brigadier Chris van der Westhuizen, who in 1993 was still a general and chief of military intelligence. So my friends Mfabana, Goniwe and Makaula had been right all along: it is virtually certain that the security services had in cold blood arranged for the assassination of Goniwe and his friends. The odd thing was that I had not even raised the issue when I was in Cradock six weeks earlier.

Notes

1 Details in Note 9 Chapter 6.

2 More so than even the Mbekis (Govan, comrade-in-arms and close friend of Mandela; Thabo, his son, the national chairman of the ANC and heir apparent; Moeletsi, Thabo's younger brother, an author and journalist), the Sisulus are the pre-eminent black political family of South Africa. Walter, also a close friend and associate of Mandela, is deputy president of the ANC; Albertina, his wife, is the deputy president of the ANC's Women's League (Gertrude Shope is president). Women have always played an important, but sometimes unrecognised, role in the liberation struggle. In the ANC's July 1991 conference, 17 per cent of the 2,000 plus delegates and 18 per cent of the newly elected NEC members were

women. Not satisfied with these numbers, they staked a claim for a minimum of 30 per cent quota, which was refused after a lively five-hour-long debate.

13

Being Super Rich in South Africa: the Menells of Anglovaal

'There is obviously a cut-off point,' she said. If they make it too difficult
for the privileged classes, then we will leave.'

Irene Menell

It was in March 1986 that I met Joe Menell for the first time. He was coming out of the UDF office on the sixth floor of the old Khotso House (which burned down later in a fire thought to be of criminal origin) when I almost bumped into him. He had just bought some 'Free Mandela' and 'Viva UDF' T-shirts which he was carrying under his arm. I was going in. It was my second attempt to catch Murphy Morobe, who was the acting publicity secretary of the UDF, while the titular, Patrick 'Terror' (nickname due to his soccer-playing skills) Lekota, one of the top leaders of the ANC, was in gaol since April 1985. The office was almost barren of furniture and empty except for a young man typing laboriously on an old typewriter and a girl who sold the posters and the T-shirts. I was not really surprised because I had read in the papers that the office had been raided twice by the police in the last two months and that Morobe himself had gone underground to avoid arrest.

Joe, probably in his early forties, was quite tall and slightly overweight. He had long, blond, wavy and dishevelled hair, thinning out on the top of his head, and clear blue eyes. He wore blue denim jeans, a white Madras cotton shirt and old brown leather boots. Slung over his shoulder was a colourful Greek bag made of coarse wool. On impulse I asked him if he was from California. I had lived in Berkeley for two years from 1981 to 1983 and he reminded me of a type of person that was common in the Bay area – tanned, laidback and casually dressed. He gave a start and said that he indeed lived in the Big Sur, which is not far from San Francisco, but that he had been born and brought up in South Africa. I told him that I was doing research for a book on apartheid. That clearly aroused his interest and he suggested that we go and have a beer together and chat. We went to the nearest cafeteria which was not far and sat down. He said that he was on one of his sporadic visits to South Africa to see his family, primarily his old mother who was in her early eighties. In California, he said, he made documentary films for PBS, the public TV channel. The last one he made was apparently on the undocumented Mexican workers who were badly exploited in the LA area. His next one would be on endangered species such as the American condor or the bald eagle, or something like that.

After these preliminaries, the conversation turned to the subject we were both interested in, namely South African politics. For Joe it was simple: the Afrikaners would never give up power unless they had to, therefore the use of force or violence would be necessary. He had had problems in the past with the government which had confiscated his passport for a while and he was not allowed to work in South Africa. We discovered that we would both be in Cape Town in about three weeks and he gave me his telephone number there. 'Give me a ring as soon as you get there,' he said as we parted.

I had been in the 'Mother City' for two days when one morning as I was walking in a busy street, I suddenly felt a hand patting on my shoulder from behind. It was Joe, looking exactly as he did in Jo'burg. He seemed genuinely pleased to see me and again we went to the nearest café and brought each other up to date on what we had done in the meanwhile. He then told me that he was involved in the organisation of a festival of South African theatre at the Lincoln Center in New York and that he was trying to get as many black South African playwrights as possible to participate. That was one of his reasons for coming back to South Africa at this time, he confessed. 'I'm going to see a play tomorrow night at the Baxter [a fine arts centre at UCT],' he said. 'Would you like to come along? You could come and have dinner with us at the house if you want, and then we could go and see the play together. Besides, I'd like you to meet my mother.' I accepted and before we separated he gave me directions to the 'farm'.

It was close to six when, after missing it once, I found the little rusty sign partly hidden behind a bush by the side of the road with a barely legible 'Glen Dirk Estate' on it. The place was in the outskirts of Wynberg, one of the good white residential suburbs of Cape Town. Two hundred metres or so on a bumpy dirt road and an old white mansion came into view. I parked the car next to two others that were there and rang the bell. A white-haired black butler opened the door and, after I introduced myself, said with a little bow that I was expected and showed me in. He took me through a big lobby into a sitting room. There were two women in the room, one was very old, the other one young, in her early- or mid-twenties at the most. They were Rachel (Ray) Menell, Joe's mother, and Sue Menell, Joe's niece, the oldest of his brother Clive's five children. The old lady was a small woman with a finely chiselled face. Her blueish white hair was impeccably permed. She was mentally very alert. Sue was tall, big-bosomed and very reserved. We made polite conversation until, ten minutes later, Joe materialised, the same debonair self, wearing exactly the same clothes as the two previous times. He asked me if I would interested in a tour of the property before it got too dark.

'The house was built in 1897,' he explained as we were crossing the big lobby on our way out. The ceilings were very high, the furniture sparse, but in mint condition. 'So, it is not an original Cape-Dutch colonial, but as close to it as you can get.' We started walking on an alley bordered by tall pines. 'The estate has about 250 hectares (600 acres) of very good land and, as you can see, most of it planted in grapevines. It's all leased out to a farmer now, we just kept the house and use it as a vacation place. Dad bought the estate planning to retire in it, but he died before he could do it.' Joe's father had emigrated to South Africa from Lithuania as a little boy with his parents to escape anti-Semitism. In 1933, with an associate called Hersov, he had founded the Anglovaal corporation and made his fortune in mining.

'You see those big trees over there?' Joe said pointing at them, 'they are horse chestnuts, some of them are over a century old.' High above, over the wooded ridges of the distant hills, white clouds tinged with gold, purple and an emerald green travelled swiftly on the sky which was quickly darkening. Suddenly, two or three big birds rose from a thicket and flew lumberingly away. 'Guinea fowl,' explained Joe. 'Mum says they gorge themselves with grapes, that's why they are so fat. They can barely fly. She enforces a strict ban against shooting them. "Not while I am still alive," she says.' We walked silently for a while. I was impressed, I had never been in such a place before. It made me think of Tara in *Gone With the Wind*. I sort of expected Scarlett to jump out from behind a bush followed by Rhett. Maybe, they would even wave at us. My daydream was interrupted by Joe who, as if he had read my thoughts, said: 'Perhaps the place can be converted into a presidential retreat one day. Wouldn't it be great if the Mandelas came to live here one day? It would be a shame to subdivide it into smaller plots.' Well, I was not sure it was a good thing for Mandela to live in a place such as this. But it was a romantic idea. I assumed that Joe thought of it as a form of poetic justice, so I didn't say anything, I didn't want to break the spell.

Back in the sitting room it was time for an apéritif. We all had a sherry. On a bookshelf against the opposite wall, some old photos in stand-up frames attracted my attention. Some of the faces on them seemed somehow familiar. I pointed them out to Joe who grinned and said: 'Oh yes, of course, that's Monty [Field-Marshal Bernard Montgomery, victor of Rommel at Alamein]. He often came and stayed at the estate in the old days when Father was still alive. He was quite old by then and wanted to get away from the cold and dampness in England, I suppose. Father liked him because he thought that he, Monty, had saved the Jews in Palestine. But I hated him. He was a very taciturn man. Just walked around the estate endlessly all by himself.' His face brightened. 'That's Henry [Ford II, the automobile magnate]. A very friendly, very jovial fellow. The typically outgoing, extroverted American, with his wife Christina. He was a very good friend of Father's.'

The old butler came to announce that 'dinner is served'. The matriarch led the way and we filed out of the sitting room, crossed the lobby again, and went into the dining room. 'Cornelius [the butler] and Raphael [another servant] have been with us for more than forty years, we consider them as almost members of the family,' Joe said. An imposing chandelier hung from the ceiling above the oval table which was covered with a white linen table-cloth and matching napkins. The cutlery was silver, the crockery fine china and the wine glasses cut crystal. The main dish, chicken casserole, was served in a silver bowl covered with a bell-shaped lid. The wine was an excellent red (Shiraz) Cabernet appropriately named *Haane Pot* (Chicken Leg). Cornelius and Raphael, impeccably attired in immaculate white jackets and gloves, waited at the table. The old lady herself served the chicken, asking each of us in turn if we preferred a 'white' or a 'brown'. Conversation was light, nothing political.

We went to the Baxter in two cars. Joe and Sue in Joe's car in front and I followed in mine. The Baxter is a modern building, but appealingly so. A large foyer at the bottom level adjoined two auditoriums, one for plays, the other for films. The galleries on the top floors are used for pictorial exhibitions. In fact, a photographic exhibition named, 'South Africa in Conflict: Protest, Resistance, Power' was being shown jointly with an Antiwar Film Festival organised by the End Conscription Campaign. When we arrived the play, *Bhopa!* written and directed by Percy Mtwa, was about to begin. The theatre was almost full, with perhaps half of the audience black, that is, mostly made up of Coloured people. The lights soon went out and the show was under way. It was clearly produced on a shoestring budget. It had a small cast of three or four actors who each played several roles. Accessories were reduced to a minimum: a few hats, sticks and false noses and moustaches. The stage was bare except for a table and a couple of chairs. The plot had to do with apartheid as lived by the members of an African family. The word *Bhopa*, which here is best translated as 'protest', also means 'arrest' or 'detention' in Zulu. The main characters of the play, which takes place in Eastern Cape, are Micah and Zweli Mangena. The former is a black master-sergeant in the South African police; he is strong and loyal, but not very bright; he does not question authority. The latter, his son, becomes active in the anti-apartheid struggle in the early 1980s. Soon the father and the son must reassess their relationship: Zweli accuses Micah of 'collaborating' with the racist regime; Micah accuses Zweli of ingratitude, he has sacrificed himself to support his family. At the end of the play the primacy of the struggle is recognised by all and *Nkosi Sikelel' iAfrika* is sung by the whole cast with many members of the audience joining in. It was not top-drawer theatre (a bit too predictable), but it was powerful emotionally and the actors were good and versatile: they could not only act, but could also sing and dance. *Bhopa!* was made into an American film in 1993, starring Danny Glover as Micah and directed by Morgan Freeman.

After the show was over we went to the bar to meet Percy Mtwa. Joe tried to convince him to participate in the *Woza Afrika* (Come

Back Africa) Festival in New York: the festival's director is Duma Ndlovu, who used to be a close associate of Steve Biko; Mbogeni Ngema will be there with his play *Asinamali* ('We Have No Money' in Zulu). Less than a month ago, Ngema was the object of an assassination attempt in Durban where his play was being shown. His would-be assassins were widely believed to be Inkatha-associated vigilantes. Then the conversation veered to white South African anti-apartheid playwrights. Apparently Ndlovu, in an interview published in *Newsweek*, had accused Athol Fugard of taking all the credit for black theatre in South Africa. He had also attacked Barney Simon, the white co-founder of Jo'burg's Market Theatre Company, whose play *Born in the RSA* would also be shown in New York. M Manaka, another black South African playwright, had said that white writers could not be legitimate witnesses of black oppression.

At some point during the conversation, a black South African journalist joined us at our table. I raised with him the issue of censorship. I told him that I was rather amazed to see books such as Lelyveld's *Move Your Shadow* and North's *Freedom Rising*, both severe condemnations of apartheid, as well as radical left-wing journals like *New Era* and *Work in Progress*, sold freely in the stores.[1] He looked at me condescendingly, like one would a very gullible and naïve person, and said: 'But it doesn't really matter, my friend. Such publications are read by a relatively small elite. It's like preaching to the already pious. What really counts is what is published in the mass-circulation newspapers and television, and there censorship is ruthless.'

Before we left, we went upstairs to visit the photographic exhibition which was described as a 'compendium of atrocities committed by the apartheid regime'. Many of the pictures were familiar, having been published earlier in newspapers and magazines: Casspirs and Buffels surrounded by heavily armed, helmeted men holding shields on their arms; soldiers and policemen clutching shotguns and *sjamboks*; mean alsatians straining on their leashes, snarling and ready to pounce; clouds of tear gas and crowds scrambling to get away from them; people dragged out from matchbox houses by uniformed men; migrant workers sitting on concrete slabs that served as beds in the seedy hostels of the townships; and so on. On a small table at the end of the exhibition was a Visitor's Book. Some of the comments in it reflected, I thought, better than anything else, what I had seen or read until then, the bitter division of white South Africans amongst themselves, even though some of the comments in the book might have been written by blacks, of course. Here is a personal selection:

> Totally biased towards the radicals, show the other side of the coin as well.
> *You mean to say you failed to see it. Look again. It's there staring you in your fucking stupid face.*

> Where are the blacks that were necklaced?
> *That's not the point. The point is the senselessness of apartheid and all that shit.*

> Africa for Africans.
> *What about White Africans?*

> Thank Heavens for the police. Without them we might already have been burnt alive.
> *You will be burnt alive anyway, you fascist bastard.*

> Please stop all this pain, so that we can share the real things – like living.
> *Give us more of that truth!*

> One solution: Revolution.
> *Revolution: No solution.*

> P W is like a mudguard: All shiny on top, all shit underneath.
> *Botha is our last chance.*

> Only Jesus is the solution.
> *Where has He been all this fucking time.*

I saw Joe again in Jo'burg two weeks later. It was Passover and he invited me to join his family and a few close friends for the *Seder* (Passover meal), which was to be celebrated at his mother's flat. I met him at the Sunnyside, an old colonial hotel near where she lived in the Houghton Estates. It was quite a shock to see Joe in a suit and tie. We had a couple of beers while waiting for another guest, an old army man, Joe said, who had served under Smuts during the Second World War. The 'Colonel' was very old indeed, very thin, stooped and walking shakily with the help of a cane. We took Joe's car and about three minutes later we were in his mother's apartment which was brightly lit for the occasion. It showed a great deal of opulence but in good taste, nothing gaudily or offensively luxurious.

Several of the guests had already arrived. Some were old friends of the matriarch, Latvian and Lithuanian Jews whose parents or even themselves had escaped persecution in the Baltic States. I was introduced to everyone, including Clive, Joe's brother, and Irene his wife. Sue, whom I had met in Cape Town, was also there. Immediately I was struck by the contrast between the two brothers. Clive looked every bit the business tycoon that he is – 'he takes care of the family's diversified business interests', was the euphemistic way Joe had described him to me at the hotel. He looked fiftyish, was very thin, narrow and tall, and had the finely chiselled good looks of his mother. He wore a dark grey, pinstriped suit and exuded the unmistakable self-confidence of the rich and powerful. He spoke in the low and measured tones of someone who was educated in expensive private schools. Irene, past her prime, but still attractive, was well groomed, vivacious, intelligent and active in politics.

We were thirteen around the long rectangular table richly festooned for the occasion. I admired the quality of all the ritual objects – the big *Seder* plate, the candlesticks, the vessels, the cups – which were of massive silver and beautifully chased. Rachel Menell was resplendent in a black brocade dress. I was placed between Irene's mother, an old Latvian lady, and Sue who was as reserved as in Cape Town. Clive, in his capacity as head of the family, officiated at the head of the table. He read in English the *Haggadah* (in Hebrew 'the Narration'), which is the story of the Jews' exodus from Egypt and of their forty years in the wilderness of the Sinai before God permitted them to enter the Promised Land. The book was passed around the table so that everyone could read a paragraph from it. Later as I munched a piece of *matzoh* (unleavened bread, as they did not have yeast in the desert) and tasted a leaf of the *maror* (a bitter herb symbolising the hardships in the desert), I remembered my conversation with Mfabana from Lingelihle: was Mandela a present-day black Moses who would lead the South African blacks to the Promised Land?

After we finished reading the *Haggadah*, I asked Irene's mother what she thought was going to happen in South Africa. She paused for a long moment and then she said: 'I've lived through two

Russian Revolutions, the First World War, the rise of fascism in Europe, the Second World War and the Holocaust, and all the wars between the Israelis and the Arabs. There is no end to it, you know, and now it is coming here. You just can't do anything to stop it. I am too old to care about myself any more. But I worry about the young ones. There is no future for them in this country.'

Then we chatted with Irene herself. The word in 1986 was that she would try to replace Helen Suzman, the veteran liberal politician, when she finally decided to retire from politics in a year or two. Irene, who studied law, was an elected Member of the Provincial Council, which was recently abolished by the central government, and had been active in efforts to upgrade the nearby township of Alexandra. She appeared to be sincere and honest, committed to the fight against apartheid. But will liberals matter in the no-holds-barred struggle ahead?

The *Seder* was the last time I saw Joe. I spoke to him once on the phone a year or so later. He told me that his mother had died of cancer a few months earlier, that it had been quite brutal. The *Woza Afrika* festival had been a triumph. Percy Mtwa was there and *Bhopa* was successful. He asked me how my book was coming along. When I told him that I felt that I didn't have enough for a good book and that I would probably have to go back to South Africa to do some more research he seemed disappointed. I wanted to see him but he said that he was very busy working on a new documentary and that after that he was planning to go on a cruise to Hawaii on a large sailboat that he owned jointly with a friend. Five more years went by and, as the saying goes, a lot of water flowed under the bridge: the economic and political situation further deteriorated in South Africa; P W Botha made an ignominious exit; F W de Klerk took over and made his famous speech; the ANC, PAC and SACP were unbanned and Mandela and other historic political leaders were liberated; solemn declarations were made that apartheid was on its way out, and indeed several legal bastions of it were scrapped. It was time to go back to South Africa to try to finish that book. . . .

A week or so after my arrival in Jo'burg in February 1992, I phoned Irene and we set up an appointment for the following afternoon at five at her house in Parktown. The taxi deposited me in a cul de sac at the end of a secluded, leafy alley. It was an old and very big house surrounded by a big plot of land. The residence on the other side of the cul de sac, Irene told me later, belonged to the Oppenheimer family, but Harry rarely stayed there, preferring a villa in Natal, near Durban, somewhere by the sea. I found that Irene had aged noticeably. The last remnants of youth had ebbed away from her, but she was her vivacious, loquacious self. 'We've been living in this house for thirty years now,' she said. 'We've raised all of our five children here.'

I saw two or three dogs, one of them a shaggy sheepdog with invisible eyes, the other a mongrel, all friendly anyway. 'No rottweilers?' I asked jokingly. Two or three days earlier I had read a story in the paper about an old court messenger mauled and mangled to death by three rottweilers in a northern suburb. They are increasingly popular among panicky whites who want to protect their properties against the burglars. 'Oh no,' she said, 'they are truly vicious, aren't they?'

The room we were in was spacious, with very high ceilings and two walls partly lined with shelves full of books. When I congratulated her on their large library, she said that they had sent thirteen cases of books to the house in Cape Town lately. After the death of the matriarch, they had taken over that house. We spoke about time inexorably churning on. Clive was sixty; Joe, seven years younger, fifty-three; she must be in her late fifties. She had tried to replace Helen Suzman after the latter retired finally about two years ago, but had lost the nomination contest to a certain Tony Leon, who was later elected. She acknowledged that Leon was bright and an up-and-coming man in the Democratic Party, but she was bitter about the way Leon had almost rigged the process. However, all that was in the past now and let bygones be bygones, you know, she had plenty of other things to do. She was still very active helping the party. There were many groups, delegations coming from Europe, the United States, Japan, and she hosted them, briefed them, organised things. She had been down to Cape Town the week before and she would be going again the following week. They had 'Nelson and Winnie' over to dinner the other night. It was a hectic life. She liked Mandela. She agreed that he was no figurehead. Clearly the boss, he had real power. But after him what? There was no heir apparent. The battle for succession would be fierce. Her favourite (not surprisingly) was Thabo Mbeki, but he was not the leading candidate, far from it. Ramaphosa was in a far stronger position, and there was Chris Hani, who could become the real power behind the throne (not any more, of course, he was assassinated in April 1993). We talked about the future of the Democratic Party. She agreed that it probably could not survive as an independent political party because the National Party had appropriated all its policies. But one could not entirely forget the authoritarian past of the Nats. It was still difficult to believe that they had become true democrats. Can a leopard change its spots? Some suspicion remained. De Klerk himself was a *Dopper*. It was possible that he had a hidden agenda: he openly rejected the idea of the majority rule. What is democracy if not domination by the majority? So there might still be a niche for the Democratic Party as the champion of liberal values.

In the meantime Clive had come back home from work. But he didn't join us. As I was on my way out an hour or so later, I saw that he was watching the news on TV in the company of Kathy, their youngest daughter. I waved to him and he waved back, but remained seated. This is when the idea first crossed my mind that he might not be very happy about my investigations. I saw Irene once more about ten days later. I had telephoned and told her that I still had a few more things that I wanted to know. She invited me over for a light lunch and I could see immediately that she was reticent, reluctant. 'We like to keep a low profile,' she said at one point.

'But, you have nothing to hide, do you?'

'No, obviously not.'

I asked her about Joe. 'Oh, he is all right. He is still in California, putting together a chat show for one of the local stations. He and Keith [Irene's and Clive's son] will be going on a two-week cruise in the Caribbean – Joe sold his half of the boat, so they will be renting one. We are expecting Joe in December. Mary [another of Irene's daughters] is getting married, he'll be coming to the wedding. Clive's very busy as usual. We've been to a party that Mandela threw for Whoopi Goldberg and Paul Simon at the house of a young Afrikaner millionaire in one of the northern suburbs. There were probably two hundred people when we arrived, we didn't stay very long.'

We spoke of literature; inevitably of Nadine Gordimer. 'She is a good writer of course. But we don't see her often, because Clive doesn't like her very much [some think that she and her husband are really Marxists]. Yes, she is a bit too conscious of style. Style is like make-up, the less you notice it the better.' She, Irene, preferred Coetzee. '*Waiting for the Barbarians* is one of my favourite novels. The best apocalyptic novel that I've ever read.' Black South African writers? There were quite a few good ones, in the 1950s and 1960s particularly – Alex la Guma, Richard Rive, Es'Kia Mphahlele, Lewis Nkosi. Then the quality went down. She had another appointment at two. I asked her point blank to tell me candidly if they would still stay in South Africa if the going got really tough.

'There is obviously a cut-off point,' she said. 'If they make it too difficult for the privileged classes, then we will leave. We know many people overseas. I like England, Clive prefers America.' Before I left I told her that I wanted to see Clive in his office at Anglovaal. She gave me the telephone number of his appointments secretary and a copy of Anglovaal's annual report. But my numerous attempts to secure a meeting with Clive were unsuccessful. I had to face the fact that Clive did not want to see me.

I decided to go to the municipal library to have a look at McGregor's *Who Owns Whom* whose 1992 edition had just come out. The McGregor has long been a kind of Bible for all those – muck-racking journalists, left-wing politicians, academic researchers, and so on – interested in the nooks and crannies of South African Big Business. It is indeed very comprehensive in its coverage but owes much of its fame to its introduction, which concentrates on the seven major groups that dominate the South African economy. The white capitalists that run the Seven Majors don't, to say the least, like the McGregor because it lists the names, not only of the controlling shareholder companies but also of the directors that sit on their boards. It is a frontal attack on the country's 'inbred corporate culture and the incestuous nature of its business activities'. It shows that the Seven Majors invest heavily in each other's companies and subsidiaries and that they exchange directorships. The new leader in the multiple directorship stakes is a certain Clem Sunter, the head of Anglo-American's gold and uranium division, who presently holds seats on the boards of 23 companies big enough to be listed on the Johannesburg Stock Exchange (JSE). Parodoxically enough Sunter, a man still young with a modern outlook, keeps a high profile and has plenty of imaginative and progressive ideas not only on how to deal with low productivity, but also how to tackle inequality and social injustice.

I found out quite a bit about Anglovaal. It is controlled by the Menell and Hersov families and is one of the Seven Majors but not one of the Big Four which are: Anglo, of course, which includes De Beers, the diamond giant, and is controlled by the Oppenheimer family; the Sanlam Group, which includes Gencor, itself a big conglomerate with mining, oil and paper interests, and the Metropolitan Life Insurance company; the Rembrandt Group, which includes Rothmans tobacco and is controlled by the Rupert and Hertzog families; and the South African Mutual Life Assurance, which includes Barlow Rand. Unbelievably, the Big Four control more than 80 per cent of all the stocks listed on the JSE. Then come Liberty Life, Anglovaal and Ventrom (not necessarily in that order), that probably control virtually the rest of the stock listed on the JSE.

Another indication of the excessive domination of the South African economy by the Seven Majors is the large number of people that work for them. Anglo and Sanlam employ, between them, over a million workers, which is half of the total employed by the private sector as a whole (the manufacturing sector employs 1.4 million people and the mining sector, 670,000; the public sector employs an additional 1.6 million people). So there is in South Africa a degree of concentration of economic power that is unheard of in market economies. The ANC's current professed strategy is, in addition to nationalising banks and mines, to break up the white corporate power through forced divestiture and aggressive antitrust laws.[2]

Compared with Anglo and Sanlam, Anglovaal is small: in 1991 it employed about 82,000 people and had a global turnover of about ten billion rands (roughly £2.3 billion). Profits after taxes amounted to about a billion rands. The Menell and Hersov families control it through Anglovaal Holdings of which they hold 51.6 per cent of the stock (which was valued at about six hundred million rands in 1991). The company was founded by the fathers of Clive Menell and Basil Hersov who are the present co-chairmen. It's become a quite diversified business empire with major investments (in that order) in: packaging and rubber, base metals and minerals, gold mining, branded consumer goods and fishing and frozen foods. Interestingly enough, about 25 per cent of revenue is generated currently from interest and financial services, which represent only four per cent of investments. Politics is inevitably a major concern these days. At the conclusion of his chairman's review in the share-holders' meeting of December 1991, Basil Hersov declared that the future of South Africa will require 'cool heads, clear minds and much determination. President de Klerk, Mr Mandela and Chief Minister Buthelezi have demonstrated these qualities and deserve the support of all South Africans in their endeavours in this regard [bringing about a non-racial, democratic and prosperous country]. . . . Compromise is essential. . . . A political settlement, however, cannot be lasting without economic changes that address the disparities in society arising from past policies.'

Well, Anglovaal, like the other Seven Majors, is obviously scrambling to show that it is a company with a social conscience. A 'consultative committee' (with several blacks sitting on it) was formed in 1991 to 'assist senior group executives to develop appropriate policies and practices'. The money allocated to the major subsidiaries to help community development projects in their respective areas was increased, and funds were distributed to 'various national charitable and educational institutions'. Dr Oscar Dhlomo, until recently Chief Buthelezi's number two man, and Enos Mabuza, who resigned as chief minister of KaNgwane (he is the founder of the *Inyandza* movement which supports the ANC), were appointed to the board of directors of the mother company, Anglovaal Ltd which until then had been lily-white.

So, Anglovaal seems belatedly applying the maxim of the late Prime Minister John Vorster, 'Adapt or Die'. The question is: Is it too little too late? I have a hunch that a lot more will have to be done including a wealth tax for the super rich to compensate for the inequities of the past.

Notes

1 J Lelyveld's *Move Your Shadow: South Africa Black and White*, Penguin, 1985, was a winner of the Pulitzer prize. J North's *Freedom Rising*, Plume, 1985, New York, is also one of the good books published in the mid eighties.

2 It seems that the white corporate bosses are finally getting the message. In June 1993 Sanlam announced that: one, it was breaking up Gencor and divesting the oil and paper companies; and two, it was beginning to sell its controlling interests in the Metropolitan Life to a black-controlled consortium. What makes this initiative even more interesting is that

Sanlam, like the Rembrandt Group, is Afrikaner-controlled. One would have expected the Anglos to take the lead. The reason is perhaps that the Afrikaners are more concerned about surviving in South Africa than the Anglos, seeing themselves as the 'white tribe' of South Africa.

14

Travel Notes One:
Kimberley and Cape Town

'When anyone tampers with your home, they tamper with your soul.
And when they tamper with your soul, that's death.'
Naz Ebrahim

I decided to take the train from Johannesburg to Cape Town to stop in Kimberley for a day or two to do some research there.[1] I enjoy travelling by train. I like the feeling of moving into a new reality slowly, gradually. Besides there is something about travelling by train that makes candid conversation a possibility. This is probably in large part due to the idea that a traveller's chance of meeting his or her fellow traveller in the future, and of being thus embarrassed of any indiscretions that he or she might have made, is very slim indeed. That is an advantage for someone looking for reliable information in an unfamiliar country.

Be that as it may, in the first leg of my journey I happened to share my compartment with a young Afrikaner soldier who had been recently commissioned second lieutenant. He was not overtly hostile or unco-operative but reserved and possibly a little suspicious. He never kept the conversation going himself or volunteered information that was not specifically asked. But he was gracious or polite enough to answer my questions succinctly, without elaborating. I thus learned that he was going to De Aar, which is an important railway junction in the middle of the Cape Province where the line branches out into three different directions: south to Cape Town, north west to Prieska and Upington and then Namibia, and south east to Port Elizabeth. From De Aar, the young officer would go to the family farm – a sheep farm – in the Karoo. It transpired that there was a kind of military tradition in his family:

his father was a major in the army before his retirement to the farm; an older brother was in the army as well; and a paternal uncle worked for the police. I asked him what he thought of the current situation. He said that the world was changing and that they had to change too. They were prepared to share the country with the blacks but that they would fight if they wanted everything. 'We are Africans too,' he affirmed. 'We have built this country and we have nowhere else to go.' It was a simple truth for him.

The train was scheduled to arrive in Kimberley at 8.45 pm. I decided to have dinner on the train. The steward placed me at the same table with a young man who also was not very communicative at first. But as the meal proceeded, possibly helped by the euphoric after effects of the wine, he opened up. It turned out that he was an Afrikaner as well working in Springbok, a mining town in Namaqaland in the north-western Cape not far from the Namibian border and the Atlantic Ocean. The area is very rich in non-ferrous materials – silver, copper and lead – and until recently, when 49 per cent was sold to private interests, the mines belonged exclusively to the state. It was a very good thing, he explained, because after the privatisation the new management made many improvements in the working conditions. His politics was more sophisticated than that of the young soldier but the message was the same. 'Oh, we'll pull through,' he said, 'we always have.' Later: 'In the Transvaal people are armed to the teeth; guns, ammunition, it's like a powder keg, ready to explode. You see, there are limits to what we can bear. We are already the most highly taxed people in the world, and they are talking of taxing us even more. People are fed up. At the end of the day there is only so much that a man can take.' What I found perturbing, even ominous was the matter-of-fact, almost casual, way that he was saying these things. There was an almost fatalistic ring to it.

At Kimberley I was one of the few passengers who disembarked. Soon they were all gone in the private cars that had come to fetch them and the station was eerily deserted. There were no taxis. I asked an Afrikaner man working at the station where all the taxis had gone and he answered that there were only two taxis in the whole town this time of the year and that one had to phone to order one. Just then a policeman came, a young Coloured man, tall and muscular, with a moustache. 'The hotel is not far,' he said, 'only two blocks away, you can easily go on foot.' I pointed at my bag and said that it was heavy and that I was not supposed to carry heavy loads because of my back. He lifted the bag – a green US army surplus bag – to see for himself how heavy it was. He then said: 'No problem, I will carry it for you.' He hoisted the bag to his shoulder and we were on our way, making small talk as we walked in the dark. The streets were empty and the town looked dead. 'This is the off season touristically,' he observed. I told him that I was not a tourist in the strict sense, that I had some research to do. He took me to the Savoy, the best, ie, the most expensive, hotel in town. I thanked him and waited until he was gone before telling the woman at the reception that I couldn't afford the R180 (£45) a night, breakfast not included. She suggested that I go to the Grand Hotel that charged only R75. She went out and came back with a tramp in tattered clothes who, she said, would carry my bag for a couple of rands. He was a rummy who reeked of alcohol but surprisingly strong. I gave him two rands, but he asked for three, he said that he was hungry. I gave him the extra rand. The Grand was an old hotel which had been remodelled recently. The room was small but it had a private bathroom with a bath, the window overlooked an inner courtyard.

As I went out the following morning, the first thing that I noticed was that there were practically no hawkers or pedlars on the pavements. The hotel was on Main Street, adjacent to Market Square which is the centre of the town. The hawkers ought to have been at their thickest here but there were virtually none. The contrast with Johannesburg was all the more striking. There the streets were literally bursting at the seams with hawkers. Like the Waikiki Beach in Hawaii at the height of the season, it was hard to find the smallest space unoccupied; the stalls were everywhere selling all sorts of consumer items, from fruits and vegetables, the commonest wares, to footwear, razors, blades, toiletries, shirts and underwear. Here the blacks appeared to be less assertive, or more subdued. Lots of Coloured people. The Boers are still very much in charge here, I thought.

I bought the local newspaper: *Diamond Fields Advertiser*, more than a century old. It had a feature called 'A Hundred Years Ago', which I read: 'Because of the influenza epidemic at the mine white workers have been doing the work of the natives and if the disease increases a serious stoppage of the mining work is imminent.' I went to the tourist office where I was furnished, by an old, colonial-looking gentleman, with a recent and illustrated brochure on Kimberley. I went through its 30 pages carefully twice. I couldn't find a single mention of a black man or woman, be he or she African or Coloured; notwithstanding the fact that large numbers of Griqua people (by far the largest component of the Coloured people; less than 10 per cent are Cape-Malay and Muslim) have lived in the area for almost two centuries; notwithstanding the fact that African labour was essential in the development of the diamond-mining industry; notwithstanding the fact that one of the most important figures of modern African political history, Robert Sobukwe the PAC leader, had lived in house detention in the Bantu location of Galeshewe for ten years or so until his death from cancer in 1978. For all intents and purposes, judging from this brochure, Kimberley could easily be a white town in the middle of a country in which the black man was unknown. The three 'sons of the soil', featured prominently in the brochure with large photographs were: Cecil Rhodes, Barney Barnato, his main rival in the diamond industry until he bought him off, and Ernest Oppenheimer, the man who took over from Cecil Rhodes – his son Harry is also present, but for some reason, no photograph.

I had come to Kimberley for two reasons, the second of which was more important: the first one was that I wanted to see with my own eyes the 'biggest man-made hole in the history of the world'; the second, I wanted to visit the house in Galeshewe where Sobukwe had died. The Big Hole, as it came to be known, is an amazing sight, one of the great monuments to human greed and, in a sense, achievement. It is more than 1,372 metres in diameter and over 2,743 metres deep, excavated entirely by the most primitive methods employed by the early diggers of diamonds in the 1870s and 1880s. Not unlike an Egyptian pyramid in reverse, it is essentially a grave, a mass grave, in fact: many thousands of men – nobody exactly knows how many – died here violently: in accidents that were a daily occurrence; because of infectious diseases; and also by the law of the gun.

'It all started here,' as the Indian pharmacist of Market Square, with whom I chatted briefly, put it in a nutshell. Indeed: the discovery of diamonds on the banks of Orange River – on a territory which was 'given' to the Griqua people because it was barren and worthless – changed the face of South Africa once and for all; gold, which was discovered a decade or so later, in the mid 1880s, in the Witswatersrand, sealed that change, made it irreversible.

Many black people came in search of work. The money would enable them to buy cattle and pay for dowries, sometimes one and the same thing. Soon, the white diggers began to agitate against the blacks. They wanted to bar the Coloureds from holding claims to dig and to regulate the African labour in the mines by a system of 'passports'. In August 1872 came Proclamation No 14 stating that any African labourer caught on the mine without a pass would be flogged. In 1875, a new Proclamation was published forbidding non-whites to hold claims or wash debris. Blacks would be tolerated in the diamond mines only as cheap, non-specialised labour. Meanwhile, the mining of diamonds had become big business: the value of diamonds exported rose dramatically from £25,000 in 1869 to £1.65 million in 1873. Living conditions in the mines were harsh even for the whites but for Africans they were abysmal. One of the important innovations introduced in Kimberley was the compounding system, according to which African labourers were put in separate labour camps (critics called them 'the De Beers monasteries of labour'), which were surrounded by barbed wire and kept out of the view of the white areas. The search for stolen diamonds involved the terrible humiliation of anal examination with an instrument called the 'speculum'. When the Africans finally rebelled in 1887 against the speculum, the method was dropped, but other draconian measures of search and control continued.[2]

I took a walk in the quiet streets of Belgravia, the old suburb of Kimberley where 'the beautiful homes reflect the opulent lifestyles of those who found fortune in the early Kimberley', as the tourist office brochure put it. I passed the Sanatorium where Cecil Rhodes had stayed during the siege of Kimberley at the beginning of the Anglo-Boer War in 1899 and the twilight of his life. As an entrepreneur, he had the unique ability to see a need before the others and to fill it, making a huge profit for himself. He was, for example, the first to have brought a large electric pump to Kimberley where the mines were flooded badly during the rainy season. He also imported the hauling equipment – the winches, the pulleys, the cables, and so on – to hoist the diamond ore to the surface. He even brought an ice-making machine for when the weather was particularly dry and hot in the summer. As a financier, he invented doing business 'in halves': the owner of a claim took one half of the profits, while the other half went to the digger who did all the work and paid all the expenses. He was barely 27 years old in 1880 when he founded the De Beers Mining Co. Five years later, he had eliminated all his competitors, including Barney Barnato (that interesting character who was part actor, part boxer and part businessman) his closest rival, and thus became the sole master of the South African diamond-mining industry. That same year, 1885, the first section of his great pet project, the Cape-to-Cairo railway, Cape-to-Kimberley, was completed. 1890 was an important year: he was elected prime minister of the Cape Colony – having been first elected to parliament in 1880 after the re-annexation of Griqualand, he had been in politics for ten years; and Zambesia (to be named Rhodesia later; the present-day Zimbabwe) was finally conquered. 1895 was a very bad year: he was one of the main conspirators behind the Jameson Raid, the unsuccessful attempt to invade the Transvaal, and was forced to resign both as prime minister and chairman of the British South Africa Company, which he had managed to have chartered by Queen Victoria herself. When he died in 1902, a disillusioned man, he was buried on the Matapos Hills in Zambesia.

Robert Mangaliso ('It is wonderful') Sobukwe belongs – with Nelson Mandela and Steve Biko; and perhaps Clements Kadalie, the union organiser of the 1920s; Chief Albert Lutuli, the ANC leader of the 1950s and 1960s and a Nobel Peace prize winner; Walter Sisulu and Oliver Tambo – to the very pantheon of black South African leaders. He was certainly one of the most influential, charismatic and inspirational African leaders of the second half of the twentieth century. He was born in 1924 in Graff Reinet in the Eastern Cape. His mother was a Pondo, one of the main tribes of the Xhosa nation; his father was Sotho. When he enrolled in 1940 in the Healdtown Institute, the biggest Methodist school in South Africa, he was one of the less than 6,000 African secondary-school students in the country. At Healdtown, young Sobukwe distinguished himself for his brilliance and command of the English language and matriculated in 1946.

One year later Sobukwe began his university studies at Fort Hare, where he first became conscious of racial discrimination and was involved in politics under the influence of Cecil Ntloko and Godfrey Pitje, two black lecturers there. He also caught the attention of A P

Mda, the ANC-Youth League's president, whose militant Programme of Action had been adopted by ANC's executive at their 1949 national conference. That same year, Sobukwe made a great speech as the outgoing Students' Representative Council (SRC) president. It is not an exaggeration to say that some of the ideas that he formulated in it are still relevant today, almost half a century later. Item: 'The Europeans and the other minorities could secure mental and spiritual freedom by learning to breathe, dream and live South Africa'. Item: 'Show the light and the masses will find the way.' In other words, the importance of providing principled leadership that involved courage, honour and imagination. He has certainly influenced greatly Steve Biko and his followers in the BC movement.

Philip Kgosana, who led that famous march of 30,000 people from Langa to Cape Town in the aftermath of the anti-pass campaign, in March 1960, was a carbon copy of Sobukwe: 'His every action, every inflection of the voice, every gesture' were unmistakably inspired by Sobukwe' writes Tom Lodge.[3]

What is remarkable is that even though Sobukwe's active career as a political leader was over on 21 March 1960, when he went to the Soweto police station and gave himself up in connection with the anti-pass campaign, his presence in black politics never faded away. He was locked up at the Pretoria Central Prison until 1963 and then sent to Robben Island where he spent six years under the especially legislated 'Sobukwe clause' of the parliament. On his release he was immediately banned and put under house arrest at Kimberley. When he died of cancer in 1978, he was only 54 years old. His funeral showed clearly the quasi-mythical place that Sobukwe had come to occupy in black politics. Political leaders of as wide a political spectrum as ANC supporters, white communists and liberals, young BC followers, even Inkatha's Buthelezi, attended the funeral. Sobukwe was a man who had a profound antipathy to violence. It is now generally acknowledged that he had no direct link with *Poqo* (the armed wing of the PAC, which espoused random violence as a vehicle for liberation), and that he knew nothing about the plans developed by Potlake Leballo and the Maseru exiles in the late seventies for a general insurrection. He was a thinker first and a poet who, like Julius Nyerere of Tanzania, translated Shakespeare into an African language; Nyerere, known as *Mwalimu* (teacher), translated *Julius Caesar* into Swahili, Sobukwe, *Macbeth* into Zulu.

That he chose to translate *Macbeth* into Zulu and not into Xhosa or Sesotho is surprising and shows a great broadness of mind, because he was a Xhosa scholar and his father was a Sesotho speaker. It is probably this quality of the man that explains the fact that he was so much feared by the apartheid regime. This is what Breytenbach wrote in March 1973 when, in the company of Sonny Leon, a Coloured leader, he went to Galeshewe to visit Sobukwe whom he very much admired: 'The regime is afraid of his kind, and when you meet the man, it is clear why. The slum where he is forced to live . . . does not succeed in detracting from his authority. The people respect him and look up to him for guidance. Even the full-time surveillance under which he is kept by the political police is a kind of back-handed compliment. . . . [His] rooms and toilet are definitely bugged.'[4]

I asked the concierge of the hotel where I was staying, an elderly black man, if the house in which Sobukwe was detained had been turned into a museum. He appeared surprised by my question. 'No,' he said, 'it is an ordinary house and other people are living in it now. Nothing distinguishes it from the other houses in the township.' In the end I decided not to go to Galeshewe to visit the house. But I promised myself that I would do so when the house was turned into a museum with some of Sobukwe's memorabilia stored in it. I was sure that that would happen one day.[5]

I left Kimberley at 9 pm only twenty-four hours after I had arrived. The train from Jo'burg was late. At the station they played music by Sinatra, Nat King Cole, Nana Mouskouri, Julio Iglesias. The second leg of my journey to Cape Town was uneventful. I had thought it wise to buy bedding for he night. The steward who made the bunk bed was white, as were, amazingly enough, most of the waiters in the dining car. In the old days, the state-operated South African Transport Company (SATC) was the biggest employer in the country (largely of Afrikaners): in 1981, it still employed 269,000 people; ten years later that number has fallen to only 160,000. As part of the privatisation drive, the company's name was changed to Transnet but the process was stopped after vociferous protests from the ANC and COSATU.

I shared the compartment with a Coloured teacher from Kimberley. We chatted a little before going to bed. It turned out that he was an ANC supporter. He did not seem overly optimistic about

South Africa's future. He was a literary fellow. 'The past bears down on South Africa's shoulders like a heavy albatross,' he said. 'Black poverty is a huge problem. So is the lack of education. The whites took everything: the land, the wealth, the knowledge.'

As I woke up in the early morning the train had stopped at Matjiesfontein, a small *dorp* (town) in the Karoo which was established in the 1880s as a health resort and which is classified a national monument now. Just behind the station is the old-world hotel surrounded by palm trees and bougainvillea. A couple of young tourists with heavy backpacks were waiting on the platform, they had probably spent the night at the hotel. We left the dry and arid Karoo behind and entered the lush, well-watered Boland region with its famous vineyards and fruit farms. I went to the dining car to have breakfast. I noticed on the walls large, old-fashioned photographs of the 1950s depicting scenes in Pretoria: blooming jacaranda trees in the streets, the gardens; the suburbs, strangely reminiscent of American suburbia: a clean-cut, short-haired man in shorts, bicycling; a little blonde girl in pigtails; a big golden 'lab', very friendly. . . .

When the train pulled into the Cape Town station it was close to twelve noon. 7 March 1992 turned out to be a gorgeous day: the air was crisp and cool, and a light breeze was blowing as if to chase the heat away. I took a cab and went directly to Sea Point where a small one-room flat was put at my disposal by my Jo'burg friends, Adele and Ellison Kahn. Ellison is a law professor at Wits, at 71 mostly retired now, but he still teaches a course or two and edits the country's leading law journal. He has received honorary doctorates from several major universities in South Africa, the last one from UCT, I believe, in 1991. He was deputy vice-chancellor at Wits for some years and narrowly missed being appointed vice-chancellor. He is predictably generous about the fact that the man who got the job is an Afrikaner, while Ellis is Jewish. 'That probably didn't play any role at all,' he said with characteristic fair play. He was well qualified for the position. An old-school gentleman, who believes in the redeeming virtue of hard work, Ellis is conservative in his political views. He comes from a wealthy family, but is low-profile about it. Partly this is due to good breeding: one doesn't flaunt one's wealth, and so on; partly it is due to necessity. When he was a young lecturer at Wits, Mandela, who was studying towards an LLB degree, was one of his students. 'He didn't strike me as an exceptionally bright student,' he said jokingly.[6] Adele is his devoted and truly indispensable wife. A sprightly, capable and energetic woman very good with the practical things of life, she created the peaceful environment in which Ellis could blossom. They have three surviving children (one daughter died in infancy from leukemia): their oldest, a son, is an academic who lives in Miami; their middle one, also a son, is a writer and editor who has made his life in London; their youngest, a daughter, is a doctor who is married to another doctor and they presently work in a rural hospital in KwaNdebele in the north. Ellis and Adele are of course worried about the situation in South Africa but they don't seriously consider emigrating: 'We are too old to leave and besides it would be very difficult to get even some of our assets out, we would simply not have enough to live on.'

Once settled in in the small apartment I felt the urge for going on a reconnaissance immediately. I wanted to see if there had been any changes since 1986 when I was last in Cape Town. So I rented a car and was on my way at about four in the afternoon. From Sea Point I drove back to the city and took the De Waal Drive, and then the M3 freeway to Rondebosch and stopped at the UCT campus. The place was empty but everything appeared to be the same: the big plaza, the ivy-covered main building at the back; the stairs leading to the equestrian statue; the unobstructed vista in front; certainly one of the most beautiful university campuses in the country. I continued on the M3, passing the affluent white suburbs of Bishops Court, Claremont, Constantia and ending in Muizenberg on False Bay. On the beach there is a long row of old-fashioned cabins made of wood and painted in various colours – red, green, blue and yellow – which reminded me of the beach in Visconti's movie, *Death in Venice*, based on Thomas Mann's book. From Muizenberg I pushed on to Fish Hoek, a resort town on the sea, and turned inland and crossed over to Hout Bay through Chapman's Peak. The view from Chapman's Peak was every bit as impressive as I remembered it. Hout Bay is a fishing harbour. There is a big emporium there that offers a large assortment of seafood: fresh, frozen and canned; also, all sorts of artefacts, souvenirs for tourists. The restaurant next to the emporium is very popular and offers fresh lobster, crab and fish with names such as *snoek*, *geelbek* and *kabeljou*. The price of lobster has more than doubled in the last six years (from the equivalent of £2.50 to £5) but it still seemed like a good bargain for a big-sized half-lobster. After lunch I continued my exploration. At the end of the harbour the tenements that served as housing for the Coloured workers of the fish factories were still there, but there has been some improvement: the road has been tarred, so there is less dust; there were no garbage piles; and the revolutionary graffiti on the walls – 'Viva UDF!', 'Viva ANC!', 'the People will rule', and so on – were gone, replaced by coloured drawings of people co-operating in community development projects and extolling the value of education for social progress. On my way back to Cape Town I passed Llandudno, another very affluent village by the sea built on the slopes of the Seven Apostles and then, practically part of Cape Town, Clifton, Bantry Bay and Sea Point. Everywhere, the beaches and coves were crowded with sun-worshippers, but no one was swimming in the sea. The Benguela current, which influences the waters here, is a cold current. The swimming is done in False Bay, on the other side, where the water is less cold due to the proximity of the warm Agulhas current.

It occurred to me that Cape Town and San Francisco (I lived three years in Berkeley, across the Bay) have a lot in common. Both cities are built on peninsulas (two in the case of San Francisco). Both have their own mountains – Mount Tamalpais may be less impressive than Table Mountain but it compensates for this with its magnificent redwood forests; there used to be forests on the slopes of the Table Mountain, but they have long since disappeared. The Mediterranean-type vegetation, scrubby with a myriad different sorts of flowers (called *fynbos* in the Cape), is similar. The two cities get a morning fog that dissipates in the early afternoon; it is called the 'tablecloth' in Cape Town because it comes down from the Table Mountain; in San Francisco, it is a 'fog bank' that rolls in from the Pacific Ocean. Each has its own notorious island prison on the Bay: Robben Island in Table Bay; Alcatraz in San Francisco Bay – the latter was closed down as a federal penitentiary in the early 1960s and later converted into a tourist attraction; the same fate seems to await Robben Island. White Capetonians – as are their Natalian counterparts – are, whether they are English- or Afrikaans-speaking, more liberal than their compatriots living in the Transvaal and the Orange Free State. But the English-speaking white Capetonians are an easy-going, relaxed, laid-back bunch of people. Maybe more than half of South Africa's 3.3 million mixed-race Coloured people live in the peninsula. They are known as a gentle people with a friendly disposition. Africans, numbering perhaps a million a half, are in a minority, but probably not for long. In the San Francisco Bay Area, the diversity of peoples is even greater. Whites, Blacks, Americans of Chinese, Latin-American, native-American, Middle-Eastern ancestry, despite the residential segregation and the occasional rioting due to racist causes, live there in much better understanding and harmony than the peoples in the Cape Peninsula. . . .

On the following morning I went looking for the area that used to be known as District Six and found it. It is called Zonnebloem now and is not far from City Hall, right next to it, in fact. It is quite a big area, still mostly wasteland, except for an Asian bazaar to the south, two or three housing schemes to the north, and the huge Cape Technikon and three isolated churches that stand eerily amongst the rubble of houses demolished fifteen, twenty years ago.[7] Here and there stick out from the scrubby bush, twisted, rusty iron bars, broken-up concrete, the foundations of old walls. One can still see patches of old asphalt which used to be the streets. I discovered where the old Hanover Street, the main thoroughfare of District Six was. One of churches – the Catholic Holy Cross Church, I believe – is so close to the Technikon, and so dwarfed by it, that it looks unreal, absurd. It is clear that the government did not dare touch it, lest it would bring down on it all the wrath of the Vatican. Somewhere in the middle of this wasteland, a couple of ramshackle shacks occupied by some squatters. . . .

I decided that I wanted to learn more about District Six and went the following morning to the South African Press Clips on Kloefnek Road to dig up some of the old stories. Here is a summary of what I've found.

For the 40,000 or so former residents of District Six, 11 February 1966 was a Black Friday. In the following sixteen years they were removed from their homes and resettled in the soulless Cape Flats – 15 to 20 miles away from their workplaces, schools and hospitals. For sixteen years these people, whose only crime was not being white, lived constantly under the sword of Damocles, waiting for their expulsion order, but at the same time fighting against it. Between 1966 and 1982, no fewer than 3,700 buildings – homes, shops, schools – were destroyed after the district was proclaimed white under the Group Areas Act. It was an act of cruelty and insensitivity that caused much anguish, misery and frustration amongst the Coloured community of the Cape but it still needs to be put in perspective: roughly during the same period, a grand total of 3.5 million people were removed from 'white' South Africa of whom 3.2 million were African and 300,000 Coloured.[8] At any rate, even if a small fraction of the total, District Six became all over the world a symbol of the hurt and distress that has resulted from all Group Area Act removals.

The government acted with typical duplicity and deceit. In October 1964, a committee was set up by the Ministry of Community Development to investigate the possibility of planning the redevelopment of the district. In June 1965, the ministry announced a ten-year plan to do just that under the Commission for the Rehabilitation of Depressed Areas (CORDA), and all property transactions were frozen. Then came the 'Big Bang' of 11 February 1966, but the government denied emphatically that there would be any mass evictions of people from District Six. A little after two years, the demolitions began and in 1969 the first mass removal of residents was under way. During the following thirteen years, the evictions and the destruction continued, sometimes alternately, sometimes simultaneously, until, in August 1982, it was over. That very same month, the first white residents moved into the 102 new homes that were built in the heart of District Six. Also in August 1982, four hectares of prime land between De Waal Drive and the area where the new Cape Technikon campus was to be built was sold to a developer for the building of up to 300 new residential units for whites.

Asked by journalists if he had any moral problems with what he was doing, Mr A Demmers, the developer, replied that he had 'no qualms' about the project. Adding: 'If I was worried about the area being white, I wouldn't have become involved.' He then explained that the area was white at first, and then the Coloureds took over and turned it into a 'slum' ('it was a disgrace'), and now the whites were taking over again. The same newspaper article reported that there was a large number of applications from whites to buy houses in a renovated District Six. Meanwhile, in 1978, District Six was renamed Zonnebloem (after the name of an educational institution run by the Anglican church) and it was announced a year or so later that about a quarter of the land was set aside for a large technikon that could have as many as 8,000 students by the year

2000. In October 1981, the government was still insisting that the Cape Technikon was to remain a white institution.

In July 1982, Naz Ebrahim, the chairperson of the District Six Rents, Ratepayers' and Residents' Association (which was founded in 1979 when there was talk about a possible change of heart on the part of the government), returned from a two-months' tour in the United States, Canada and Britain where she had gone to publicise the plight of District Six and generate support. When she had left, she was still living in Manley Villa in Rochester Road in District Six. What she still did not know when she arrived back in South Africa was that her house was one of the last to have been vacated a fortnight earlier, and that her new home was Flat R1, Yusuf Gool Boulevard, Gatesville, in the Cape Flats. A few days later Naz Ebrahim published a short article in the *Cape Argus* in which she gave eloquent expression to the human tragedy that is the story of District Six. 'There is a saying,' she began, 'that "You can take the people out of the heart of District Six, but you will never take District Six out of the hearts of the people".' She described District Six as a place where 'East and West met. Saints and sinners, raconteurs and rascals, princes and paupers, and all sorts of people promenaded in endless procession along its bustling thoroughfare – Hanover Street. . . . Hanover Street, the street they said would never die, disappeared. . . . The groan of brick and mortar structures crumbling and the din of the bulldozer was a living nightmare. . . . And now that the [white] tenants have moved into the resurrected homes in Ashley and Constitution Streets, the last glimmer of hope fades. . . . A once closely knit community is scattered throughout the Cape Flats. . . . District Six is dead.'[9]

On the day following Naz Ebrahim's article in the *Argus*, (28 July 1982) Colin Eglin, a leading liberal politician and Progressive Federal Party (PFP) MP for Sea Point, wrote a letter to Naz Ebrahim that was given broad publicity:

Dear Naz

I know that I express the feelings of thousands of citizens of Cape Town when I say that we are deeply, deeply ashamed.

Because of the privilege and comfort and security which the race laws of our country confer on us we have not shared the dull ache of your experience.

But we admire your courage.

We understand your anguish.

We respect your anger.

We know that no amount of sophistry or tortuous logic can ever justify what the powerful have done to the powerless, the strong have done to the weak, here in the heart of Cape Town.

What was once District Six is an ugly scar on the side of Devil's Peak. Even if one day it is covered by smart town houses for well-off whites or by a modern technikon used to train the children of those who drove you and 40,000 others out of Cape Town to the plains of the Cape Flats, it will remain a monument to racial bigotry and a constant reminder of one of the most sordid chapters in the political life of our country.

We would like to say that we are sorry. But in the circumstances that would sound trite.

We cannot promise that justice will come one day. But we can, and will, try.

Yours sincerely,

Colin Eglin

No doubt, an eloquent and charitable letter. But it is also a revealing letter. Revealing of the entire position of the English-speaking white community in South Africa for close to a hundred years, since the Union Constitution of 1910. What is that position? It is, I believe, in a nutshell, to be found in the second paragraph of the letter: 'the privilege and comfort and security which the race laws of our country confer on us'. That is the key. And what is the key word in that key part of sentence? It is 'confer'. True: the ruling Afrikaners conferred on the Anglos 'privilege and comfort and security', and they took it. They did not say: 'we cannot accept this because it is immoral'; they did not say: 'we will bring the economic life of this country to a halt' – they had the muscle to do it; they did not say: 'we will not serve in the same parliament as you or, not serve in the same army as you.' They did not say and do all these things. So they stand before history as, at a minimum, guilty by omission. Very few English whites put their lives on the line – like John Harris who blew up Jo'burg's railway station in the early 1960s and was hanged for it. A small number of women (mostly those associated with the Black Sash movement) did what they could. But, as Rian Malan mentions in *My Traitor's Heart*, most English whites are seen by Afrikaners, not entirely wrongly, as *soutpiels*, or 'salt dicks', because they were traditionally with one foot in South Africa and the other in England – 'a straddle so broad that their cock dangled in the sea'.[10] These days most *verligte* Afrikaners regret what they have done to their Coloured cousins. The first time I went to see him at his Saffier farm outside Paarl in the Boland, in March 1986, W A de Klerk, told me: 'We've always had a close, even intimate, relationship with the Coloured people. . . . We were nursed by our *ajas* [Coloured nannies] to whom we were closer than to our biological mothers. And what did we do? We took their political rights away and then we chased them from our midst.'[11]

Real change of heart on the part of the government did come . . . in 1988. It declared that, in the following year, District Six was to become an 'open area'. In 1989, the first Coloured families returned to District Six. That same year the Hands Off District Six association launched a campaign whose purpose is to stop the profiteers from cashing in on the value of the land whose price has shot up dramatically. The association is working on many fronts: it wants to establish the principle that the former residents of District Six be given first refusal rights to any housing scheme to be developed in the area; they also want to make sure that the houses are affordable for the Coloured community. Given the new mood in the country, they are likely to achieve a measure of success in their objectives. After February 1990, the new administrator of the Cape, Kabus Meiring, declared that District Six could be the showpiece of new South Africa, a symbol of the healing of the wrongs of the past. In April 1992, there still was not any visible building activity in the wastelands of what was District Six, but that is not necessarily a bad sign.

In the afternoon I went to the University of Western Cape (UWC) in Bellville looking for Peter Vale, who is the co-director of the Centre of Southern African Studies, which he helped to establish with the help of the Rockefeller Foundation, I believe. I could not locate him but I found a campus in turmoil. I was astonished to see Jake Gerwel, the rector of the university, in the lobby of the Economic and Management Sciences Building (in which Vale's centre is located) arguing with a group of male students who were trying to enforce a boycott against attending classes; he was accusing them of intimidating the female students who wanted to get in. In the big auditorium of the main hall, an SRC meeting was in progress. The place was packed and speaker after speaker blasted the University administration for deciding not to re-admit the students who had failed to pay back their debts. The decision was made after much soul-searching because the university found itself in the middle of a serious financial crisis. Due to its aggressively democratic admissions policy (a kind of affirmative action), which had enabled many poor blacks of under-privileged backgrounds in rural areas to be accepted, by making many bursaries available to them. So the university had grown at a much faster pace than anticipated but the government had refused to increase its subsidies to match the needs. Faced with a real prospect of bankruptcy, the university administration was forced to increase the fees and, to drive the message home that it meant business, it had refused to re-admit those students who had been unable to reimburse their loans. That was of course a paradox that flew in the face of the very principles of open admissions that Jake Gerwel and his colleagues had espoused in the first place, and that is why they were accused of betrayal by the students. There were also accusations of falling standards from certain quarters. So, it was a complex, complicated and painful situation.

When I first visited UWC in 1986, it was in the process of establishing its reputation as a serious left-wing intellectual centre. The university was created in the 1960s – the heyday of Verwoerdian dogma of separate development – to serve the Coloured community which, in contrast to the Africans and Indians, did not yet have its own university. For the first ten, fifteen years of its existence, most of the administrators and lecturers were Afrikaners. This situation was facilitated by the fact that the mother tongue of the large majority of the Coloureds is Afrikaans. Things began to change significantly in the early 1970s when the university became associated with the rise of Black Consciousness movement. Several important BC leaders, such as Peter Jones (a close friend of Steve Biko's – they were in the same car and arrested together the last time Biko was gaoled and tortured to death), who helped to set up the first South African Students' Organisation (SASO, founded by Biko) branch at UWC; Johnny Issel, who was eventually elected national patron of the UDF; and Trevor Manuel, presently a bigwig with the ANC, were all connected with the UWC.

In 1986, my contact at UWC had been Chris Heymans, a *verligte* Afrikaner, who taught in the political science department. On the phone he had warned me to 'be careful and not to get lost' in Nyanga or Guguletu, the two African townships not far from Belville. The situation was tense due to the fighting in Crossroads (see Chapter 10). Heymans had been waiting for me in his office with four of his students, two of whom were African and the other two Coloured. They seemed reluctant to talk about South African politics and appeared to misrepresent much of what was going on in sub-Saharan Africa. We spoke about countries such as Angola, Mozambique and Ethiopia, and I was amazed by the absence of a real grasp of the problems. They kept repeating slogans like 'American imperialism' and 'neo-colonialism' as if they were valid substitutes for analysis. They believed in a sort of naïve way in a socialist paradise to come. I was disappointed.

Later, we had gone to see Graeme Bloch, a young Marxist historian and a former member of the Western Cape executive of the now-dissolved UDF. Long, curly hair and round, wire-rimmed glasses à la Trotsky, he looked the part. I made the mistake of touching, in passing, on our common Jewish heritage. He bristled and I sensed immediately that I had made a mistake. 'It's absolutely irrelevant,' he said coldly and decisively. 'Whether one is born black or white, rich or poor, in China or in the United States, has nothing to do with it.'

'It' probably referred to a combination of the spirit, the mind, the soul. It was true in theory, but in practice? Anyway, I didn't say anything and he gave me a classically Marxist analysis of certain aspects of the South African reality which goes like this: 'The TBVC states are reactionary structures created by monopoly capitalism to exploit black workers. They fired 23,000 workers at the Impala platinum mines [in Bophuthatswana] recently, just because they refused to return to work before their demands for the abolition of the *Induna* [headman – workers living in males-only hostels are organised by tribal origin] system and for the recognition of NUM were met. The *Induna* system is a disgrace and do you know what their excuse is for not recognising the NUM? Bop is an independent country and doesn't recognise South Africa-based unions. That, however, did not prevent the mine managers from concluding an accord with the white Mineworkers' Union which is based ... in Johannesburg! When Ramaphosa (then general secretary of the NUM) went to Lebowa, he was arrested and gaoled by the homeland authorities. At the Phalaborwa iron mines, 3,000 workers went immediately on strike. There were bloody clashes with the police. Incidents such as these occur all the time. The mine managers know that, when push comes to shove, they can always fire the recalcitrant workers and replace them by others from Malawi and Mozambique. That's no problem with the chronic unemployment that is ravaging the region. So their policy is to make a few minor concessions and most workers will give in because they've no other choice. Those who insist on substantial demands will be fired. But with the emergence of NUM that policy is now doomed.'

Curious to see if his views had changed in the meantime, I looked Graeme up when I was at the UWC but I was told that he was in England on a sabbatical year. I was disappointed because I knew that in 1989 he had married Cheryl Carolus, a rising Coloured political star who, at the July 1991 conference of the ANC had been elected to its National Executive Committee at age 35 (she is also a prominent Communist Party member).

Peter Vale invited me to come to his house in Muizenberg on Saturday because I had told him that I was leaving on the following Monday. I met his wife, Louise, who is also involved in grass-roots development projects. We went to the beach but did not stay long because it was blowing very hard. Back in the house we had Chicken Biriyani and then we had a long chat in the yard. Peter used to teach at Rhodes in Grahamstown but, when the opportunity came to start a new centre at UWC with the help of the Rockefeller Foundation, he took it. Having published in the prestigious *Foreign Affairs* journal, he is well connected with the political crowd in Washington. He told me that he was the only African representative in the North-South Group set up by the Council of Foreign Relations to promote worldwide economic development. We spoke first about UWC and the South African universities in general:

'UWC is a child of apartheid but it was able to shake off its shackles and become the intellectual home of the left. It was an extremely important moment in the liberation of the people and of ideas in this country. In the past many youths were denied access to university education simply because they were poor and lived in the rural areas. The UWC changed that. It is the role of the university to respond to the state, to oppose it when necessary, and UWC took a very tough line in the 1980s; but like the other universities in the country, it was caught off guard by FW's speech in February 1990. My own feeling is that it remains ANC-dominated, but if the PAC and AZAPO are excluded from a CODESA-type settlement, they will retreat to the progressive radical universities like UWC, as well as UCT, Wits, Fort Hare, University of the North at Turfloop and so on. Already the Coloured students of UWC feel victimised because they cannot go about their business of getting a good education. As a result of this, we might see in the future an exodus of Coloured students to UCT and Stellenbosch which would turn UWC into an African-dominated university. One potentially dangerous development from all this is that the Afrikaans-speaking universities – Pretoria, RAU, Stellenbosch, Potchefstroom – will maintain themselves as centres of educational excellence, especially in the sciences, while in the English-speaking universities the standards might go down.'

We then spoke about the AIDS situation which, while not as preoccupying in South Africa as in the rest of the continent, is serious enough and is probably bound to get much worse. A study by the Metropolitan Life estimated that at the beginning of 1993 about 300,000 people were HIV-positive and that, in about 5,000 cases, the virus had already erupted into full-blown AIDS. Some specialists argue that the disease has now moved from the pre-epidemic to the epidemic phase and that 'it will hit its murderous stride' towards the end of the century, just as the new multi-racial democracy will be trying to find its wobbly feet. At that time it is possible that about three million people will be infected with the virus and about 160,000 will be sick with the disease.[12]

'Unless a cure is found soon,' Peter Vale said gloomily, 'all other problems that we have may pale to insignificance.'

I shuddered at the thought of what a major epidemic of AIDS combined with large-scale violence could do to the social fabric of South Africa.

Notes

1 This is the first of the three Travel Notes chapters that are part of the same field research trip that I undertook in March and April 1992, during which I covered roughly 3,000 miles and visited, friends, contacts, towns, universities, black townships and squatter camps.

2 The best book on the terrible conditions that prevailed in the mines is: C Van Onselen, *New Babylon, New Nineveh: Studies in the Social and*

Economic History of the Witwatersrand, 1886–1914, 2 vols. Ravan, 1992, Johannesburg. Van Onselen is also the author of *Chibaro, African Mine Labour in Southern Rhodesia, 1900–1933*, Pluto-Ravan, 1976, Johannesburg. See also B Kennedy's *A Tale of Two Mining Cities: Johannesburg and Broken Hill 1885–1925*, Donker, Delta House and Melbourne UP, 1984, Johannesburg, Cape Town and Melbourne.

3 Tom Lodge, whom I visited at his office at Wits both in 1986 and in 1992 (in between he l'ved a few years in New York – worried for his family after the assassination of Daniel Webster, a colleague, he left South Africa but came back after the liberalisation of February 1990), gave me a copy of his review article, 'A Liberal of Another Colour', in: *Transformation*, 16, 1991, on B Pogrund's book, *Sobukwe and Apartheid*, P Halban and Jonathan Ball, 1990, Johannesburg and London. The quotes and Sobukwe's short biography are from that review article.

4 B Breytenbach, *A Season in Paradise*, first published by J Cape in 1980. The quote is on page 199.

5 That appears to be happening now, in 1993. Nelson Mandela visited Galeshewe in May to address a large crowd there.

6 What I did not know then is that Ellis has published a juicy collection of anecdotes and portraits of personalities in, Ellison Kahn, *Law Life and Laughter*, 1991, Cape Town.

7 Technikons are post-secondary school institutions that prepare students for employment in commerce and industry. There are about a dozen in the country of which those of Pretoria, Witwatersrand and the Cape are the biggest.

8 On the painful subject of the forced removals, see Note 1 at the end of Chapter 9.

9 In March 1991, Mrs Ebrahim found in herself the courage to visit the wasteland that used to be District Six. She found the bits of asphalt covered by earth and bush that was all that remained of Rochester Street and stopped at the spot where her six-bedroom house used to stand. To the journalists who were accompanying her she said: 'When anyone tampers with your home, they tamper with your soul. And when they tamper with your soul, that's death.' Ten years later the wound was still open and festering. See *The Sun*, 15 March 1991, Cape Town, page A10.

10 Malan, *My Traitor's Heart*, page 75.

11 See Note 4 Chapter 3.

12 See also Mary Crewe, *AIDS in South Africa: the Myth and the Reality*, Penguin, 1992.

15

Travel Notes Two: Port Elizabeth, Uitenhage, Fort Hare and Grahamstown

'They still see us as people who, given half an opportunity, will steal their children's lunch boxes while they are on their way to school.'

Revd Arnold Stofile

A small article in the *Cape Times* caught my attention in April 1992. Entitled 'Judge Presents Case for Second-tier Rights', it said that Judge P J J Oliver, a well-known personality, had expressed support for 'justiciable', that is, enforceable by law, 'second-generation rights' such as the rights to food, to shelter, to education and to health services (first-generation rights being the democratic rights to life, to liberty, to free association and speech and to property).

I was astonished to see that article because the distinction is an old Marxist one and, as everyone knows, Marxism as an ideology has collapsed in much of the world. But I then realised that in South Africa the Communist Party is one of the very few in the world that is actually thriving. South Africa is a special case where second-generation rights could be seen as a means of righting the wrongs of the past. They could be seen as a vast affirmative action programme, whose purpose would be the narrowing of the huge gap between the haves, largely white, and the have-nots, largely black. They could be seen as a moral obligation as well as enlightened self-interest because the wounds of the country would never heal otherwise, they would continue to suppurate.

One of the places where the yawning gap between the haves and the have-nots is the most glaring is the Eastern Cape. Some of the most miserable African townships in South Africa are in the Port Elizabeth/Uitenhage area. I was shocked to read in the *Monitor*, at about the same time, an article on the *Ukuhleleleka* (the word means marginalised people, the under-class, in Xhosa) of Port Elizabeth. It said that about half of all dwellings in the African townships of PE and Uitenhage were shacks of only one or two rooms in size. These rudimentary structures were mostly built by their occupiers and were made of perishable materials. They were often packed on top of each other in areas of very high population density. PE's Soweto-on-the-Sea squatter camp, for example, had a population density of about 700 persons per hectare, 'an astronomical figure for an area of single-storey housing'. It went without saying that there was neither electricity nor water-borne sanitation. Each one of the 135 or so water taps was shared by over 600 residents. . . . [1]

It had taken me two days to cover the 600 miles that separate Cape Town from Port Elizabeth. I had taken my time, stopping the first night at Mossel Bay and then continuing on the Garden Route which is strongly recommended to well-heeled tourists who are also nature lovers. Thus, I passed the famous Wilderness Beach – miles and miles, as far as the eye can see, of unrestricted beach of fine golden sand with, on the dunes, at respectable distances one from the other, the comfortable summer or retirement houses of the well-to-do. Pavement cafés were teeming with young people at Knysna and at Plettenberg Bay, which has the reputation of being the playground of the rich. If the luxurious residences on top of the hills and the number of BMWs and Mercs parked in front of the restaurants were any indication, that was certainly the case. In the four-star hotel on the tip of a rocky promontory, an all-white crowd of tourists and local people sat drinking and chatting under colourful parasols while their children splashed and cavorted in the pool. Black waiters moved to and fro, stepping carefully over the sprawling bodies, to bring refreshments to the holidaymakers. I left the N2 highway to take the Nature Valley's Road to the Tsitsikama National Park, which is a forest and coastal park. I admired the little coves, the breakers pounding on the boulders and exploding into small hyperborean fireworks. The temptation to spend the night in one of the cottages that lined the coast was strong but I pushed on, I wanted to be in Port Elizabeth before the day was out. At Humansdorp, which is at about an hour's drive from PE, I left the N2 again to have a look at a string of lovely villages – Jeffrey's Bay, St Francis Bay, Oyster Bay – that dotted the coast.

Travelling on the Garden Route makes one realise even more acutely how the South African whites wanted to create a paradise here at the southern tip of the African continent exclusively for themselves and how painful must be the prospect of losing it.

Dusk was falling when I checked in at the Humewood Hotel on the Summerstrand in Port Elizabeth. As I watched from the window, some elderly people were strolling on the esplanade taking in the cool air of the evening. . . .

New Brighton is the biggest and the oldest black township in Port Elizabeth. In addition to it, there are, among the older townships of the PE/Uitenhage area places such as KwaZakhele, Zwide, Walmer and KwaNobuhle. In recent years, new ones like Motherwell, Kwa-Magxaki, Kwadesi and Tyhoksville have come into being. Part of these townships, or adjoining them, are the shanty towns of Red Location, Soweto-on-the-Sea, Veeplaas and Langa. Malabar and Calvin Park are the Indian and Coloured townships of Port Elizabeth.

Friday France, a researcher for the *Monitor* and a lanky black man in his early thirties, took the wheel of my car and we left the offices of the Human Rights Fund in the direction of New Brighton. It was the start of two days to be spent in the townships there. Red Location is a shanty town in New Brighton which derives its name from the fact that the corrugated-iron barracks used by British soldiers during the First World War had corroded owing to the salt and dampness that came from the sea and gave them a greenish-reddish colour. The barracks were in a truly terrible shape, nowhere near being fit for human habitation, but the place was bursting at the seams with people and garbage piled here and there on the dusty dirt road.

'Unemployment around here is about 80 per cent,' Friday said, 'much higher than the national average for blacks, which is of about 50 per cent.' The shocking in this country has become commonplace, I thought. I asked him where Little Soweto was. He told me that Little Soweto was another name for Soweto-on-the-Sea. 'It is not far, we will go there next,' he said.

I remembered how, six years ago, on a grey and drizzly morning, I had come upon the dismal squatter camp by chance. It was a Sunday and I was staying at the Edwards, an old colonial hotel in the middle of the town on a knoll overlooking the harbour. After an extraordinarily rich buffet brunch for only eight rands (about

£2), I had decided to drive up to Uitenhage to have a look. I had barely crossed the central business district and left PE behind, when a truly nightmarish spectacle had come into view on the right side of the highway. It was a huge, sprawling shanty town surrounded by high, barbed-wire fences. Myriads of plastic wrappers caught in the wires flapped madly in the howling wind. Others, mixed with pieces of paper and cardboard, flew about in circles forming maelstroms, and zigzagged in the no-man's-land between the fence and the first shacks, and up and down in the narrow alleys between them. I had been so shocked by that affront to humanity that I had stopped the car to have a better look. I had watched for a while but couldn't see any movement in it. I had assumed that men, women and children were all huddled inside their shacks to protect themselves from the elements. A military vehicle – a Buffel, I believe – was parked further down the road, under a bridge. The hatches facing the camp were open and three or four soldiers were watching with their binoculars. They were young conscripts who did not appear to be overly enthusiastic about what they were doing.

Suddenly Friday pointed to smoke billowing at a distance. 'A fire,' he said. 'A commonplace occurrence around here. It usually starts when a primus stove is overturned by accident and the shack is destroyed. If it's windy, like it is today, two or more shacks will be destroyed, because the fire will spread to the neighbouring shacks. There is no fire-fighting department nearby, so by the time they come it is usually too late.' We arrived where a throng of gawkers had gathered around the blaze. Woefully ineffective-looking plastic buckets of water were passed along. There was no big excitement, except for the few people busy dragging household items from the shack next in line of the fire. Strewn on the ground were a couple of mattresses, clothing, a broken armchair, a table, kitchen utensils and provisions. Three shacks were already burning and a fourth was threatened by the leaping flames. There was an unmistakable air of resignation and fatality to it all; it was just one more disaster in a life that was made up of disasters, in a life that was a constant struggle of survival.

An unmarked car with two burly white men in civilian clothes in it pulled up behind us. 'Policemen,' said Friday. One of them was talking on the phone. 'He is probably calling the fire department,' he added. Other than phoning, the two men didn't take any action, they just sat in the car watching. It was for them a routine incident.

'Let's go and have lunch,' I told Friday. 'We will continue in the afternoon.'

The place Friday took me to, a block away from the HRF offices, was darkly lit and air-conditioned and looked more like a singles bar than a restaurant. The waitresses, mostly heavily made-up blondes in their twenties, wore mini skirts and see-through blouses. The food was of passable quality but the prices were inflated to include (presumably) the viewing pleasure. I was saddened to see Friday taken in by such a vulgar sting operation. After leaving a big tip so as not to embarrass Friday, who seemed to be a regular, we left. As we walked back to the car and I breathed – with gratitude – the fresh outdoor air, I told him the way I felt. I concluded my remarks by an explanation of why I thought Steve Biko was a great man: because, I said, he understood that the most important thing for the black man was to liberate his mind, his soul, his spirit.[2] That is why he emphasised black pride, black self-respect and black self-reliance. I realised that I was being patronising and was afraid that Friday might be offended by my remarks. But he was not. In fact it was the opposite that happened: I won his trust and from then on he told me things about his private life that he wouldn't normally tell a stranger. He had been arrested in the June 1986 general State of Emergency and spent three years in gaol. While he was in prison his wife had left him. After his release they had separated and were in the middle of a divorce now. They had two children who lived with their mother. It was a complicating factor in his life. 'And I am not an exception,' he said, 'several of my friends found themselves in the same situation'. That was the hidden face of apartheid, the side that is in the shadows, the side that touches the soul. Friday made more than R2,000 working for the HRF, close to what he would be making if he were a white man. It is not a bad salary but he still could not afford to buy a car. He lived in New Brighton in a small house.

In the afternoon we went to the Enkathazweni Community Centre in New Brighton. It is a large brick building that houses the offices of the civic associations and of the ANC. Friday was talking to some friends when Harry Fazzy, a veteran of the struggle and the recently elected chairman of SANCO, arrived in the company of three or four other people.[3] Friday introduced me to Fazzy, who had spent about a third of his life (24 years) on the Island, as he put it. He was a union organiser in the early days, then he became an ANC activist, and finally a civics organiser. We talked for a while with Fazzy. What struck me most was his wisdom, his dignity and, more particularly, the lack of hatred in his heart. The latter was a quality that one often finds in the old-timers who were 'prison graduates', ie, who had spent a long time in gaol.

In Veeplas, one of the worst shanty towns that I had seen so far, groups of children in torn, tattered clothes played in the dust. Older people sat in the shade of their shacks, getting drunk on cheap, homemade beer. As we drove on, I suddenly recognised ahead of us the road that I had been on six years ago on the perimeter of Soweto-on-the-Sea. I was outside then, looking in; now I was inside, looking out. It was, briefly, a strange feeling. I saw in my mind's eye the image of the myriad plastic wrappers fluttering on the barbed-wire fences. The fences were gone now, they had been removed. Under blue skies and without them, the squatter camp despite all its wretchedness looked, somehow, less hellish.

The next day we first went to Malabar, the Indian township of Port Elizabeth. The larger, better houses were on the hill, the smaller, poorer ones on the flats below. They were all Indians of course: women in saris, children in short pants, babies in prams – I saw few men, I deduced that unemployment must be less severe among them. Suddenly I was hit by the absurdity, the unreality of this Indian township in the middle of Africa. It was as if, by a stroke of a magic wand, it had been – lock, stock and barrel – flown in on a flying carpet. A young boy came to enquire if we were from the *Mercury* (one of the two dailies in PE). He said that they had published a story recently about African squatters who were beginning to invade the hill – in full view of the more affluent houses.

We passed central Uitenhage, which is an industrial town, part of the PE/Uitenhage conurbation. It comes third in terms of economic importance – after the Pretoria/Witwatersrand/Vaal (PWV), which generates more than two-thirds of South African GDP, and Durban/ Pietermaritzburg; Cape Town comes fourth. In Langa, Friday showed me a section called Kabah which was bulldozed to the ground in 1985-6 'because it was too close to the white areas'. Its residents were moved to the nearby Tyhoksville, one of the newer townships. 'Kabah is the local [African] version of Cape Town's District Six,' Friday said. Tyhoksville was a depressing sight: some decent houses on the flats but the surrounding hills were covered by shanties. Friday appeared to know everybody. He kept meeting friends – former UDF, MDM (Mass Democratic Movement) activists now unemployed, who survived thanks to their girlfriends who worked as secretaries and salesgirls. One of the tragedies of apartheid is the collapse of the old family and community values. Even the traditional African system of *Ubuntu* (a combination of mutual help, co-operation and solidarity) is badly shaken.

We went next to Addo, about 35 miles east of PE, because Friday wanted to show me the wattle-and-daub houses that people lived in. In his mind these were even worse than the matchboxes in the townships. I told him that this was not necessarily the case, that they had a potential for better, more comfortable living if certain improvements were made in the way they were built. Not far from Addo was the police station where, during the Emergency, Friday was held for several months before being transferred to a regular prison. As we drove past it, Friday pointed to some windowless corrugated-iron prefabs at the back of a brick, one-storey building and said, 'These are the cells where they used to keep the prisoners, I was held in the second one on the left.' A little further, in a sports field by the side of the road a rugby match was in progress. One of the teams was fully white, the other fully black. Virtually all of the forty or fifty spectators were white. As we stood watching, a scuffle suddenly broke out between some white and some black players. It was eventually brought under control and the match resumed, but it was a tension-charged atmosphere. I could sense a lot of frustration and repressed anger, especially on the white side. Friday grew uneasy. 'Let's get out of here,' he said twice. In the car he explained that 'these are very conservative *boere* [farmer] communities, all these sudden changes, it's been very hard on them.'

On our way back we passed by Kwamagxaki, one of the newer townships, where the private sector was building some nice houses. 'Would you like to live in one of these houses,' I asked Friday.

'Yes, but I could never afford them,' he answered. 'They cost 60, 70,000 rands [about £12 – 15,000]. Only businessmen and professionals, such as doctors and lawyers can afford them, and they are a very tiny minority.' It was early evening when we returned to the Humewood and dusk was falling. We sat on the terrace outside and had a couple of beers and watched the sun set over the sea. I invited Friday to stay and have dinner with me but he declined, saying that he had to meet his girlfriend. So we drove back to New Brighton where I dropped him off on the main road somewhere. He gave me instructions on how to get back on the highway that would take me back to Summerstrand. 'I doubt we will see each other soon,' he remarked as we parted.

'Of course we will,' I said, 'it's a small world.' We exchanged the triple-hold comrade handshake. 'Don't forget Biko', I added before getting into the car. 'No, I won't,' he said. I waved one last time and took off. It was badly lit in the township. I drove slowly to avoid an accident. I was not afraid but still I was relieved when I reached the highway. . . .

I stopped briefly at Fort Beaufort, a small town, to see Jessica Landman, whose name had been given to me by Evelyn Sagor in Cape Town because she was a social worker involved in community development projects in New Town, the local Coloured township. Jessica, an Afrikaner in her mid-thirties and a mother of two children, turned out to be a very earnest woman trying her best to help the township's residents with her work, but she had not completely overcome her Afrikaner attitudes – the idea that Coloured people are more developed than the Africans, for example. The same probably could be said about her husband, who studied at the nearby Fort Hare University for a postgraduate degree in agronomy. Jessica took me to New Town on the morning following my arrival.

In marked contrast with Tini Budu, the African township with its 40,000-plus residents, only 3,000 people lived in New Town. Jessica arranged for tea at the Reverend's house and from the discussion that we had there, I learned, to my utter astonishment, that its small size did not prevent New Town from having a substantial amount of factionalism and intrigue among its leadership. More serious was the lack of any serious attempt at integration, or even communication between the white, Coloured and African communities of Fort Beaufort. Relations between the whites and the Coloureds appeared to be friendly enough, at least without overt animosity. But those between Africans on the one hand, and the whites and the Coloureds, on the other, were strained, owing probably to the demographical imbalance. So, the fear of being swamped by the Africans and the old habits and reflexes explained the lack of integration. For example, the chairman of the local management committee, who seemed a friendly and moderate fellow, told me about a school-building project in New Town. It didn't occur to him that the building of yet another segregated school was not in keeping with the spirit of the times. Like in the other African townships across the land that I visited, some nice houses were being built in Tini Budu which would be made available primarily to Africans working for the government: teachers, nurses, social workers. When I said that I wanted to visit Tini Budu it created quite a fuss. It was clearly a problem. Half-hearted efforts were made to find contacts there but they were not successful and the idea was soon dropped. . . .

Ciskei, the last of the four TBVC states to achieve so-called independence in 1981 is very close to Fort Beaufort. Precisely half an hour after taking my leave from Jessica I was already at Fort Hare University. It was four o'clock in the afternoon and it was a sunny, balmy day. The campus covered a large area and appeared to be well maintained. Students strolled between the teaching halls and between the latter and the residential buildings. The proportion of female students seemed quite high. I went to the admin building but Arnold Stofile, with whom I had an appointment at 4.30, was not there. He is the director of public relations at the university and a leading ANC member (in July 1991, in the last elections to the Executive Committee, he received the tenth largest number of the votes, ahead of such people as Joe Modise, the Umkhonto commander, and Alfred Nzo, the former general-secretary; but of that I was not aware at the time). While his staff were looking for him, one of his assistants took me to an exhibition by black painters and sculptors at the Oppenheimer Art Centre. The quality of the works shown there made me almost grateful to Stofile for being late. It was very rewarding to see work that reflected suffering and hope in such a creative and imaginative manner.

Somebody came to fetch me at the Art Centre. Stofile was back. He apologised for being late (maybe I should open a parenthesis here to note that appointments in Africa are not set in concrete the way they are in the West, it is the physical presence that counts more. So one ought not get discouraged, and be patient if the person one has an appointment with is not there on time. More often than not he will appear eventually and the meeting will take place). Francis Wilson (a professor at UCT) was right: Stofile was the man to see. He is extremely outspoken and very articulate but also bent on hyperbole. We spoke about the military leader of

Ciskei, Brigadier Oupa J Gqozo, an opponent of the ANC, who came to power in March 1990 in a coup that overthrew Lennox Sebe (before that he was for many years military attaché to South Africa; he put that time to good use by forging close links with the South African military).

'Gqozo, Mangope and Buthelezi all belong to the same camp,' said Stofile, 'the camp of those who want to balkanise South Africa because it suits their own parochial interests. We want a wholly united country in which the present boundaries of the ten bantustans are not taken into account at all. Gqozo is just a Pretoria stooge. He would've been killed long ago by his own military, by his own police, if there were no South African troops there to protect him. He has no popular support whatsoever. The best way to describe him is that he is a man riding the proverbial tiger; he can't get off from it because, if he does, he gets killed by the tiger. You are asking me about the difference between Gqozo and Bantu Holomisa [the military leader of Transkei, the largest of the TBVC states, who took over from the corrupt Matanzima brothers in 1987]: I will tell you, it is the same as between the Indian Ocean and the Sahara desert. Gqozo is an out and out agent of Pretoria. Holomisa consults with us and the other liberation movements [a PAC congress was held in Umtata, Transkei's capital, in April 1992]. He doesn't see Transkei as a legitimate entity, but as a transitional structure that was forced upon the people. He just keeps the fire going for the time being. As far as he is concerned, the sooner Transkei is reincorporated into South Africa the better.'

After that, the conversation shifted to the more general subject of the transition to a democratic South Africa. He was annoyed by what he saw as a lack of trust for the ANC on the part of the outside world. 'They believe far more easily what De Klerk is saying than what Mandela is saying. It is not that what Mandela is saying doesn't make sense. It does when the Americans say it, when the Germans say it, when the French say it, but not when we say it, and that is that democracy is about majority rule. The white world still doesn't trust us because they still see us as monkeys running up and down the street, they still see us as people who, given half an opportunity will steal their children's lunch boxes while they are on their way to school – I'm putting it in very crude terms of course, but that's the gist of it. Otherwise how can you explain the failure of the international community – call them the capitalist world if you like – to understand the need to continue the financial and trade sanctions until the point of irreversibility [in the transition to the majority rule] is reached? Mandela said it many times, the present situation is not at all irreversible, but they don't believe him.[4] The government pretends they've closed the books on apartheid, but what is the reality? The bantustans are still there. The system of separate departments for education, health, municipal services, etc is still there – did you know that there are fourteen separate departments of education in this country? There are no massive public works programmes to create jobs for the 45 to 50 per cent of black workers who are currently unemployed, no massive house-building programme for the seven million people who live in shacks.

'The government has not even conceded the principle that the people who were forcibly removed from the areas in which they lived, sometimes for generations, should get their land back, or at least be properly compensated. More than two years after February 1990, the police continue to kill and torture our people in the prisons and police stations. So, apartheid is not dead, it is still very much alive and the present situation is not at all irreversible. The transfer of real power does not appear to be on their agenda; the white minority is still unwilling to relinquish power. The Nats want to force us to strike a deal with them which would leave the large majority of our people out in the cold. We cannot afford to strike such a deal. They've agreed to free elections, but not before the ANC has been weakened to such an extent that it cannot win an outright victory at the polls. Violence is the main weapon that they are using against us to achieve that aim. They want to create a situation in which white authority will remain intact, whether directly or by proxy. The reason is that they are afraid of what might happen to them if they lose; they've got blood on their hands, you see, they are guilty of serious crimes against humanity. But we are looking into that to see how we can accommodate that fear, but it is difficult. Mandela offered them a block of sixty seats in parliament – without having a mandate from the ANC leadership to do so, and they've refused, so it became a non-issue before we could take him to task over that. The ANC leadership knows exactly how much it can afford to compromise and which are the principles that cannot be bargained away. But we keep our cards very close to our chest, we cannot afford to divulge our plans, because we are suspicious of them – and they are suspicious of us.'

It was dark by the time I arrived in Grahamstown, which is an hour and a half from Fort Hare. Grahamstown, the capital of the Border Region, used to be a military outpost in the old days. After the British settlers arrived in the early nineteenth century, there were fierce battles between them and the native people, the Xhosas. With its old pubs and inns, churches and monuments, its Victorian architecture, the city still has a very English atmosphere; it is also the site of the Rhodes University. During my three days in Grahamstown, I stayed with Robert Berold who owns a little house there. Robert is a humanist in the fullest meaning of the word. A literary man, a poet (he is the editor of *Coin*, the foremost poetry magazine of the country), he could easily have had a brilliant academic career, but he chose instead to devote much of his life to help the poor blacks of Grahamstown. It was in 1984 that, with an associate, he launched his first Power Station project: a small wooden toy manufacturing workshop in an abandoned municipal power station, which provided employment for five people. From this modest beginning, the Power Station grew rapidly to, roughly eight years later, 65 full-time and 30 part-time employees working together in five producer co-operatives – making ceramics, screen-printed textiles, puppets and papier-mâché wastepaper baskets. But, as I found out later, what made the Power Station truly special was the remarkable extent in which it was run democratically.

The majority of the workers at the Power Station are women. This is no coincidence but a deliberate decision based on the fact that, in South Africa today, many of the women cannot count on the men to raise their children. One thing that could become a problem at the Power Station is that the salaries depend on production level and revenue, and therefore are variable. In a good month a worker will make R600 (about £130) but in a bad month only half of that which is utterly insufficient to make ends meet. Then the management has to make advance payments and that creates a problem of indebtedness. Robert explained that their aim was to achieve economic viability in a self-reliant situation both of which depended on professional skills and, even more so, on educational levels. If the latter was so low among the township people, it was because not only were wealth, power, income and land so unfairly and unequally distributed in South Africa, but also literacy, skills and knowledge.

Elvis Maholo, the translator-cum-public relations-cum mainten-ance man at the Power Station took me to Joyce Makeleni, one of the veterans, so that I could talk to her. She belonged to the group that was making papier-mâché wastepaper baskets. Seven or eight women worked in a big room, around a long rectangular table. The atmosphere was distinctly relaxed. Joyce's two-year-old baby was brought in from the crèche so that she could breastfeed her. 'She is a delicate child,' Joyce said by way of explanation, 'and she doesn't like the bottle. She also has a tight chest. I had to take her to the doctor not long ago.' Joyce, who was born on a farm in the countryside near Port Alfred but grew up here in Grahamstown, has two other children. She lives in the Mfumlani, one of the several black townships in the Grahamstown area, sharing a two-room house with another woman. She has one room for herself and her two children – her third child is with her mother who also lives in the township, but in a separate house.

'We used to live together,' she said, 'but it was not possible after I had my third child, it was too hard on her.' She pays R50 a month for her room. Her children are from two different men. She left the second one, the father of the last two of her children, a petrol-station attendant, because he was a gambler. He would waste his money in the casino, 'instead of buying food for his children'. This brutal man beat her up badly recently because she refused to go back to him. Joyce is quite happy at the Power Station, 'because I had no job'. The lady she worked for before, a potter, had let her go because she was seven months pregnant. 'She said that business was slow and that could not afford to employ two helpers any more. She said, "Come back after your child is six months old." I told myself: I don't think this lady needs me any more, because I can't wait for six months before starting working again. So I got this job. It's hard because we are working for ourselves. If you are working for a boss you know that you will get your salary; here you know that if you don't work hard, you will not get your salary. Also, you have problems if you don't have enough orders. You are worried because you know that you will not get enough salary.'

Recently, Joyce had had a hard time meeting her bills. One of her creditors threatened 'to put me with the lawyer's if I don't pay'.

Last month was a very bad month, she made 'a very little salary', about R250, and she needs around R500 to make ends meet. 'When you have young children, it is very difficult,' she said. 'They are sick all the time and you have to pay for the doctor.' If she made R800, she said, she could qualify for a loan to buy a four-room house with water and toilets inside. That is her dream. Now it is one room with tap water outside and a bucket toilet also outside. There is no electricity in the township.

Life in Mfumlani is dangerous: 'You can get a robbery even if you are sitting inside your house. . . . The people with the combis, they are fighting now. You are afraid, you don't know which way you can go.' (These are the famous 'taxi wars' between companies that often have political affiliations. It is very big business involving thousands of combis that transport black workers between their workplaces in the white cities and the townships where they live.) I asked Joyce what she would like to see changed if there was an ANC government tomorrow. 'One thing we all wish,' she said, 'is that a new government has a better feeling for everybody. It mustn't think this one must get better, this one must be pressed down. We must all be the same.'

It was eleven o'clock in the morning when I knocked on the door of Rachel Breytenbach's house. It was a beautiful early autumn day, sunny but not too hot. It was quiet, the only sound I could hear was the twittering of the birds. The street was wide, the houses, separated by the usual bougainvillea bushes and gum trees, were old. The woman who opened the door was petite, fair-complexioned and thick-haired. She had limpid blue eyes and something earthy emanated from her. She wore a loose, shapeless smock, had sandals on her feet. Rachel is the only sister of Breyten Breytenbach, the great poet who is also a painter and, until recently, was the *enfant terrible* of Afrikaans letters. He was also 'one of the fiercest and most uncompromising critics of apartheid' as his close friend, André Brink once put it.[5]

I had long been fascinated by Breyten; I wanted to know more about the deep, psychological forces that moved him, and that is why I had come to see his sister Rachel in Grahamstown. I thought that he was one of the genuine white heroes of the liberation struggle, a man in the same league as Beyers Naudé, Helen Joseph, Bram Fisher, and Albie Sachs. He was only twenty years old when he went into voluntary exile to Paris in 1959. He quickly made a name for himself as a painter. By 1964, *Catastrophes*, a book of short stories, and *The Iron Cow Must Sweat*, a volume of poetry, established him as one of the rising stars of Afrikaans literature. He married Ngo Thi Hoang Lien (Yolande), a young woman of Vietnamese origin while he was still in his twenties. The law against mixed marriages was in effect then and she was not allowed into South Africa until 1972. *A Season in Paradise* is about the 'unforgettable' three months that they spent touring the country and visiting friends and relatives.[6] It was during that visit, in a symposium at UCT organised by the *Sestigers*, that he made the fiery speech that is still remembered today. 'We are a bastard people with a bastard language,' he said. 'Our nature is one of bastardy. It is good and beautiful thus. But instead of being proud of it, we feel threatened. We built walls. Not cities, but city walls. And like all bastards – uncertain of their identity – we began to adhere to the concept of purity. That is apartheid. Apartheid is the law of the bastard.'

In August 1975, Breyten returned to South Africa, but this time disguised as a priest and with a false passport. He was now a founding member of *Okhela*, a shadowy white revolutionary organisation operating from Europe and had come to establish contacts and recruit members. But he had been betrayed and had been tailed throughout his three weeks in the country. He was arrested at Jan Smuts airport as he prepared to board the plane for Paris. An interesting twist to the story is that his own brother was a member of the security police that arrested him. After a trial that became a *cause célèbre*, he was found guilty of treason and sentenced to nine years in imprisonment, of which he served seven, before being released and put in a plane back to Paris. The story of his incarceration is told candidly in *The Confessions of an Albino Terrorist*.[7]

In 1986 he was allowed to come back to receive the prestigious *Rapport* prize awarded by the biggest-selling Afrikaans Sunday newspaper. He took advantage of the opportunity to tour the country, blasting apartheid wherever he went. In Pretoria, at his acceptance speech, before a captive audience of five hundred members of the Afrikaner establishment, he accused the Dutch Reform Church of having 'manoeuvred God around like a Casspir'. Adding for good measure: 'Pretoria, that megalomaniacal symbol of racist oppression, should be blown up with dynamite, razed to the ground.' The verbal eruption caused a furore after Breyten left the country and a hunt for scapegoats was on as to who was responsible for letting the 'traitor' back into the country again. H Pakendorff, the editor of *Vaderland*, a liberal daily paper, was sacked. For a while it looked as if even 'Wimpie' de Klerk, the editor of *Rapport* and older brother of F W who at the time was the most powerful politician after Botha himself, might be in danger of losing his job too, but he was eventually spared.

I asked Rachel why Breyten had not come back to South Africa to live after February 1990. She sat on a sofa next to a bookcase and I on an armchair facing her. On the wall above the bookcase hang two of Breyten's early paintings. The house was sparingly furnished. 'Half of it is rented to two students, from the university where I work as a laboratory assistant.' She spoke with a certain directness that is a trait of the Afrikaner personality. 'He was so young when he left,' she said. 'He could not come back for thirteen years and that is a very long time. Then he returned for three months. That is all he was allowed to stay. . . . Then there was the tragedy of the prison, and that was another seven years. He came back again in 1986 for the *Rapport* prize. He actually spoke to me about it, you know: when you come back to a place you were born in and grew up in, you can smell it, you can feel it, everything is so familiar, and yet you feel sad too, because you also realise that you don't belong there any more. And that's the very tragic thing that happened to him. . . .

'The last time I saw him was in December of last year [1991]. I saw him in Cape Town, he also came to Grahamstown, but only for a day and he was very busy – there was this poetry symposium at the university. Things are always happening when Breyten is around and he can be very impulsive; he has lost the concept that people have their own lives to live too, when he wants to see you you must be there for him. We met once more after that in Cape Town and went to Stellenbosch, Paarl and Dal Josaphat [the Coloured township near Paarl] to visit a painter called Botha who lives there. From there we crossed the mountains to Montagu to visit one of our brothers who lives there. Breyten was born in Bonnievale, not far from Montagu, where our family had a farm. So, you see, he was thrown back into a sentimental, emotional world, into something that is very deeply rooted, this is where you come from. I know part of him would like to be here. If he could have a place of his own in the country where he could stay for longer spells with Yolande, I think that's what he needs. He is confused, very confused.'

I wanted Rachel to tell me about the relationship between Breyten and his older brother who worked for the security police. As a prelude to that I asked her about the family. I mentioned that Breyten had written affectionately about her in *A Season in Paradise* (he is very fond of nicknames; in that book he refers to Yolande by about thirty different nicknames, Rachel qualifies for three: 'Baby', 'Puddles' and 'Pinkydoll').

'We are five children in the family,' she began. 'I am the youngest and the only sister. All the brothers had a very good relationship with their mother. . . . When she died [Breyten was in prison and he was not allowed to attend the funeral] a lot of the feelings for the mother came my way [she chuckled]. Not always very good, you know, it can be quite demanding sometimes. . . . They are very different, one can hardly imagine brothers so different one from the other.'

As tactfully as I could, I broached the subject of the brother who worked for the security police. 'Yes,' she agreed, 'it was very difficult, but that situation has changed fortunately. In 1986, when he came for that *Rapport* prize – Father was still alive then – one day I called his older brother and I asked Breyten to talk to him; he did and he was so happy after that. It was a big relief for him, they had not spoken to each other for so many years. His older brother did go to prison to visit him, but that's not really talking. And then our father died [in December 1988, just before Christmas]. I didn't think that Breyten would come [all the way from Paris], but he did and I remember how we were all sitting around the table after the funeral, and it was midnight and they could not stop talking; it was like a dam bursting from all sides; they were all trying to explain how they felt, and so on.'

'It seems that the last time he came [December 1991] he was quite worried about the direction that things were going, fearing that one form of dictatorship would be replaced by another. He said "We shall have to fight for our freedom all over again",' I said.[8]

'Yes, I've picked that up,' said Rachel. 'You see, we don't go into long political discussions when we are together, I don't know if it is an old Afrikaner custom or what, but we will rather talk about family affairs and life in general. What happens is that when there are close friends around, this is when the conversation gets heavily political, and I am usually there listening. Last December we spent an evening together with André [Brink] and Alta [Brink's wife; the Brinks are originally from Grahamstown where they own a big beautiful house; he taught at Rhodes for many years before taking a post at UCT] and they talked politics all night. The problem with Breyten is that while he has a different perspective living outside the country and that is useful, he also is not here long enough to absorb the intricate problems. It's like when you visit a very sick person rarely, the effect on you will be bigger than if you see him all the time. After Mother died, Father had a stroke and I was the only one who was staying with him at the time, and I became used to his condition; for Breyten it was very different: each time he saw him it was a big shock.'

We had orange sodas. I asked her about Breyten's paintings on the walls. 'His painting keeps him very busy,' she said, 'In Europe he is much better known as a painter than a writer, or a poet. He was always successful with his painting. They like his work in Europe, especially in Holland. He is very much in tune with European sensibilities, but I don't think he does it deliberately. He is quite honest in that way. He gives expression to his feelings of the moment. He now has a studio in a little farm that he purchased in Spain, near Barcelona. Painting is his real work; he makes his living from painting, people don't always understand that. They are always asking him to come to South Africa, but that's always taking time away from his work, and you need a lot of time to paint.' She made comments on some of the pictures on the walls: 'That one was done after he came out of prison, that's why it's grey and depressing [he was allowed to write in prison, in fact he wrote *A Season in Paradise* there, but for some reason not to paint]; that one is from Spain, it is very bright and colourful.' Breyten's work is sometimes compared with that of Hieronymus Bosch: 'a dazzling marriage of the real with the mystical and the imaginary,' as Brink put it once, perhaps with a touch of hyperbole.

Rachel next produced an album of photos and there he was: Breyten in Paris, in the kitchen of his small apartment with Yolande; Breyten in Simonstown near Cape Town on the terrace of a villa overlooking the bay which belongs to Suzanne Fox (daughter of Uys Krige, a famous Afrikaner writer) and her husband who is a well known architect; Breyten eating grapes somewhere in the countryside. 'He is very fond of grapes,' Rachel said. 'It must have something to do with his homesickness.' She pointed to another photo. 'That one is very typical of him. You'll always find him with a little notebook on his lap. That's the way he works, writing down his ideas as they come. He doesn't go into an office and close the door behind himself.'

I asked Rachel if Breyten was worried about getting old, obsessed by the idea of death. 'He is vain,' she said and laughed. 'But he is fortunate because he is in very good shape, he does a lot of exercise and he is very fit [in one of the pictures he was in swimming trunks and he looked like someone who does quite a bit of weight-lifting], I think that's the Buddhist side of him, but I wouldn't say that he is afraid of death. He is like the rest of us, we get impatient because time is running out and that we are not that young any more. He missed part of his life in prison; when I went to visit him in Paris after his release he was in a very bad way.'

I asked her about Yolande. 'She is a very special person,' Rachel answered, 'and they've been together such a long time. They have a peaceful and mature understanding. She is a very warm and giving person; sort of reserved, not showing much, but extremely giving; she is quite attractive too. How come they don't have any children? Well, I think you've to begin with their lifestyle in Paris, it was very bohemian . . . then there was the prison, and then it was too late – for a woman, you know, you get past the age. I don't think it's a problem, they don't talk much about it. I suppose she must miss not having children of her own because she comes from a big family. I remember she once told me about my own daughter, "It's sad to have only one child." So she must have strong motherly feelings that she couldn't give expression to. I think what happened was that all those feelings went Breyten's way, and he thrives on that.' She laughed.

'I heard that he was disappointed by the way he was treated by the ANC, that he expected more recognition,' I said.

'Yes, but you must also remember that he is an Afrikaner, and that plays a role too. The Afrikaner is quite different from the English-speaking South African person. It's a whole way of growing up that's different. It's a very different culture. My daughter goes to school here in Grahamstown and I can see clearly the difference between that world and the world that I come from which is more innocent in a way, more expressive, more emotional, more intense.

In fact, I came to Grahamstown to escape all that, I couldn't take it anymore.'

She took a volume from the shelf near her. 'That's his first novel,' she said, '*In Memory of Snow and Dust*. It came out in 1989; he wrote it in English, he is writing in English now. I will be honest with you. I have struggled through it, but I don't always understand what it is all about, it gets very complicated. I asked him the last time he was here, but he never talks much about his work. I think the problem is he doesn't like to spend much time on his writing, it must flow like water from a tap.' She took another slim volume. It was *Sinking Ship Blues*, a well-known poetry book. 'The poetry I can relate to 100 per cent,' she said brightening. 'I remember Breyten once reading his own poems on television, it was a very moving experience. He writes poems in English too now, but never in French, even though he's lived in France most of his life.'

Wanting to leave her on a cheerful note, I said: 'Next time you talk to him, tell him that that photo of his on the cover of his books gives a very misleading impression of him. I thought he was a hunched-up little guy before you showed me the pictures in the album.'

She chuckled. 'Come to think of it, he does look like a hunched-up little guy, you're right. Yes, I'll certainly tell him.'

Notes

1 A significant study with a substantial bibliography: R Riordan's, 'The *Ukuhleleleka* of Port Elizabeth,' in the *Monitor*, June 1988, pages 2–16.

2 BC is a rising force in South Africa. A recent good book on it is: N Barney Pityana, Mamphela Ramphele, M Mplumwana and L Wilson, *Bounds of Possibility: the Legacy of Steve Biko and Black Consciousness*, David Philip, 1991, Cape Town and Johannesburg. See also: B Goba, 'The Black Consciousness Movement: Its Impact on Black Theology', in: J Mosala and B Tihagale (eds), *The Unquestionable Right to Be Free: Essays in Black Theology*, Skotaville, 1986, Johannesburg. More on Steve Biko and BC in Note 3 of Chapter 6.

Two beliefs that are central to the BC philosophy are: one, it is only when you arrive at a deep sense of your own humanity that you can appreciate the humanity of others and are ready to build a community of human beings based on social justice; and two, non-racialism does not mean much if the appalling inequalities in the South African society which were produced by apartheid are not tackled significantly. BC philosophy permeates the thinking of not only the PAC and AZAPO but also of many ANC intellectuals. Pallo Jordan, for example, may or may not be aware of it, but the two beliefs mentioned above underpin his remarks about the whites not seeing the blacks as belonging in the same 'moral universe' as them. See Chapter 17.

3 About the civics in general and SANCO in particular, see Chapter 3 and Note 1 at the end of the chapter.

4 Nelson Mandela, in his speech to the United Nations in New York in September 1993, has called for the lifting of the remaining sanctions.

5 More on Breytenbach in Chapters 5 and 14.

6 Details in Note 4 Chapter 14.

7 Published by Faber & Faber in 1984.

8 In December 1993 it has come to my knowledge that Breyten Breytenbach has written a book about this visit (*Return to Paradise*, published by Harcourt Brace, 1993), which deals with many of the themes that we took up with Rachel. He ends the book: 'Why will I not return to stay? Too late now. Foreigner here. Painted monkey. Bitter dreams. No roots. Attachment too painful. Deathwish . . .' The quote is from the excellent review by Lynn Freed in the *International Herald Tribune* of 9 December 1993.

16

Travel Notes Three: Umtata, Empageni and the Berg

'The life of a Zululand sugar baron is very sweet. In Zululand, the sun always shines, the rains seldom fail, the flowers bloom all year, and there are always enough Zulus to cut your cane and serve your gin and tonic at sunset.'

Rian Malan

My main reason for wanting to go to Umtata was to visit Cecil Cook's Transkei Appropriate Technology Unit (TATU). I had learned about it from Bill Davies, a professor of development studies at Rhodes University in Grahamstown. Bill is involved in something called the Regional Development Forums (RDF) whose goal is the upliftment of poor people living in the townships and villages in rural areas. I went to see Bill in his office at Rhodes. He is an intense man very much committed to what he is doing.

'The poor blacks have been so demoralised, so dehumanised by apartheid that you have to start right at the beginning, by enabling them, by helping them to build capacity,' Bill said. Empowerment will have to wait until that has been achieved because if it came before only chaos can be the result. Indeed, if the RDFs have sometimes run into difficulties in their dealings with the civics, it is because the latter wanted, in addition to their political role of advocacy of the township people's rights to better housing and services, to operate as development agencies as well, something they were not qualified to do.[1] To make things worse, the civics are sometimes beset by substantial corruption and jockeying for power.

An important element, according to Bill, which has not received the attention it deserves is the fact that the urban agglomerations of the hinterland – towns such as Graff Reinet, Cradock, Fort Beaufort, King William's Town, and even Grahamstown; there are about 35 of them in the Eastern Cape alone, whose populations range from fewer than 5,000 to more than 100,000 – have a stagnant and even declining white population and a larger and rapidly growing black population. Under the old apartheid system the whites provided the capital and the know-how and, therefore, the jobs; the blacks provided their labour. That system is crumbling now and is supposed to be replaced by a new one in which the blacks will take over. But the problem is that, for the time being, and probably for a long time to come, they have neither the capital nor the know-how to do so. It can be imagined that to a certain extent the capital will be provided by the state and foreign donors, such as the World Bank, but the skills – and this is where the enablement, the capacity-building part comes in – will have to be created and this is what the RDFs are trying to do. Bill then gave me an example of what he meant in practice.

Recently, the Independent Development Trust (IDT), which he called a remarkable South African institution, received a R750 million grant from the government to launch a nationwide project to provide serviced sites for blacks living in shanty towns. Each site will have a portable toilet, a water tap *and* a water meter. These sites will be provided free to the families that qualify for them (there is a whole set of elaborate criteria), but they must pay for the water and R48 per month for the services, such as refuse removal, emptying bucket toilets and so on. Furthermore, the recipients of the sites are responsible for the building of their own housing. The problem is that many of these people do not have the income that would qualify them for a commercial loan. If a relapse to the ugly shanty town situation is to be avoided (which would be ironic because the serviced sites project was started precisely as a solution to the shanty town problem), a way must be found to build cheap, but still acceptable, decent housing on the sites. Bill argues that the answer is wattle-and-daub housing, whose cost per unit would not exceed R1,000, and this is where TATU comes in, because it is involved in generating alternative technologies that could reduce the building costs quite dramatically. Indeed, one of TATU's significant accomplishments lately has been the reduction of the cost of a 50-square-metre school classroom from R48,000 to R15,000 through 'labour contributions, site-fabricated soil-cement bricks, and the use of village-based builders'. TATU's methods and innovations in poor areas to generate development that is sustainable could certainly be of great use to the Regional Development Forums.

I left Grahamstown early in the morning, again on the N2 and soon reached the unmarked Ciskei border at the Great Fish River. The same rolling hills dotted with villages that looked picturesque from a distance and that I had seen after Fort Beaufort on my way to Fort Hare unfurled before my eyes. In less than an hour, I crossed the whole width of this so-called independent state and arrived in King William's Town, a pleasant enough looking town near Bisho, the Ciskei capital. Another hour or so of travelling inside the white corridor between Ciskei and Transkei, I reached the Transkei border at the Great Kei River. Here 'independence' is, ostensibly, taken more seriously: there is a substantial concrete building where the travellers' passports are checked, desultorily it is true, by the South African police.

Not surprisingly, the Transkeian countryside was quite similar to that of Ciskei. The sprawling campus of the University of Transkei (Unitra) is on the N2, about seven miles from the centre of Umtata. It was built in the 1970s in a contemporary sort of style; it is not ugly, but lacks originality or character. I parked the car in a huge parking lot under the broiling sun and set about looking for the admin building where the PR department is normally located. In an esplanade on top of the main plaza several hawkers had set up shop selling food, tobacco, fruit and cold drinks. The PR people were friendly and hospitable, and knew about TATU. They told me where it was and then somebody took me to the political science department to see if someone was available there that I could talk to. The building was jam-packed with students who were sitting on the floors, stairs, and passageways of the building. The lack of maintenance was in evidence from the chipped furniture, the worn-out and grimy carpeting. I ended up in the office of Xoliswa Jozan-nes, a fairly junior lecturer. She told me that Transkei had achieved 'independence' in 1976 and that the Matanzima brothers, who were in power for more than a decade, were dictatorial and corrupt but that they followed a policy of Africanisation in which the state played a leading role. Bantu Holomisa, the young military leader who took over in 1987 after the Matanzimas fled, reversed that policy and opted for a free enterprise system that opened Transkei to foreign investment, that is, largely, to white South African businessmen. But a common characteristic of both regimes was that 'independence' had not changed much for the ordinary people; only a small elite of top civil servants had benefited from it becoming enormously rich, thanks to nepotism and corruption. The rural areas still depended largely on the money remittances of the migrant workers. Except for a large irrigation scheme in the northern district and some assistance to 'progressive farmers', these rural areas remained pretty much the same as they were before 'independence'. Transkei was ANC country and Holomisa was very supportive of the organisation.

When I arrived in TATU at about ten o'clock in the following morning, Cecil Cook was not yet there. 'He often works at home in the mornings,' his secretary said, 'because he is constantly solicited in the office,' and gave me some literature to read. I was astonished to discover that more than 130 people worked here in several departments such as carpentry, metalwork, brickmaking, farming, and so on. I went walking around. It was an active, industrious place, like a beehive. The atmosphere seemed relaxed and the workers happy to be there. Cecil came at about eleven. He is an American with a long history in international co-operation and an unusual personality that combines the mystical and visionary with the pragmatic and practical. The former attribute is represented, as it were, by a florid pepper-and-salt beard; the latter, by the ubiquitous American baseball cap that he wore most of the time.

Our first conversation in his office took a distinctly philosophical turn. Cecil is concerned about the future of humanity on earth. He is convinced that the future of our planet does not belong to a high-tech, urban-industrial, largely Euro-American, civilisation, but that the survival of mankind depends on the development of a 'third way' (TATU also means 'three' in Xhosa): a post-modern, post-urban/industrial civilisation, which would be mixed, integrating the strengths of both the high-tech and the pre-industrial civilisations. Since I happen to agree, broadly speaking, with that view, we hit it off immediately and derived a lot of pleasure talking for the next couple of hours about the Club of Rome and its Limit to Growth ideas which had been the rage in the 1960s before being debunked in the 70s after scientists showed that their numbers were wrong. Their prediction that certain non-renewable resources, such as oil and some non-ferrous minerals would be depleted in less than a century, proved to be widely off the mark, for example. They also might have exaggerated the growth (exponential) of pollution and its uncontrollability. But they certainly did a great job of awareness-creation and consciousness-raising. The general public and governments now acknowledge readily that these problems exist, that they are serious and that they could become dangerous if they are not tackled with foresight and determination.[2]

I had dinner with the Cooks that night. They told me that both he, a former Christian, and his wife, a former Jewess (also American) had converted into the Baha'i faith which is based on the belief of human brotherhood and the necessity of a world government to promote peace and social justice on our planet. The Baha'i religion was founded in Persia in the second half of the nineteenth century by Mirza Husain Ali, known as Baha'u'llah, who based himself on the teaching of the prophet Bab, who was executed at the age of 30.

Also invited to dinner was Ezra Sigwela, a former journalist who now worked for the Transkei Council of Churches (TCC). He was involved with TCC's Dump People Project in Umtata. It tried to help poor and homeless people. Ezra, who is in his early fifties now, went through some really bad times in the sixties and seventies when the going could be rough for the anti-apartheid activists. It all started with his making the 'mistake' of writing a couple of articles for *New Age*, the Communist journal. He was arrested in 1964 and detained for thirteen months during which time he was tortured by the security police; later he was sentenced to an additional fourteen months in prison. In 1969, while he was working for the Xhosa Development Corporation, he was arrested again for sheltering an ANC cadre and was sentenced to ten years' imprisonment, nine of which he spent on Robben Island. In 1980, he was again picked up by the police, just before his twins were born, because he was helping Ciskei refugees. This time he went to court and eventually won his case, but not before spending another seven months in gaol. In 1986, he was, again, taken into custody for five weeks: they wanted to know about his work for the TCC. After that it was thought safer to get him out of the way for a while: he was sent to the United States to study theology. He came back in 1989 and has been working for the TCC ever since. It was quite a story. But also one, alas, very common in South

Africa. I found it remarkable that, after all the pain and suffering, Ezra did not harbour any resentment or hatred in his heart.

In the afternoon, Cecil asked X, one of his social workers whose name I have regrettably forgotten, to take me to Nyandeni, a village where TATU was involved in some community projects. He put a Toyota pickup truck at my disposal and off we went with X, a friendly and talkative woman of about forty and an expert driver. After about half an hour of fast driving on dusty tracks, I noticed not far from the road two or three huts and a little boy who ran off when he saw the car. That suggested that there were people around and I asked X to stop so that we could go and talk to them. Two women and four or five children were on the other side of the huts. One of the women was busy bathing one of the children in an iron basin. The other woman crouched next to her, looking after the other children. Two more smaller red and yellow plastic buckets lay around, as well as a pile of cow dung. X spoke to the women in Xhosa, making occasional clicking sounds and they responded in a friendly way.

They didn't seem upset by our unannounced visit. The two women were the grandmothers of the children, not the mothers, one of whom had gone to fetch wood in the forest and the other worked as a casual domestic worker in Umtata. One of the huts was an abandoned rondavel, its thatched roof had caved in and one of the walls had collapsed. The second one was a wattle-and-daub hut with a metal roof, on top of which two or three bricks were placed to prevent it from flying away when the wind blew fiercely, a common occurrence in these mountains. The third structure was a new rondavel presumably built to replace the one which had fallen apart. The woman who sat next to the basin took the baby boy, who had been bathed, dried and clothed, and in a few effortless movements put him in a piece of cloth which she then wrapped around her back to carry him in the African fashion. With a khaki-coloured traditional turban on her head, bead necklace and bracelets around her wrists and ankles, and loop earrings, she cut a very exotic figure. The children did not look underfed or malnourished. One of the women was a widow. The husband of the other one and the fathers of the children were all migrant workers. They sent money once in a while, but irregularly; they came back only for about three weeks at the end of the year. Life, one of the women said, revolved around looking after the children, hoeing the small patch of land around the huts, fetching water from the river or the communal tap both quite a distance away – they had, therefore to use the same water to wash themselves and the children, to clean the house, and so forth – firewood was harder and harder to find, so that they were using cow dung as a substitute. Their daily diet consisted mainly of mealie meal, pumpkins and beans; when sometimes there wasn't enough food to go around, they had to ask for help from relatives. It was very spartan inside the rondavel where one of the families lived: sleeping mats, a few bundles placed against the wall on the dirt floor; a simple wooden table and two or three chairs in a corner; and that was all. Yes, they had heard about the sweeping political changes that were happening in the country, but they didn't know what it all meant. They sometimes listened to a Mandela speech on the radio, but they didn't really understand what he said. No, nothing had changed in their lives after Holomisa had taken over from the Matanzimas. It was the same thing for them.

I left them feeling that these people were in the business of survival and that they were not holding their breath for anything to happen that could affect their lives positively. They vaguely hoped that something good might happen, but they didn't count on it. Maybe that's the definition of a true realist.

The sky lowered and became a menacing grey as we continued our journey towards Nyandeni. Before long it started raining and it was damp, dark and foggy when we reached the village, which was scattered over a large area but we couldn't see much because of the fog. We stopped by a small house with a yard closed off by a broken fence where a skinny cow was grazing. A young woman wearing a headscarf came out of the house. X knew her well because she once joined a sewing class organised by TATU. She lived in that small brick house with her two young children. She told X that her sewing machine had broken down a long time ago and that she couldn't get it fixed because she couldn't take it to Umtata. There was no regular transport link between the village and Umtata. Her story was similar – disturbingly so somehow – to that of the two old women that I had just seen: husband in Jo'burg, remittances of money, brief visits at the end of the year, news from the radio, not much hope that things were going to change for the better – there used to be an ANC branch in the village, but it had 'disappeared'. It had got dark inside the house and I could barely see her face.

The older one of her two children, a girl of about ten, went into the bedroom (the house had only two rooms) and came back with an oil lamp, which she lighted. From the open door I could see the cow grazing. A mangy dog passed by. A couple of chickens strayed into the room but nobody paid any attention.

'There is a primary school in the village,' the woman said, 'and a church. If I have a serious problem I go and talk to the priest.' She was a good Christian. She showed us the Bible which was the only book that she had in the house, which was modestly furnished: a square table with an oilcloth on it, four chairs, a cupboard. The floor was in cement, there was a sink and running water, but the toilet was outside. They went to bed at about eight o'clock and got up as soon as there was light outside. She has to milk the cow, prepare breakfast, and get the kids off to school. Then she will work in the field – hoeing, weeding, watering. The rest of the day is taken by household chores. She has some friends and they do get together during the day, but never after it gets dark. The loneliness in the dark, in the meagre light of the oil lamp, that's the toughest part. . . .

It was stormy weather when I left Umtata early in the morning. The hills were covered by a mantle of fog and visibility was poor. Flashes of lightning tore the leaden sky, followed, at irregular intervals, by claps of thunder. It had not rained for months, I was told, and it was as if suddenly some invisible floodgates had opened in the heavens above to punish the humans for some serious offence that they had committed. The countryside was littered with the carcasses of abandoned vehicles. A man on horseback looked like a ghost from a long bygone era. A shepherd boy and his flock seemed lost in the middle of the hills.

Before Mount Frere, the next sizeable town, I passed several villages where clusters of women waited for transport. I gave them lifts as much as I could. Some were going shopping, others to work. One bright-eyed young woman worked as a cashier in a department store in Mount Ayliff, the next biggish town after Mount Frere. Her home was in the village of Qumbu, about 60 miles away, so she had no choice but to rent a room in Mount Ayliff where she stayed during the week and at the weekends she went back to Qumbu. Much of what she made, R300 (about £80) a month, went for rent, food and transport costs. She hoped to find a job in the big city

(Durban, Port Elizabeth); she took correspondence courses in business administration. It was a story that I heard often: they are all
attracted by the city lights like moths by the glare of a lamp. 'There
are no jobs in Transkei' was a constant lament, like a dirge in a
funeral. They all dreamed of becoming nurses, social workers,
teachers, office workers. It represented for them a good, steady
income, job security, a loan for a house, a down payment for a car,
furniture.

Suddenly a hailstorm hit the car. Ice nuggets as big as small
marbles struck the roof in waves and the road was soon covered
by a white carpet that snaked around the hills for miles and miles.
I crossed into Natal briefly before entering another part of the
Transkei (all ten bantustans are made up of bits and pieces of land;
KwaZulu, for example, is made up of ten pieces, Bophuthatswana,
eight). After Umzimkulu, the last substantial town in the Transkei,
it was Natal for good. What a contrast! As soon as I crossed the
'border', it was as if I had entered the countryside of a mountain
state in America; in Colorado or Wyoming, for example. Pine and
fir forests on the rolling hills, immaculate corn fields, beautiful
farmsteads, modern villas. Another thunderstorm hit as I was near-
ing Durban. Lightning fell so close to the car that I could see the
balls of fire and feel their jolt. It was like being in the middle of a
battle with artillery shells exploding all around me. It was with
relief that I checked in at a guest house near the university.

Jeremy Evans is a young researcher at the University of Natal who
works on the delicate subject of *Muti* murders. Simon Bekker, the
director of the Centre for Social and Development Studies, with
whom I had a chat, had suggested – after I told him that I was
interested in looking at the South African reality from as many
different angles and perspectives as possible – that I should go and
see him. He also gave me an article on the subject.

Muti is one of those words difficult to translate into English; but
it connotes the idea of magic and witchcraft and, therefore, derives
from a belief in the supernatural. The practitioners or professionals
of *muti* are the *inyangas* and *sangomas*, that is, roughly speaking,
witch doctors, wizards and diviners; with a sub-group of medicine
men, healers and herbalists. It appears that 10,000 *inyangas* and
sangomas are practising in the greater Johannesburg area alone.
'They are supported by a nationwide network of 40,000 traders in

healing and magical herbs,' writes Rian Malan, adding that 85 per cent of all black households consult an *inyanga* or *sangoma* 'at least occasionally' to deal with problems in the areas of love life, evil spirits, health and happiness, success in one's chosen profession or in business, and so on.[3] The personality and the presence of a person can be enhanced by medicines called *intelezi*, prescribed by the *inyangas* and *sangomas* and prepared by the healers or herbalists. The debate on whether or not the *inyangas* and *sangomas* are charlatans or bona fide traditional doctors and psychologists misses the point and is misleading because they derive much of their effectiveness from the belief that the people have in them. For our purposes here, suffice it to say that they have nothing to do with killing human beings.

It goes, of course, very differently with the *muti* murders. Jeremy Evans, in his scholarly article, '*Muti* Murders: Ritual Responses to Stress', gives a fairly typical example of a *muti* murder that took place in KwaNgqobeni in Zululand:

A group of people led by Ntambo [faction leader] decided to gain the upper hand in a conflict that threatened to break out with the local group of comrades. During a meeting it was decided that one of the comrades should quickly be killed to provide ingredients for a powerful medicine that would strengthen Ntambo's group. A young comrade, about fourteen years old, was caught and mutilated. *Intelezi* was made with his head, left arm and foot and his genitals, and the concoction was cooked over a slow fire. Each member of Ntambo's group took his turn to hold a blanket over his head and absorb the steam from the *muti*. After they had been (thus) strengthened, the group were attacked by the comrades who were superior in numbers and in weapons. Ntambo's group won the battle.[4]

In the same article, Evans maintains that *muti* murders have increased dramatically lately: in Umlazi (the biggest black township in Natal), for example, during a period of intense conflict in the late 1980s, dismembered bodies with missing genitals, internal organs, hands, feet and sometimes even heads, were discovered at least one every two weeks (about 25 a year). Presently, that number is down to about 12 to 15 per year but these are only the reported cases, the actual number of incidents is probably much higher. In the Umbumbulu district on the south coast, an area badly affected, an average of six dismembered bodies are found every month. *Muti* murders increase significantly during periods of intense conflict because human *muti* is supposed to enable those who profit from it to appropriate the power in their victims' genitals, brain and other organs. The more powerful the victim, therefore, the more effective the *muti* that derives from him. By that factor alone, *muti* murders involving white victims should be on the increase too, (because whites are seen as very powerful) but that has not been the case until now, so other dissuasive factors (fear of retribution, bad publicity in the West) must have been at work.

After I left Evans, I continued thinking about the subject: however one rationalised the *muti* murders as being part of the traditional thought system, 'perceived by their adherents to be more or less commonplace, rational and moral', as Evans wrote, the fact remains that they *are* barbaric, and conjure up in the Western mind images of cannibalistic savagery. And therein lies the paradox: certainly, the subject of *muti* murders is a legitimate field of research; but, on the other hand, the temptation is there for white South Africans to overdo it, ie, to exaggerate and amplify its importance, so that the African society is portrayed as being ruled deep down by some cruel and primitive impulses. The truth is that I hesitated before I decided to include the subject in this book because of my sympathy for the black cause. Is it possible for the white South African researchers and journalists, considering what is at stake, to remain objective? I wish I knew the answer to that question, but my intuitive reaction is that it probably isn't. . . .

Empageni, despite its African-sounding name, is a white town (the local black township is called Ngwelezane). Rian Malan describes it thus:

> The town rises like an island from the sea of green cane, and the sky above is often stained by the smoke from a fuming sugar mill. It is sugar that creates the wealth that gives white Empageni its prosperous gloss, its look of a boomtown in the American Sunbelt. There's a brand-new mall downtown, vaguely Moorish in architecture, and one or two multi-storey office blocks on the main street. The parks are clean, the schools spacious, the streets and driveways full of shining new Toyotas, Hondas and BMWs.

A blight of split-level ranch homes is spreading out across the surrounding countryside. In white backyards, uniformed black maids are hanging out the washing, bare-chested black garden boys trimming the hedges, and the white madams are . . . seated on a comfortable sofa in [their] living room[s], sipping tea. [As for Ngwelezane] The government has built no new houses for twenty-six years, because Pretoria's mad scientists don't want more blacks in 'white' South Africa.[5]

I had left Durban early in the morning and drove north along the coastal lowlands stopping at the big bridge that spans the mighty Tugela River to watch its muddy waters flow into the nearby Indian Ocean. On the other side of this river, I thought, is Zululand, the traditional territory of the Zulu kingdom which was founded by the legendary King Shaka. This is the river that the powerful army commanded by Lord Chelmsford had crossed more than a century ago to defeat King Cethswayo's army and bring to an end the independence of the proud Zulu nation. At Gingindlovu, just before Empageni, I had turned inland to have a look at the lush, green sugar-cane fields which belonged to white sugar barons. 'The life of a Zululand sugar baron is very sweet,' writes Malan. 'In Zululand, the sun always shines, the rains seldom fail, the flowers bloom all year, and there are always enough Zulus to cut your cane and serve your gin and tonic at sunset.'[6]

I had not come to Empageni to visit the town, however, but to see Dan Taylor who worked at the Centre for Low Input Agricultural Research and Development (CLIARD), which was based at the University of Zululand. Dan turned out to be a genial fellow of about 35. In his office, quite barren except for a few maps and old photographs of African chiefs on the walls, we spoke about Kwa-Zulu and Mangosuthu Gatsha Buthelezi, its undisputed leader.

'Much of the land in Zululand is too dry and of too poor quality,' Dan said, 'to be farmed by traditional techniques alone and what we try to do here in CLIARD is to come up with methods of cultivation which use little water and save on chemical fertilisers.' Dan told me that in the grand apartheid era the land was controlled by the department of Development Aid – with some areas of free-hold tenure. Much of this land [which is made up of Zululand and other enclaves in Natal] was turned over to the KwaZulu government, but the department still holds on to some land that was purchased from white farmers for consolidation purposes. In KwaZulu, a system of patronage exists between the government and the chiefs, who are responsible for allocating the land to the villagers. In exchange for their political support, the chiefs receive generous salaries and other perks from Ulundi. Inkatha draws much of its support from the homeland's civil service. Inkatha membership makes it easier to acquire a business licence, land for farming, and so on. Schoolchildren are automatically members of Inkatha and their membership fees are included in their school fees. Inkatha's main problem is that the youth is increasingly turning its back on Inkatha and joining the ANC, which offers it a better hope for the future. Many of the older generation who grew up with Radio Zulu may still feel an affinity with Inkatha, but not the young people. The large majority of the rural people are apolitical, more concerned with bread-and-butter issues. But the KwaZulu government has done very little to improve the quality of their lives, so they see it as a failure.

People are also disillusioned because they harboured the hope of the Zulu nation rising from the ashes, like the mythical phoenix to defeat the *boere* tyranny. What they see instead is that the KwaZulu government is nothing but a pawn in the hands of an oppressive regime. At the university, the ANC has majority support, then come PAC and AZAPO. Inkatha has a very small presence. The majority of the students are still Zulus, but a large and growing minority are not; the university is trying to move away from its tag of being a Zulu institution. The townships in Natal used to be Inkatha strongholds but that has been challenged successfully by the ANC, which has gained ground and Inkatha did not like that, hence the violence. The United Workers Union of South Africa (UWUSA), launched by Inkatha in 1986 with a great fanfare, is generally seen as a kind of sweetheart union. It has never opposed management, it has never done anything for the workers, even Inkatha supporters admit that COSATU offers them a better alternative. In a general election and in Natal as a whole – assuming that political violence and intimidation were brought under control – Inkatha probably would not get more than 20 to 30 per cent of the votes. Inkatha is seen as a predominantly ethnic organisation and many people are against that. The ANC would win the election because it would carry the big townships such as Umlazi, KwaMashu and Edendale. The Nats, or a new centrist party led by De Klerk, would do well in the white and Indian areas but that would not be more than 15 per cent of the total votes.

Later, Dan took me on a tour of the nearby rural areas in one of CLIARD's four-wheel-drive vehicles. Soon after leaving the main road we were in traditional Zululand: dry, dusty tracks, flat at first but steep and with big pot holes later on. We stopped to talk to two Zulu women hoeing in a small patch of land. As in the rest of tropical Africa, in Zululand too much of the work is done by women. Dan spoke some Zulu, so we engaged them in conversation. They were friendly and cheerful and laughed easily. It was a potato patch they were working on and, predictably enough, they complained about the lack of rain. Dan asked them a few questions about manure and weeding, and then we moved on. He pointed, here and there, to small fields of bananas, cassava, maize and beans around the huts and shacks. The more we pushed inland, the more we could see the damage wrought by drought, erosion and flooding: dry river beds, boulders displaced by the storm waters, ditches and crevasses and scrubby vegetation.

I noticed a compound with several dwellings by the side of the track and asked Dan if we could go in to pay them an impromptu visit. He was reluctant at first but, as I insisted, he gave in. I was startled to find out that the place was crowded: a group of five young men huddled in a corner drinking beer while one of them played on an old guitar, they were the only ones who wore decent clothing; some of the women, in rags, prepared food, others looked after babies; seven or eight half-naked children hung about or played with wire toy cars that they had probably made themselves. They all seemed baffled by our appearance. Despite Dan's greetings and explanations in Zulu they remained reserved, apathetic and even suspicious. Our attempts to break the ice met with only limited success. Suddenly I saw in Dan's eyes that he was afraid. I remembered that there was always an element of unpredictability in situations such as this, experienced 'Africa hands' knew that. In South Africa, being at the wrong place at the wrong time can be fatal. The young men stopped making music and drinking, stood up and came to join us. They were unemployed. Luckily, some relatives worked on the Reef and sent some money and this was how they managed to survive. They also grew some food around the compound. Sometimes one of them would find casual work in Eshowe or Empageni. They were not threatening but there were gaps in the conversation, periods of uneasy silence. Dan continued to be uncomfortable, so after a while we left.

Once in the car I asked him what was the matter, why was he so nervous. The only white men who appear suddenly and without warning are the police, he said. As a rule, one has to be with a black person that they know. Maybe they thought we were spying on them.

On our way back to the campus, we came across a group of a dozen or so schoolchildren who were returning to school after the lunch recess. They looked good in their school uniforms: white shirts (some of the boys wore ties) and blue skirts for the girls and well ironed grey trousers for the boys; in spite of the dust on the road, their shoes were well polished. They waved back at us when we waved and the boys broke into a grin and the girls giggled, they seemed a happy and relaxed lot. They were the generation of the nineties and the future belonged to them. . . .

Ted Tollman (a relation by marriage of the Jo'burg Kahns) had to make at least ten phone calls before he could secure a place for me at one of the hotels in the Drakensberg (the Berg) mountains where I had decided to spend the four days of the Easter holidays. The Berg, in northern Natal, is one of the places well-heeled South Africans go on holiday – other places include the Natal coastline on the Indian Ocean, Sun City in Bophuthatswana, the Cape Peninsula, the Kruger Park and the lush, tropical valleys of the Northern Transvaal. There are a dozen or so good hotels on the Berg, as well as chalet-type cottages that can be rented by the weekend or for longer periods. For the less affluent there are the camping sites and the inns in the national parks and nature reserves.

Ted is a professor of architecture at the University of Natal; Shirley, his wife, is a psychologist who teaches at the same university. They are decent, liberal people who live in a big old house on Chelmsford Road near the university. They invited me to dinner one night. My impression at the end of my visit was that, despite the brave façade that they put on, they were worried about the future. They told me that two of their white acquaintances had been murdered lately. 'So people are afraid,' Ted said. 'Criminal and political violence have increased sharply. We don't feel safe.' A certain weariness, pessimism transpired from their comments.

They were 'hanging in there', because it was too late for them to start all over again elsewhere. Like the Kahns in Jo'burg.

The Champagne Sports Resort was even more luxurious than I expected: manicured lawns, swimming pool, tennis courts, a bowling alley, big tropical plants, colourful parasols in the shade of which people sat sipping drinks and chatting while the children splashed and cavorted in the pool. The room I stayed in was spacious, nicely furnished with Scandinavian-looking furniture and had colour television. The cost was R150 (£35), including breakfast and a meal, buffet type and of excellent quality. In the dining room all the patrons were white, except for two Indian families who had come en masse: grandparents, parents and children; all the waiters were black, and the managers, again white.

I spent the following three days exploring the region, which was quite big: it took me two hours to drive to the Rugged Glen Mountain Resort. The Mont-aux-Sources, the Cathedral Peak and the Cathkin Peak hotels had magnificent views of the mountains by the same name. The Mountains of the Dragon, being in the 3,000 to 3,500 metres range (the higher peaks are in the neighbouring Lesotho, but even there they are all under 4,000 metres), they are not as spectacular as the central European Alps, which are 700 to 800 metres higher. They have no jagged peaks covered by permanent snow and glaciers but they are massive and cover a very large area. In the Zulu villages on the rolling hills I saw some rare specimens of the low-slung (shorter than a man, like the Masai huts), thatch-roofed rondavels, but mostly the dwellings were small wattle-and-daub huts.

Zulu children followed the passing cars trying to sell primitive but charming clay or loam sculptures: small stylised animals like horses and Zebu cows. I gave a lift to three boys who seemed thrilled to travel by car. One of them offered me a horse as payment for the ride: 'It's for nothing,' he said. 'You can have it if you want it.' As I am typing these lines, the little horse with an arched neck but no mane, small holes in places for eyes, short stubby legs and a curved tail, but no ears (they were broken in the transport), is standing on my desk, as if keeping an eye on what I am writing.

Saturday night. The pub of the hotel is bursting at the seams with young people. They are truly packed like sardines in a tin, there must be at least two hundred of them standing, sitting, playing billiards, smoking, drinking, dancing to the throbbing music oozing from a jukebox in a corner. I made a point of searching carefully but, with the exception of the barman, I couldn't see a single black face. They were all the sons and daughters of the South African moneyed class living it up. As I stood there watching, a big Merc pulled up and two girls, one perhaps sixteen the other eighteen, came out of it and went into the pub. They were both clothed in the latest-fashion designer jeans and blouses. The big Merc pulled out ponderously, almost majestically; presumably it would return at closing time to collect the girls. I walked in the direction of the cottages. I saw light in some of the windows. Silhouettes of women tidying things in the kitchen. Men, women and children in the living rooms watching television, having a good time. The very image of affluent normality itself. I sat on an old bench and gazed at the starry sky. The almost-full moon was rising over the tips of the tall fir trees. In the small chapel nearby someone played the piano, practising the hymns of Easter Sunday. I could see the shape of the distant mountains in the dark. It was cool, but not cold. And so peaceful.

Notes

1 More on the civics in Chapter 3 and Note 1.

2 See Donella H and Dennis L Meadows *et al*, *The Limits to Growth: A Report for the Club of Rome's Project on the Predicament of Mankind*, Universe Books Publishers, 1972, New York, which is still a very stimulating book.

3 R Malan, *My Traitor's Heart*, Vintage, 1991, page 228.

4 Unpublished mimeographed paper, Centre of Social and Development Studies, University of Natal, 1991.

5 R Malan, *My Traitor's Heart*, pages 182–4.

6 R Malan, *My Traitor's Heart*, page 181.

17

Wrapping It Up With Pallo:
a Question of Moral Universe

*'The biggest obstacle is psychological ... the decision makers [of the
major conglomerates] ... don't see the blacks as living in the same moral
universe as themselves.'*

Pallo Jordan

I first met Pallo Jordan in 1987, when I was a visiting scholar at the
Institute of International Studies of the University of California at
Berkeley. The institute had organised a conference on South Africa
and Pallo was invited as a guest of honour. Unless my memory
betrays me, he gave one of the two keynote speeches at the conference. He was at the time the deputy director of the ANC's Department of Information and Publicity (DIP). He struck me as a very
bright, but also shrewd, person; well in control of his emotions,
with a good sense of humour. He has deliberate, almost ponderous,
manners which, combined to his big, soft dark-brown eyes, high
curved brow and a full black beard, give him the appearance of a
sage. He is that, but not to the point of overlooking the fact that
politics is essentially a power game and, therefore, the art of the
possible. Thus he is a pragmatic man but also a Marxist at heart, I
believe. A Marxist in the sense that a dose of Marxist analysis is
inevitable if one wishes to understand the problems of poverty,
inequality and exploitation. The question of policy, ie, how to
address these problems is largely a different matter altogether, of
course – particularly in view of what has happened in the Soviet
Union and Eastern Europe. At any rate, Pallo comes from a relatively privileged background: his father was a university lecturer
and his mother a teacher and both were involved in the black
politics of their day.

Wrapping It Up With Pallo 249

He received a solid education at the University of Wisconsin at Madison and at the London School of Economics and started working full time for the ANC in 1975. For a few years he was in charge of Radio Freedom based in Luanda. He was then moved to Lusaka to head DIP's research unit. In 1985 he was elected to the National Executive Committee and promoted to deputy director of the DIP. When Johnny Makatini died in 1989, Thabo Mbeki was named chief of foreign affairs and Pallo replaced Thabo as director of the DIP. In July 1991, in the new elections to the NEC at the national convention in Durban, Pallo received the fifth largest number of votes – after Hani, Thabo, Joe Slovo and Patrick (Terror) Lekota. He is presently seen as one of the four or five most influential leaders of his generation. He could make a good minister of Foreign Affairs one day.

I saw Pallo twice, once in early February 1992, soon after my arrival in South Africa, and once at the end of April, just before I left the country, both times in his office at Shell House, national headquarters of the ANC, 51 Plein Street, in central Johannesburg. The building, a twenty-storey skyscraper, was sold to the ANC – at a very 'reasonable' price, the rumour goes – after the petroleum giant decided to pull out from South Africa because it was getting too much flak from anti-apartheid campaigners at home. Pallo's office, on the nineteenth floor, is surprisingly modest, crammed with electronic equipment and piles of documents. The telephone rang constantly: many were overseas calls from journalists looking for quotes and information. I remember one of them asked sensitive questions about ANC's finances: where the money came from and how much its executives were paid, and so on. Pallo was a bit nonplussed at first and tried to evade the questions by saying that it was classified information. But when the journalist insisted (in the name of freedom of information, something like that), he promised to send him a copy of the latest treasurer's report (which probably did not contain most of the answers the man was looking for, but it was a diplomatic way of getting around the problem without antagonising him.

The first time I saw Pallo he said that they would try to organise some visits for me in Soweto and in the townships of the Vaal Triangle to the south of Jo'burg – Sebokeng, Sharpeville – but nothing came of it. Sakkie Macozoma, his deputy I believe, who was put in charge of it, had other more important things to do, he later told me on the phone. My second meeting with Pallo was the productive one: we spent about two hours together discussing SAIRR's *Race Relations Survey 1991–2* which had just come out and that I had just finished reading . . . What follows is a summary of that conversation.

I began by mentioning Revd Beyers Naudé's comment in the introduction. (like Helen Joseph and Bram Fisher, Naudé is revered by the blacks. A former secretary-general to the South African Council of Churches, he could easily have become a top member of the Afrikaner power elite but instead chose anti-apartheid militancy). In view of the 'political conflict, economic crisis, poverty, unemployment, lack of housing and the educational mess in South Africa, the churches are overwhelmed by the vastness and apparent insolubility of the problem.' And then, to drive Naudé's point home, I read Pallo the conclusions of several studies mentioned in the survey that supported Naudé's comment.

Item one: an Econovision study that found:

By the end of 1990 about four million adults were without formal employment, and that unemployment will grow by 700,000 in 1991 and 1992 . . . Only 9 per cent of the people entering the labor market between 1985 and 1990 were employed in the formal sector. Jobs in the key manufacturing sector grew only by 0.3 per cent in the 1980s decade . . . The 'lost generation' – millions of poorly educated, unemployed, young black people with a high frequency of crime, violence, political radicalism and general anarchism – could grow by half a million within a mere two years. Some 90 per cent of those currently unemployed were estimated to be below the age of 30 . . . The shortage of executive and skilled workers is expected to reach 921,000 by 2005, while the surplus of semi-skilled and unskilled workers will rise to 11,570,000.

Item two: Ina Perlman, the executive director of Operation Hunger, has declared that malnutrition and hunger in South Africa was now 'emphatically the worst situation in ten years'. 25,000 people are dying of hunger each year. Operation Hunger was feeding 1.6 million people daily, partly due to the harsh drought experienced 1991–2.

Item three: the catastrophic housing situation. According to an

Urban Foundation study, seven million people lived in shacks. The backlog was more than one million houses, while altogether 40,464 houses were built for Africans in 1990, and indications were that the number built in 1991 would be even less than that figure . . . The 1991–2 budget allocated about one billion rands (about £200 million) for African housing, a little more than one per cent of the total. The government has set aside two billion rands more for the construction of 100,000 serviced sites (30-by–60 foot plots with access to communal water tanks and portable bucket-system toilets). The people are expected to build their own houses on the sites.[1]

Item four: the lack of electricity. ESCOM admits that between 60 and 70 per cent of the South African population does not have access to electricity. Of the 271 black townships nationwide, only seven are fully electrified – possibly another 70 to 80 are partly electrified. ESCOM has launched a crash programme of township electrification that could result in total electrification in ten years' time.

Item five: the very unequal distribution of health resources. The whites who are less than 15 per cent of the population consumed more than half of all public and private health services in 1990–91. 69 per cent of the whites were members of a health care scheme, as opposed to 33 per cent of the Indians, 30 per cent of the Coloureds, but only 5 per cent of the Africans.

Item six: the gap in education. The difference in per capita expenditure in education between the whites and the Africans was reduced from 18 to 1 in 1969–70, to 4 to 1 in 1989–90. But that did not fundamentally redress the particular backlog in education. African schools remained overcrowded, badly equipped and many of the teachers were underqualified. The quality of education in the black universities of the homelands was much lower than the white universities. Even in the liberal English-speaking universities the percentage of African students was less than 15 per cent: at Wits, for example, 2,599 out of a total of 19,148 were African in 1990; at UCT, 1,378 out of 13,545. In Afrikaans-speaking universities, the numbers were much worse, of course: at the University of Pretoria, only 293 out of 23,323 were African, barely more than one per cent; at Stellenbosch, only about five per cent of the students (686 out of 14,122) were Coloureds whose mother tongue is Afrikaans – the number of Africans was insignificant.

Item seven: land ownership. Suffice it to say that in the formerly white South Africa (87 per cent of the total amount of land), Africans don't own any land because it was taken away from them.[2]

'So here we are, Pallo,' I said. 'That's an incomplete list of the African grievances. Now, what about the willingness of the whites to address them? One would assume that, because of strong guilt and shame feelings that should be present, the whites would be prepared to make great sacrifices. Is this the case? The existing evidence, while less than conclusive, does not point in that direction. I gave Pallo three examples from the Survey, the first one, a University of Stellenbosch study, for example draws attention to the fact that 'South Africa is a fairly middle-income country in the same league as Algeria and Hungary, with a per capita income of $2,290, has limited resources with which to solve social problems. The output of the whole South African economy is smaller than that of most cities in industrial countries with populations of five million or more. The resources available for addressing poverty are not as great as often thought.'

What is the 'message' of this statement? It is, I believe, do not expect too much, because trying to address seriously poverty in this country can only mean one thing: the impoverishment of all. I find that message misleading, and even dishonest, because an average per capita income of $2,290 is meaningless. What is meaningful is that the average white *family* has probably a standard of living which is fifteen, twenty times higher than that of an African family (partly because Africans have much larger families). In terms of purchasing power parity South African whites probably have a standard of living comparable to that of the American whites, whose lifestyle they like to emulate.

The second example is a recent statement by Chris Stals, the governor of the South African Reserve Bank, that stresses the importance of maintaining 'standards': 'Rising labor costs are the country's major problem. Unit labor costs rose by 17.2 per cent in 1989 and 16.3 per cent in 1990. This is what is pushing up our rate of inflation, this is the malignant disease that erodes our competitiveness vis-à-vis the rest of the world.'

What is the message this time? It is this: we in South Africa have first-world standards, not third-world standards. Indeed, a 10 per cent rate of inflation is unacceptably high for a first-world country.

But not for a hybrid first-third world country with 45 to 50 per cent unemployment!

Turkey, for example, a country which has averaged an annual GDP growth of more than five per cent in the last decade or so, has had, during the same period, an average inflation rate of about 50 per cent. Now, inflation is considered a serious problem in Turkey and the government is trying to combat it but not at the expense of economic growth and job creation (unemployment is about 10 per cent). In a highly inegalitarian society whose economy has been stagnant in the last ten years or so, fighting inflation cannot be priority number one. This is South Africa, Mr Stals, not Taiwan or Malaysia.

A third example is to be found in a story in the *Financial Mail*, according to which, '1991 has been a good year on the whole for the country's twenty richest families. Their listed holdings on the JSE had risen by 57 per cent, from R6.9 billion in 1990 to R10.8 billion in 1991 [£1.5 billion to £2.4 billion].' Even if the 16–17 per cent inflation figure is discounted, that still leaves about 40 per cent real growth. Not bad in a country suffering from severe recession for almost ten years. . . .

So, Pallo, what do you say? Given all that I told you, are South Africa's problems insoluble, or not?

Pallo remained silent for a while, as if overwhelmed by the immensity of the problems. He then broke into a grin and said: 'I might be an incorrigible nineteenth-century rationalist, but I believe that no human problem is insoluble. The South African problems will need a huge amount of resources to be dealt with effectively. They will also require a very long time. But it can be done. The biggest obstacle, in my view, is not even the economics of it per se (even though it is formidable) – it is psychological: the major conglomorates in this country – the industrial giants, the insurance companies – have enormous reserves at their disposal in the form of pension funds, and so on, which they refuse to mobilise for the welfare of the black people. In fact, they've been sitting on the fence for a long time, not investing in South Africa in a way which is commensurate with their possibilities; they've even been exporting capital.[3] Ostensibly, they're doing this because of the instability, the uncertainty, and so on. Which is true at a certain fairly superficial level of consciousness. A much deeper level of explanation, I believe, is that the decision makers of those corporations, the owners and the managers, who are all white, don't see the blacks as living in the same moral universe as themselves. They see them as people apart. They have one set of standards for themselves, and another for the black community. There is a weird paradox in this country: the most affluent section of the population – that with the highest share of national income, that with the best jobs, the best education and best opportunities in life – is also the one which benefits the most from the largesse of the state in the form of entitlements such as free schooling, free books and free hot meals for their children, farming and housing subsidies, and tax rebates if their income falls below a certain level.

'It is the opposite for the poorest section of the population: those who are unemployed, those who have the worst-paying jobs, those who have no education to speak of, and no opportunities in life, have to pay for everything and receive no subsidies. In most societies it is the disadvantaged that are helped by the state; here in South Africa it is the already privileged! Historically the group which has received the largest amount of financial and technical assistance from the state is the white farmers who are among the most prosperous people in the country. The people in positions of power and influence in the government, in the business community, don't find that odd at all. They find it absolutely normal. They expect it even! So, it *is* a weird paradox, and the only explanation that I can think of is that they don't see us as living in the same moral universe as themselves.

'You mentioned the *Financial Mail* article about the country's richest twenty families. There has always been in this country the moral dilemma of extreme wealth co-existing with extreme poverty. What makes it worse here is that the economic divide coincides with the racial divide. Virtually all the shares listed in the Johannesburg Stock Exchange are owned by foreigners and a few hundred South African whites. In 1990, Africans owned less than 4 per cent of all businesses. In 1991, only 4.5 per cent of all top civil servants were black and only 0.6 per cent were African! In October 1991, a proposal was made at a conference in the Eastern Cape to levy a special tax equal to one-third of one's assets (after a threshold to be determined) and payable over ten years as a means to eliminate, or rather to make more bearable, the economic disparities created by apartheid. Immediately there was a storm of indignation, with newspaper headlines proclaiming that 'The ANC Wants to Soak the Rich!' In fact, the proposal was based on what the German government had done after the Second World War – a government of Christian Democrats, mind you! Their thinking was that the burden of the war had to be shared, it was a question of solidarity. The Adenauer government submitted the special equalisation tax to the Bundestag which approved it. Compare this with what the De Klerk government is trying to achieve. The real meaning of all those constitutional proposals to share power is to seal off their ill-gotten wealth from redistribution. What they are really saying is this: "We don't mind doing a bit of sharing, but it will have to come from future economic growth. What is ours is ours." That's the reason for all this focusing on the future. J O Thompson, the chairman of the Anglo-American Corporation, said in July 1991 that six years of an annual growth at 5 to 6 per cent would create jobs in the formal and informal economy for 2.5 million people, as well as generating an additional R55 billion in revenue for social investment. Dr Stals warned in April 1991 that South Africa would plunge into ungovernability by 1996 if the annual growth rate remained at around 1 per cent while the population increased by 2.5 per cent a year.

'We don't deny that economic growth is indispensable,' Pallo concluded, 'but it must be combined with a willingness to share, a willingness to correct the inequities of the past, on the part of the whites. Redistribution through growth is not enough, it must be supplemented by growth through redistribution.'

I asked Pallo how the two could be combined in an effective way. 'A massive housing building programme,' he said, 'would kill two birds with one stone: provide decent dwellings for millions of squatters, and create jobs which, with a multiplier effect in the rest of the economy, could run in the hundreds of thousands. And it won't have any adverse effects on our balance of trade because all the materials needed – wood, bricks, corrugated iron, cement – are indigenous. But they are not interested in doing it, because they see it as an inflationary and risky policy.

'Then there is the crucial land question. Africans were dispossessed of their land and reduced to a state of servitude by a series of racist laws that were passed between the early 1900s and the 1950s. Whole communities were removed from their ancestral lands to clear white South Africa of black spots and were dumped in the bantustans created for that purpose. More than 3 million Africans were evicted from places that they had been living for generations. Furthermore, the prohibition for African farm workers to unionise made it possible for white landowners to kick out tens of thousands of workers without any compensation whatsoever when they mechanised their farms. We proposed a Land Claims Court to be established to deal with all these issues, but there is bloody-minded resistance on the part of white farmers. For example, even land which belongs to absentee landlords and which has been lying fallow for years is rapidly being turned into 'game parks' in an attempt to avoid expropriation. We are against wholesale expropriation without compensation, because we think it would create terrible dislocation, and this is why we proposed the Land Claims Court. But the government came up with this White Paper on Land Reform which is nothing but an attempt to prevent land redistribution under the cover of free market proposals. This is ridiculous because there has never been anything "free market" about white agriculture which has always been pampered. That is why it has a debt of R17 billion [£3.3 billion] which it will never be able to repay.'[4]

'There is one thing that I have a hard time understanding,' I told Pallo, 'and that is how come white liberals in this country have tolerated for such a long time starvation wages for agricultural and domestic workers? Because compared to them workers in the manufacturing sector and the mines are a true labour aristocracy.'

'The reason is simple really,' said Pallo. 'They just didn't want to dip deeper into their pockets. The liberal parties did not agitate for higher wages because it was not popular with the electorate, so it was a non-starter. But things are beginning to change. The only way to prevent exploitation is to enact legislation that protects the worker and the precondition of that is the existence of unions that would put pressure on the bosses and the government. There have been unions for domestic workers for some time and modest gains were made. Agricultural workers and farmers are just beginning to unionise. It will take time.'

There remained the big question of political violence. Why it persisted? Why was it proving impossible to stop it? 'Musa Myeni [director of International Relations of Inkatha],' I said, 'has threatened not long ago to deploy 100,000 fighters in Soweto and 150,000 in the rest of the country if the ANC did not end the violence.'[5]

Pallo chuckled softly and then said: 'Political violence originates from the fact that the major political players have different agendas. We, in the ANC, stand for a non-racial, united and democratic South Africa which would be just and fair for all its citizens. De Klerk's Nationalists, Big Business, the secessionist right wingers, Inkatha and some other reactionary homeland governments, they all have their own separate agendas with some convergent and divergent elements in them, which explains the fluidity of the political alliances between them. The central point is that as long as political violence continues it is impossible to hold general elections leading to majority rule. It is certainly not in our interest to postpone the elections. It is in the interest of those who fear the outcome of those elections. Of those who believe that they need more time to weaken the ANC. Of those who hope to forge an alliance of conservative and reactionary forces that will beat the ANC at the polls. But it is all wishful thinking. Because it is not going to happen. History teaches us that in the long run the party that leads the struggle for the liberation of its people will win. The tyrants, the dictators, the oppressors, the traitors must lose in the end. That's what history teaches us.'

As I left Pallo, feeling admiration for his intelligence and moderation, and went down the elevator, I remembered the results of a poll that was also mentioned in the SAIRR Survey: 63 per cent of the white, but only 44 per cent of the black respondents thought that even if a new constitution was agreed on it would not bring peace and harmony to the people of South Africa. Other polls also indicated that a very small percentage of whites – about three per cent – trusted or supported the ANC. That percentage rose to about five per cent in September 1993 and may rise further. However, it does seem to indicate a long, painful transition to a truly democratic and non-racial South Africa.

Notes

1 See also the first section of Chapter 16, my conversation with Bill Davies and the work that is being done in Cecil Cook's TATU.

2 See also the introduction to Chapter 9.

3 This is beginning to change. See Note 2 on Chapter 13.

4 See also the introduction to Chapter 9.

5 As mentioned earlier, the question of violence is a make or break one in South Africa. See Chapter 7 Note 3 on Chapter 8 and Note 4 on Chapter 11.

Part Two

A Supplement: A Brief Introduction to South African History and Politics

18

Early Days

The Strandlopers were probably the first inhabitants of South Africa. They were a prehistoric coastal race who lived on the Cape coast up to the time of the arrival of the white man in the middle of the seventeenth century. They were possibly the ancestors of both the Bushmen (also known as the San people) and the Hottentots (also referred to as 'Khoi-khoi' or 'Man-man') who are thus probably related.

The rest of the South African territory was occupied by the Bantu (plural of Muntu, which means simply 'Man' in the Nguni languages), tribes whose slow migration south from Central Africa may have started a thousand years ago, if not earlier. The South African Bantu are divided broadly into four ethno-linguistic categories the first two of which are much larger. They are: firstly, the Nguni peoples which include the Zulu-, Xhosa-, and Swazi-speaking peoples, plus the Ndebele of the Transvaal; secondly, the Sotho-Tswana peoples which comprise the North Sotho (mainly Pedi-speaking), the West Sotho (or Tswana) and the South Sotho; thirdly, the Shangana-Tsonga peoples in the Northern Transvaal; and fourthly, the Venda people, who are the smallest of the four groups.[1]

The three small ships, led by Jan van Riebeek, belonging to the Dutch East India Company (DEIC) arrived at what was later to become Cape Town in 1652. It was not, of course, the first time that the white man had come in the area. The Portuguese explorers, for one, had rounded the Cape of Good Hope much earlier but it was the first time that the white man had come to stay. The idea was to set up a sort of a way-station to cater to the vessels that plied the East Indian route. The company needed fresh produce for its sailors, primarily vegetables and meat, in the long voyage to the East Indies.

At first the colony grew slowly: towards the end of the seventeenth century, there were barely a thousand settlers. They owned about 300 slaves, an equal number of horses, 4,000 heads of cattle, and 50,000 sheep.[2] 'Life was nasty, brutish and short' in those days, to use Hobbes's famous phrase, particularly for the slaves.

Two epoch-shattering events happened in Europe in the late eighteenth and early nineteenth centuries whose ripples came to be felt on the shores of the Cape Peninsula: the French Revolution and the subsequent Napoleonic Wars. The British Empire, the great victor of the Napoleonic Wars, became the dominant superpower of the world, a position it was to hold throughout the nineteenth century, until the advent of the First World War, in fact. The British became interested in the Cape merely as a means to keep the route to India ('The Jewel in the Crown') open. They defeated the Dutch easily and took over the colony, extending in the following decades their hegemony to the vast territories of the interior.

Meanwhile, it is important to note, as some historians have done that, in the eighteenth century, the small Dutch colony was an isolated place, not only geographically, but also culturally, in the sense that it largely missed the great intellectual and spiritual currents of the time which were revolutionising Europe: the Age of Reason – also known as *'Le Siècle des Lumières* – dominated by the *philosophes*, such as Voltaire and the *Encyclopédistes*, such as Diderot, was an unusually fertile period in the history of ideas. The vital issues of liberty, equality and democracy; of separation of church and state; and of representative government; were discussed ad infinitum, and the seeds were sown for the eventual abolition of the absolutist regimes. All this the people living in the small Cape Colony largely missed.

In the economic realm, the doctrine that prevailed at the time – until the advent of industrial capitalism in the late nineteenth century – was mercantilism, according to which a nation's wealth was largely determined by the degree of its control of international trade routes. The mercantilist era was preceded and made possible by the great Spanish and Portuguese discoveries and conquests. Vasco da Gama first rounded the Cape in 1498; Magellan completed the first circumnavigation of the globe in 1521; Cortez and Pizarro conquered Mexico and the Peru at the beginning of the sixteenth century and destroyed the Aztec, Inca and Maya civilisations there; and so on. Mercantilism's golden age arrived with the invention, at the end of the sixteenth century, of the joint stock (chartered) companies. Thereafter, in the following one hundred years or so, these companies acquired enormous wealth and power, becoming truly states within states. The domination of the Dutch, British and French chartered companies continued until, in the middle of the eighteenth century, the states began to reassert their primacy.[3]

The DEIC was incorporated in 1602. Soon its activities expanded to a very large area in the East Indies, including Java (where Batavia, the company's headquarters was based), Sumatra, Borneo and the Celebes Islands. The company controlled the lucrative spice – cloves, nutmeg, pepper, coffee – trade between Europe and the East Indies, as well as exploiting gold and diamond mines in Borneo. Such was its success that 'within thirteen years [of its foundation] the Company owned 800 vessels and their profit for the first six years reached the astronomical figure of 76 million dollars, equivalent in our money to three billion dollars.'[4]

In the 1640s the DEIC began thinking about establishing a 'revictualling station' in the Cape, which happened to be halfway between Holland and the East Indies. The company needed fresh meat and vegetables to fight against scurvy, which was claiming many lives among their crews in the long voyage to the East and back. So, about ten years later, it organised a group of settlers who started a 'vegetable garden' that produced 'cabbages, pumpkins, turnips and onions' in large quantities.[5] In due time a storehouse, a granary and a hospital were added to it. They also bartered tobacco for beef with the Hottentots, who were unable to put up much resistance against the encroachment of their territory by the newcomers. The main reason was that the latter had firearms and horses. The Bushmen proved to be even less of a challenge: many of them were killed in a smallpox epidemic imported by Dutch sailors, the rest retreated into the Kalahari desert. A key element in the early expansion of the Cape Colony was that it was free of malaria and sleeping sickness.

In 1685, after the Revocation of the Edict of Nantes by Louis XIV, about 200 French Huguenots arrived in the small colony. They brought with them wine-making skills that did not yet exist there. DEIC records show that by the end of the seventeenth century more than half a million vines had been planted in the Cape. Inevitably, the 'easy promiscuity' of the colonists and the sailors with the Malay and African women slaves resulted in a growing population of brown, or mixed race, people (who later were classified as Coloureds by the social engineers of apartheid), many of whom became skilled craftsmen, making a lasting contribution to Cape-Dutch culture. They also played a big role in the development of the Afrikaans language and literature. Afrikaans, which in the beginning was only a spoken language, was fertilised by the Malays and Africans.

The DEIC control of the colony was never very firm. Many settlers severed their ties with the company and became 'Free Burgers'. From roughly the middle of the eighteenth century the Boers ('farmers' in Afrikaans) in search of new grazing land for their ever-expanding herds of cattle, started testing the eastern frontier (the Great Fish River) on the other side of which was another nation with great herds of cattle, the Xhosa, and war (known as the Kaffir Wars) became a constant feature in the border area.[6] On and off it continued for more than fifty years between 1770 and 1835, when the Xhosa were definitively defeated with the help of the British troops.

Notes

1 'Peoples and Languages', in *South Africa 1992, Official Yearbook*, South African Communication Service, Pretoria, pages 21–23.

2 T C Robertson, *South African Mosaic*, C Struik, 1978, Johannesburg, page 14. This is a big illustrated book.

3 I used G R Elton, *Renaissance and Reformation, 1300–1648*, Macmillan, 1976, for this paragraph.

4 R Seth, *Milestones in African History*, Chilton Books, 1969, Philadelphia, page 56.

5 T C Robertson, *South African Mosaic*, page 10.

6 For a fair treatment of the epic history of the Xhosa people, see N Mostert, *Frontiers*, published in 1992 and obtainable from the Frank R Thorold bookshop in Johannesburg.

19

The Imperial Century

'There is only one way out of the troubles in South Africa: reform or war. And of the two war is more likely.'

Alfred Milner,
British High Commissioner to South Africa,
1897–1905[1]

To understand British colonial policy in South Africa, it is helpful to have some knowledge of the dominant position occupied by Great Britain in the nineteenth century and also a grasp of the meaning of the concept of imperialism.

Great Britain was the global superpower of the time. It would not be an exaggeration to say that it combined the powers of *both* the United States and Germany – or Japan – in our era. 'The British stood at the threshold of a colossal boom. . . . They were soon to manufacture every kind of capital goods to become . . . the workshop of the world. At the same time they emerged victorious and aglow from the unexampled struggle of the Napoleonic wars, to stand alone among the Powers of Europe. . . . During the sixty years of Victoria's reign the Empire had grown by more than ten times . . . to a quarter of the land mass of the earth, and a third of its population.'[2]

Historically, European imperialism has been divided into two distinct stages: that of the 'Old Imperialism', whose origins go back to the establishment in the late sixteenth and early seventeenth centuries of the joint stock, chartered companies; and that of the 'New Imperialism', which began with the famous (or rather notorious) 'Scramble for Africa' in the 1870s and ended after the

Second World War, in the early 1960s, with the accession to independence of most African colonies.

Old Imperialism in Britain

Many historians readily agree that in Great Britain Old Imperialism was characterised by a certain moral streak which manifested itself in a form of paternalistic humanism that was later lost. In Britain, the first three decades of the nineteenth century belonged to Tory conservatism. In Europe, the downfall of Napoleon and the Congress of Vienna of 1815 had resulted in the 'Restoration' of the *anciens régimes* and, for the next fifteen years, politics was dominated by the strong personality of Metternich, the Austro-Hungarian chancellor, who was an arch-conservative and very much opposed to all the ideas embodied by the French Revolution. He favoured political absolutism and was against self-determination for the peoples who were part of the Austro-Hungarian Empire. In Britain, Edmund Burke's *Reflections on the Revolution in France*, a very largely negative assessment of the Revolution, was very influential among the members of the political establishment: 'In 1815, the Tory Cabinet, fresh from its triumph over Napoleon and the French Revolution, was less inclined than ever to offer any measures of reform in the liberal direction. The period of 1815–22 was marked by an extreme conservatism.'[3]

British liberalism began to gain ground in the late 1820s and early 1830s. The liberal opposition to the Tories came from four sources principally: firstly, from philosophers and poets such as William Godwin, Thomas Paine, Jeremy Bentham, Shelley and Byron; secondly, from Roman Catholics fighting for political emancipation in England and Ireland; thirdly, from Protestant missionaries mobilised against slavery and the mistreatment of 'natives' in the colonies, and fourthly, from the rising new class of industrial capitalists. Some of the results of all this agitation were quite spectacular. There were a series of political reform bills between 1832, when only 3 per cent of the population could vote, and 1844, when male suffrage became universal (women, in 1902). An important reform that is of particular interest in the framework of this book was the Abolition of Slavery Act of 1834 at significant cost to the Treasury, since slave owners had to be compensated. The London Missionary Society became increasingly vocal in the defence of the 'natives' (human) rights'. The *quid pro quo* was, of course, relentless proselytisation. The Aborigines Protection Society, for example, decreed that: 'The complete civilization and the real "Happiness of Man" can never be secured by anything less than the diffusion of Christian Principles; and the diffusion of true Christian Principles could best be achieved by the exertion of British Authority.'[4]

Meanwhile, several revolutionary movements broke out in Europe in 1848, which were all crushed eventually. But they still signalled the advent of the age of nationalism. By 1870, the unifications of Germany and Italy were almost complete. In Great Britain, liberal democratic ideas continued their lopsided progress. The Industrial Revolution made the British Empire the dominant economic force of the world. By the late 1850s, Great Britain was supplying a significant chunk of the world's needs in textiles, iron and machinery.

New Imperialism in Britain

Contemporary scholars see New Imperialism as having been far more cynical, selfish and self seeking, as well as more racist, in its attitudes than Old Imperialism. Paradoxically enough, scientific and technological advances appear to have contributed to a deepening of racism: 'Rapid transformation in steamship and, toward the end of the century, the revolution in tropical medicine enabled large numbers of English women to make semi-permanent homes in areas where they had been absent. Once nearly universal, concubinage came to be frowned upon, if not exactly rare.'[5]

It all started in 1870, when John Ruskin, an influential literary figure and intellectual, was given a prestigious chair at Oxford University. He chose 'Imperial Duty' as the topic of his inaugural lecture. It was a huge success and Benjamin Disraeli, twice prime minister, in 1868 and in 1874–80, became an ardent defender and foremost champion of 'Empire'. 'It was a broad phenomenon which found artistic expression in Rudyard Kipling's poems, political expression in Joseph Chamberlain's movement to make the Empire a great economic unit . . . commercial expression in such organisations as the British South Africa Company of Cecil Rhodes, and diplomatic expression in the treaties with other imperialist powers.'[6]

The imperial idea was reinforced by a rascist pseudo-theory which came to be known as Social Darwinism, according to which the 'most favoured races' were the 'fittest to survive in the everlasting struggle for existence'.[7] This 'hymn' to racial superiority notwithstanding, New Imperialism was fuelled primarily by important economic necessities: 'The old panacea of Free Trade was losing its effect. Only Empire, it seemed to many businessmen, could restore the proper status quo: with new markets, with new sources of raw materials, and with convenient barriers ... against foreign competition.'[8] Lord Carnarvon, Disraeli's colonial secretary, believed that the Empire's colonies should be grouped into larger sub-units, and that Africa 'South of the Zambezi' should be amalgamated into such a unit.

Nonetheless, support for the 'Imperial Idea' was never unanimous. Important sections of the British opinion were either sceptical about it or opposed to it. The Liberals, led by William Gladstone (four times prime minister – 1868–74, 1880–85, 1886 and 1892–94), never accepted it wholeheartedly or unconditionally. As a general policy, the Liberal Party stood for free trade and for gradual parliamentary reform; it also favoured self-government in the colonies. Gladstone was a foremost defender of morality in government. As early as in 1838, when he was only 29 years old, he had published *The State in its Relation with the Church*, a work in which he argued for an 'ideal union' between the state and the church, which would create 'an Anglican utopia of moral policy in the United Kingdom'. Later, during his long political apprenticeship under Peel, Gladstone learned to blend his moral concerns with more pragmatic considerations. The following remarks, that he made in a letter to a colleague, might be worth quoting: 'No government ought to commit itself in any case except where it is righteous, and ... no cause is really righteous with reference to its being taken up by governments, unless the objects that are being contemplated are practicable and attainable.' For Gladstone, 'native societies [had] to be handled with humane guardianship until under British rule and tutelage [they] could, at some rather distant future date, be emancipated and enjoy their own national independence.' He believed that the British 'settlement colonies' such as Canada, Australia and South Africa deserved a special treatment. For the latter he accepted the principle of 'responsible government' as a means of teaching them local 'home rule'. 'The British settlers are still Britishers overseas,' he declared, 'and very much part of a worldwide British family.' Gladstone shared 'the Greek ideal of mutually responsible policies ... [whose] goal was a constantly evolving and adjusting empire of family association.'[9]

After Gladstone's defeat in 1886 (over the Irish Home Rule issue), the following two decades (except for the brief interlude in 1892–94)

were again dominated by the Conservatives – the Salisbury governments of 1886–92 and 1895–1902, and the Balfour government of
1902–6. It was during the second Salisbury government that the
arch-imperialist Joseph Chamberlain, the colonial secretary, pur-
sued his expansionist policies in Southern Africa. If the Liberals
were swept back into power in 1906 with an overwhelming majority
at the polls, part of the reason was their unequivocal condemnation
of the Anglo-Boer War of 1899–1902. Indeed, Queen Victoria's long
and glorious reign had ended in the midst of what was supposed
to be a 'little war' to subdue those 'uppity Boers' in South Africa,
a war which had instead dragged on and on, exposing 'the military
weakness of an army that had become used to cheap victories against
outgunned native opponents, and divided British opinion terribly.'[10]

Old Imperialism in South Africa

At first, the British were interested in the Cape only as a staging
post to India. The idea was to guard the road to India and when
they came in 1806 with a fleet of 63, they had every intention of
staying permanently. At the time, the Dutch colony spread over an
area of about 100,000 square miles and was populated by about
26,000 whites, 30,000 slaves, and 20–30,000 people of 'uncertain
status' (Hottentot natives and mixed-race people).

After they defeated the Dutch and took over, the British wanted
to maintain a stable and reasonably prosperous colony at the lowest
possible cost. This policy had two main components: taxing moderately the colony's modest exports – in those early days, wine, wool
and ostrich feathers principally; and avoiding problems with the
Bantu Africans, who lived beyond the north-eastern frontier, and
with the Boers within the colony. It proved to be an impossible
task. Virtually from the beginning, 'English evangelicism, with its
emphasis on the welfare of the Coloured peoples, [clashed] with
the dour fundamentalism of the Boers. Disturbing rumours reached
London about Afrikaner mistreatment of the Hottentots, and by the
1820s the London Missionary Society (LMS) had gone sternly into
action.'[11] In fact, as early as in 1812, James Reed, the first representative of the LMS in South Africa, had secured in the 'court of law'
some convictions of Boer employers who had 'mistreated' their
Coloured servants. A far more serious incident had taken place in
1815, when 'a Boer named Bezuindenhout, charged by a magistrate
with cheating and abusing a servant, refused to appear in court,

and was killed in a gunfight with the soldiers – Hottentot soldiers no less – sent to arrest him. Swearing revenge, his brother precipi- tated a small rebellion which was quickly and forcefully put down with the public hanging of five white men. The site of their execution, Slagter's Nek, is one of the Afrikaner shrines of contem- porary South Africa.'[12] The unfortunate fact that the gallows col- lapsed in the first attempt and that the prisoners had to be hanged again made – understandably – things worse. In 1819, James Reed was replaced by Dr John Philip, who remained the local superin- tendent of the London missions until his death in 1851. He was vociferous in the defence of native rights, and outspokenly critical of Afrikaner attitudes. T R H Davenport affirms: 'He was capable of making the wrong allegations as well as the right ones [in the service of his cause and] . . . became the *bête noire* of white settlers for the damning criticism of their labour relations in his *Researches in South Africa*,' which was published in London in 1828 and which quickly became the 'Bible' of the humanitarian and liberal circles there.[13]

The British tried very hard to 'civilise' the Boers. D Harrison writes: 'In 1822 the Governor of the Cape Colony, Lord Charles Somerset, issued a proclamation that English was to be the only language of the courts and schools, even though Dutch settlers outnumbered the British by eight to one. He imported English, and especially Scottish, teachers and ministers to put their stamp on education and religion. . . . Many [Afrikaner] parents simply kept their children away from school to avoid having them educated in English. In 1829, in the government schools in Cape Town there were 675 pupils; eleven years later the combined attendance was eighty-four.'[14]

Meanwhile, the first large group of English colonists had arrived in the Cape in 1820. There were about 5,000 of them of whom, four years later, a few hundred left the Cape to establish a small settle- ment in Port Natal (Durban). As mentioned earlier, slavery was abolished throughout the British Empire in 1834. For some Boers that proved to be the straw that broke the proverbial camel's back. In the next two years an estimated four to five thousand Boers voted with their feet and left the Cape Colony, crossing the frontier in search of greener pastures and to escape what they believed was unbearable British tyranny. In the following decade or so, some eight to ten thousand more followed in their footsteps. Even if the majority stayed behind ('There were Boers in the Cape Peninsula

who lived exquisitely, in lovely oak-sheltered towns like Stellenbosch or Paarl, in wide-stoeped homesteads of the wine valleys, or
fine old houses with floors of red tile and furniture of stink-wood,
among the gardens of Cape Town'), the exodus, which came to be
known as the Great Trek, became the central mythical event of
Afrikaner history.[15]

The *Voortrekkers* (those Boers who chose to leave) soon clashed
with the powerful Zulu kingdom which claimed as its own all the
territories that are part of the Natal province today. After suffering
hundreds of casualties in the initial encounters, the Boers were able
to inflict a bad defeat on the army of the Zulu King Dingane on
the banks of the Nkome River (later renamed Blood River).[16] Three
years later the Boers proclaimed the independent Republic of Nat-
alia. The British, however, did not like the idea of the Boers having
direct access to the sea – they feared that they, the Boers, might be
able to secure help from Germany, the competing continental power,
and challenge their supremacy in South Africa. And so they
annexed Natal as a new British colony in 1843, declaring also, for
good measure, British sovereignty in all the territories between the
Orange and the Vaal rivers to the north. To show the Boers that
they meant business, they dispatched the following year a sizeable
expeditionary force to Port Natal. Once more, the Boers had no
choice but to move out. They went north, crossing the Orange and
Vaal rivers, and established in 1852 another republic, which they
called the Transvaal. Two years later, for reasons of economy primarily, the British decided to grant independence to the Orange
territory, which thus became the second Boer republic of the
Orange Free State.

The Transition from Old to New Imperialism

Sir George Grey, governor of the Cape Colony between 1854 and
1861, is seen by some as an important transitional figure between
Old and New Imperialism in South Africa. In 1854, 'representative
government' (the stage prior to 'responsible government', which
came in 1872) was granted to the Cape Colony. The Cape Constitution of 1853 envisaged a House of Assembly which would be
elected on the basis of property qualifications and which thus,
theoretically at least, was colour-blind. But in reality the governor,
was in favour of a policy called 'amalgamation' of blacks and
whites: 'By building schools and hospitals that would demonstrate

the superiority of [white] civilisation ... by establishing courts to which natives might bring their disputes, and above all by asserting his own personality in place of the crumbling authority of the chiefs,' he said, 'the policy will achieve his aims.'[17] In 1857, there was a strange and tragic cattle-killing incident which resulted in the death by starvation of several thousand Xhosa tribesmen. The latter killed their cattle and burnt their crops because they were told by the wizard that gods demanded the sacrifice for the liberation of their land from white occupation. It is possible that the incident further reinforced in Grey's mind the idea of white superiority.

'The natives will become part of ourselves,' he declared on one occasion, but only as 'useful servants, consumers of our goods, [and] contributors to our revenue.'[18] Finally, Grey was probably the first exponent of the idea of a 'federation' uniting the two British colonies with the two Boer Republics. In the early 1860s, the entire population of the Cape Colony was still about half a million of which about 180,000 were whites; the Transvaal had a population of about 20,000 and the Orange Free State far less.

In the early 1850s it was discovered that the coastal plain of Natal was well suited to the sugar-cane crop. Since a stable labour force was needed to work in the plantations and the Zulus could not be relied upon to provide it, the problem was solved by 'importing' large numbers of labourers from India, in a succession of shiploads beginning in 1860. They were 'indentured' – under contract for a specific period of time and intended to go back after that and were mostly 'low-caste Hindus from Madras', even though later some 'Gujerati traders' were allowed to come as 'passenger Indians'. In theory, the Cape system of a non-racial political franchise and representative government was extended to Natal Colony as well. In practice, however, the property requirements to be part of the franchise were so restrictive that, for all intents and purposes, the vote was limited to the whites. Self-government was granted to Natal only in 1893, twenty-one years after the Cape. Interestingly enough, that was the year Mohandas K Gandhi arrived in Natal on a legal assignment ... and decided to remain in the colony on learning that the disenfranchisement of Indians was intended. It is in South Africa that Gandhi developed his methods of passive resistance (*satyagraha*, the soul force). He is the founder of the Natal Indian Congress and of the journal *Indian Opinion*, of which he was the first editor.[19]

New Imperialism in South Africa

'When Gladstone resumed office in December 1868, a new policy began to take shape, in which federalism came to be associated with the transfer of power to the Cape. That policy was continued by Disraeli and his colonial secretary, Lord Carnarvon. Africa south of the Zambezi was to be integrated into a single imperial unit. The two independent Boer republics, especially the Transvaal and the still independent Zulu kingdom, stood in the way of that grandiose project.

Sir Garnet Wolseley, an experienced colonial hand, was sent to South Africa, ostensibly as governor of the Natal Colony, but his real mission was to bring the two Boer republics back into the British fold. At the time, the Transvaal and the Free State were poor and sparsely populated and therefore thought unlikely to show much resistance. Once on the spot, Wolseley named a certain T Shepstone, a former secretary of Native Affairs in Natal, as special commissioner and dispatched him to Pretoria at the head of a small military contingent. Shepstone's specific instructions were to 'annex the Transvaal'. He did just that in April 1877, without encountering any belligerent reaction from the Boers. The British could now turn their attention to the Zulu kingdom which enjoyed an independence of sorts in their traditional area north of the Tugela river. King Mpande had kept a low profile during his long reign between 1839 and 1873, but his successor Cetshwayo was accused – it was a blatant excuse, of course – of being 'less respectful of the Imperial power' and a 16,000-strong British army was sent into Zululand in 1879. Despite the ambush of their advanced corps at Isandhlwana where some 900 Redcoats lost their lives, Cetshwayo was defeated at Rorke's Drift and Ulundi and his capital burned to the ground.

The British appeared well poised to realise their grand design, but that was counting without the resilience of the Boers who, under the leadership of Paul Kruger, had been quietly preparing for a rebellion. The Boers had hoped that, with the fall of the Disraeli government in 1880 and the return of Gladstone, the Transvaal's and the Free State's independence would be restored. When no such thing occurred, the rebellion was on. After some initial skirmishes, a major battle was fought at Majuba Hill, which is on the border between Natal and the Transvaal. It was a true disaster for the British who lost 280 men as well as their commanding officer. To the surprise of some who thought that the British would teach the Boers a lesson that they would never forget, Gladstone offered

peace negotiations, and after making some relatively minor concessions, the two Boer republics recovered their independence. It
can, fairly safely, be assumed that had this first Anglo-Boer War
(1880–81) had taken place a decade or so later, that is, after the
importance of the gold reserves in Witwatersrand became known
(it did in 1886), its outcome would have been very different. But
the Boers were, as they would be time and again at critical junctures
in their tortured history, lucky, and luck is an important factor in
the history of nations.

In 1869, a lot of excitement was generated by the discovery on
the banks of the Orange River, not far from Kimberley, of a huge
diamond weighing 85.4 carats – it was later named the Star of
South Africa and given to Queen Victoria as a present (it is still
with the British Crown Jewels). In 1877, Cecil Rhodes returned to
South Africa very much under the influence of John Ruskin's ideas
and utterly convinced that the British were destined to rule the
world, because they were the 'possessors of a superior civilisation.'
He once said (some fifteen years later, when he was prime minister
of the Cape Colony): 'I contend that we are the finest race of the
world, and that the more of the world we inhabit, the better it is
for the human race.'[20] He firmly believed that he himself had a
central role to play in that 'moral purpose'. Meanwhile, he had
become the diamond king and richest man in South Africa.

When the richness of the Witwatersrand gold reserves became
known in 1886, the gold rush to the Transvaal was on. The Boer state
was invaded by a horde of businessmen, prospectors, adventurers,
speculators, prostitutes and African workers. Soon, out of a sprawling mining camp of tents and corrugated-iron-roofed shacks, grew
the city of Johannesburg (which the Zulus called *Egoli* or the City
of Gold) which, in less than a century, was to become sub-Saharan
Africa's most important financial and industrial centre. The white
adventurers were called Uitlanders (foreigners) by the Boers who
disliked their loose morals but their main fear was that they might
be outnumbered and lose their country – in 1890 there were probably no more than 50,000 Boers in the whole of the Transvaal.

In a time of fixed gold prices, the main preoccupation of the
mining companies was how to keep the costs of production down.
That required the fulfilment of two conditions: cheap and plentiful
labour and reasonably priced dynamite (a lot of it was needed to
open up the deep-level gold mines of the Rand). The mining com-

panies were able to reach an agreement among themselves to keep the wages down. But the price of dynamite they could not control because it was manufactured locally by French and German companies and supplied by the Boer government under a system of monopolistic concession (other such concessions concerned liquor and the building of the railways). Involving the payment of large bribes to Boer officials, the system was corrupt and resulted in a high price for the dynamite. So, it was a big problem for the 'Randlords' but it did not keep them from amassing colossal fortunes by founding gold production companies and selling their stocks on the European (London mainly, but also Paris and Berlin) exchanges. Many early investors made mind-blowing profits very quickly. In February 1893, for example, the Rand Mines sold in London 400,000 new shares valued at £1 each. In the summer of 1895, less than two and a half years later, the same shares were worth 45 times as much![21]

In Johannesburg, Cecil Rhodes was able to enlarge his already considerable fortune but he never became the pre-eminent financier of the gold industry. That position was for a long time occupied by the firm Wernher, Beit and Co (known as the 'Corner House' on Market Street). Rhodes apparently did not mind, being preoccupied by much bigger ambitions of a different sort. In addition to his dream of unifying the African continent under British tutelage by means of the Cape to Cairo Railway, he now wanted to open for white settlement the vast territory between the Limpopo and the Zambezi rivers, which is a huge and well watered plateau 4,000-feet high and benefiting from a splendid climate. What made this project even more attractive was the fact that a certain Rider Haggard had published *King Solomon's Mines* in 1886, a book in which he claimed that the region was rich in gold and other precious metals. The southern part of the territory was inhabited by the Zulu-related Matabele who had come here under the leadership of Mzilikazi, a former commander of the great Zulu King Shaka. In the northern part lived the more peaceful Shona-speaking peoples. Rhodes concocted some clever schemes to penetrate the territory.

In those days, the Matabele King Lobengula was courted by many 'chasers of concessions'. Even Paul Kruger, the wily president of the Transvaal, had concluded a Treaty of Friendship with him in 1887. Rhodes, too, began by securing a similar treaty less than a year later 'on behalf of the British Crown'. Later, he sent Dr L S

Jameson, a political protégé of his and a close friend, to Lobengula with the mission of obtaining a mineral concession. He offered in exchange royalties, rifles and a number of other gifts. When the news arrived that Jameson had been able to obtain the concession, Rhodes passed on to the next phase which was crucial: to secure a royal charter of incorporation for his company. Only a chartered company could give him the 'full licence to own and operate in an independent country.' After some complex wheeling and dealing in London, which included some direct and some indirect bribes in high-up places, the British South Africa Company was incorporated with the blessing of Queen Victoria herself who signed its charter in October 1889. Rhodes was named both chairman and managing director.[22]

He was now well positioned to reach the pinnacle of political power in the Cape Colony. He befriended J H Hofmeyer, the leader of the Afrikaner Bond, a cultural organisation, which was founded by the Cape Afrikaners to further their ambitions of cultural autonomy. Rhodes pretended to support those ambitions and, with the support of leading Afrikaners, had no problem in getting himself elected prime minister of the Cape Colony in July 1890. Despite his famous slogan: 'Equal rights for all civilised men below the Zambezi', it soon became clear that Rhodes did not believe in the essential equality of whites and non-whites. Two of the first pieces of legislation introduced by his government were the Master and Servant Act and the Franchise and Ballot Act, which raised the property requirements and thus reduced the number of non-white voters. His government was also responsible for the Glen Grey Act, whose purpose was to regulate the lives of the Bantu of Eastern Cape by creating Native Reserves for them, which later became the Bantustans of Ciskei and Transkei. Their disenfranchised inhabitants were forced to pay a labour tax if they were unable to find work outside their specified districts – the idea being to force them to work in the mines.

In September 1890, the preparations for the conquest of Zambesia were completed and a Pioneer Column of about 200 carefully selected white settlers, protected by five hundred Bechuanaland police, left for Matabeleland. They reached their destination some six months later and founded a new city they called Salisbury, in honour of the then British prime minister. Jameson was appointed administrator general and, when it was discovered that the land

had great agricultural potential (no gold or precious metals, alas),
huge tracts of it were sold cheaply to raise money for the upkeep
of the territory. But there was a problem: the Matabeles, who were
a warlike people, were raiding the peaceful Shonas and thus 'inter-
fering with the integrity of the labour supply' of the settlers. The
decision was made in Cape Town to deal with them and the Matabele War was on. Lobengula had never a chance against Jameson's
heavily armed troops and Bulawayo, his capital, was taken in November 1893.

'The Jameson Raid was the real declaration of war in the great
Anglo-Boer conflict,' said Jan C. Smuts, prime minister of the Union
of South Africa in 1919–24 and 1939–48.[23] In the few years preceding
the Raid, relations between the mining barons (dubbed mischiev-
ously 'gold bugs' by the Liberal British press) and the Boer government of the Transvaal had deteriorated seriously. The former
complained about chronic corruption and excessive taxation; the
latter mistrusted the gold magnates and thought that all they cared
about was making big profits. The high price of dynamite and the
system of monopolistic concessions continued to be a festering sore.
The issue of the Uitlanders' franchise was not resolved. The Boers
fearing (correctly) that they were running the risk of becoming a
minority in their own country, had in 1888 raised the residency
requirement for voting from 5 to 14 years. The Cape government
presented the problem to London as one of suppression of the
political rights of Her Majesty's subjects. In Jo'burg a Reform Committee was formed which, with the help of the Chamber of Mines,
collected some 13,000 signatures on a petition demanding the right
to vote for the Uitlanders. In reality, the petition was part of a
conspiracy: it would be used later to prove that there had been
a spontaneous uprising against Boer tyranny, and that the British
government had to intervene to protect its citizens living in the
Transvaal. The three leading proponents of the conspiracy were
Rhodes, Alfred Beit of the Corner House, and Joseph Chamberlain,
the newly appointed colonial secretary of Salisbury's government.

'Rhodes had purchased 5,000 rifles and a million rounds of
ammunition. . . . The plot reached its critical point in mid-December
1895, with Jameson's arrival at Pitsani (Mafeking), the relief party's
jump-off point across the border in Bechuanaland. Some 500 men
assembled. . . . Everything was ready.'[24] In Jo'burg, however, things
were beginning to fall apart: the members of the Reform Committee

themselves were not so bullish any more about the chances of the insurrection succeeding. Besides, they were divided among themselves: some wanted an independent Uitlander republic, others preferred to remain a British colony. Several messages were sent to Jameson to postpone the invasion. But Dr Jim, as he was known then, was in no mood for foot-dragging; he decided to go ahead anyway. He and his party covered the 170 miles between Pitsani and Johannesburg in less than two weeks. But the Uitlanders failed to rise. In the meantime, the Boers had learned about the invasion and had plenty of time to mobilise. Jameson's much smaller force had absolutely no chance against Kruger's 6,000 commandos and the raid ended in ignominy for Jameson, who was taken prisoner and gaoled in Pretoria.[25]

At first, the failure of the Jameson Raid looked like a major disaster for the British government, which was universally censured for its heavy-handed imperialism against an independent white republic. In Zambesia, moreover, both the Matabeles and the Shonas took advantage of the situation to rebel and many Europeans were killed in the outlying farms. Rhodes was exposed as a Machiavelli-like character who plotted the whole affair and was forced to resign both as chairman of the British South Africa Company and as Cape prime minister. But when the Kaiser sent a telegram of congratulations to Kruger on his narrow escape, British opinion swung back in support of the raid which was now seen as a swashbuckling exploit for the just cause of British imperialism. Sir (later Lord) Alfred Milner, an experienced colonial administrator who had served in India for forty years, was sent to the Cape as the new high commissioner to pick up the pieces. New Imperialism was on the march again.

Milner believed that imperialism was a 'great movement of the human spirit'. He too had a great vision, a grand design: to restore British supremacy in the whole of Southern Africa, which then would be an integral part of a united British Empire. His secret ally in this project was none other Alfred Beit of the Corner House, who earlier had supported Cecil Rhodes and who was the richest of all the gold magnates. In 1899, the gold mines of the Rand were already producing twenty million pounds' worth of the precious yellow metal a year, compared to only five million pounds for the Cape's diamonds. With the value of the gold reserves estimated at 700 million pounds, the Transvaal had become the greatest gold power in the world.

Milner's strategy for achieving his goal was to work up a crisis that could be used as a *casus belli* against the Transvaal. *Faute de mieux*, the issue of the Uitlanders' electoral franchise was revived and political agitation soon reached a breaking point in Johannesburg. A last-ditch effort to avoid war was made in June 1899 at the Bloemfontein Conference, but it all came to naught when Milner, supported by Chamberlain, asked for 'immediate and substantial representation' for the Uitlanders. The old fox Kruger, who knew perfectly well what was happening declared: 'If we give you the franchise tomorrow, we may as well give up the Republic.... It is our country that you want.'[26] War came on 11 October, at the expiration of Kruger's 48-hour ultimatum accusing the British of interference in the internal affairs of the Transvaal and with massing troops in Northern Natal. Chamberlain, who was apparently busy drafting his own elaborate ultimatum, was relieved to discover that he would not have to make it public after all.

The Anglo-Boer War (1899–1902) is clearly made up of two parts: the first, which lasted about a year, is distinctly conventional; it began with the Boer sieges of Ladysmith in Natal, Kimberley in the Cape and Mafeking in the Transvaal, and ended up with the capture by the British army of Johannesburg and Pretoria. The two Boer republics were annexed in October 1900 and the war was declared to have been won. It turned out to have been a very premature declaration of victory, to say the least, for in fact the longest, costliest, bloodiest, most cruel part of it, the guerrilla war imposed on the British by the Boer commandos that lasted close to two years, was still to come.

At the outset of the first part of the war, the 45,000-strong Boer army, divided into largely autonomous cavalry commandos of between one and five thousand men, had numerical superiority and won big victories at Colenso (Natal), Magersfontein (Free State) and Stormberg (the Cape). In the battle of Colenso alone, the British suffered 2,000 casualties. The fortunes of war turned in February 1900 with the battle of Paardeberg in the Free State. The British army, led by Lord Roberts, trapped the 4,000 men of Piet Cronjé most of whom were made prisoners of war, including the Boer general himself. From then on, British victories began to fall in like dominoes: the reliefs of Ladysmith and Kimberley, and the capture of Bloemfontein were accomplished in less than a month. In May, Roberts's army crossed the Vaal river and entered the Transvaal. As they approached Johannesburg, the big question in everyone's mind was: 'Are the Boers going to blow up the mines?' They did not. The Boers had decided against doing it, because they realised that the destruction of the mines would antagonise European opinion – many capitalists in Paris and Berlin, not to mention London, had heavily invested in the mines. Johannesburg and Pretoria fell like ripe apples in June and in July. The 3,000 British prisoners of war held in Pretoria were released. Old President Kruger, after having spent weeks as a fugitive in a railway carriage, crossed the Mozambique border in October and sailed into exile in Europe. Lord Roberts left South Africa in January 1901 and was given a hero's welcome in London. Lord Kitchener (of Khartoum fame), who had been the chief of staff, replaced him. But by then the second phase of the war had already started.

The news of the British victory was received with jubilation by the Africans who had cheered them whenever they entered the Boer cities. They were hoping that the magnanimous British would put an end to their days of oppression and misery. After all, that was the official position of Chamberlain and the British government. But they were wrong. As Thomas Pakenham puts it: 'Now the Africans found that their celebrations of Roberts' victory, celebrations which included widespread burning of passes, had been premature. . . . So the first step of Roberts' military government of Johannesburg was to get them off the pavements and back into their locations.'[27] Kitchener's attitude was no different: the tenth point of his ten-point peace plan prepared in February 1901 was the following: 'As regards the extension of the franchise to the Kaffirs in the Transvaal and the Orange River Colony, it is not the intention of His Majesty's Government to give such a franchise before a representative government is granted to those colonies.'[28]

Two Boer generals are generally credited with having started the second part of the Anglo-Boer War: Christiaan de Wet from the Free State and Koos de la Rey from the Transvaal. Soon Louis Botha, who had taken over as Commandant-General at Piet Joubert's death, as well as Christiaan Beyers, Smuts, Hertzog and one or two others followed suit. After President Kruger's flight, the mantle of overall political leadership had fallen on Marthinus Steyn, the president of the Free State. A critical *krijgraad* (council of war) was held in

November 1900 where the momentous decision to continue the war, and more specifically to invade the Cape and Natal, was made. The decision to invade the two colonies was taken for two reasons, the second of which was far more important: one, the British would have to stop their policy of farm-burning, because that would not be tolerated by British opinion, the colonies being technically on British soil; and two, the staunch belief that the invasion of the Cape would not fail to start an insurrection among the numerous Boers living there. Between December 1900 and September 1901 several epic attempts were made to invade the Cape but they all failed miserably, because the forces involved were too small and because the *volk* failed to rise. It is true that by that time the 250,000-strong British army may have appeared to the latter as invincible.

Meanwhile, Kitchener was experimenting with a few strategic innovations of his own. The first one was a gigantic line of block-houses linked by barbed wire and miniature forts within range of rifle fire from each other; at its peak the blockhouse line was 3,000 miles long and was used to trap commandos who would either be captured or killed; the total number of fighting men thus incapacitated was called a 'bag'. The strategy proved to be an effective one: as the blockhouse line swept the country, the totals of monthly bags kept rising: 859 in January 1901, 1,772 in February, 1,472 in March, 2,437 in April, and so on.[29] Kitchener's second innovation was the infamous concentration camps. Tens of thousands of Afrikaner women and children (and their African workers and servants; there were separate camps for them) were 'given a few minutes to clear their homes, and then driven off in wagons' to the camps. In August 1901, there were '93,940 whites, 24,457 blacks in the so-called "camps of refuge".... Every month the death toll rose, relatively as well as absolutely: May, 550; June, 782; July, 1,675. Crisis was becoming catastrophe.... At least 20,000 white and 12,000 Coloured people had died in the concentration camps, the majority from epidemics of measles and typhoid that could have been avoided.'[30] A third innovation was the quite large-scale use of native troops. Kitchener, who had served as *sirdar* (governor) in Sudan, had no use for the prevailing nonsense at the time that this was 'a white man's war': 'Africans serving in Kitchener's ninety-odd columns must have been enormous: 20,000 perhaps.'[31]

Ruthless, even perhaps inhuman, as some of Kitchener's policies were, they had one undeniable advantage (from the British perspective): they worked. By the end of 1901, the Boer forces had been reduced to about 25,000 ragged, bedraggled men. The situation became indeed so hopeless for the Boers that in April 1902 they accepted to engage in peace talks during which the issue of the natives' political rights came up again. Chamberlain, to be entirely fair, made some half-hearted attempts at gaining some improvement in their condition: 'We cannot consent to purchase a shameful peace by leaving the coloured population in the position in which they stood before the war.'[32] But he had both Kitchener and Milner against him, and in the end he was persuaded that it was better to leave 'the question of political rights of natives to be settled [later] by the colonists themselves,' i.e., after they were granted representative government. Some historians, rightly or wrongly, argue that it was then that the political fate of the blacks was sealed for almost a century.[33] Besides, at the same conference a unique opportunity to 'defangle' the Boers, was probably missed when their offer of surrendering large chunks of territory, *including* the Witwatersrand, the richest part of the country, in exchange of total independence in the thus severely shrunk present-day Transvaal and Orange Free State, was rejected out of hand for the sake of safeguarding white unity. As mentioned earlier, Milner's grand design was to unify the whole of Southern Africa, which then would be an integral part of the British Empire.

After the war, Milner, financed by Beit and some other 'gold bugs', continued his policy of white unity. Like Lord Somerset almost a century before him, he tried hard to anglicise the Boers by imposing the use of the English language in the schools. He also, in an effort to outnumber the Boers, made an attempt to bring large numbers of British settlers to South Africa (the first census taken in 1904 in the Transvaal showed that there was an almost equal number of English- and Afrikaans-speakers there). Milner's policies were not so unrealistic as they were made out to be by later historians and given time they might have succeeded. But he was forced to resign in 1905 over the issue of the flogging of the indentured Chinese workers who had been brought in to supplement the African labour in the mines, which was in short supply. Another stroke of good luck for the Afrikaners was the victory of the Liberals in the British general elections of 1906. In fact, the mood of British public opinion had been changing since the publication in 1902 by a certain J A Hobson – who had been a correspondent for the *Manchester Guardian* in South Africa during the Anglo-Boer War – of *Imperialism*, a book in which he accused the British government of being in cahoots with 'a small confederacy of international financiers working through a kept press', and with condoning the fact that 'Kaffirs ... everywhere in white man's South Africa [are] the hewers of wood and the drawers of water.'[34] The Biblical expression caught the imagination of the journalists, who used it widely, and the Liberals decided to grant self-government to the Transvaal and to the Orange River colony. The subsequent elections were won by the Boer parties and the colour bar was entrenched in the Union Constitution of 1909. It was to serve later as the legal basis for an avalanche of segregationist labour laws that were passed in the late 1920s and early 1930s. The Africans were removed from the common roll of the Cape Colony in 1934. The Coloureds' turn came twenty-two years later, in 1956.

Notes

1 T Pakenham, *The Boer War*, Weidenfeld and Nicolson, 1979, page 577.

2 J Morris, *Heaven's Command: an Imperial Progress*, Harcourt Brace Jovanovich, 1973, New York, pages 22–3 and page 539.

3 H W Littlefield, *History of Europe since 1815*, Barnes and Noble, 1963, New York, page 20.

4 J Morris, *Heaven's Command*, page 50.

5 J Cell, 'The Imperial Conscience', in P Marsh (ed), *The Conscience of the Victorian State*, Syracuse UP, 1979, page 204.

6 H W Littlefield, *History of Europe since 1815*, page 75.

7 J Cell, 'The Imperial Conscience', page 204.

8 J Morris, *Heaven's Command*, page 390.

9 D Schreuder, 'Gladstone and the Conscience of the State', in Marsh (ed), *The Conscience of the Victorian State*, pages 91 and 99.

10 J Cell, 'Imperial Conscience', page 208.

11 J Morris, *Heaven's Command*, page 54.

12 M Strage, *Cape to Cairo: the Rape of a Continent*, Harcourt Brace Jovanovich, 1973, New York, page 26.

13 T R H Davenport, *South Africa: a Modern History*, University of Toronto Press, 1977, page 34. Davenport is considered the foremost contempor-

ary South African historian. A third edition of his book was published in 1986 in the Cambridge Commonwealth Series.

14 D Harrison, *The White Tribe of South Africa*, University of California Press, 1981, Berkeley and Los Angeles, pages 48–9.

15 J Morris, *Heaven's Command*, page 51.

16 'Under General Pretorius, the Boer force numbered about 800 of which 464 were fighting men with shotguns; they also had three cannons. The 10,000 Zulu warriors were all armed with short stabbing spears and cowhide shields. In the end, numbers proved no match against superior weaponry. The Zulu lost 3,000 casualties against only three wounded for the Boers.' D Harrison, *The White Tribe*, page 17.

17 J Cell, 'The Imperial Conscience', page 197.

18 J Cell, 'The Imperial Conscience,' page 197.

19 T R H Davenport, *South Africa*, page 91.

20 C Wheatcroft, *The Randlords*, Atheneum, 1986, New York, page 138.

21 C Wheatcroft, *The Randlords*, page 133.

22 Cecil Rhodes's story is told in fascinating detail in Strage, M, *Cape to Cairo: the Rape of a Continent*.

23 C Wheatcroft, *The Randlords*, page 181.

24 M Strage, *Cape to Cairo*, pages 98–9.

25 Despite the raid, or perhaps partly because of it, Dr Leander Starr Jameson went on to have an extraordinary career. He was sentenced to a fifteen months' term after the Boers turned him over to the British government but he was released after four months. He returned to South Africa and served with distinction as a doctor in the Boer War. He was then elected to parliament in 1900 and in 1904 he became prime minister of the Cape Colony. In 1911 he was knighted and, when he died in 1917, he was buried on the Matapos hills in Rhodesia (Zimbabwe now) alongside his mentor and friend Cecil Rhodes. Kipling's famous poem 'If...' is said to have been inspired by him. See C Wheatcroft, *The Randlords*, page 190.

26 T Pakenham, *The Boer War*, pages 66–8. Thomas Pakenham is the foremost historian of the Boer War. The following four or five pages on that war are based on his monumental book.

27–33 T Pakenham, *The Boer War*, pages 429, 491, 499, 510, 518, 548, 563 and 564.

34 J A Hobson's *Imperialism* became a very influential book. It was, among others, used heavily by V I Lenin in his writing. See C Wheatcroft, *The Randlords*, page 204.

20

The Afrikaner Era

*'The primary consideration is whether Afrikanerdoom will reach its
ultimate destiny of domination (baaskaap) in South Africa.'*
J C van Rooy, chairman,
Afrikaner *Broederbond* 1934[1]

The Era of the Generals
In 1904, just before he died in exile in Switzerland, Paul Kruger
wrote a letter to General Louis Botha in which he warned his people
against disunity: 'Do not forget,' he wrote, 'that a grave warning
lies in the words "divide and rule". Never let these words apply
to the South African [read Afrikaner] nation. Then our people and
our language will endure and prosper.'[2]

But that solemn warning went unheeded and the Era of the
Generals began – a period which started with the proclamation of
the Union of South Africa in 1910 and ended with the arrival to
power of Dr D F Malan's purified National Party in 1948 – called
after the three former Boer Generals – Louis Botha, (J B M) 'Barry'
Hertzog and Jan Christiaan Smuts – that have dominated it. It is
an era of great achievements for the Afrikaner nation but also one
marked with discord and disunity – an era of *Broedertwis* (Quarrel
among Brothers) as the Afrikaners themselves call it. A bitter
struggle developed between the forces that favoured white unity,
represented by Botha and Smuts, and the anti-English, Afrikaner
supremacists led by D F Malan – and less so by Hertzog.

After the Union was achieved in May 1910, the first general
elections were won by Botha's South African Party. Botha became
prime minister; Smuts, minister of the Interior and Hertzog, minister of Justice. Botha, who had coined the motto of 'Forgive and

Forget', wanted white unity, that is, unity, not only among Afrikaners – contrary to the legend the Boers had been badly divided
during the Anglo-Boer war: there were those who had stayed put,
the Cape Loyalists; those who had fought on the British side, the
National Scouts; those who had rapidly surrendered, the 'hands-
uppers'; and those who had fought to the bitter end, the 'bitter-
enders' – but also between the Afrikaans- and the English-speakers.
Botha did not have time to bring his policy to fruition. His white-
unity policy received a fatal blow when the First World War broke
out. The Union of South Africa being part of the British Commonwealth, he had no choice but to enter the war on the side of the
British. That position was strongly opposed by Hertzog who, in
1914, resigned from the government and the party to launch his
own National Party which coined its own counter motto: South
Africa First. The National Party stood, among other things, for
a compulsory mother-tongue education in primary schools and
bilingualism in the public service. When Botha attacked German-
occupied South West Africa (Namibia) at the demand of the rather
insensitive British, a very serious *Broedertwis*, known as *Die Rebellie*,
broke out which was led by a trio of former Boer generals – de la
Rey, Beyers and de Wet – who conspired to overthrow the government. The rebellion failed as things went wrong practically from
the beginning: de la Rey was accidentally shot at a roadblock which
had been set up to catch a gang of robbers that had been terrorising
the area; Beyers drowned trying to cross the Vaal river; and de Wet
was captured and sent to prison. The government had survived
but at a high price. Deep divisions continued to persist throughout
the war. Botha, who realised that his dream of reconciliation was
dashed, died in 1919 a disillusioned man and was succeeded by
Smuts.

The political crisis was compounded by an economic and social
one. There was the big problem of the poor whites brought about
by the Boer farmers' inability to recover from the devastation
wreaked by the Anglo-Boer War. To make a very bad situation even
worse, there was a long period of drought and crop failures. In
large numbers, the impoverished Boers left the rural areas in search
of work in the cities, in the factories and especially in the mines,
where they clashed with the gold magnates who naturally preferred
the much cheaper African labour. In 1920, the gold mines were
employing 180,000 Africans and 21,000 whites whose average wage

was sixteen times higher than that of the Africans. A confrontation was inevitable; it exploded in January 1922 after brewing for some months. It was no trifling affair, as shown by the following account of it by D Harrison:

By early January 1922 twenty thousand white miners were on strike.... Witwatersrand came to a virtual standstill. Next the white miners organized themselves into white commandos.... The crucial issue [was] competition with the blacks, and ... the need of maintaining the color bar that the mining houses were now trying to repudiate.... On 29 January the strike unions called on workers and sympathizers to join forces with the National and Labour parties in the struggle to overthrow Smuts and install a government 'calculated to promote the interests of the White Race in South Africa'. A mass meeting of strikers, inspired perhaps by recent events in Russia, proclaimed a People's Republic. Armed groups of miners began roaming the streets, looting and fire raising and attacking native compounds.... Smuts called up Citizen Force Units of the Army ... the final assault ... began with a softening up [of the main strike headquarters at Fordsburg] by the artillery's thirteen pounders and ended with a bayonet charge by the Durban Light Infantry.... During the fighting, forty-three members of the Defence Forces and twenty-nine policemen had been killed. Thirty-nine miners or 'revolutionaries and suspected revolutionaries' had died and so had forty-two ordinary civilians. About five-hundred had been wounded. Some thirty Africans had been killed in indiscriminate acts of racial violence. Nearly five-thousand people were arrested.[3]

Just before the strike some important political developments had taken place. The Unionist (pro-British) opposition had joined Smuts' South African Party, while Hertzog's Nationalists, who supported the strike, had formed a pact with F Creswell's Labourites. The general election of 1924, to the surprise of many, was won by the Hertzog-Creswell alliance and the following ten years in power were spent consolidating white workers' interests. A deluge of new laws were passed by the parliament to that effect as well as to expand the public sector to provide jobs for the poor Afrikaners (no longer called Boers because they had become urbanised. Today

'Boer' has come to mean 'oppressor' to the blacks). In 1933, Hertzog, worried about developments in the Cape where Malan and his Nationalist supporters were gaining ground, dissolved the pact and joined forces with Smuts to form the United Party. Two years later, Malan left the alliance to create his own purified National Party.

The Broederbond or Afrikaner Supremacy on the March

The Afrikaner *Broederbond* was founded in 1918 with several purposes in mind: to help the Afrikaners who had fallen on hard times after the Anglo-Boer War; to promote a national identity and culture, and economic empowerment at the national level.[4]

The creation in 1929 of the Federation of Afrikaans Cultural Associations (FAK) made it possible for the *Broederbond* to focus on economic and political matters. The level of success achieved was beyond the wildest dreams of its founders. In 1948, they captured the biggest prize: the state. The fact that, in 1948, all the members of the Malan government (with the exception of one) were *Broeders* shows clearly the incredible distance travelled by the organisation in less than two decades. By 1966, the year of Verwoerd's assassination, the *Broederbond* had accomplished its goal of complete control of South African society – with the notable exception of Big Business. It was able to do this: firstly, by using state power to pack the civil service, the army, the police and the intelligence services, with their own people; secondly, by infiltrating and eventually dominating the Afrikaner church and schools, two essential institutions; and thirdly, by enlarging considerably the public sector. The story of how they did it will be told briefly in the following pages.

In the late 1920s, a new ideological movement was born in the Cape province that was led by Malan (who was the chairman of the National Party there). Other prominent members included Verwoerd, T E Donges, N J van der Merwe, J G Strijdom (a future prime minister) and C R Swart. A common characteristic of all these men was that they had *not* fought in the Anglo-Boer War. They became the leading apostles of a new exclusive nationalist ideology and bitterly opposed Hertzog's and Smuts' policies of national unity of all the South African whites. Malan and his followers believed in a pure Afrikaner nationalism and, in the early 1930s, they were all recruited by the *Broederbond* to form its intellectual core. It was in 1933 that the first circular dealing specifically

with black problem was sent to the *Broederbond*'s general membership (which, in 1935 stood at 1,395 males organised in 80 cells; by
1965, the numbers were 6,966 and 484 respectively). The circular
emphasised that the total segregation between the whites and the
blacks should now be 'the immediate practical policy of the state'.
'A native,' it said, 'will be allowed . . . to go temporarily to white
areas to work in farms, in towns and cities. But he will not be
allowed to take his family.'[5] The seeds of grand apartheid had thus
been sown; they would germinate into a huge forest in the following
thirty years or so.

From the biggest affiliate of the FAK, the Afrikaans Language
and Cultural Society of the Railways (ATKV), came the seemingly
innocuous (it certainly was at the time) idea of celebrating the
hundredth anniversary of the Great Trek of 1836 by having a couple
of oxen-drawn wagons cross the country, all the way from Cape
Town to the site chosen for the building of the megalo-maniacal
Voortrekker Monument in Pretoria. The Afrikaner popular response
was beyond the organisers' wildest imagination: people lined up
in the streets of the towns and villages visited by the wagons
dressed in period costumes; men let their beards grow for the
occasion; there were patriotic speeches, festivals, songs, and so on.
Soon, the original two wagons were multiplied by four and they
went around visiting all the holiest shrines of Afrikanerdom such
as: Slagter's Nek (where five Boers had been hanged by the British
about a century ago); the grave of Captain Jopie Fourie who had
been executed for his role in the 1914 *Rebellie*; the monument erected
at the site of the Battle of the Blood River in Natal to honour
Piet Retief and the seventy burghers treacherously murdered by
Dingane, the Zulu king; and so on. The eight wagons finally converged on Monument Koppie in Pretoria, where a huge crowd
estimated at 200,000 had gathered in anticipation of the grand finale,
which was to be held on 15–16 December 1936. Hertzog, the prime
minister, could not participate in the ceremonies, because his presence would require the playing of the national anthem which, under
the constitution, was the British 'God Save the King' and that was
simply anathema in the circumstances; it would have caused bloody
riots. So Hertzog, and Smuts by solidarity, had to stay away from
the 'Sacred Happening' which everyone knew was organised by the
Broederbond and the Nationalists. Some historians go so far as
believing that the Hundredth Anniversary Trek was an important

factor in the watershed Nationalist election victory in 1948, that came more than a decade later.

On the eve of the Second World War (as had been the case with the First), the Afrikaners were sharply divided among themselves on whether the country should enter the war on the side of the Allies or remain neutral. A vote taken by the government had resulted in a deadlock: Hertzog and six ministers had voted to stay out of it; Smuts and six others for siding with the Allies. The matter was taken to the House of Assembly, which voted in favour of Smuts, 80 to 67. Hertzog had to resign and Smuts became prime minister for the second time. Hertzog then joined forces with Malan to form the *Herenigte* (Reconstituted) National Party. But it proved to be an uneasy and a short-lived alliance. Having failed to secure the new party's chairmanship at the 1939 Bloemfontein Congress (his own backyard, he was born there) following a *Broederbond*-inspired smear campaign that painted him as a freemason, Hertzog retired from active politics and 'died a lonely, bitter and dejected man in November 1942'.[6]

⅄ The *Ossewabrandwag* (OB, the Oxwagon Guard), a pro-German fascist organisation, was launched in February 1939. With the traditional anti-British Afrikaner sentiment exacerbated by the war and bolstered by the initial German victories, the OB grew rapidly. So much so in fact that in August 1940, its leader Hans van Rensburg 'offered to stage a rebellion against Smuts, placing its 160,000 members and 15,000 soldiers (known as *Stormjaers*) . . . at the disposal of Hitler'.[7] It appears that the Nazis accepted the offer and an attempt (a weak one, it is true) was made in 1941 to overthrow Smuts and replace him by a puppet government favourable to the Germans. Operation Weissdorn was entrusted to a secret agent named R Leibbrandt, who 'was landed by a German yacht in June 1941 with the express purpose of assassinating Smuts and staging a coup d'état with the help of the most militant *Stormjaers*'.[8] But Leibbrandt's plan was too extreme (it involved the assassination not only of Smuts, but also some of Smuts' closest associates (even apparently Malan himself) and a panicked van Rensburg blew the whistle in time for it to be foiled. Leibbrandt was captured and sentenced to death, but not executed, Smuts being a friend of his father's. After the failure of the conspiracy, Malan broke the alliance that he had made with the OB, and as the prospects of a German victory in the war became dimmer, so did OB's fortunes in South Africa. Soon after the war ended, OB was no longer a factor.

The fact that achieving domination, or hegemony, in a society requires above all the control of the schools and the church, goes a long way to explain why educationists – teachers, school administrators, principals, inspectors – and churchmen formed such a large part of *Broederbond* membership in the crucial decades of the 1930s and 1940s. Of course, as mentioned earlier, the *Broederbond* supported the Nationalists who pushed for mother-tongue tuition in separate schools; as opposed to the Unionists' dual-medium instruction within the same premises. In 1939, a Christian National Education Conference was organised by the FAK, which laid the foundations of an education programme that became official policy after 1948. Smuts's unexpected defeat sealed, as it were, the growing estrangement between the English- and Afrikaans-speaking South Africans.

Afrikaners are Calvinist Protestants and their church, the DRC, is subdivided into the *Nederduitse Gereformeerde Kerk* (NGK), which is by far the biggest; the *Gereformeerde Kerk* (GK) also known as the *Dopper* church, which is the most conservative and the *Hervormde Kerk* (HK), the most liberal, organised as a white mother church and sister churches for the blacks. For a long time the DRC went along with the official policy of racial segregation, espousing dogma such as the Afrikaners being sent by God to the Dark Continent to save the heathen souls from damnation, and so on. The persistent attacks from Anglican, Catholic and Methodist churches were largely ignored. To be fair, there was some occasional opposition within the DRC. In 1954, for example, a certain A Geyser, a brilliant young theology professor at the University of Pretoria, after 'intensive study', came to the conclusion that there was 'no scriptural justification' for apartheid. A far bigger challenge came in 1960, in the aftermath of the Sharpeville Massacre. The conference organised jointly at Cottesloe, Johannesburg, by the World Council of Churches and eight major NGK churches of the Transvaal and the Cape found that apartheid 'was not compatible' with the scriptures. What came to be known as the DRC Revolt was short-lived, however. The rebels were fiercely attacked by Verwoerd, then prime minister and at the peak of his powers, and by the conservative forces within the DRC led by A P Treurnicht, then editor of *Kerkbode*, NGK's official journal and, from 1983, when he broke away from the National Party, and until his death in April 1993, the leader of the Conservative Party, the 'respectable' right wing. Most of the rebels quickly recanted, admitting that they had made a mistake. Among the few diehards who did not was Beyers Naudé who went on to found the Christian Institute and its progressive journal *Pro Veritate*, of which he became the editor.

In the 1943 general elections, Smuts' United Party (UP) won a big victory: 89 seats, against only 43 to Malan's HNP; nine seats went to the English-speakers' Labour Party, which was a UP supporter; so Smuts had a huge majority in parliament. However, behind the bright façade, the reality was far murkier. For years, his own intelligence services had been warning Smuts that the *Broederbond* was carrying out a systematic plan to destroy him and his party and it was making dramatic progress. Partly because Smuts believed in his own invincibility and partly because he did not want to get entangled in a confrontation with the DRC and the civil service which formed the bedrock of *Broederbond*'s support, he did not pay much attention. Only towards the end of the war did he become convinced the *Broederbond* had become a real threat that had to be dealt with but, by then, it was too late. At the UP Congress that was held in Bloemfontein in December 1944, he attacked the organisation violently: 'The Afrikaner *Broederbond*,' he declared, 'is a dangerous, cunning, political, Fascist organisation of which no civil servant could be allowed to be a member.'[9] He forced the civil servants to choose between belonging to the *Broederbond* and working for the government. More than a thousand resigned from the *Broederbond*, albeit reluctantly and filled with rancour; only a hundred or so did the opposite: they quit their jobs, rather than leave the *Broederbond*.

Smuts's last three years as head of government were spent basking in the glow of his international recognition as a world-class statesman. In 1946, he was invited to San Francisco and given the exceptional honour of writing the preamble to the United Nations Charter. A year later, the British Royal Family paid a long visit to South Africa as his personal guests. He was a personal friend of Churchill's. But, like the other two Boer generals Botha and Hertzog, his end was tragic. He too was rejected by his own people and died a lonely man because he had lost touch with them. He suffered an unexpected defeat of staggering proportions in the general election of 1948. The final tallying of the votes gave the UP 65 seats, against 70 to Malan's HNP; N C Havenga's Afrikaner Party won 9 seats; the Labourites, 6 and Native Representatives, 3. Overall totals were: pro-UP forces, 74; pro-HNP, 79. As if to rub more salt into his wound, Smuts himself was defeated in his own constituency of Standerton by one of the civil servants who had preferred to resign rather than quit the *Broederbond*. Smuts, now old and disillusioned, retired to his farm and died two years later, in 1950. The Era of the Generals was over. A new chapter would now begin in Afrikaner history that would take them to the apex of their power.

The Verwoerdian Era: The Coming of Age of Apartheid

It is impossible to exaggerate the role that Dr Hendrik F Verwoerd played in the building of grand apartheid in South Africa.[10] He has been called the 'Promethean Afrikaner', the 'Architect of Apartheid' and, for a while, there was serious talk about a Verwoerdian vision. He was undoubtedly a very charismatic figure endowed with extra-ordinary leadership qualities (a great orator, he could speak for hours without notes) and he dominated white politics for close on two decades. In short, he was a very determined man who had what it took to impose his flawed vision on his people.

Verwoerd was born in Holland in 1901 and brought to South Africa by his parents as a three-month-old baby. In his early twenties, he went to Germany to study and came under the influence of Hegelian nationalist and idealist thought. After having earned a doctoral degree in psychology he returned to South Africa and joined the faculty at Stellenbosch University, then as now the Mecca of the Afrikaner intelligentsia. In the mid 1930s, he became the editor of *Die Transvaler* and a member of the Executive Committee of the *Broederbond*, both very influential positions which he used to the hilt to propagate the philosophy of separate development. He was not alone of course. In 1945 appeared G Cronjé's book, *A Home for Posterity*, whose main message was 'the Bantu must undergo their own "Christian National Development" and have their own fatherland in which they can enjoy national self-determination'.[11] *A Home for Posterity* was an important milestone. Separate development was now a serious ideology which was further refined by the intellectuals of South African Bureau of Racial Affairs (SABRA), a *Broederbond*-connected think tank founded in 1950 at Stellenbosch University. After a few years of study, SABRA came to the conclusion that the African homelands had to be granted full independence. That conclusion was at first rejected by Verwoerd who believed that white guidance was necessary for the 'proper development of the Bantu'. Later, however, he agreed with SABRA's views and the Promotion of Bantu Self-government Act was passed in 1959. But, even if it were a strictly economic undertaking, the policy was doomed because the enormous financial resources that were necessary to give it substance were never allocated to it.

With the appointment of Verwoerd as minister of Native Affairs in 1950, a torrent of legislation began to pour through the white parliament to promote, codify and entrench grand apartheid. Among the most important of the new laws passed were: The Population Registration Act and The Group Areas Act, both in 1950; The Bantu Education Act in 1953 and The Resettlement of Natives Act in 1954. In 1958, Verwoerd became prime minister (succeeding J G Strijdom who had died in office). Apartheid laws continued to be steamrollered through parliament, especially after the Sharpeville Massacre in 1960. State security became the primary concern. Under the provisions of The Criminal Act of 1965, for example, 'witnesses' could be detained up to 180 days without being brought before a magistrate; the notorious Section Six of The Terrorism Act of 1967 did away altogether with *habeas corpus* and suspected terrorists could now be held in gaol for years without trial. As a result of all these repressive laws, African resistance was all but crushed by the late 1960s.

The first attempt on Verwoerd's life came in 1960 when he was shot in the head by a 'deranged' white farmer. Miraculously, he not only survived but made a full recovery which he later attributed to God's will so that he could pursue his work. That belief was widely shared at the time. His narrow victory on the Republic issue in 1961 was the high point of his political career. South Africa severed all its remaining ties with the UK. On his return from the Commonwealth conference from which South Africa was expelled, he was received as a hero. The second, and successful, attempt on his life came in 1966. Earlier in that year he had decided to seek a fresh mandate from the electorate and had won the subsequent general election in a landslide, increasing National Party's majority from 105, against 49 to the United Party; to 126 against 39. Verwoerd had concluded, quite rightly, that the result of the election constituted a vote of confidence for his policy of separate development and was preparing for a new big push when Fate decided otherwise.

It happened on 6 September 1966. Verwoerd had just taken his seat in the House of Assembly when one of the messengers crossed the floor and suddenly, as he reached the prime minister, pulled a big knife from under his coat and plunged it several times into the neck and chest of Verwoerd, who died on the spot. The assassin, Dimitrio Tsafendas, a man of mixed race with a Greek father and a Mozambique mother, was found to be 'deranged' at his trial. In 1993 he is still languishing in a prison cell in Pretoria.

The forced removal of blacks from places they had been living in for generations was at the very heart of the separate development policy. A grand total of more than 3.5 million non-whites (of whom more than 3 million were Africans) were thus expelled from their lands in rural areas and from 'locations' in urban areas between 1960 and 1983. It is a huge subject to which I cannot hope to do justice in the limited space of this chapter.[12] So I choose to give briefly two specific examples of the ruthlessness and fanaticism with which the ideology of grand apartheid was put into practice. The first concerns the expulsion of the Coloured people from the common roll of voters (the Africans were expelled in 1936) and the second has to do with Bantu education whose negative consequences are probably among the most damaging of those wrought by apartheid because the most lasting.

By the early 1950s the Coloureds had been part of the common roll in the Cape for more than three-quarters of a century; in fact, since responsible government had been granted to the Cape Colony in 1872. The Malan government did not waste much time in declaring that that situation was unacceptable because it contravened one of the basic tenets, indeed the very essence, of the separate development policy. The Coloureds would have to be taken out of the common roll and be put in a separate one under which they would still be able to elect their four (white) representatives to the House of Assembly. So far so good, but there was a problem: the question could not be dealt with, as usual, with the passing of a new law in parliament. Franchise laws were entrenched in the constitution and any change therein required a two-thirds majority, which the Malan government did not have. There were also massive public protests organised primarily by the Torch Commando (an association of war veterans) and the Women's Defence of the Constitution League (out of which came the Black Sash, committed to the defence of the Africans' human and legal rights). So, a few years went by without a resolution of the crisis. In 1954, Malan, now eighty years old, resigned and was succeeded by the advocate J G Strijdom, who quickly found a way around the impasse. He enlarged the Appeals Court and appointed five new judges to fill the vacancies, and he increased the size of the Senate from forty-eight to eighty-nine members. In February 1956 it was all over; despite an epic five years' battle, the Coloureds were no longer part of the common roll.

Verwoerd believed that there was no point in educating blacks, Africans in particular, for jobs that would not be available for them anyway. This is what he had to say about the Bantu Education Act of 1953: 'Good racial relations cannot exist when education . . . creates the wrong expectations on the part of the Native. . . . [Education] has to train people in accordance with their opportunities in life. There is no place for the Natives in White South Africa above the level of certain forms of labor. . . . European education for blacks can only lead to discontent, frustration and ultimately social upheaval.'[13]

After the Act was passed, the overall responsibility for African education was taken away from the provincial administrations and given to a central Department of Native Affairs. All public schools were required to register with the Department and had to follow the curricula prepared by it; the training of black teachers also was taken away from the provinces. In 1958, a new Department of Bantu Education was created. The consequences of these reactionary policies were tragic. The number of Africans who passed the Matric (high school diploma) plummeted: from 259 in 1953 to 115 in 1961. Between 1954 and 1965, school expenditures per black pupil fell from R8.7 to R4.9; that of a white pupil rose from R50 to R75. As for higher education, the two black colleges – Fort Hare, affiliated to Rhodes University, in the Eastern Cape and the University College of the North in the Transvaal, affiliated with Wits, which had enjoyed a good reputation all over Africa, were also taken over by the Department of Bantu Education and turned into 'bush colleges'. Under The Extension of the University Education Act of 1959, three more segregated institutions of higher learning were founded: the University of Western Cape at Belville near Cape Town for the Coloureds; a college for Indians at Westville, near Durban in Natal; and the University of Zululand in Empageni.

The Birth and Growth of the Reform Movement: The Pre- and Post-Soweto Periods

The originator of the Afrikaner reform movement is not, as is generally believed P W Botha, but B J Vorster who succeeded Verwoerd after his assassination. Vorster clashed with the *Broederbond* right wingers over two policy issues: the partial desegregation of sports; and the establishment of relations with moderate African regimes, including the exemption of black diplomats from residential segregation and other forms of petty apartheid. By the late 1960s the international sports boycott against South Africa was already in high gear and the country's sportsmen were beginning to feel the sting of almost complete isolation. The situation was deemed to be demoralising and dangerous by Vorster and some others in the power elite. Not long after he took over, the government came up with a two-tier sports policy: at the national level, different racial groups would be allowed to compete against one another; at the international level, the South African teams could be multi-racial; however, no mixing of the races would be allowed at provincial and local club levels. The new policy was approved by the parliament in 1971, but it did not really serve any useful purpose because by the mid 1970s the issue was no longer a question of sports boycott *per se* but a boycott of grand apartheid, of which the sports boycott was but one component.

Meanwhile, Vorster had been quite active on the African political scene, achieving even, for the time, some spectacular results. He was, for example, credited with persuading Ian Smith of Rhodesia to accept discussions with Harold Wilson, on how to end the civil war and the Unilateral Declaration of Independence (UDI). There were discreet contacts with Houphouet Boigny of Ivory Coast. Dr Banda's Malawi agreed to exchange ambassadors. Insignificant as they may well appear today, these reforms were enough for some extremists such as Albert Hertzog (son of Barry, the former prime minister), Jaap Marais and Louis Stofberg to break away from the National Party and form their own *Herstigte* (Purified) National Party, the HNP.

After the Soweto uprising of 1976, things would never be the same again in South Africa. Many *verligte* (liberal) Afrikaner intellectuals realised this early and began searching for ways of getting out of the impasse short of giving away the store, i.e, of losing their dominant political position. A leading *verligte* scholar and intellectual was Gerrit Viljoen, a distinguished professor of classics who, in 1967, had become the first rector of the newly created Rand Afrikaans University in Johannesburg. In 1974, Viljoen had been elected chairman of the Afrikaner *Broederbond* defeating, after an arduous battle, the conservative candidate A P Treurnicht. To Viljoen, some of the old tactics of grand apartheid, such as making life as difficult as possible for as many Africans as possible in the townships, with the aim of having them return to the homelands, did not make much sense any more. He suggested that instead of constant harassment, a new deal in the form of the urban renewal of the townships should be offered to Africans. He also stressed the need to develop the homelands and to abolish many of the petty apartheid rules – such as segregated restaurants, cinemas, hotels, parks, etc- which were unnecessarily humiliating to blacks.

'But,' Viljoen cautioned, 'an authoritarian structure is at its most vulnerable when it embarks on self-analysis and the correction of its shortcomings. Then precautions must be taken against confusing your own people and undermining their instinct for self-preservation, and also against provoking expectations on a revolutionary scale among those affected by the system. At the same time the necessary corrective measures must be identified and implemented carefully. Too little too late can be counterproductive and look like concessions made under pressure.'[14] This, in a nutshell, summarises the essence of reform policy in the decade and a half from the mid 1970s to February 1990, when Mandela was released from prison and the ANC and the other black opposition movements were unbanned and allowed to return home.

With Vorster's resignation in 1978 over what came to be known as the Muldergate scandal (C P Mulder was Information minister and chairman of the party for the Transvaal province; his ministry was shown to have set up a secret slush fund to buy favourable media attention in South Africa as well as abroad), the stage was set for a fierce succession struggle, which was won by P W Botha, thanks to the support of R 'Pik' Botha, who became minister of Foreign Affairs. P W, who was born in 1916, was a machine politician. When offered a job by Malan as party organiser at the precocious age of twenty, he had not hesitated to drop out from university to take it. He was 32 when first elected to parliament from George, a coastal town in the Western Cape. In 1966 had come his big break: just a few months before his assassination, Verwoerd had entrusted him with the crucial portfolio of Defence. In the following twelve years, during which he was uninterruptedly Defence minister, Botha transformed a relatively small and import-dependent army into a formidable and largely autonomous fighting machine. The main instrument by which he achieved that feat was Armscor, a state corporation which has the monopoly for manufacturing arms and munitions in South Africa; in the 1980s Armscor became a major arms exporter to Latin America and other parts of the world.[15]

In November 1979, after a much publicised visit to Soweto, Botha agreed to meet with South African business leaders led by Harry Oppenheimer (the son and successor of Ernest, the founder in 1917 of the Anglo-American Corporation, Anglo for short).[16] The meeting took place at Carlton Hotel in central Johannesburg with Botha accompanied by his whole cabinet and Harry Oppenheimer by some of the 180 or so prominent businessmen that he represented, including some major Afrikaner business figures such as Rembrandt's Anton Rupert. The conference went well and at its conclusion a new Spirit of Carlton was hailed by ecstatic media, perhaps a trifle prematurely. The euphoric feeling intensified when the reports were published of two government commissions which had long been working on issues involving, directly and indirectly, black labour: the Wiehahn Commission on trade-union rights, and the Riekert Commission on influx control and pass laws. The former recommended that the colour bar should be relaxed, indeed removed, for most jobs in the mines and the factories, and that black trade unions should be recognised officially (by registration) under certain conditions, the most important of which being that they stayed out of politics and were subject to outside auditing. The latter advised the acceptance of the permanence of African workers in the townships, implying thus the possibility for those to buy property and to bring in their families. In retrospect, it is clear that the Wiehahn commission, in particular, has paved the way for a tremendous rise in black labour power in the next ten years or so.

With hindsight, it appears that the decision to co-opt the Coloured and Indian populations by offering them the carrot of political representation in separate chambers of parliament was taken sometime in late 1980. It was during that year that the Senate, the upper house of the white House of Assembly, was abolished and replaced

by a President's Council, whose role was declared to be to transcend
political and racial barriers and help formulate a new constitutional
framework. The language used to describe the council is a good
sample of the Afrikaner newspeak that was common in those days
and which did not have any connection whatsoever with reality.
One observer described it as 'a motley collection of colored politicians, white businessmen and academics and a Nationalist hard-
core of senators and MPs.'[17] It was apparent, from its first session,
in February 1981, that the council was not the appropriate forum
(to say the least) to initiate drastic constitutional reform. To test the
waters on his reform policies, Botha called a snap election in April
that he won in a landslide. That must have convinced him that he
was on the right track and that the project to co-opt the Coloured
and the Indian communities into the white hegemonic system (in
a junior, powerless capacity) was a good one. African political
rights, explained Chris Heunis, the minister of Constitutional Development, would be at the appropriate time the object of a separate
dispensation. In fact, what the government had in mind, and was
hoping to achieve, was: firstly, to keep the majority of rural Africans
out of the picture by having them exercise their political rights in
the 'independent' homelands; and secondly, to devise a system of
local autonomy, with some form of regional and central representation to be worked out later, for the Africans living in the townships. Black protest against the new constitutional arrangements,
the 'Boycott the Constitution Campaign', was vigorous, but unable
to stop the realisation of the project – the boycott was successful in
the sense that it discredited the new constitution and parliament,
preventing them thus from acquiring legitimacy. In a whites-only
referendum, about two-thirds of those who voted (the turnout was
high) supported the new constitution. However, in the subsequent
elections for the Coloured House of Representatives and to the
Indian House of Delegates, a very small percentage of the two
electorates bothered to vote – about 30 and 20 per cent respectively,
most because they disagreed with the project, some because they
were afraid of the consequences. In an almost comical case, a candidate for one of the Cape seats in the new House of Representatives
won with a grand total of . . . 94 votes.

Because it was essentially flawed the new constitution of 1983
had two major consequences whose dramatic effects continue to
this day: firstly, the breaking away, under the leadership of Dr

Andries Treurnicht (died in April 1993), from the National Party of an important faction of right wingers who went ahead to form the Conservative Party; and, secondly, the explosion of the violence in the townships. For Treurnicht and Co the inclusion of non-whites at the national political level, even in a junior and powerless capacity, was dangerous. Carel Boshoff, a distinguished professor of theology at Pretoria University, and his wife, Verwoerd's daughter, founded the Afrikaner *Volkswag*, a conservative counterpart of the *Broederbond*, and the Afrikaner Women's Federation. Boshoff's goal is the creation of a Boer Volkstaat, which he called Oranjia, in the arid north-eastern Cape. As for the explosion of the violence in the townships, it led to the two States of Emergency of March 1985 and June 1986. The latter, which lasted more than three years, a general State of Emergency, was serious and led to the arrest of more than 15,000 black activists. The mainstream print media were severely muzzled during that period.

In the general elections of May 1987, not only was the National Party able to maintain its huge majority, but Treurnicht's Conservatives, confounding the predictions of the pollsters, beat Colin Eglin's Progressive Federal Party (PFP), replacing it thus as Official Opposition in the white parliament. That there had been a massive lurch to the right was confirmed by the results in Natal. In that traditionally liberal bastion (the large majority of the whites are English speakers who supported until then the New Republic Party, NRP). The PFP-NRP alliance had won 13 seats in 1981, against NP's 7; in 1987, the result was more than reversed: 6 for the alliance (PFP, 5 and NRP only 1), 14 for the NP. So, normally P W Botha's hand ought to have been greatly strengthened but, paradoxically enough, it is the opposite that happened, for by that time another crucial phenomenon had become determinant: the international sanctions which were hurting the South African economy badly – the gross domestic product declined on average one per cent a year between 1983 and 1990 while, simultaneously, the African population (28 million out of a total of 35 million) was growing at 2.6 per cent a year. It was obvious that things could not be allowed to continue like this.

With the collapse of the Soviet empire and Communism in Eastern Europe, the Afrikaner power elite decided to take the plunge and launch a process of negotiation that could in the end lead to black majority rule but – and this is a very big but – with the appropriate guarantees that the whites' position as a privileged minority would be maintained. It was clear that P W Botha was not the man to bring about the quantum leap in the Afrikaner mentality that such a change required. He was too old and he belonged to the old school. A much younger, more flexible, man with a modern outlook was needed. Surprisingly enough, that man turned out to be, not the genial Pik Botha, the perennial Foreign Affairs minister, or Barend du Plessis, the minister of Finance and (presumably) the leader of the *verligte* faction within the National Party caucus, but F W de Klerk, the leader of the party in the Transvaal and head of (again presumably) the *verkrampte* (reactionary) faction. In August 1989, he replaced P W Botha, who had a stroke and was forced to resign. In February 1990, the ANC, PAC and the Communist Party were unbanned, and Nelson Mandela was released. A new era began in the history of South Africa.

Notes

1 I Wilkins and H Strydom, *The Super-Afrikaners: Inside the Afrikaner Broederbond*, Jonathan Ball, 1978, Johannesburg, page 2.

2 The letter was sent on 29 June 1904, from Clarens in Switzerland where Kruger had taken refuge. I saw it in the Kruger Museum in Pretoria.

3 D Harrison, *The White Tribe of Africa*, pages 79–81.

4 There exist two excellent books on the history of the *Broederbond*: I Wilkins's and H Strydom, *The Super-Afrikaners* and J H P Serfontein's *Brotherhood of Power*, Rex Collins, 1979. The section on the *Broederbond* is based on Wilkins's and Strydom's book.

5–6 I Wilkins and H Strydom, *The Super-Afrikaners*, pages 191 and 72.

7–8 P J Furlong, 'Pro-Nazi Subversion in South Africa, 1939–41'. Mimeographed paper presented at the annual African Studies Association meeting in Madison, Wisconsin, USA, in October 1986, pages 9–10.

9 I Wilkins and H Strydom, *The Super-Afrikaners*, page 81.

10–11 An excellent summary of Dr Verwoerd's life and accomplishments is W A de Klerk's 'The Promethean Afrikaner' in *The Puritans of Africa: a History of Afrikanerdom*, Penguin Books, 1976, pages 229–79; the quote is on page 219.

12 For more on the forced removals, see Note 1 at the end of Chapter 9 and the section on District Six in Chapter 14.

13 I am indebted to my friend Ian Wyllie, the former editor of Durban's *Sunday Tribune*, for drawing my attention to this text.

14 Viljoen made that statement during the speech he made on the occasion of his election to the chairmanship of the *Broederbond*. The idea apparently belongs to Alexis de Tocqueville, the author of *Democracy in America*.

15 A good biographical summary of P W Botha is D Geldenhuys's and H Kotze's, 'Man of Action', in *Leadership*, No. 2, 1985, Cape Town and Johannesburg, pages 30–47. Deon Geldenhuys, a political science professor at Rand Afrikaans University (RAU) published the influential *The Diplomacy of Isolation* in 1984.

16 Ernest Oppenheimer took full control of De Beers in 1929. He entrenched further De Beers' formidable hold on the diamond industry by creating the Central Selling Organisation which presently controls about 90 per cent of the world's total sales of diamonds. He died in 1957. The Oppenheimers' story is told in D Pallister, S Steward and I Lepper, *South Africa, Inc. The Oppenheimer Empire*, Simon & Schuster, 1987, New York.

17 D Harrison, *The White Tribe*, page 280.

21

The Liberation Struggle

The people shall govern. . . .
the people shall share in the country's wealth. . . .
all land shall be shared among those who work it. . . .
there shall be houses, security and comfort. . . .
Slums shall be demolished and new suburbs built where all shall have
transport, roads, lighting, playing fields, churches and social
centers. . . . 'These Freedoms We Will Fight For, Side By Side,
Throughout Our Lives, Until We have Won Our Liberty.'
The Freedom Charter,
the Congress of the People,
25–26 June 1955

It is probably appropriate to begin this chapter with an important historical event that happened roughly during the second and third decades of the nineteenth century and which is believed to have had a crucial bearing on the subsequent development in the central South African region. That historical event – known as the *Mfeqane* (the Crushing) in Nguni and *Difaqane* (the Hammering) in Sotho – concerns the incessant military campaigns of the famous Zulu king, Shaka (dubbed by some historians the Black Napoleon) that provoked a chain-reaction of displacement among the peoples living in the region, ultimately causing the depopulation of large chunks of South African territory, which in turn is thought to have facilitated the task of the invading whites.[1]

The Early Innocent Years

I told briefly the story of the discovery of diamonds in north-eastern Cape on the banks of Orange River and in the Kimberley area in the late 1860s and early 1870s in Chapter 14. Gold was discovered on the Reef in the mid 1880s and the availability of cheap and plentiful labour was an important factor for the gold mines. A commentator wrote: 'What the abundance of rain and grass was to New Zealand mutton, what plenty of cheap grazing was to Australian wool, what the fertile prairie acres were to Canadian wheat, cheap native labour was to South African mining.'[2] As a result of concerted policy, not only were African wages reduced significantly by the early 1890s but a pass system was put in place that effectively controlled the movement of African labour – the idea behind the policy being to stop rival mining interests from stealing labourers from each other by offering higher wages. As for Natal, a ruthless system of forced labour (called *Isibalo*) was in operation, which relied on poll, hut and labour taxes for its existence. It and other grievances, such as a growing land shortage, cattle disease and crop failures, finally drove the Zulus to the Bambata rebellion of 1906 in which some 3,000 Zulus and 30 Europeans were killed.

It is generally believed that *Imbumba Yama Afrika* (Union of Africans), which was founded in the Cape Colony in 1882, was the first African political organisation. The first African newspaper was started in 1884 by a certain D D T Javabu, who was also its first editor. These were the days when a small minority of Africans in the Cape Colony (plus a tiny number in Natal, a total of perhaps 12,000 people) were part of the general political franchise (the common roll), even if they were not permitted to stand for election. In the first decade of our century this small elite was mainly preoccupied with the enlargement (in the Cape and Natal) and the extension (to the Transvaal and the Orange Free State) of the political franchise. They did this, despite the negative signals that they were getting, because they had faith in the British sense of fair play. Among those negative signals were: the fact that no clause for black emancipation was included in the Peace Treaty of 1902 at the end of the Anglo-Boer War; the Lagden Commission's proposals in 1905 of territorial separation between whites and non-whites and, in the following year, the School Board Act passed by the government of the Cape Colony, restricting the access of non-whites to public education.

In 1909, the South African Native Convention, which was held in Bloemfontein, protested against the British treachery of not keeping a promise to extend the franchise to the Boer republics of the north. That did not stop the Cape parliament from passing the Land Act of 1913, which prohibited Africans from buying land outside the reserves. In one fell swoop, 87 per cent of the country was declared White South Africa, off limits to blacks except as guest workers. The writing was on the wall but the small African elite still clung to their illusion that they might somehow be able to reverse the policy by petitioning the British government in London. Meanwhile, the South African Native National Congress was founded in 1912 (its name was changed to African National Congress, or ANC, in 1921). The ANC, except for a brief interlude under J Gumede's presidency, was a decidedly mild and bourgeois movement in the first three decades of its history, until the end of the Second World War, in fact. Its first president was J Dube, a schoolmaster from Natal who had been educated in America. Its second, S M Makgatho, an estate agent from Pretoria. These two men strongly believed in the British sense of equity and justice and two delegations were duly dispatched to London in 1914 and 1919 to ask for British intervention to set things right in South Africa. In 1923, the ANC adopted a Bill of Rights in which it was stated that: 'the Bantu have, as subjects of His Majesty King George, the legal and moral right to claim the application or extension to them of Cecil Rhodes' famous formula of "equal rights for all civilised men south of the Zambezi".'[3]

The Birth of the Labour Movement.
The Slow Coming of Age of the ANC

In the early 1920s, two new organisations came into being that began to make a difference insofar as black labour was concerned: the Industrial and Commercial Workers Union (ICU), led by Clements Kadalie, a schoolteacher from Nyasaland (now Malawi) and a man of great charm and charisma; and the Communist Party of South Africa (CPSA).[4] Virtually from the beginning the Communists were very influential with the ICU, but they could not change it from a diffuse mass organisation into a tightly structured trade union. The ICU had grown considerably during a period of modernisation of South African agriculture: 'Sharecropper arrangements were transformed into rent-paying tenancies and squatters were being squeezed off the land. . . . Rural Africans in their desperation turned to the ICU, joining it in their thousands.'[5] In the mid 1920s, its high point, the organisation had a working class membership, and at that stage explicitly socialist goals. Later, however, considerable tension developed between the CPSA and the ICU, with the Communists accusing the ICU leadership of using the organisation to enrich themselves. In the showdown that ensued the Communists were expelled from the ICU whose ideology veered to the right. That – given what was happening at the time: the Hertzog-Creswell government busily passing legislation entrenching white workers' privileges – proved fatal to the ICU, which collapsed, its membership dwindling from a high of about 100,000 in 1927, to 3 or 4,000 by the end of the decade. The CPSA was by now far more interested in the ANC, which appeared to have a promising future.

With the election of J Gumede as its president in 1927, the ANC appeared poised for a radicalisation of its positions. Gumede was a man who had been influenced both by Garveyism (the American Negro ideology based on racial pride and exclusiveness) and by Communist internationalism which, in the aftermath of the Bolsheviks' victory in Russia, was extremely influential in the progressive European circles. In South Africa, the CPSA maintained: 'An independent native republic [would be] a stage towards a workers' and peasants' republic.'[6] But the ANC's radicalism turned out to be short-lived. When Gumede wanted to organise a people's campaign in support of the Communists' Native Republic slogan, he was defeated in 1930 and replaced by P I Seme who was a moderate. As with Kadalie's ICU, the ANC's swing to the right discredited the organisation and its support waned.

African resistance probably fell to an all-time low in the decade of the 1930s. That sorry state of affairs had relatively little to do with what was happening in South Africa proper. The 1930s is the decade of the Great Depression, the most severe economic crisis of modern times. As a result of it, Fascism was on the rise in Europe and all liberal and progressive forces were trying to unite in an ultimately unsuccessful effort to stem the tide. In South Africa, the situation was similar: the CPSA concentrated all its energies in fighting the Afrikaner white supremacists who were out to capture the white labour movement. In order to do that an all-white People's

Front was created to combat the Fascist tendencies of the white workers. In 1936, came the shock of the Africans' removal from the general electoral franchise in the Cape. The response of the ANC consisted largely of 'wordy protests . . . delegations, vague calls for African unity and national days of prayer'.[7] That situation was to continue basically unchanged until the outbreak of the Second World War during which there was a big jump in the numbers of Africans working in the manufacturing sector.

Meanwhile, Dr A B Xuma, a man of remarkable professional achievement (he had studied medicine in both America and Europe before opening a successful private practice in Johannesburg), had succeeded the lacklustre P I Sema as president of the ANC. Xuma's forte was his talent for organisation and, under his leadership, the ANC gradually regained some of the ground that it had lost in the 1930s. In 1943, a document inspired by the Atlantic Charter of 1941 and entitled African Claims was published by the ANC. It called for full citizenship and equal opportunity for all South Africans. Smuts was put on the spot but he turned a deaf ear to African aspirations of freedom and equality. It was as a reaction to his rejection that the younger generation of ANC's leadership founded the Youth League. Meanwhile, ANC's dues-paying membership had reached 5,500 in 1947 and there were many more sympathisers.

It was during the Second World War that there was a big spurt in the black labour movement. Throughout the 1930s, minor black unions such as the Laundry Workers' Union and the Furniture, Mattress and Bedding Workers' Union had continued to exist, as had the more important multi-racial unions like the Food and Canning Workers' Union and especially the Garment Workers' Union, whose general secretary was a well-known white Communist, E S ('Solly') Sachs. After having battled the Powers That Be for years, Sachs was finally banned under the Suppression of Communism Act of 1950 and forced to go into exile (he died in London in 1975). During the War two things of importance happened: one, the manufacturing sector overtook for the first time the mining sector in terms of their respective contributions to the economy as a whole and, two, owing to the induction of large numbers of white men into the army after the Smuts government entered the war on the side of the Allies, there was an important influx of African workers into the manufacturing sector. The whites – the Communists, as well as the socialists and the liberals – became again involved in the organisation of black labour unions. The Council of Non-European Trade Unions (CNETU) was from its inception dominated by Communists and, by 1945, it claimed to have a total membership of 158,000 organised in 119 unions. In 1941, the CNETU had been instrumental in creating the African Mineworkers' Union (AMU) whose membership grew to about 25,000 in the next three years. For the first eight years of its history the AMU was led by J B Marks, a well-known and respected Communist who also was a member of the ANC's executive committee. In 1946, the AMU made two big demands: a minimum daily wage of ten shillings and family housing for its workers – which implied that the much-hated males-only hostel system inside the mining compounds would be abolished and the families would be allowed to come and live with the bread-earners outside the mines. After four months of stonewalling by the Chamber of Mines, about 60,000 miners went on strike with the full support of the CNETU. But the Smuts government used brutal force to crush the strike and 12 miners were killed and about a thousand injured. As a result of the strike, the AMU was dissolved and the CNETU seriously weakened.

The 1950s and 1960s (the heyday of Afrikaner power, see the preceding chapter) are the lean decades of the African labour movement. Most African unions were not strictly speaking outlawed but they were not officially recognised either. They continued to exist in a sort of limbo and kept a low profile. The corporate bosses tolerated them as long as they did not overstep certain limits; they could always rely on the government to intervene forcefully if things got out of hand, ie, if the workers went on strike. That situation went on until the Durban strikes of 1973 which rapidly spread to other cities. This time the bosses asked the government not to intervene, because alienating black workers no longer suited their interests. More and more they needed the black skilled workers to meet the demands of a rapidly expanding economy.

The big event of the post-Second-World-War years was the rise of the ANC's Youth League. After Anton Lembede's untimely death in 1947, Walter Sisulu, Oliver Tambo, Nelson Mandela and Robert Sobukwe took over. The Defiance Campaign of 1950–52 was a benign – but psychologically rewarding and emotionally uplifting – affair, despite the 8,000-plus activists that were arrested and sentenced to short terms of prison. The campaign consisted of breaking relatively minor apartheid regulations, such as visiting black townships without a permit and entering and demanding service in premises reserved for whites, such as post-office counters, and trains.

The idea of a Congress of the People was first floated in August 1953 at Cradock by Professor Z K Matthews, one of the only two African university professors in South Africa at the time, and adopted in March 1954 by the national executive of the ANC. A Congress Alliance was set up which was made up of the ANC, the South African Indian Congress (SAIC), the South African Coloured Peoples Organisation (SACPO) and the Congress of Democrats, an organisation of whites which was created after the banning of the CPSA in 1950. A National Action Council was formed which launched an appeal for freedom volunteers who would canvass the country to collect people's demands for a Freedom Charter. Some 10,000 volunteers were in the end enlisted in the effort; they were sent to the townships and the villages, to the factories and the mines and even to the farms (but that was more difficult owing to the harassment by the Boer farmers), to collect people's demands.

African women became heavily involved in the Congress of the People campaign. The newly formed Federation of South African Women led by Lilian Ngoyi, Albertina Sisulu and Elizabeth Mafekeng made an important contribution. The congress was asked to address the triple oppression of black women: by capitalism, by racism and by sexism. About a year later, in 1956, 20,000 women, many with their babies strapped to their backs, marched to the Union Buildings in Pretoria, the seat of government, to demand an end of their obligation to carry passcards (*Dompas*) and to segregation in education. In March 1955, just three months before the congress was held, the Communist-affiliated South African Congress of Trade Unions (SACTU) was founded and the task of collecting the workers' demands for the Freedom Charter was entrusted to it. The Communist journal of *New Age* also played an important role in publicising the congress.

Finally, there was the election of the delegates that were to represent all the social, economic and professional categories of the people: the farm labourers, the factory workers, the mine workers, the teachers, the traders, the students, the women, etc. The Congress of the People Campaign culminated in a giant mass rally at Kliptown, Soweto, in which more than 3,000 delegates from all over the country participated. The Freedom Charter was presented to the people's delegates and adopted by the ANC at its national conference on the following year. It still constitutes the basic Manifesto of the people's demands in South Africa. There have always been reservations and differences concerning its contents: Professor Z K Matthews, for example, was not happy with its appeal to the nationalisation of the means of production. Chief Albert Luthuli (the ANC president from 1952 to 1967 and a Nobel Peace prize winner) gave eloquent expression to those concerns: 'The Charter produced in Kliptown is,' he said, 'line by line, the direct outcome of conditions which obtain – harsh, oppressive and unjust conditions. It is thus a practical and relevant document.' However, he went on, 'the Freedom Charter is open to criticism. It is by no means a perfect document. But its motive must be understood, as must the deep yearning for security and human dignity from which it springs.'[8]

The government's response to the Congress of the People was a massive crackdown less than a year later: 156 Congress leaders – Chief Luthuli; Joe Slovo and his wife Ruth First (assassinated in Maputo, Mozambique some 25 years later by a parcel bomb that almost certainly was sent by BOSS, the South African Bureau of Security Services); Moses Kotane, a prominent Communist; Helen Joseph, one of the pioneers of the anti-apartheid struggle and a figure revered by militant Africans; Yusuf Dadoo, the SAIC president; Mandela, Tambo and so on – were arrested and charged with high treason. Even though all of the accused were found not guilty in the end, the long trial (it lasted four and a half years) drained the energies of the opposition movement.

The Liberation Struggle Becomes Violent

In 1959, a major split occurred in the ANC with the Africanists breaking away because they disagreed with ANC's policy of non-racialism. Robert Sobukwe, whose influential life is described in Chapter 16, and his followers believed that non-Africans should not be allowed to play a leadership role in the liberation struggle. They insisted on a strictly African leadership and founded their own Pan-Africanist Congress. Barely more than a year passed when the PAC, in an effort to upstage the ANC, decided to go it alone in the protest campaign against the pass laws which was scheduled to begin in three weeks' time. The campaign resulted in the famous Sharpeville Massacre in which 69 Africans were killed by the police and about 200 wounded. That was on 21 March 1960, which was a watershed event in the liberation struggle.

The Sharpeville Massacre shocked world opinion. There were front-page reports in major American and European newspapers, prime-time television coverage. A significant flight of capital took place. There was talk that it might be 'the beginning of the end'. The response of Verwoerd's government was brutal and effective: a general State of Emergency was declared and the ANC and the PAC were banned. The eruption of the volcano did not happen. Frustration, even desperation, played a big role in the creation of the *Umkhonto we Sizwe* (Spear of the Nation) by Mandela and some other Youth Leaguers; it was a decision not presented for approval to the ANC's National Executive Committee.

A few months later, just before Christmas 1961, Johannesburg, Durban and Port Elizabeth were rocked by a series of explosions. The attacks were carried out by *Umkhonto*. But the latter was not the only group to resort to violence. Virtually at the same time as *Umkhonto*, another organisation, called *Poqo* ('Pure' in Xhosa) dedicated to violent action had been formed by the PAC. *Poqo* was potentially more dangerous for the whites because it subscribed to the theory that random violence was a more effective strategy because it sowed panic in the white areas. Again, initially the whites feared that the government might not be able to deal with the violence. Again, the government proved the opposite. Some 3,000 *Poqo* suspects were arrested and many of their leaders sentenced to long gaol sentences. *Umkhonto's* turn came a couple of years later when the entire leadership of the ANC was captured in a raid on a farm in Rivonia, a Johannesburg suburb, and sentenced to life imprisonment.[9]

With the banning of the ANC, and the PAC after Sharpeville, (the SACP had been banned in 1953), a political vacuum was created in the liberation struggle into which moved the Black Consciousness movement whose origins can be traced back to Anton Lembede and Robert Sobukwe. But it was Steve Biko who really started it in the late 1960s with his creation of the all-black South African Students Organisation (SASO).[10] Biko was dissatisfied with the National Union of South African Students (NUSAS), which he felt was dominated by white liberals. So, in the following few years, he went around the country preaching the BC gospel. BC was clearly influenced by two intellectual and ideological currents: firstly, the black-American emancipation movement defined by the slogans Black Power and Black is Beautiful and secondly, the writings and speeches of African revolutionaries and nationalists such as Amilcar Cabral, Frantz Fanon, Kwame Nkrumah and Julius Nyerere.

By 1973–4, the Black Peoples Convention (BPC), a political umbrella organisation and Black Community Programmes (BCP), its social equivalent based on principles of self-help and self-reliance, were founded and operating. It was in 1973 that Biko, who was born in King William's Town in the Eastern Cape in 1946, was first banned for five years. In 1975, he was arrested and imprisoned for 137 days. One year later, he was arrested again and held in solitary confinement for 101 days. Two more arrests came in March and July 1977. Finally, in August of that same year, he was stopped in a car at a roadblock in the company of his friend and fellow-activist Peter Jones and taken into custody for the last time. He died in his prison cell on 12 September barely 31 years old. He had been tortured to death by the security services in Port Elizabeth.

Scarcely a month after Biko's violent death, and despite the international outcry, the Vorster government cracked down on the BC movement: BPC, SASO and the Black Women's Federation were banned; the black newspaper *The World* was closed down and its editor, Percy Qoboza, arrested. The repression spread to the white supporters of the BC such as Beyers Naudé of the Christian Institute and Donald Woods of the *Daily Dispatch*. But this time it did not take long to fill the void left by the banning of the BC organisations. In April 1978, the Azanian Peoples Organisation (AZAPO) was founded that took the BC ideology beyond the ideas of black awareness and black self-reliance and into the harsher world of Marxist class analysis to explain the South African situation. Meanwhile, of course, the Soweto uprising had broken out in June 1976 – perhaps the single most important event in the black liberation struggle.

The Soweto uprising began as a march of secondary-school-children protesting about a government decision to have certain subjects taught in Afrikaans. What happened was that on 13 June 1976, at a meeting of the South African Students Movement (SASM) convened at Naledi High School, a 'Soweto Students' Representative Council (SSRC) was formed . . . which planned the fateful demonstration for June 16. On that day 15,000 children converged on Orlando West Junior Secondary School, only to be confronted by a hastily summoned and aggressive police detachment which, when tear gas had failed to disperse the students, fired into the crowd, killing two and injuring several more. . . . By midday rioting had broken out in several parts of Soweto . . . and two white men were attacked and killed.'[11]

The uprising spread rapidly to other African townships in the Transvaal and the first ANC leaflets calling for the grown-ups to join the children in a revolutionary onslaught against the apartheid regime began circulating at the end of July. This was when a Black Parents' Association (BPA) was formed, not to join the uprising, but to help the victims of the violence. September witnessed an ominous new development in Soweto: the conservatively oriented African migrant workers living in the male-only hostels began attacking the young revolutionaries. This young-radical versus adult-conservative split was encouraged and exploited by the government. The Soweto uprising entered its final phase with persistent attacks on the *shebeens* but it never really ended. For years after that school attendance was poor and sporadic. The slogan 'Liberation Before Education' took hold among the township youth, the result of which is what came to be known as the 'lost generation', an important destabilising factor in the present day negotiation process for a new democratic South Africa.

What were the causes of the Soweto uprising? In its immediate aftermath there was a general consensus among the *cognoscenti* that it had been brewing for a long time, waiting for a last straw. In fact, there are three major post-mortems of the Soweto uprising: the first is a conservative one; the second attributes a big role to Black Consciousness ideology and the third is basically Marxist.[12] The conservative explanation not surprisingly found its fullest expression in the report released by the government commission of enquiry which claimed that the main reason of the uprising was lack of communication: the government had been unaware of the degree of dissatisfaction caused by its insistence that maths and social studies be taught in Afrikaans. That, plus the usual economic grievances arising from low wages, housing shortages, the alleged corruption of local authorities etc, were exploited by professional agitators who had acted on orders from the ANC. J Kane-Berman, a former journalist, currently the director of SAIRR, concluded that BC was the single most important factor. The SSRC, he argued, had close ties with the BC movement. Three Marxist analysts, J Brickhill,

A Brooks and B Hirson saw the Soweto uprising as a *revolution manquée*, owing to the absence of a working-class party to provide the missing link between the workers and society; they blamed the ANC for its less than full commitment to the uprising. The truth is probably a combination of two latter explanations.

From 1983 to 1990, the liberation struggle was dominated by the UDF, created to fight the tricameral constitution, and, less so, by the BC-oriented National Forum. The Boycott the Constitution Campaign was successful in the sense that it drew the attention of the world to the fact that the African majority was once more excluded from the political process. Again the townships exploded in an upsurge of violence that has continued ever since.

I now return to developments on the equally important labour front which I left at the point of the Durban strikes of 1973–4.

The Rising Clout of Black Labour

The Durban strikes of 1973–4, in which about 60,000 workers struck successfully, are historically important because in their aftermath came the first real change in the trilateral black labour/white big business/Afrikaner state relations. Even before the strikes big business started negotiating with independent black unions, and the government, under pressure from big business, offered official recognition to the black unions under certain conditions. Some moderate unions belonging to the Federation of South African Trade Unions (FOSATU) accepted the government's offer; others, such as the more militant South African Allied Workers Union (SAAWU) for example, rejected it.[13]

The rise of the black labour movement in the late 1970s and early 1980s has been truly phenomenal: in 1976 there were a measly 75,000 workers organised in 25 unions; by the end of 1987 the corresponding numbers were 1.5 million and 260 respectively. Despite this tremendous growth, however, about three-quarters of the African workers remained at that stage un-unionised. Among the significant developments of the period stand out: the creation by the Council of Unions of South Africa (CUSA), a BC-oriented group, in August 1982, of the National Union of Mineworkers (NUM), which rapidly became the biggest and most influential union in the country; and the merging, after more than two years of union talks, of FOSATU, NUM and a number of independent unions to form the giant COSATU. At that juncture, the remaining pro-BC unions reorganised themselves into the National Council of Trade Unions (NACTU). In the second half of the 1980s, other powerful black unions, such as the South African Railways and Harbours Workers Union (SARHWU) and the National Union of Metal Workers of South Africa (NUMSA) came into being and joined COSATU.[14]

From its very inception, COSATU has been very active politically, but the degree of its militancy grew dramatically after the general State of Emergency of 1986. At its first annual congress held in July 1987, its then president, Elijah Barayi (now John Gomomo) declared unambiguously that the organisation could not be expected to keep out of politics, 'because for us blacks politics is a bread-and-butter issue'. At the same meeting, the Freedom Charter was officially adopted as a document symbolising and representing the hopes and aspirations of the black people in South Africa. A month later came the big confrontation between the NUM, led by its secretary-general Cyril Ramaphosa, and the Anglo-American Corporation. At its peak, more than 200,000 workers, mostly gold mine workers from the Rand, joined the strike. After stormy negotiations that lasted three weeks, the outcome was a technical victory for Anglo-American – the strike was broken when Anglo threatened to close down some uneconomic shafts and to dismiss the striking workers, but a moral and political victory for NUM and COSATU. They gained significant raises in wages ranging from 15 to 23 per cent and other advantages.[15] The clout of COSATU continued to grow in the late 1980s and early 1990s. Its secretary-general, Jay Naidoo, is seen as one of the most important political players in South Africa. On 5–6 November 1991, COSATU was able to paralyse the country for two days when it called a massive strike in protest of the VAT that had been introduced by Barend du Plessis, the then Finance minister.

In conclusion, a new era has begun in the political history of South Africa. An introduction to that era is to be found in the first chapter of this book. Good reading!

Notes

1 See 'From Dawn of History to the Time of Troubles', first chapter of Davenport's *South Africa: A Modern History*, in the third Cambridge edition, 1984.

2 The quote is originally from C W de Kiewet's classic work, *A History of South Africa, Social and Economic*, Oxford University Press, 1942; in C Wheatcroft, *The Randlords*, page 17.

3 J Leatt, T Kneifel and K Nurnberger (eds), *Contending Ideologies in South Africa*, David Philip, 1986, Cape Town and Johannesburg, page 91.

4 This section is based on 'Black Protest Before 1950' which is the first chapter of Tom Lodge's *Black Politics in South Africa Since 1945*, Ravan, 1985, Johannesburg. I saw Tom twice in 1986 and 1992. His book is considered by many as the best on the subject.

5–7 T Lodge, 'Black Protest Before 1950', *Black Politics*, pages 5–6, 9 and 11.

8 R Suttner and J Cronin, *30 Years of the Freedom Charter*, Ravan, 1986, Johannesburg, page 115. This is a magnificently illustrated book on the Congress of the People and the Freedom Charter.

9 The Rivonia Trial is covered in more detail in Chapter 6.

10 On Biko and the BC movement there is the substantial Note 2 at the end of Chapter 15.

11 T Lodge, *Black Politics*, page 328.

12 The three post-mortems in question are: the Report of the Commission of Inquiry into the Riots at Soweto and Elsewhere (known as the Cillié Commission Report) 1977, Pretoria; J Kane-Berman, Soweto: *Black Revolt, White Reaction*, Ravan, 1978, Johannesburg; and A Brooks and J Brickhill, *Whirlwind Before the Storm*, IDAF, 1980 and B Hirson, *Year of Fire, Year of Ash*, Zed, 1979.

13 The rise and composition of black labour is a complex and sometimes confusing subject. For a detailed account see J Baskin, *Striking Back: A History of COSATU*, Ravan, 1991, Johannesburg. Two good introductions are: 'Introduction: Trends in Organised Labour' in *South African Review* 3, 1986, pages 1–20 and S Friedman, 'The Trade Union Movement', in M A Uhlig (ed) *Apartheid in Crisis*, Random House, 1986, New York, pages 176–89.

14 Not to be upstaged, Buthelezi's Inkatha launched the United Workers of South Africa (UWUSA) with great fanfare at a rally at the Durban soccer stadium in May 1986. Seven years later, UWUSA is nowhere near COSATU, or even the BC-oriented NACTU, for that matter, in strength.

15 The strike has been covered extensively in South African and Western print media. See, for example, 'South Africa: Black Miners Seek pay Rise', in *Africa Research Bulletin*, 16 March 1987 and 'South Africa: Bread, Butter and Rights' in the *Economist*, 18 July 1987.

Postscript

It was one of the leading stories on the BBC evening news yesterday (28 November 1993): 'The Afrikaner Broederbond is to open its membership to women and to people of all races.' I confess I was astonished even if only briefly. For, on second thoughts, the logic of that decision imposed itself on me. Indeed, given the fact that the Nats have for some time decided that their political salvation lies in non-racial politics, it made sense that the 'Brotherhood' should at some point follow suit. So far so good, but I was still impressed by the incredible ideological distance travelled by the Afrikaner power elite inside Broederbond in the last seven or eight years – the February 1990 revolution was in the making for several years before it actually burst into the open. After all, this was the same organisation that owed its very existence to the exclusive goal of Afrikaner hegemony, and which had worked with almost superhuman determination and singlemindedness to achieve that goal by conceiving, developing and putting into practice the misguided ideology of grand apartheid.

These days, the Nats, under the clever and inspired leadership of F W de Klerk, to save their political skins are counting on a special relationship, in the form of a durable and mutually rewarding political alliance, with the three-million-plus Coloured community (less importantly with the million-strong Indian community too) that would form a political power bloc in the country only second in strength to the ANC, which would be unable to ignore it. The rationale behind this 'grand design' is that such an alliance is 'natural' since the two communities share a cultural (notably linguistic) heritage. It is indeed possible that the policy has a future and might work, but only after the April 1994 elections. At present both communities are confused and divided against themselves: the Afrikaners, between the National Party and the Afrikaner *Volksfront*; the Coloureds, between the same National Party and the ANC. The Coloured (and Indian) community will naturally assume a wait-and-see attitude until well after the elections. They will judge the ANC on how well it will be able to work with the NP in the transitional period of 1994–9; they might wait until after the elections of 1999 before making up their collective mind definitively. As for the Afrikaners, my tentative guess is that a significant majority will eventually drop the *Front* and fall back into line behind the NP. The relevant development in that respect is that about half of their own supporters reject the idea of an independent *Volkstaat*.

Meanwhile, if the results of a nationwide poll carried out in September 1993 are to be believed, the ANC may well be headed for a landslide victory in April '94: close to 60 per cent of the 2000 respondents to the poll (a particularly credible one because it was specially weighted to include urban and rural areas, the hostel and shack dwellers in the townships, and the domestic workers in the white suburbs) said they were going to vote for the ANC, as opposed to less than 15 per cent for the Nats. The Freedom Alliance – which comprises Buthelezi's Inkatha Freedom Party, the Conservative Party and some conservative homeland parties – came in third with a little over ten per cent. The Democratic Party and the Pan-Africanist Congress were next with about three per cent each (amazingly the South African Communist Party received less than one per cent). Assuming, therefore, that the ANC can 'bring out the vote' (the numbers above are based on a voter turnout of 80 per cent; obviously, the larger the turnout, the better for the ANC), it can expect to win between 230 and 240 seats out of 400 in the national assembly; Nelson Mandela would become president and, probably, Thabo Mbeki first deputy president; the movement would also be entitled to 19 out of 30 cabinet posts. The NP could win between 60 and 70 seats, the second deputy presidency for F W de Klerk, and four cabinet posts. The Freedom Alliance, if they stick together, could end up winning about 50 seats and three or four cabinet posts; but it is doubtful that Inkatha will, when push comes to shove, choose to fight the elections in an alliance with the white right-wingers; because, even if it goes it alone, its chances of winning more than 5 per cent of the total vote – the threshold to participate in the government – are good (not so for the CP). Among the others only the PAC in my opinion can reach 5 per cent of the vote.

The interim constitution grants the new nine provinces relatively strong powers even though, when all is said and done, the new South Africa will be essentially a unitary state. What will happen in the provinces? The same poll predicts that probably the governments of six out of the nine new provinces – the Northern, Eastern and Western Transvaal; the crucial PWV (Pretoria-Witwatersrand-Vaal) area; as well as the Eastern Cape and Orange Free State – will be controlled by the ANC. KwaZulu-Natal is a toss-up: the poll gave both the IFP and the ANC just under 40 per cent support, but the conventional wisdom is that time is probably working to ANC's advantage. The NP can expect to win big in the Western Cape, where the whites and the Coloureds together form about three-quarters of the population, and fairly big in the Northern Cape where the same two groups are more than half the population – but it is well to bear in mind that even in these two provinces the ANC will gain in the long run.

I wish to make two observations at this juncture, which I think are important. The first one is that, luckily, the ANC appears unlikely to win a two-thirds majority overall, which would enable it to write (or rewrite as the case might be) the new constitution by itself. So the chances of that task being carried out in the same spirit of cooperation, compromise and good will are fairly high. A crushing domination by the ANC would sow panic among the whites and cause large-scale emigration, something that must be avoided at all costs. My second observation has to do with my fear that violence will get out of control during the election campaign, including the elections themselves. That would make 'fair and square' elections impossible and rob the ANC of its legitimate victory at the polls. Such an outcome would certainly cause tremendous anger and frustration among the black masses, and the black townships would explode in massive unrest. That in turn could lead to a military coup d'état which could plunge the country into a protracted civil war. So, on the well-tested theory that prevention is better than cure, important measures must be taken to nip the nascent violence in the bud, so to speak. A strong message needs to be sent to the potential perpetrators of violence – including probably: Terre Blanche's AWB, the rogue elements within the security services (the infamous 'third force'), Inkatha's and the ANC's warlords and vigilantes, PAC's African People's Liberation Army – that they will be watched closely and if need be incapacitated. But that alone will probably not be enough: in addition to strong-arm tactics internally (if Abe Lincoln did so during the American civil war, there is no reason why de Klerk and Mandela cannot resort to them temporarily in South Africa), an international peace-keeping force under the authority of the United Nations will be needed to dissuade the potential mischief-makers.

Now, having discussed the possibility of things going wrong, I must hasten to add that I don't believe that they will do so. Certainly, there will be some violence and resistance from the Afrikaner right-wing, but its magnitude will not be so great as to invalidate the elections, which will take place as planned, and the ANC will emerge as the big victor as widely anticipated, and the NP will come in a distant second. Then what? What is likely to happen in the crucial five years following the elections? I would like to elaborate a little, speculate even, on this critical transitional period.

If I had to choose one single word to capture the essence of South Africa's transition to democracy, that word would have to be: change. South Africa has already changed a great deal between February 1990 and December 1993. It will change considerably more after the April 1994 elections. Some of the change will be fast, momentous and fundamental; some of it will be painstakingly slow, but equally significant; some, inevitably, will be superficial, even cosmetic. Political change will belong to the first category: black South Africans and the parties that represent them will become the dominant political force in the country. Social, economic and cultural changes will belong the the second and third categories: notable progress will be made in the fields of education, housing and welfare; the townships will be upgraded, some of the land returned to its rightful owners, the gap between wages and salaries for whites and blacks will be further narrowed, schools will be built and teachers trained, some wealth will possibly be redistributed, and the scary black unemployment rate somewhat reduced. In short, a remarkable effort will be made to meet – half way, or more – the needs, the aspirations and expectations of the poor masses. But will it be enough? That is the question to which I turn now. I will try to address some of the objective and subjective difficulties that probably lie ahead.

Objectively, the biggest difficulty has to do with what may be termed as the patience factor – which will be in short supply on the black side. It is generally agreed that South Africa needs a real GDP growth rate of about 5 per cent a year for about ten to fifteen years to deal effectively with its daunting social problems. That average rate, which could generate two to three million new jobs during that period of time, is well within the South African possibilities; this is a country well endowed with natural and human resources and which has a good industrial and technological base. Many countries – not only the much-celebrated four 'Asian Tigers' (Taiwan, South Korea, Hong Kong and Singapore), but also Malaysia and Turkey, not to mention Mainland China – sometimes less well endowed than South Africa in resources, have achieved a real GDP growth rate of 5 per cent or more over long periods of time; South African can do it too. Moreover, if the gods are merciful and the gold prices remain firm (in the, roughly, $400 an ounce range), during the next five to ten years, that could generate billions of extra dollars to be used for the social and economic uplift of the very poor. But all this will take time and the poor masses, who have had it bad for too long, may not be prepared to wait. That is why an extra effort may be needed from the whites to accelerate things. The problem is that that extra effort might not be forthcoming. The onus of the sacrifices to be made will fall, not on the rich – they somehow always find a way to stay rich – but on the white middle and upper-middle classes who already think that they are overtaxed. These can be expected, under the banner of the need to 'maintain standards', to wage a fierce battle to protect their privileges. To use that shopworn but effective metaphor, there will be blood on the floor. An undesirable, but necessary, outcome of this confrontation, which can be viewed as a competition for scarce resources, is that some form of authoritarian government might be inevitable for some years to keep things under control. That is a regrettable outcome, but the legacy of apartheid is a terrible one and the slate cannot be wiped clean quickly and easily.

Again, it will take time to heal the wounds of apartheid. Apartheid can be compared to an awful war which has caused much destruction; not only material destruction, the hearts and souls of the black people were affected too. The whites who are the originators of the war have not suffered from it (they have torn one another apart in other wars); on the contrary, they have benefited enormously from it. Now the physical and psychological damage from the war must be fixed, the horrors of apartheid put right. To conclude, the first elected government of South Africa that (hopefully) will come to power on the days following 27 April 1994 will be faced with a very tough assignment. Success is by no means a foregone conclusion. It will, at best, be a tough balancing act; a fragile, delicate equilibrium that will be very difficult to maintain; and things could go wrong any time. What if they do? Various scenarios can be envisaged.

Clarence Makwetu, the PAC president, has declared that the really important elections will be those of 1999. He probably said this in part to prepare the supporters of his movement for the expected dismal performance of the PAC in the 1994 elections – the polls indicate that it may win anywhere between 2.5 to 7 per cent of the vote; my guess is that it will be closer to the upper limit. Beyond that many people think that he has a point. It is probable that some major political realignments will take place between 1994 and 1999. The ANC-SACP-COSATU alliance could crumble as a result of the government clamping down on dissent, strikes, crime, etc. Some speculate that the ANC itself will break up with the radical-left forces leaving the organisation and joining the PAC and AZAPO (the SACP will probably stay out, preferring to remain an independent vanguard party) in a left-wing alliance. I think it is inevitable that a number of people will leave the ANC over the transitional period, but whether or not that will amount to a real break-up remains to be seen. Moreover, this will be compensated by many new people joining the organisation. COSATU too might suffer the same fate, with some of the more radical (or moderate, depending which way the labour confederation moves) unions leaving it, possibly, to join NACTU. The speed and magnitude of the realignments will, more or less directly, depend on the extent to which the ANC-dominated government will be able to tackle the nation's problems. It is possible that in the very long run, that is beyond 1999, a liberal-democratic centre will emerge including the ANC, NP, DP and, possibly, Inkatha. In other words, mainstream politics will consist of democratic competition between right-of-centre and left-of-centre political forces. This is, of course, the best that could happen to South Africa and it is my wish that it happens; but, to be realistic, I must recognise that such an outcome is still in the domain of wishful thinking and a very long way off.

I would like to end this postscript on a more personal note based on my belief that the rational, the impersonal, the detached analysis, the broad outline can only go as far to capture reality, or rather, truth or meaning. Human lives, after all, are primarily lived at the personal, or individual, level, even if the societal level is made up by a multitude of bilateral and multilateral relationships. I will thus focus below on the feelings and the hopes, on the *mea culpas* and *cri de coeurs*, of a few distinguished people and comment upon them. √The following quote from Alan Paton's *Cry, the Beloved Country* (first published in 1948):

> ... I have one great fear in my heart, that one day when they are turned to loving, they will find that we are turned to hating.

has been, over the years, chosen by many authors and writers to dramatise the situation in South Africa. We must admit that Reverend Msimangu's fear is, more topical than ever today. Many black people, young people mostly, and with good reason, 'are turned to hating'. That's unfortunate, but luckily not the whole story. There are also a lot of people, the majority probably, who are prepared to forget, if not exactly to forgive, not yet at any rate, and build a common future. The reality of the life of these people is well captured in the following quote by Charles E Cobb, Jr, a journalist with the *National Geographic*, who is the author of the 'Twilight of Apartheid' published in the issue of February 1993:

> Despite dire headlines, black South Africans manage much normalcy in day-to-day living. Babies are born, families raised, weddings and birthdays celebrated. There is work and play, warmth and love.

And so it was, and so it is. And that is why I am ultimately cautiously optimistic about the future, as are many of the thinking blacks and whites in South Africa. They know, as Aggrey Klaaste, the editor of the *Sowetan*, said in the same National Geographic story mentioned above that: 'In the end we will have to run this country together. We know that.'

I only wish there were many more Afrikaners who felt like the journalist and author Rian Malan who wrote in the *A Spirit for Our Time: South Africa's Promise* (Published by the Millennium Group, 1992, Cape Town):

So it seems to me that there are adjustments I've got to make in coming to terms with Africa. Like accepting that I am going to have a lot less in the future than I have now, and just grin and bear it. Like readjusting my expectations of life, my levels of comfort, to what this country can actually sustain ... (I)t seems to me that this is the price we are probably going to have to pay.

But it will come. I am confident that there will be more in the future, for what is the alternative? I would like to conclude this section with the following quote from J S Naipaul's *Guerrillas*:

When everybody wants to fight there's nothing to fight for. Everybody wants to fight his own little war, everybody is a guerrilla.

As I write the final lines of this book I am invaded by an almost religious mood. I have no doubt in my heart that during my researches and travels there South Africa has become part of me and I have come to love that country. I have made many friends there, both black and white. But there is a more profound, philosophical reason for my infatuation with South Africa. I increasingly feel that our Western world has entered a phase of deterioration and disintegration on the moral, ethical and spiritual planes. We live in societies in which the primacy of the things of the mind, of the soul and of the heart are no longer recognised. We live in societies where, increasingly, sophisticated and ruthless marketing techniques, very effectively using the mass media (especially television), are turning human beings into dumb consuming machines. Quality is becoming scarce: the world is becoming a more homogenised and mediocre place almost by the day. Places like South Africa – where human beings are confronted with real challenges – hold out for me the hope that perhaps everything is not lost and that a new society, where true human values – such as friendship, honour, courage, wisdom, pride, frugality, knowledge, tolerance and solidarity – have their rightful place, can exist. This may not be immediately visible, or even perceptible in South Africa, because the improvement of the material conditions of the poor blacks is at the top of the agenda. But it 'ain't' so. The real battle in South Africa is a battle for true human values. It is a spiritual battle where white and black South

Africans together can show the world the depth of the human potential for good. It is in that sense that I too feel South African. More than thirty years ago John Fitzgerald Kennedy, standing by the wall that separated east and west Berlin, shouted: 'Ich bin ein Berliner!' It was a commitment to freedom and human decency. A message to the world at large that America stood for those values. It was the beginning of the sixties, a time when it was still possible to think that what is important is not to endlessly blabber about the world, but to try to change it, to make it a better world for the generations to come. Such ideas have almost become a laughing matter today and the young are confused and disoriented and suffer from a deep malaise, because there are no true ideals anymore, nothing to look up to. So the battle for quality, for human values in South Africa will be watched closely by all those who care about such things. So, go for it South Africa! My best wishes to you in your efforts to create a new society in which it will be good to live.

ZE, Geneva
December 1993

Selected Bibliography

I General

Arnold, G, *South Africa: Crossing the Rubicon*, Macmillan, 1992
Cowell, A, *Killing the Wizards: Wars of Power and Freedom from Zaire to South Africa*, Simon & Schuster, 1992, New York
Malan, R, *My Traitor's Heart*, Vintage, 1991
Mallaby, S, *After Apartheid*, Time Books, 1992
Sampson, A, *Black and Gold*, Coronet Books, 1987, London
Sparks, A, *The Mind of South Africa*, Heinemann, 1990, London

II Historical

Davenport, T R H, *South Africa: A Modern History*, Univ of Toronto Press, 1977; Cambridge UP, 1984
Harrison, D, *The White Tribe of South Africa*, Univ of California Press, 1981, Berkeley and Los Angeles
Mostert, N, *Frontiers: the Epic of South Africa's Creation and the Tragedy of the Xhosa People*, Pimlico, 1993, London
Pakenham, T, *The Boer War*, Cardinal, 1991, London (first published by Weidenfeld and Nicolson in 1979)
Pallister, D, Steward, S and Lepper, I, *South Africa Inc: The Oppenheimer Empire*, Simon & Schuster, 1987
Serfontein, J H P, *Brotherhood of Power*, Rex Collins, 1979, New York
Wheatcraft, C, *The Randlords*, Atheneum, 1986, New York

III Political

Adam, H and Moodley, K, *Democratising Southern Africa: Challenges for Canadian Policy*, Canadian Institute for International Peace and Security, 1992, Ottawa

Callinicos, A (ed), *Between Apartheid and Capitalism: Conversations with South African Socialists*, Bookmarks, 1992, London, Chicago

Horowitz, D L, *A Democratic South Africa?* Univ of California Press, 1991, Berkeley and LA

Ellis, S and Sechaba, T, *Comrades Against Apartheid: the ANC and the South African Communist Party in Exile*, J Currey, 1992, London

Innes, D, Kentridge, M and Perold, H (eds), *Power and Profit: Politics, Labour and Business in South Africa*, Oxford UP, 1992, Cape Town

Lodge, T, *Black Politics in South Africa Since 1945*, Ravan, 1985, Johannesburg

Lodge, T et al, *All, Here and Now: Black Politics in South Africa in the 1980s*, Hurst, 1992, London

Ottaway, M, *South Africa: the Struggle for a New Order*, Brookings, 1993, Wasington, DC

Schrire, R, *Adapt or Die: the End of White Politics* in South Africa, Hurst, 1992, London

Van Zyl Slabbert, F, *The Quest for Democracy: South Africa in Transition*, Penguin, 1992

IV Social/Economic/Labour/Human Rights

Baskin, J, *Striking Back: A History of COSATU*, Ravan, 1991

Berger, I, *Threads of Solidarity: Women in South African Industry, 1990–1980*, Indiana Univ Press, 1992, Bloomington

Hugo, P, *Redistribution and Affirmative Action: Working on the South African Political Economy*, Halfway House, South Africa, Southern Book Publishers, 1992. Distributed by Lakeside Publications, Haslemere, England

James, W G, *Our Precious Metal: African Labour in South Africa's Gold Industry, 1970–1990*, D Philip, Cape Town, 1992; Indiana University Press, 1992, Bloomington

Jones, S and Müller, A, *The South African Economy, 1910–1990*, Macmillan, 1992

Jones, S (Ed), *Financial Enterprise in South Africa Since 1950*, Macmillan, 1992

Letsoalo, E M, *Land Reform in South Africa: a Black Perspective*, Skotaville, 1987, Johannesburg

Van Onselen, C, *New Babylon, New Nineveh: Studies in the Social and Economic History of the Witwatersrand, 1886–1914*, (2 vols), Ravan, 1992

Platzky, L and Walker, C, *The Surplus People: Forced Removals in South Africa*, Ravan, 1985

Sachs, A, *Advancing Human Rights in South Africa*, Oxford UP, 1992, Cape Town

Smith, D M (Ed), *The Apartheid City and Beyond: Urbanisation and Social Change in South Africa*, Routledge, London, New York, 1992

V Biographical/Leadership

Kamsteeg, A and Dijk, E, *FW de Klerk: Man of the Moment*, Vlaeberg, 1990, Johannesburg

Meer, F, *Higher than Hope: a Biography of Nelson Mandela*, Hamish Hamilton, 1990, London

Mzala, *Gatsha Buthelezi – Chief with a Double Agenda*, 1988; translated into French under the title of: *Afrique du Sud: Buthelezi et l'Inkatha: le Double Jeu*, l'Harmattan, 1993, Paris (Mzala is probably a pseudonym)

Pityana, N B, Ramphele, R, Mplumwana, M and Wilson, L, *Bounds of Possibility: the Legacy of Steve Biko and Black Consciousness*, David Philip, 1991, Cape Town and Johannesburg

Pogrund, B, *Sobukwe and Apartheid*, P Halban and J Ball, 1990, Johannesburg and London

Van Zyl Slabbert, F, *The Last White Parliament*, H Strydom, 1985, Johannesburg, Sidgwick and Jackson, 1986 London

VI Statistical/Who's Who

Gastrow, S (ed), *Who's Who in South African Politics*, 4th Revised Edition with an Introduction by T Lodge, Hans Zell, 1993, London and New York

South African Institute of Race Relations, *1991–2 (Annual) Report on Race Relations*, 1992, Johannesburg

List of Acronyms and Abbreviations

AMU	African Mineworkers Union
ANC	African National Congress
APLA	African Peoples Liberation Army
ATKV	Afrikans Language and Cultural Society of the Railways
AWA	African Writers Association
AWB	Afrikaner Resistance Movement
AZAPO	Azanian Peoples Organisation
BC	Black Consciousness Movement
BCP	Black Community Programmes
BLA	Black Local Authorities
BPC	Black Peoples Convention
CASE	Community Agency for Society Enquiry
CBD	Central Business District
CBM	Consultative Business Movement
CLIARD	Centre for Low Input Agricultural Research and Development
CNETU	Council for Non-European Trade Unions
CODESA	Convention for a Democratic South Africa
CORDA	Commission for Rehabilition of Depressed Areas
COSAG	Concerned South Africans Group
COSATU	Congress of South African Trade Unions
COSAW	Congress of South African Writers
CP	Conservative Party
CPSA	Communist Party of South Africa
CRADORA	Cradock Residents Association
DEIC	Dutch East India Company
DP	Democratic Party
DRC	Dutch Reform Church
ESCOM	Electricity Supply Commission
FAK	Federation of Afrikaans Cultural Associations
GK	*Gereformeerde Kerk*

HK	*Hermvorde Kerk*
HNP	*Herenigte* (Reunited) National Party (Malan)
HNP	*Herstigte* (Purified) National Party (Jaap Marais)
HRF	Human Rights Fund
ICU	Industrial and Commercial Workers Union
IDASA	Institute for a Democratic Alternative for South Africa
IDT	Independent Development Trust
IFP	Inkatha Freedom Party
IMF	International Monetary Fund
JSE	Johannesburg Stock Exchange
KTC	Kapstaad (Cape Town) Camp
LMS	London Missionary Society
MDM	Mass Democratic Movement
NACTU	National Council of Trade Unions
NASASA	National *Stokvels* Association of South Africa
NEC	National Executive Committee (ANC)
NECC	National Education Crisis Committee
NGK	*Nederduitse Gereformeerde Kerk*
NLC	National Land Committee
NP	National Party
NSMS	National Security Management System
NUM	National Union of Mineworkers
NUSAS	National Union of South African Studies
PAC	Pan-Africanist Congress
PE	Port Elizabeth
PFP	Progressive Federal Party
PTA	Parents Teachers Association
RAU	Rand Afrikaans University
RDF	Regional Development Forum
SABC	South African Broadcasting Corporation

SABRA	South African Bureau of Racial Affairs
SACBC	South African Catholic Bishops Conference
SACC	South African Council of Churches
SACP	South African Communist Party
SACPO	South African Coloured Peoples Organisation
SACTU	South African Congress of Trade Unions
SADF	South African Defence Force
SAIC	South African Indian Congress
SAIRR	South African Institute of Race Relations
SANCO	South African National Civics Organisation
SARU	South African Rugby Union
SASM	South African Students Movement
SASO	South African Students Organisation
SBDC	Small Business Development Corporation
Soweto	South West Townships
SRC	Students Representative Council
SSC	State Security Council
SSRC	Soweto Students Representative Council
TATU	Transkei Appropriate Technology Unit
TCC	Transkei Council of Churches
TEC	Transitional Executive Council
UCASA	Urban Councils Association of South Africa
UCT	University of Cape Town
UDF	United Democratic Front
UF	Urban Foundation
UNHCR	United Nations High Commission for Refugees
UNISA	University of South Africa
USSALEP	United States-South Africa Leadership Exchange Programme
UWC	University of Western Cape
UWUSA	United Workers Union of South Africa (Inkatha)
Wits	Witwatersrand University

Index